SUPPOSITION
ARE PHY...

IF SO AU...
WILL BE...
EXTENT, why? / BECAUSE THE NOTION
OF NORMATIVITY ISN'T GROUNDED IN
PHYSICALITY → IF I INTENDED TO DO
X, THEN IF I STILL
INTEND TO DO THE SAME
THING I SHOULD DO X

WANTING; IS THAT REDUCIBLE?
↳ RELATED TO INTENTION

→ ON PHYSICAL GROUNDS
WANTING

SKEPTICISM
IS ABSURD IN CONTEXT OF MEANING

EVEN

IF IT WERE A FACT THAT I MEANT
ADDITION BY "PLUS" THEN EVERY FACT
UNDERNEATH THAT WOULD ALSO BE A
FACT, TOO. IS IT THE CASE THAT ALL
GENUINE FACTS MUST BE REDUCIBLE?

ALL MEANING NEED BE IS A PARTICULAR
POLICY REGARDING RIGHT OR WRONG ANSWERS;
EVERYTHING ABOUT HOW I ACTUALLY ADD CAN BE
COVERED BY DISPOSITIONS

I COULD HAVE NEVER COMPLETED
A SINGLE ADDITION & IT WOULD
STILL BE POSSIBLE FOR ME TO MEAN
ADDITION BY PLUS. IF THIS IS POSSIBLE
THEN WHAT IS IT REDUCIBLE TO?

RULE-FOLLOWING AND MEANING

Edited by

Alexander Miller and Crispin Wright

McGill-Queen's University Press
Montreal & Kingston • Ithaca

Introduction and endmatter © Alexander Miller 2002
Chapter 2 © The Aristotelian Society 1984
Chapter 3 © Kluwer Academic Publishers 1984
Chapter 4 © Kluwer Academic Publishers 1984
Chapter 5 © Blackwell Publishers 1984
Chapter 6 © *Journal of Philosophy* 1985
Chapter 7 © Oxford University Press 1989
Chapter 8 © Blackwell Publishers 1989
Chapter 9 © Oxford University Press 1989
Chapter 10 © Oxford University Press 1990
Chapter 11 © *The Philosophical Review* 1990
Chapter 12 © *Midwest Studies in Philosophy* 1994
Chapter 13 © Oxford University Press 1995
Chapter 14 © University of Calgary Press 1997

ISBN 0-7735- 2381-2   (hardcover)
ISBN 0-7735- 2382-0   (paperback)

Legal deposit second quarter 2002
Bibliothèque nationale du Québec

Published simultaneously outside North America by Acumen Publishing Limited

McGill-Queen's University Press acknowledges the financial support of the
Government of Canada through the Book Publishing Development Program
(BPIDP) for its activities.

National Library of Canada Cataloguing in Publication Data

Main entry under title:

Rule-following and meaning

Includes bibliographical references and index.
ISBN 0-7735-2381-2 (bound).—ISBN 0-7735-2382-0 (pbk.)

1. Meaning (Philosophy) 2. Language and languages—Philosophy. 3.
Wittgenstein, Ludwig, 1889-1951. I. Miller, Alexander, 1965- II. Wright, Crispin,
1942-

B840.R84 2002   121'.68   C2002-900571-X

Designed and typeset by Kate Williams, Abergavenny.
Printed and bound by Biddles Ltd., Guildford and King's Lynn.

CONTENTS

ACKNOWLEDGEMENTS

We are grateful to Philip Pettit, whose idea it first was that a collection such as this might be useful, and to Steven Gerrard at Acumen for his enthusiasm and commitment to the project. Thanks, too, to Jim Edwards and Bob Hale for their advice on choosing the selections. Finally, we are indebted to Dean Burnett and Rob Thomas, computing officers in the School of English, Communication and Philosophy at Cardiff University, for their help in producing electronic copies of the chapters from hard copy.

We are grateful to the following publishers and copyright holders for permission to reproduce the following:

"Scepticism and Semantic Knowledge" by Graeme Forbes, first published in *Proceedings of the Aristotelian Society*, 1983–4, pp. 223–37. Reprinted by permission of Blackwell Publishers.

"The Individual Strikes Back" by Simon Blackburn, first published in *Synthese* 58 (1984), pp. 281–301. Reprinted by permission of Kluwer Academic Publishers.

"Wittgenstein on Following a Rule" by John McDowell, first published in *Synthese* 58 (1984), pp. 325–63. Reprinted by permission of Kluwer Academic Publishers.

"Wittgenstein, Kripke, and Non-Reductionism about Meaning" by Colin McGinn, taken from Colin McGinn, *Wittgenstein on Meaning* (Oxford: Blackwell, 1984), pp. 150–64. Reprinted by permission of Blackwell Publishers.

"Kripke on Wittgenstein on Rules" by Warren Goldfarb, first published in the *Journal of Philosophy* (1985), pp. 471–88. Reprinted by permission of the *Journal* and the author.

"Critical Notice of Colin McGinn's *Wittgenstein on Meaning*" by Crispin Wright, first published in *Mind*, 98 (1989), pp. 289–305. Reprinted by permission of Oxford University Press.

"Meaning and Intention as Judgement Dependent" by Crispin Wright, taken from Crispin Wright, "Wittgenstein's Rule-Following Considerations and the Central Project of Theoretical Linguistics", in A. George (ed.), *Reflections on Chomsky* (Oxford: Blackwell, 1989), pp. 246–54. Reprinted by permission of Blackwell Publishers.

"The Rule-Following Considerations" by Paul A. Boghossian, first published in *Mind*, 98 (1989), pp. 507–49. Reprinted by permission of Oxford University Press.

"The Reality of Rule-Following" by Philip Pettit, first published in *Mind*, 99 (1990), pp. 1–21. Reprinted by permission of Oxford University Press.

"Truth Rules, Hoverflies, and the Kripke-Wittgenstein Paradox" by Ruth Garrett Millikan, first published in *The Philosophical Review*, 99, no. 3 (1990), pp. 323–53. Reprinted by permission of the editors of the *Review*.

"Kripke on Wittgenstein on Normativity" by George M. Wilson, first published in *Midwest Studies in Philosophy*, 19 (1994), pp. 366–90. Reprinted by permission of the editors of *Midwest Studies*.

"Meaning, Use and Truth" by Paul Horwich, first published in *Mind*, 104 (1995), pp. 355–68. Reprinted by permission of Oxford University Press.

"Kripke's Normativity Argument" by José L. Zalabardo, first published in the *Canadian Journal of Philosophy*, 27, no. 4 (1997), pp. 467–88. Reprinted by permission of University of Calgary Press.

Alexander Miller
Crispin Wright

THE CONTRIBUTORS

Simon Blackburn is Professor of Philosophy at the University of Cambridge. Previously, he taught at the University of North Carolina, Chapel Hill. His books include: *Spreading the Word*; *Ruling Passions*; *Think*; and *Being Good*.

Paul A. Boghossian is Professor and Chair of the Department of Philosophy at New York University. He is the author of many articles on philosophy of language and mind.

Graeme Forbes is the Celia Scott Weatherhead Distinguished Professor of Philosophy at Tulane University. He is the author of: *The Metaphysics of Modality*; *Languages of Possibility*; and *Modern Logic*.

Warren Goldfarb is Professor of Philosophy at Harvard University. He is the author of a number of works on Wittgenstein, philosophy of logic, and philosophy of mathematics.

Paul Horwich is Professor of Philosophy at the Graduate Center, City University of New York. He was formerly Professor of Philosophy at University College London. His books include *Truth* and *Meaning*.

John McDowell is Professor of Philosophy at the University of Pittsburgh. His books include: *Mind and World*; *Mind, Value and Reality*; and *Meaning, Knowledge and Reality*.

Colin McGinn is Professor of Philosophy at Rutgers University. His books include: *Wittgenstein on Meaning*; *The Subjective View*; and *Mental Content*.

Alexander Miller is Senior Research Fellow in Philosophy at Cardiff University. He is the author of *Philosophy of Language*, as well as a number of articles on the philosophy of mind and language, metaphysics, and metaethics.

Ruth Garrett Millikan is Professor of Philosophy at the University of Connecticut. Her books include: *Language, Thought and Other Biological Categories*; *White Queen Psychology and Other Essays for Alice*; and *On Clear and Confused Ideas*.

Philip Pettit is Professor of Politics and Philosophy at Princeton University. Previously, he was Professor of Social and Political Theory at the Research School of Social Sciences, Australian National University. His books include *The Common Mind* and *Republicanism*.

George M. Wilson is Professor of Philosophy at the University of California, Davis. Previously, he taught at the Johns Hopkins University. His main areas of specialisation are philosophy of language and mind, and film aesthetics.

Crispin Wright is Professor of Logic and Metaphysics at the University of St Andrews, Visiting Professor at Columbia University, New York, and a Fellow of the British Academy. His books include: *Wittgenstein on the Foundations of Mathematics*; *Frege's Conception of Numbers as Objects*; *Realism, Meaning and Truth*; *Rails to Infinity* and *Truth and Objectivity*.

José L. Zalabardo is Lecturer in Philosophy at University College London. Previously, he taught at the University of Birmingham. He is the author of *Introduction to the Theory of Logic*, and a number of articles on metaphysics and the philosophy of language and mind.

CHAPTER ONE

INTRODUCTION
Alexander Miller

One of the most widely discussed books in recent Anglo-American philosophy is Saul Kripke's *Wittgenstein on Rules and Private Language*.[1] Kripke's Wittgenstein's skeptic, drawing mainly on materials from Wittgenstein's *Philosophical Investigations* and *Remarks on the Foundations of Mathematics*, argues for a "skeptical paradox" about meaning: there is no fact of the matter in virtue of which an ascription of meaning, such as "Jones means addition by '+'", is true or false; and so, since nothing turns on the nature of Jones or of the '+' sign in particular, there is no fact of the matter as to whether any speaker means one thing rather than another by the expressions of his language.[2] KW then attempts to neutralise the impact of the skeptical argument. Even though there are no facts in virtue of which ascriptions of meaning are true or false, the "insane and intolerable" (*K*, p. 60) conclusion that "all language is meaningless" (*K*, p. 71) can be avoided via KW's "skeptical solution" to the "skeptical paradox": ascriptions of meaning can be viewed as possessing some non fact-stating role, so the propriety of ascribing meanings to linguistic expressions isn't threatened by the argument to the skeptical paradox. It emerges that the "skeptical solution" is available only for languages spoken by linguistic *communities*. A corollary of KW's neutralisation of the skeptical paradox is thus that there can be no such thing as "solitary" language.

Although many of the contributions to this volume question in passing whether KW accurately captures the views of the actual, historical

---

1. Where bibliographic information is not given, it appears in the Guide to Further Reading (p. 295).
2. Kripke is careful not to present this as straightforward exegesis of Wittgenstein. He writes "the present [work] should be thought of as expounding neither 'Wittgenstein's' argument nor 'Kripke's': rather Wittgenstein's argument as it struck Kripke, as it presented a problem for him"(*Wittgenstein on Rules and Private Language* (hereafter '*K*'), p. 5). In what follows I'll just speak of "Kripke's Wittgenstein", and abbreviate this by "KW".

Wittgenstein,[3] the volume is not intended to be a contribution to the already vast literature on matters of exegesis and the interpretation of Wittgenstein. Rather, it aims to give a representative sample of the most important *philosophical* reactions to the questions raised by KW's arguments; even if the selections were to tell us little about *Wittgenstein's views*, they would have much to teach us about some of the most fundamental questions of contemporary philosophy of mind and language, those concerning the metaphysics and epistemology of meaning. This introduction has four sections. In section 1, KW's argument for the skeptical paradox is outlined in as neutral a set of terms as possible.[4] The skeptical solution is given a brief exposition in section 2. Section 3 comments on George Wilson's "revisionist" interpretation of KW and Section 4 comments briefly on the question of the relevance of "rule-following" to the issues concerning meaning.

1. THE SKEPTICAL PARADOX

The conclusion of KW's skeptic's argument is that there is no fact of the matter in virtue of which sentences such as "Jones means *addition* by '+'" or "Smith means *green* by 'green'"are either true or false. The general strategy adopted in arguing for this conclusion is as follows. First, it is argued that if the species of fact in question is to be found, then it must be found within some set of particular areas. Once this has been done, our knowledge-acquiring powers are imagined to be idealised with respect to those areas: we are given *unlimited epistemic access* to the areas in question. Given this, and the ensuing argument that even under *these* conditions the sought after meaning-facts still elude our grasp, and any particular claim about the character of these meaning-facts still cannot be justified, it follows that there simply were *no* such facts there in the first place. For if there were any such facts, given unlimited epistemic access we would surely have found them, and would surely have been able to justify at least some claims concerning their character. But we cannot do this. So, the argument goes, there cannot be any such facts.[5]

KW's skeptic outlines his argument with an example from simple arithmetic, and asks "In virtue of what fact did I mean, in the past, the

---

3. See in particular, Ch. 3 (Blackburn), Ch. 4 (McDowell), Ch. 6 (Goldfarb), Ch. 7 (Wright). Wilson (Ch. 12) argues that the ease with which critics such as these establish that KW does not accurately portray Wittgenstein's views may depend upon a misinterpretation of KW's views themselves: see section 3 below.

4. Absolute neutrality is, however, impossible. For example, Wilson, and the commentators who support him, would question whether KW's skeptical solution can properly be described as *non-factualist*. See n. 3.

5. Thus, as many of the contributors take pains to stress, the skepticism propounded by KW's skeptic is *constitutive*, rather than *epistemological*, in nature. See e.g. Wright (Ch. 7), p. 109, and Boghossian (Ch. 9), pp. 150–51.

addition function by my use of the '+' sign?".[6] In order to make the question vivid, he imagines the following example. Suppose that "68 + 57" is a computation that I have never performed before. Since I've performed at most a finite number of computations in the past, we can be sure that such an example exists (even if you have performed this computation before, just suppose, for the sake of argument, that you haven't; the argument would work just as well for any other computation which you haven't actually performed). Also, the finitude of my previous computations ensures that there is an example where both of the arguments (in this case 68, 57) are larger than any other numbers I've previously dealt with (again, even if this is not the case in the present example, we can easily enough imagine one for which it is the case, and nothing turns on this).

Now suppose that I perform the computation and obtain "125" as my answer. After checking my working out, I can be confident that "125" is the correct answer. It is the correct answer in two senses: first, it is correct in the *arithmetical* sense, since 125 is indeed, as a matter of arithmetical fact, the sum of 68 and 57; and it is correct in the *metalinguistic* sense, since the "+" sign really does mean the addition function. (You can imagine how these two senses of correctness might come apart: if the "+" sign really stood for the subtraction function, 125 would still be the sum of 68 and 57, but the correct answer to the question "68 + 57 = ?" would now be "11"). But is my confidence that I have given the correct answer justified? KW imagines a "bizarre skeptic" arguing that it is not:

> This skeptic questions my certainty about my answer, in what I just called the "metalinguistic" sense. Perhaps, he suggests, as I used the term "plus" in the past, the answer I intended for "68 + 57" should have been "5"! Of course the skeptic's suggestion is obviously insane. My initial response to such a suggestion might be that the challenger should go back to school and learn to add. Let the challenger, however, continue. After all, he says, if I am now so confident that, as I used the symbol "+", my intention was that "68 + 57" should turn out to denote 125, this cannot be because I explicitly gave myself

---

6. Kripke says that the problem is set up in this way, with respect to past meanings, in order to enable the skeptic to intelligibly formulate his argument at all – the skeptic at this point does not call our present meanings into question, so that he can present his skeptical argument to us: "Before we pull the rug out from under our own feet, we begin by speaking as if the notion that at present we mean a certain function . . . is unquestioned and unquestionable. Only past usages are to be questioned. Otherwise, we will be unable to formulate our problem"(*K*, pp. 13–14). Of course, once the skeptical conclusion has been established with respect to past meanings, it can be generalised to encompass present meanings too, for we can always imagine ourselves running the skeptical argument tomorrow about what we presently mean by the "+" sign. Note, though, that both Forbes (Ch. 2), and Boghossian (Ch. 9) argue that the fundamental question raised by the skeptical argument does not concern transtemporal identity conditions for meaning, but rather conditions for meaning something by an expression *at a particular time*.

instructions that 125 is the result of performing the addition in this particular instance. By hypothesis, I did no such thing. But of course the idea is that, in this new instance, I should apply the very same function or rule that I applied so many times in the past. But who is to say what function this was? In the past I gave myself only a finite number of examples instantiating this function. All, we have supposed, involved numbers smaller than 57. So perhaps in the past I used "plus" and "+" to denote a function which I will call "quus" and symbolize by "$\oplus$". It is defined by

$$x \oplus y = x + y, \quad \text{if } x, y < 57$$
$$= 5 \qquad \text{otherwise.}$$

Who is to say that this is not the function I previously meant by "+"?

$(K, \text{pp. 8–9})$

The challenge is thus: cite some fact about yourself which constitutes your meaning *addition* rather than *quaddition* by the "+" sign. Any response to this challenge has to satisfy two conditions $(K, \text{pp. 11, 26})$. First, it has to provide us with an account of the type of fact that is constitutive of the meaning of "+". Second, it has to be possible to *read off* from this fact what constitutes *correct* and *incorrect* use of the "+" sign – it must show why the answer to the problem "68 + 57 = ?" is *justified*.[7]

KW's skeptic is thus challenging us to provide an acceptable answer to the question: In virtue of what fact are you now justified in answering "125" to the query "What is 68 + 57?" In accordance with the general strategy outlined above, KW's skeptic begins his argument that this challenge cannot be met by allowing us unlimited epistemic access to two areas, and inviting us to find a suitable meaning-constituting fact from within either of those two areas. The areas in question are (a) *our previous behaviour, linguistic and non-linguistic*; and (b) *the entire contents of our previous mental histories*.[8]

Nothing from the finite pool of my previous behaviour will do, since ex hypothesi I have never dealt with numbers larger than 57, and "+" and "$\oplus$" have the same extensions for numbers smaller than 57. Anything which is a "correct" answer to "$x + y = ?$" will also be a "correct" answer to

---

7. The exact nature of this "reading off" requirement, and its relation to the normativity of meaning, is a matter of extreme controversy. For discussion see e.g. Ch. 9 (Boghossian), Ch. 13 (Horwich), and Ch. 14 (Zalabardo).

8. Note that although KW's argument has obvious affinities with Quine's "argument from below" (*Word and Object* (Cambridge, MA: MIT Press, 1960), Ch. 2)) for the indeterminacy of translation, it is much stronger than Quine's argument, insofar as it allows us access to a wider range of facts in our search for the facts that constitute meaning. Quine rules out an appeal to facts of the sort mentioned in (b) from the start, whereas KW's argument is that even if we suppose ourselves to have idealised epistemic access to these sorts of fact, we will still be unable to find a fact which can constitute our meaning one thing rather than another. See *K*, pp.14–15, 55–8.

"$x \oplus y = ?$" so long as $x, y < 57$. Enlarging the pool of previous behaviour won't make a difference, since no matter how it is enlarged, a "deviant" interpretation of "$+$", such as that which takes it as standing for the quaddition function, will always be possible; even if we enlarge the pool of previous behaviour so that we have encountered numbers larger than 57, there will always be some number which is larger than those we have previously encountered, and the skeptic can use this to construct an analogue of the quaddition interpretation.

At this point, the skeptic imagines the following protest:

> [O]ur problem arises only because of a ridiculous model of the instruction I gave myself regarding "addition". Surely I did not merely give myself some finite number of examples from which I am supposed to extrapolate the whole [function] . . . Rather I learned – and internalized instructions for – a *rule* which determines how addition is to be continued. What was the rule? Well, say, to take it in its most primitive form: suppose we wish to add x and y. First count out x marbles in one heap. Then count out y marbles in another. Put the two heaps together and count out the number of marbles in the union thus formed.   (*K*, p. 15)

Isn't it this fact about what I had previously learnt and internalised that constitutes the fact that I meant *addition* and not *quaddition*? Alas, the skeptic has a response to this suggestion:

> True, if "count", as I used the word in the past, referred to the act of counting (and my other past words are correctly interpreted in the standard way), then "plus" must have stood for *addition*. But I applied "count", like "plus", to only finitely many past cases. Thus the skeptic can question my present interpretation of my past usage of "count" as he did with "plus". In particular, he can claim that by "count" I formerly meant *quount*, where to "quount" a heap is to count it in the ordinary sense, unless the heap was formed as the union of two heaps, one of which has 57 or more items, in which case one must automatically give the answer "5".   (*K*, p. 16)

Thus, if I follow the "counting" rule properly, I really ought to answer "5" when asked "$68 + 57 = ?$". We are back to where we started: citing something like a *general thought or instruction* in response to the skeptical challenge won't work, because the skeptic can always respond by giving a deviant interpretation of the symbols of the general thought or instruction itself. And the point can be generalised: any set of instructions that come before the mind require interpretation as much as the linguistic expression whose understanding they are supposed to facilitate, and are thus as susceptible to deviant interpretation as that original expression. Clearly, invoking instructions for interpreting the instructions will send us off on a fruitless infinite regress. Kripke takes himself here to be expounding Wittgenstein's remarks in the *Philosophical Investigations* on "a rule for interpreting a rule":

> [A]ny interpretation still hangs in the air along with what it interprets, and cannot give it any support. Interpretations by themselves do not determine meaning (*PI*, §198).[9]

It thus looks as if no fact about my previous behaviour will do the trick. Does the search within our *mental histories* fare any better ? Does the possession of some *mental image*, or some other specific mental item possessed of its own distinctive qualitative character provide what we are after? It seems not.

Firstly, it is not a *necessary* condition for understanding that some particular item come before one's mind when one hears or uses a given expression. As a matter of empirical fact, it seems to be the case that no one "mental entity" comes before one's mind when one correctly understands a linguistic expression. And even in cases where there does seem to be an empirical regularity between a particular expression and a particular such item we can still perfectly well *conceive* of someone understanding the expression in the absence of that item (indeed, we can conceive of someone understanding the expression even when *no* such item is present at all). It is no more necessary for understanding an expression that I have an inner mental picture before my mind than it is that I have a concrete physical picture ready to hand – just as I can perfectly well understand "cube" without having a drawing of a cube in front of me on the table, so I can understand it without having to call up a mental image.

Secondly, neither is it a *sufficient* condition for meaning a sign in a particular way that some item, be it a picture or otherwise, come before one's mind. The essential point is that the picture does not by itself determine the correct use of the associated word, because the picture thus associated is really just another sign whose meaning too requires to be fixed. There is no logical route from the properties of an image or picture to the meaning of an associated word, because of the possibility of deviant applications of the word consistent with some interpretation of the picture; the relation of any picture or image to the associated word can be construed in such a way that any future pattern of use of the expression can count as correct. Whatever comes before the mind can be made to accord with a deviant application of the expression. Thus, mental images set no standards for the correct use of an expression; one cannot "read off" from a mental image what counts as the correct use of an associated expression. In order to drive this point home, we can imagine

---

9. Note that some care is required in pinning down exactly what the "regress" here involves. See Wright's remarks on this in Ch. 7, pp. 125–6.

someone in the hands of an omnipotent but curious experimenter, conditioned by the experimenter to have the image of a cube every time he hears the word "cube". But again, this will not be sufficient to determine what he understands by the word in question. We might of course admit that images *naturally suggest* certain applications, but the important point is rather that they do not logically determine them. It is possible that two people might understand a word differently even though the same images always occurred to them on hearing it.[10]

KW's skeptic considers a further reply, which, drawing on the subject's past mental life, might be adduced in response to the skeptical argument. This is that in the paragraphs above we have concentrated too exclusively on what might be called "quotidian" states of mind – states such as mental images, sensations, headaches and other introspectible mental states with their own distinctive phenomenological character. Perhaps meaning addition is not a state of these kinds but rather an irreducible state, "a primitive state . . . a state of a unique kind of its own" (*K*, p. 51). This response, however, is castigated by KW on the grounds that it is "desperate" and leaves "completely mysterious" the character of the primitive state thought to constitute understanding.[11] For one thing, it is not an introspectible state and yet its possessor is thought to be aware of it with a degree of certainty whenever he has it. How could this be possible? It is also completely mysterious, moreover, how "a finite object contained in our finite minds" could be such as to reach out to an indefinitely large number of future uses of an expression and determine whether or not they are correct in the light of that expression's meaning. It is a mystery what the relationship is between these future uses and the putative primitive state; the response as it stands gives no clue as to what the nature of this relationship is, or how it is forged.[12]

---

10. I am here merely summarising the rich battery of arguments that Colin McGinn, drawing extensively on Wittgenstein's texts, develops against the suggestion that understanding might be constituted by the occurrence of mental images, etc. See McGinn's *Wittgenstein on Meaning*, pp. 1–7 for some excellent exposition. Kripke spends relatively little time on this suggestion since, as he writes, "this particular Wittgensteinian lesson has been relatively well learned, perhaps too well learned" (*K*, p. 48). This seems right: none of the contributors to this volume attempts an answer of *that* sort to the skeptical argument.

11. The full passage in *K* from which these quotes are taken is reproduced by Boghossian in Ch. 9, p. 178.

12. Many commentators find this "anti non-reductionist" argument of Kripke's, as it stands, unconvincing. See e.g. Ch. 5 (McGinn) and Ch. 9 (Boghossian). Other commentators attempt to develop non-reductionist accounts of meaning that nevertheless answer to substantial epistemological constraints. Thus, Wright (Ch. 8), explores a "judgement-dependent" conception of meaning that is at once non-reductionist but accommodating to the "non-inferential and first-person authoritative" nature of knowledge of meaning; and Pettit (Ch. 10) develops an account that eschews reductionism (p. 203) whilst accommodating the idea that rules are "directly and fallibly readable". Note, though, that Pettit would not want to claim that rules are "*sui generis*" (p. 195). For approaches to non-reductionism, different from those proposed by McGinn, Boghossian, Pettit, and Wright, see Ch. 4 (McDowell) and Ch. 6 (Goldfarb).

KW's skeptic also considers a suggestion that at first seems to issue in a plausible refutation of his skeptical argument. The suggestion is that in limiting us to facts concerning our *past* actual behaviour and our previous *occurrent* mental states, KW's skeptic has already guaranteed himself success: rather, we should consider *dispositional* facts about language users. These will enable us to distinguish between the hypothesis that I meant *addition* in the past and the hypothesis that I meant *quaddition* in the past. The claim that I meant *addition* would be true if I was disposed in the past, when asked to compute "*x* + *y*", to produce the *sum* of the two numbers. Similarly, the claim that I meant *quaddition* would be true if I was disposed, when faced with the same query, to respond with the result of *quadding* the two numbers. Thus, were my knowledge-acquiring powers concerning my dispositional properties sufficiently idealised, I would no doubt see that I was disposed to give the answer "125" to the query, even though in fact I never did because I was never asked to. The skeptic's claim that I meant some function other than addition would thus be refuted.[13]

KW's skeptic, however, has two powerful-sounding objections to the dispositionalist account. The first objection is that it completely fails to take account of the *normativity* of meaning. In effect, it fails to satisfy the second of the two conditions laid down earlier on any candidate fact for meaning addition. We say that a competent language speaker *ought*, given his previous meanings and his intention to remain faithful to them, to respond to e.g. arithmetical questions in certain determinate ways, and we believe that the response he ought to give is logically independent of the response that he *did* give, or *would have given*, had he actually been faced with the query. But the dispositionalist account leaves no room for such a distinction between the answer he ought to have given and the answer he would have given, for according to the dispositional account the answer he ought to have given simply collapses into the answer that he would have given. In a nutshell, the dispositionalist response appears to involve the unacceptable equation of *competence* and *performance*. Kripke sums the problem up as follows:

> Suppose I do mean addition by "+". What is the relation of this supposition to the question how I will respond to the problem "68 + 57"? The dispositionalist gives a *descriptive* account of this relation: if "+" meant addition, then I will answer "125". But this is

---

13. Boghossian shows in Ch. 9 (p. 164) that causal-informational and conceptual-role theories of content, of the sort widely discussed in contemporary philosophy of mind and language, are in fact species of dispositionalism of the sort attacked by KW's skeptic. Boghossian also convincingly argues that the questions KW raises concerning linguistic meaning arise with equal force for mental content (pp. 148–9). On this latter point, see also Sartorelli, "McGinn on Content Scepticism and Kripke's Sceptical Arguments". Note, too, that since beliefs and desires rationalise behaviour in part at least in virtue of their content, our picture of ourselves as intentional agents is threatened by the arguments of KW's skeptic.

DISCEPTNIST
theory of names vulnerable
to skeptical argument

INTRODUCTION

not the proper account of the relation, which is *normative*, not descriptive. The point is *not* that, if I meant addition by "+", I *will* answer "125", but rather that, if I intend to accord with my past meaning of "+", I *should* answer "125". Computational error, finiteness of my capacity, and other disturbing factors may lead me not to be *disposed* to respond as I *should*, but if so, I have not acted in accordance with my intentions. The relation of meaning and intention to future action is *normative*, not *descriptive*.   (*K*, p. 37)

This problem shows up further in the fact that intuitively we want to be able to leave room for the possibility that someone is *systematically mistaken*, in the sense that he is disposed to make mistakes. For example, someone might be disposed to systematically miscarry when carrying out addition problems, and we want to leave room for the possibility that such a person means addition but is giving answers out of line with those that he ought to give; we do not want to be committed to the conclusion that he in fact means some different arithmetical function and is after all counting correctly.

The second problem for dispositions is that they are, like the totality of our previous linguistic behaviour, finite.[14] For example, it simply is not true that I am disposed in such a way that I will always give the sum of two numbers when faced with "What is $x + y$?"; some numerals will simply be too long for me to handle and some will be so long that I will die before having an opportunity to respond to the query. Given this, it is easy for KW's skeptic to construct deviant interpretations that are nevertheless compatible with all of the dispositional facts concerning me – e.g. perhaps I meant *skaddition*, where this is defined as:

$$x * y = x + y, \quad \text{if } x, y \text{ are small enough for me to handle,}$$
$$= 5, \quad \text{otherwise.}$$

I would then be unable to cite any fact about my dispositions that could constitute my meaning addition and which would be incompatible with the hypothesis that I meant skaddition. Dispositions are thus unable to fix the meaning of the "+" sign.[15]

---

14. Note, though, Kripke's important remarks on the "finitude" objection at *K*, p. 52, n. 34, where he seems to suggest that the finitude problem is not the most fundamental of those he raises.

15. The contributors to this volume differ in their estimates of the plausibility of KW's anti-dispositionalist arguments. Boghossian argues in Ch. 9 that KW's arguments fail but then proceeds to develop an anti-dispositionalist argument of his own. McDowell and Pettit find dispositionalism implausible for roughly Kripkean reasons. Goldfarb, Blackburn, and Wright all raise worries about KW's arguments, though none of them wishes ultimately to defend dispositionalism. Forbes (Ch. 2), Millikan (Ch. 11), and Horwich (Ch. 13) all, in their own ways, defend dispositionalist accounts of meaning in the face of KW's arguments. Zalabardo (Ch. 14) questions the "standard" interpretation of KW's "normativity" objection to dispositionalism – which he attributes to Boghossian, Wright, Blackburn, and McDowell, and proposes an interpretation of his own.

KW's skeptic considers a reply to the skeptical argument which has it that a choice between the incompatible, but apparently equally acceptable, hypotheses that it was *addition* that was meant and that it was *quaddition* that was meant, could be made by some kind of appeal to the *simplicity* of the respective hypotheses: perhaps it is the simplest function that should be deemed to have been meant. KW's skeptic, however, is scornful of this suggestion, but not merely because "simplicity is relative, or that it is hard to define, or that a martian might find the quus function simpler than the plus function" (*K*, p. 38). These are indeed problems, but KW suggests that the difficulty with the suggestion is in fact more basic, and that it relies on a misunderstanding of the nature of the conclusion of the skeptical argument. The conclusion proper of the skeptical argument is not that there are two competing genuine hypotheses about what was meant: that conclusion is only supposed to be a "dramatic device", designed to facilitate the statement of the skeptical argument. The real conclusion of the skeptical argument is that no content can be attached to the hypothesis that a determinate meaning is attached to a given expression. Keeping the real nature of the skeptical conclusion in mind then helps us to see that the appeal to simplicity considerations is misplaced:

> Now simplicity considerations can help us to decide between competing hypotheses, but they can never tell us what the competing hypotheses are. If we do not understand what two hypotheses *state*, what does it mean to say that one is "more probable" because it is "simpler"? ... if two competing hypothesis are not genuine hypotheses, not assertions of genuine matters of fact, no "simplicity" considerations will make them so. (*K*, p. 38)[16]

So none of the facts we have considered – facts about our previous behaviour, facts about our behavioural dispositions, facts about general thoughts or instructions, facts about "quotidian" mental states such as mental images, facts about *sui generis* and irreducible states of meaning and understanding, or facts about "simplicity" – appear to be plausible candidates for constituting the fact that we mean *addition* rather than *quaddition* by "+". We appear to be facing the conclusion that there is no fact of the matter as to what we meant in the past by "+", and since our present understanding of "+" will be up for retrospective viewing in the future, it follows that there is no fact

---

16. Wright, "Kripke's Account of the Argument against Private Language", p. 773 n. 5, argues that this rebuttal of the simplicity suggestion *begs the question* because it *assumes* non-factualism about ascriptions of meaning, a thesis which, at the relevant stage in the dialectic, is still up for proof. It is unclear whether Wright's point is decisive, though. KW's skeptic does not need to assume that non-factualism about meaning-ascriptions is true, but just that we have as yet no account of what meaning-facts could consist in. Making this weaker assumption doesn't appear to beg any questions.

of the matter as to what we mean at present by "+" either. And, since the skeptical argument could, without any loss, be rerun against anyone else and any other linguistic expression, it follows that there are no facts of the matter as to what anyone means by any expression. The notion of meaning has apparently, as Kripke puts it, "vanished into thin air" (K, p. 22).

2. THE SKEPTICAL SOLUTION

Kripke distinguishes between two ways in which the skeptical argument might be responded to. One way he describes as a "straight solution". This would consist of a demonstration of the thesis that the skeptic called into question: the production of a suitable meaning-constituting fact of the sort the skeptic questions. On the other hand there is what Kripke describes as a "skeptical solution". Such a solution would consist of two parts: first, an admission that the sort of fact questioned by the skeptic is in fact non-existent; second, an argument to the effect that an area of discourse does not have to be viewed as fact-stating in order for it to enjoy a tenable position within our lives. In the case of ascriptions of meaning, KW argues that our practice does not require for its tenability the sort of justification which the skeptic demands, namely, an account of their truth-conditions or facts which would render them true or false. We can justify our practice of ascribing meaning and understanding in other terms. It is this latter sort of solution, a skeptical solution, which Kripke sees Wittgenstein himself advocating in the *Philosophical Investigations*.[17]

KW thus admits, at the outset of the skeptical solution, that sentences ascribing meaning do not have truth-conditions, that there are no facts or states of affairs in virtue of which such sentences have truth or falsity conferred upon them. As textual support for his claim that Wittgenstein rejected the idea that sentences had to be viewed as possessing truth-conditions in order for our practices with them to be deemed legitimate, Kripke cites Michael Dummett's claim that the emphasis in Wittgenstein's early work, the *Tractatus Logico-Philosophicus*, upon facts and truth-conditions, was replaced in the later *Philosophical Investigations* by a completely different emphasis.[18] In the later work, the emphasis is on describing the conditions under which sentences are deemed to be *justified* or *assertable*, and on the *role* or *utility* that so deeming them assertable under

---

17. Talk of a "skeptical solution" is a direct reference to Hume's *Enquiry Concerning Human Understanding*. Kripke takes Hume to be arguing that e.g. there are no facts in virtue of which statements about causal relations are true or false, but to be attempting to neutralise this conclusion by arguing that such statements can be viewed as having some legitimate non fact-stating role. See *K*, pp. 66ff. For discussion of the analogy with Hume, see e.g. Blackburn (Ch. 3).
18. The reference is to Dummett's paper, "Wittgenstein's Philosophy of Mathematics", in his *Truth and Other Enigmas* (London: Duckworth, 1978).

those conditions has within our lives.[19] Thus, the change in emphasis which Kripke sees Wittgenstein as recommending is this: we are enjoined not to look for "entities" or "facts" corresponding to sentences ascribing meaning but rather to look at the circumstances under which such ascriptions are actually made and the utility that resides in ascribing them under these conditions. If these conditions and the corresponding role and utility can be specified adequately, then, KW suggests, we will have provided a skeptical solution to the problem raised by the skeptical argument.

What are the relevant conditions, utility and role? Consider the sentence "Jones means *addition* by '+'". If Jones is considered in isolation from any linguistic community – as a speaker of a solitary language – then the conditions under which this will be asserted will correspond to those under which Jones himself would assert "I mean addition by '+'". There will thus be no distinction between the assertion conditions of "Jones believes that he means *addition* by '+'" and "Jones means *addition* by '+'". Thus, whatever seems right to Jones will be right, "and that only means that here we can't talk about 'right'" (*Philosophical Investigations*, §258). So, in the case of an individual considered in isolation, the skeptical solution will be powerless to salvage any point to our practices with the notion of meaning, since any such reconstruction must respect the fact that the meaning an individual speaker attaches to an expression is normative with respect to his inclinations to apply it in certain ways. Kripke takes this to be the upshot of Wittgenstein's famous claim that "to think one is obeying a rule is not to obey a rule. Hence, it is not possible to obey a rule 'privately': otherwise thinking one was obeying a rule would be the same thing as obeying it" (*Philosophical Investigations*, §202).

Matters stand differently when Jones is considered, not as a solitary individual, but as a member of a linguistic community. The utterance of "Jones means addition by '+'" is then considered to be justified when Jones has performed satisfactorily often enough with "+", where this is taken to involve nothing more than that Jones has satisfactorily often enough come up with the answer that most of the rest of his fellow speakers in the community are disposed to give. The utterance of the sentence thus marks the community's acceptance of Jones into its midst, and it marks also the community's conviction that Jones can generally be trusted to act as they do in transactions which involve the use of the "+" sign. The utility of uttering ascriptions of meaning under such conditions is clear. They allow us to discriminate between those people we can trust in our transactions involving "+" and those we cannot. More generally, they allow us to discriminate between people who are members of our general linguistic community and those who are not. A grocer who "means addition by '+'" is one who can be trusted to treat me as I expect when

---

19. It is unclear whether the notion of justification or assertibility conditions which Dummett discerns in the later Wittgenstein can actually be used by KW in the context of the skeptical solution. See e.g. McDowell's remarks in Ch. 4, at p. 51.

I go in to his shop to buy five apples. And note, crucially, that in the communal setting there is a distinction between the conditions under which it is assertable that Jones believes that he means addition and the conditions under which it is assertable that he actually does mean this; it might indeed be the case that Jones believes that he means addition, but at the same time the rest of the community finds that his use of the "+" sign is out of step with theirs, so that the assertion conditions for "Jones means addition by '+'" are not in fact met.

To sum up then, the skeptical solution admits that discourse involving meaning is not fact-stating, but attempts to legitimise it by finding it a non fact-stating role to play.[20] This involves spelling out the assertability conditions of ascriptions of meaning, and showing that asserting them under these conditions plays a useful role in our lives. It emerges that these assertion conditions involve an essential reference to a linguistic community, since the community underwrites the "seems right/is right" distinction essential to any conception of meaning. The preservation of a legitimate role for ascriptions of meaning is thus claimed by KW to deliver a demonstration of the impossibility of a solitary language.[21]

3. KRIPKE'S WITTGENSTEIN AND MEANING-SKEPTICISM

George Wilson (Ch. 12) argues that most commentators misinterpret Kripke's Wittgenstein when they view him as *accepting* the conclusion of the skeptical argument and then trying to rehabilitate the notion of meaning by proposing a non-factualist account of ascriptions of meaning. Wilson rejects this: according to him, *Kripke's Skeptic* argues as follows:

(NS) If X means something by a term $^\wedge A^\wedge$, then there is a set of properties, $P_1, \ldots, P_n$, that govern the correct application of $^\wedge A^\wedge$ for X.

---

20. Hardly any commentators think that the skeptical solution is plausible. See e.g. Boghossian's arguments against "semantic irrealism" in Ch. 9 and in "The Status of Content". See also Wright's "Kripke's Account of the Argument Against Private Language". Many of the objections raised depend on construing the skeptical solution as a form of "semantic non-factualism", a construal which Wilson argues against in Ch. 12 and in his "Semantic Realism and Kripke's Wittgenstein": see section 3, following.
21. Kripke attempts to use these remarks in an exegesis of Wittgenstein's famous "private language argument". But the issues about the relationship between arguments against solitary language (a language which is in fact spoken only by a solitary individual) and arguments against private language (a language which is necessarily unintelligible to everyone except its speaker) are very complicated. See Goldfarb's remarks in Ch. 6, and also Wright's "Does PI §258–60 Suggest a Cogent Argument Against Private Language" for some useful discussion. Blackburn, Goldfarb, and Boghossian, in Chs 3, 6 and 9 respectively, all argue that even if the skeptical solution could be sustained, it would not provide any compelling reasons for thinking that a solitary language is impossible.

(G) If there is a set of properties, $P_1, \ldots, P_n$, that govern the correct application of $^\wedge A^\wedge$ for X, then there are facts about X that constitute $P_1, \ldots, P_n$ as the conditions that govern X's use of $^\wedge A^\wedge$.

(BSC) There are no facts about X that constitute any set of properties as conditions that govern X's use of $^\wedge A^\wedge$.

So, (RSC) No-one ever means anything by a term.

According to Wilson, however, *Kripke's Wittgenstein* emphatically does *not* accept the "radical skeptical conclusion" (RSC), but rather denies this, and uses this as a lever to reject the "classical realist" conception of meaning embodied in (NS). Thus, KW, according to Wilson, argues as follows:

(G), (BSC), not (RSC); so, not (NS).

Wilson's interesting interpretation of KW deserves a fuller examination than I can even start to attempt to give here, so I will limit myself to pointing out one possible problem with Wilson's interpretation. This is that it appears to sit ill with Kripke's remarks about the distinction between "straight" and "skeptical" solutions to the skeptical paradox about meaning. According to Kripke "[A] proposed solution to a skeptical philosophical problem [is] a *straight* solution if it shows that on closer examination the skepticism proves to be unwarranted"(*K*, p. 66). That is, a straight solution is one which finds fault with the skeptic's reasoning or by denying one of the premises in the skeptic's argument. In contrast "A *skeptical* solution of a skeptical philosophical problem begins on the contrary by conceding that the skeptic's negative assertions are unanswerable"(*K*, p. 66). That is, a skeptical solution begins by accepting the negative *conclusion* of the skeptical argument. The problem for Wilson's interpretation of KW should now be clear. According to Wilson, KW blocks the inference to (RSC) by denying (NS): (NS) is false, so although the inference from (G), (NS), and (BSC) to (RSC) is valid, the skeptic has no *cogent* route to the conclusion (RSC). But this means that, by Kripke's lights, KW is proposing a *straight* solution to the skeptical solution: one which finds fault with the skeptic's reasoning or with one of his premises. But of course, Kripke clearly intends his Wittgenstein to be proposing a *skeptical* solution to the skeptical paradox. It seems to me, then, that Wilson's interpretation, interesting as it may be as a potential piece of *Wittgenstein* exegesis, does not sit well with *Kripke's Wittgenstein's* take on these matters.[22]

---

22. I do not claim that this point is decisive against Wilson's, merely that he owes us an account of Kripke's distinction between 'straight' and 'skeptical' solutions which meshes with his interpretation of KW. For more on the issues raised by Wilson's interpretation, see also the papers by Byrne, Davies, Kremer and Soames ("Facts, Truth Conditions and the Sceptical Solution to the Rule-Following Paradox") listed in the Guide to Further Reading (p. 295).

4. RULE-FOLLOWING AND MEANING?

KW appears to raise a question about the factuality of ascriptions of meaning. But what has meaning got to do with rule-following? Paul Boghossian, in chapter 9, argues that the answer is "nothing" and that the "the rule-following considerations" is "strictly speaking a misnomer"(p. 151) for the discussions of meaning of the sort collected in this volume. Boghossian says that many writers assume that there is a connection between rule-following and meaning because, according to them, "expressions come to have [meaning] as a result of people following rules in respect of them". But this won't do, since on an ordinary understanding, following a rule is an intentional act, "an act among whose causal antecedents lie contentful mental states". Far from explaining meaning, then, the notion of rule-following presupposes it. Hence the "misnomer" accusation.

However, one does not need to hold the explanatory claim – that expressions acquire meaning in virtue of our following rules in respect of them – in order to appreciate the intimate connections between the notion of meaning and the notion of rule-following. The notion of intending to follow a rule in a certain way is *analogous* to meaning something by a linguistic expression. Suppose I intend to follow the rule "add 2" when writing out the following arithmetical series: 2, 4, 6, 8, 10, ... Intuitively, later on in the series, certain continuations (e.g. 24, 26, 28) are determined to be correct by the rule which I intend to follow, and certain continuations are determined to be incorrect by that rule (e.g. 34, 35, 37). This is the analogue of the applications of a predicate being determined as correct or incorrect by the meaning of the predicate. Just as KW's skeptic will claim, of a predicate, that there are no facts of the matter as to which applications are correct and which are incorrect, he will also claim that there are no facts of the matter as to which continuations of the arithmetical series are correct or incorrect. "The Rule-Following Considerations" is thus an entirely apt title for the debates about meaning brought into such sharp focus by Kripke's reading of Wittgenstein.

CHAPTER TWO

SKEPTICISM AND SEMANTIC KNOWLEDGE

Graeme Forbes

I

This paper is about the 'skeptical paradox' which Saul Kripke extracts from the one hundred or so sections of Wittgenstein's *Philosophical Investigations* preceding §243, and focuses on the dispositionalist response to the skeptic, which seems to me to be a better response than Kripke is willing to allow.[1]

The paradox is: '. . . no course of action could be determined by a rule, because every course of action can be made to accord with the rule' *(Investigations* §210). When someone masters a concept, we think of him as grasping a content or meaning which will guide his future applications of the concept and against which those applications will be assessed as correct or incorrect. The challenge the skeptic poses is that of specifying a fact about the subject *in virtue of which* his later applications are correct, or incorrect. Perhaps, for example, the subject's understanding has degenerated over time, so that the applications he now makes he would once have rejected. The problem is not an epistemological one: the point is not that the subject cannot be *sure* that his understanding of the concept has not changed, but rather that there may be no such distinction as the purported one between a situation in which his understanding stays the same and one in which it changes. Thus, the skeptic's questions are not about how the subject *knows* that his understanding is the same as it was previously, for he holds that there is nothing *to* know here; instead, they are about what *makes*

---

1. I shall be referring to *Wittgenstein on Rules and Private Language* by Saul A. Kripke (Oxford: Blackwell, 1982), and to *Wittgenstein on the Foundations of Mathematics* by Crispin Wright (London: Duckworth, 1980). Page references to these works in the text are given just by a number in parentheses, the context making it clear which book is intended.

16

it the case that it is the same as it was. Let us introduce some terminology. For any class of entity, we can distinguish between identity *at* a time and identity *through* time for entities of that class. In the present case, then, the skeptic is raising a query about intrasubjective crosstemporal identity of content (meanings, understanding): he is saying that it is not possible to give an account of what such identity consists in, or, that there are no coherent transtemporal identity conditions for contents applicable to individuals on a one-by-one basis.[2]

Arithmetical examples are helpful. Suppose someone is given a table on which are written all truths of the form '$x + y = z$' for x, y greater than or equal to 9. He is then taught to add two natural numbers of arbitrary length in standard notation by following the procedure, roughly, of writing one numeral under the other (preserving the order of digits and aligning on the right), adding zeros on the left of the shorter number to make both numbers the same length (when necessary) and then adding corresponding digits by referring to the table, carrying 1 and entering only the right digit when the table gives a two-digit answer. The content of addition remains the same for a subject if he would attempt to follow these rules were he to take himself to be adding two numbers. How, then, can every course of action be made to accord with these rules? The problem is that the rules themselves have to be understood by the subject. Suppose that after midnight on 31 December 1982, the subject, in writing one numeral under the other, reverses the order of the digits in one or both numbers, but claims to be doing the same thing as he did before. This could show that he has developed a misunderstanding about what it is to preserve the order: he comes to think it sufficient for this that an end-digit remains an end-digit and a surrounded digit remains surrounded by the same digits, though not necessarily on the same sides. The skeptic is asking for an account of what such change of understanding consists in: what relevant feature of the subject when he was successfully taught addition has altered? The difficulty is to specify a fact whose sufficiency does not itself involve an assumption about how the subject understands something; for such assumptions only postpone the question of what constancy of understanding consists in. That is, either there is a level at which such assumptions do not have to be made, in which case we should give the account for that level straight away, or else there is no account; at best, we can say that the transtemporal relationship of sameness of content is 'primitive', which does not seem very different from an admission of defeat.

---

2. The 'identity conditions' terminology is mine. Passages which support this reading of Kripke can be found on p. 8, p. 9, p. 12, p. 13, e.g. '[The skeptic] puts the challenge in terms of a skeptical hypothesis about a *change* in my usage'(p. 13, my emphasis).

II

On Kripke's reading, then, the skeptic wants to know what the intrasubjective transtemporal identity conditions of meanings are. Crispin Wright's reading, at least in emphasis, is different. According to Wright (pp. 33–7), Wittgenstein is opposing the idea that at a *particular* time my grasp of the content of a concept is a determinate state wholly transparent to myself, even if I cannot convey it to anyone else: I know how I now understand addition because I know how I now intend 'preserving the order'. My grasp of a content at a particular time may be thought to consist in a grasp of a certain pattern, the preserving of which constitutes correct application in terms of my present understanding; but Wittgenstein insists that the idea of 'grasping a pattern' is itself without content. Thus, contrary to what was said above, we are not to concede that the subject's present understanding can be taken for granted, and ask what would make it the same as his original understanding: the problem is one of the (intrasubjective) identity conditions of contents or meanings *at* a time.

In fact, Kripke regards beginning with the puzzle about transtemporal identity conditions as a dialectical manoeuvre, to avoid pulling the rug out from under our own feet (p. 13): without transtemporal identity conditions, there can be no fact about what the subject meant in the past, and 'if there can be no fact about . . . [what] . . . I meant in the *past,* there can be none in the *present* either'. But the claim that there is no fact about what the subject meant in the past is ambiguous between the claim that he had no determinate understanding in the past and the claim that, although he had such an understanding, there is no fact about whether it is the same as his present one. The context dictates that it is the second reading which is intended, and from this, nothing follows about determinacy of understanding *at* a time. Indeed, the semantic case is precisely the one where, although the question of crosstemporal identity conditions clearly arises, some philosophers have felt it possibly unanswerable, despite holding the view that identity conditions at a time *can* be given. Thus, adapting a proposal of Hartry Field's, we might argue that for any concepts c_1 and c_2 of a subject S at a time t, if $r[c_1/c_2]$ is the proposition obtained by substituting c_2 for any occurrence of c_1 in r, then c_1 and c_2 are the same in S's scheme of concepts at t iff: for any proposition p, the subjective conditional probability of r given p is the same for S at t as the subjective conditional probability of $r[c_1/c_2]$ given p. However, as Field himself notes, identity conditions of this nature cannot be straightforwardly adapted to crosstemporal ones, for even if c_1 and c_2 are the same concept, the probability of r given p at one time and that of $r[c_1/c_2]$ given p at another can be quite different if the subject's beliefs about the world have changed. So it is conceivable that what I *now* understand by some concept is well-defined (without reference to anything 'outside' me), as is what I will understand by it tomorrow, but there is no fact about whether or not these two understandings are the same.[3] In fact, it will emerge below that identity at a time is a more fundamental problem than identity through time for conceptual content, in view of which it seems that, whatever the fact about what Wittgenstein really meant – if there is such a fact – Wright's interpretation is more direct and more challenging.[4]

III

If understanding or grasping a concept is a state of mind, then since there is no shortage of theories about what it is for an individual to be in a given state of mind, should not the transtemporal identity conditions of the entities any such theory appeals to provide an answer to the skeptic? Suppose, for instance, that a (non-experiential) state of mind is a dispositional state; then would skepticism not be refuted by a general theory of the transtemporal identity conditions of dispositions? It looks as if a skeptic who concedes the notion of understanding at a time concedes everything, since although it may be difficult to give an account of what it is to be in a given dispositional state at a time, once such an account is available, it is improbable that there will be much further difficulty about what it is for such a state to persist. For instance, if x's being in a particular dispositional state at t consists in certain counterfactuals being true of x at t, then there may be nothing more to that state's persisting than those counterfactuals continuing to be true.

In Kripke's exposition, the suggestion that understanding is a dispositional state is rejected by the skeptic. To see why, it is necessary to introduce a further aspect of the paradox. According to Kripke, the paradox can only be resolved by explaining not just what 'meaning the same' amounts to when applied across time, but also by showing how the analysis leads to a sense in which a correct application of a concept *is justified*. The idea is, apparently, that without transtemporal identity conditions, any application is just as good as any other, e.g., in the case of addition, the answer obtained by inverting is no worse than the answer obtained in the conventional way. But according to Kripke, a dispositional theory does not provide any sense in which, say, '68 + 57 = 125' is justified and '68 + 57 = 143' is not, for the dispositional view is 'simply an equation of performance

<hr>

3. See 'Logic, Meaning, and Conceptual Role', *The Journal of Philosophy* 74 (1977) pp. 379–409, especially pp. 398–9.

4. Wright sometimes writes as if the problem is one of transtemporal identity, e.g. p. 389: 'Objective conceptual stability means: objectivity in the idea of when an expression is applied in the same way . . . as previously.' Perhaps the trouble arises here from running objectivity and stability together.

and correctness' (p. 24). Just because the subject is and was disposed to give the answer '125', it does not follow that this answer is justified in terms of the rules he learnt (p. 23).

Why does this mean that my belief that 68 + 57 = 125 needs a justification which the dispositional theory is impotent to provide? Suppose, more generally, that we are in doubt as to how to apply a concept in some particular case where we are sure that there is a proper application but unsure what it is. For a particular answer to be correct or justified in this situation is just for it to be the one which is dictated by the content of the concept. But as soon as we say this, we see that the problem of justification has nothing to do with grounding the application of *trans*temporal identity to the content of a concept: justification of the answer I give at present is provided by what I at present understand the concept's content to be, and an answer could be justified in *these* terms even if my understanding of the content is unstable through time, and *even* if questions about stability through time do not make sense. The objection to Kripke's skeptic is therefore that his demand for an explanation of the idea of justification is not relevant to his demand for an account of transtemporal identity, since the justified/unjustified distinction is settled at the point of explaining understanding at a time.[5]

If this is correct, then Kripke's claim (p. 22) that the dispositionalist response to the skeptic 'immediately ought to appear misdirected, off target' on the grounds that the dispositionalist cannot distinguish between performance and correctness – i.e. cannot distinguish between giving justified answers and saying the first thing which comes into one's head – can be interpreted in two ways. One is that the dispositionalist must identify any *sequence* of performances as the ideal manifestation of some single disposition; but this claim would have little plausibility unless another claim, which Kripke may be interpreted as intending as well, is also correct: that the dispositionalist must regard any performance *at* a time as an ideal manifestation of some single disposition at that time. For if a distinction can be made at a time between ideal and imperfect manifestation of a disposition, transtemporal identity conditions for dispositions would determine whether or not a sequence of performances was the manifestation of a single disposition and so determine such matters as whether or not the sequence represents 'improvement'. Since it is really not at all obvious that the dispositionalist can never justify classifying some performance as non-ideal in certain respects, it is doubtful if the dispositionalist response to the skeptic should *immediately* appear 'misdirected'.

---

5. We certainly *also* intend that our various applications of a concept be mutually consistent, but this is an issue separate from the question of the justifiability of a particular application in terms of the content of the very concept being applied.

IV

If this account of the situation is correct, then the main burden of the skeptic's case will be borne by his detailed objections to the dispositionalist account, these having to be understood as criticisms of the idea that my understanding of a concept *at* a time is a dispositional state. At this point, questions about transtemporal identity drop out as irrelevant, even though the *evidence* that a particular state obtains at a particular time consists in facts about performance at various times. The objections which Kripke advances focus on the fact that in applying a concept, things may go wrong in certain ways, e.g. we may make mistakes, or encounter 'external' obstacles (such as death). Thus our actual performances may fall short of ideal performance in a variety of respects; but the skeptic says that the dispositionalist does not have at his disposal the materials to make the distinction between a performance which constitutes imperfect manifestation of grasp of one content rather than ideal manifestation of grasp of another. In fact, Kripke suggests (p. 30) that the dispositionalist will have to see all performances as ideal manifestations, so the objection, more accurately, is again that the dispositionalist must identify correctness with performance.

To assess the significance of these points, it is helpful to look first at simpler examples of dispositional states, and at what analysis of the obtaining of such a state might be given. Common salt is water-soluble but not benzene- or petrol-soluble: it is disposed to dissolve in the first, but not the second or third, of these liquids. This is a consequence of a combination of factors. Water dissolves salt because the electric charge on a water molecule is not evenly distributed, which means it will orient itself in one direction in the presence of a positive ion and in the other in the presence of a negative ion, in each case a net attraction resulting. A salt crystal is an arrangement of sodium (positive) and chloride (negative) ions held together by electrostatic forces, which are not strong enough to combat the attractive forces which arise when such a crystal is in the presence of water molecules; thus the crystal dissolves. No such forces arise when salt is in petrol or benzene. In the light of this, we can see that it would be wrong to identify the persistence of the disposition of water-solubility in salt with the persistence of some physical state of salt, for if appropriate contingent properties of water altered in some way, salt might no longer dissolve in it. There is certainly a physical mechanism whose being activated when salt is put in water explains why salt in fact dissolves in water, but it does not have to be any particular mechanism, nor need it be unique. So a first thought is that the disposition exists if the counterfactual 'if salt were put in water it would dissolve' is true, and persists so long as it remains true, which gives an existence and an identity condition abstracted from the specific natures of salt and water.

However, this simple counterfactual analysis of the concept of water-solubility is open to objections like those advanced by the skeptic against the

[margin note: THESE COUD BE ANALOGIZED TO THE PARTS OF AN ADDITION]

[bottom handwritten note: SUPPOSE IT DOES NOT DISSOLVE, IS IT NO LONGER SALT?]

dispositional account of understanding. For example, if salt were put in a saturated solution of water, it would not dissolve. Alternatively, suppose God has the intention concerning some salt, that if it is put in water he will distribute the electric charges on the water molecules evenly, or in some other way, without violating the laws of nature, eliminate the relevant attractive forces before they have time to affect the salt crystals; it might be that: (i) God has this intention for all time and all salt, or (ii) He has the intention for some times and all salt, or (iii) He has the intention rarely and for just a few salt crystals. The simple counterfactual analysis can be maintained in the face of these examples only with difficulty: it seems better to say that the proper counterfactual analysis of water solubility is something like 'if salt were put in water, then *ceteris paribus* it would dissolve', the idea being that if the water is saturated or if God is going to play tricks, other things are not equal.

Since it seems clear that the skeptic has some sort of counterfactual account of dispositions in mind, the problem for the mental and the physical cases appear similar. Why say that salt is water-soluble but in certain circumstances this disposition is not manifested, when we could instead say that it has some rather more complex disposition whose *analysis* would include such counterfactuals as 'if salt were in water at time t then it would not dissolve', where t is a time at which God intends to depolarize all salt-containing water? For this disposition, whatever it is, would then be perfectly manifested in the circumstances we imagined. Kripke's skeptic objects to the dispositionalist about understanding that it is not possible to classify a particular performance as an imperfect manifestation of some disposition unless one first specifies the disposition whose ideal manifestation the performance fails to match; but to specify that disposition is to give its counterfactual analysis, and if we have yet to say which performances fall short of the ideal, we cannot formulate the counterfactuals. Thus there is a circularity in application which blocks the ascription of any disposition other than the vacuous one, that the object is disposed to do exactly what it does and nothing else. However, if the situation with salt's behaviour in water is the same, this problem cannot be insuperable.

Our ascription of dispositions to objects is underpinned by certain conceptions which resolve the threat of circularity just described. When we say that salt is S-soluble, where S is some substance, we have the conception of a state which grounds the disposition in salt and whose properties will lead, through interaction with states of S, to salt's dissolving in S. When we say that salt will dissolve in water *ceteris paribus,* we are adverting to a possibility admitted by this conception, the possibility of interference with the interaction between the relevant state of salt and that of water, whatever these states may be: we can distinguish between a closed system, where just the relevant states interact, and one in which there is disruptive causal influence from 'outside', where 'outside' includes other states of the objects in question, whose causal powers to interfere are activated by some other agent (if they were directly activated just by salt's being put in water, rather than by a detour e.g. through God's intentions, then salt would not be water-soluble). Hence, given a sequence of experimental results in which some substance sometimes dissolves in water and sometimes does not, we have to ascribe dispositional states to a number of entities simultaneously, and if we do so guided by the conceptions just sketched, it is *intelligible* that the substance should be classified as water-soluble. Of course, it is another question whether the experimental results *confirm* this classification: that will depend on independent confirmation of the other dispositional states ascribed to make sense of the sequence of results. But the skeptic's argument is about the intelligibility of the ascription of a disposition to dissolve in water to a substance which sometimes does not.

This could all be conceded by the skeptic if the case of understanding is in some way special. But the problems in this case appear exactly parallel. For instance, a subject, if queried about the sum of two numbers, may give no response because he has fallen asleep or because he has died. However, we would not reclassify a drug formerly regarded as a stimulant simply because a subject who absorbed it failed to exhibit stimulated behaviour, if in the circumstances the subject also absorbed a depressant or received some lethal shock. The conception of interference applies quite straightforwardly to these examples, in which we are simultaneously ascribing dispositions to the drug and to other entities: the other drug, the shock, the subject's body. Our chosen ascription can be justified e.g. by independent confirmation that shocks of that type are indeed lethal. And it does not need much independent confirmation that death will interfere with arithmetical computations.

One special phenomenon arises in virtue of the fact that, when behaviour manifests understanding, it is intentional under some description; for when behaviour is under the agent's intentional control, the possibility of making a mistake arises, a possibility with no parallel in the case of non-sentient things – Kripke mentions as an example (p. 29) that when asked to add certain numbers, some people forget to carry. Now a man may interpret '+' to mean addition and would give the right answer if he were not also disposed to make such a mistake: but how can we discern in his performances two dispositional states, one which embodies his interpretation of '+' and one which embodies his tendency to err? Kripke argues (p. 30) that we can only explain an outcome as the product of a mistake if we first know how he interprets '+'. If we think that his interpreting '+' as addition is a dispositional state, the state of being disposed to compute the (correct) sum of two numbers, then his behaviour as we observe it does not justify ascription of *that* disposition, but we cannot say that his behaviour is the product of that disposition and one to make a certain mistake, until we *do* ascribe that disposition, an ascription we will therefore never be in a position to make.

However, the fact that the notion of making a mistake makes cross-reference back to what we take his interpretation of '+' to be is no more an obstacle to simultaneous ascription of both dispositions than is the fact that the idea of a state which interferes with the behaviour of salt in water makes cross-reference back to what we take the disposition of salt in water to be. In the previous cases of simultaneous ascription of dispositions, there was no problem about independently checking each of the ascribed dispositions, even though the independent checks will themselves involve further simultaneous ascriptions. But the same is also true of hypotheses about mistakes: if someone has just forgotten to carry, then *ceteris paribus* he should change his mind about the answer when reminded, or when the problem is given to him again with the sum of the digits in the troublesome column computed separately and the left digit of the answer highlighted. And extreme degrees of unresponsiveness imply intellectual limitations whose manifestations would not be limited to just the operation of computing sums. So the dispositionalist need have no difficulty at all with the idea that one man may intend '+' to stand for addition and make mistakes, while another may mean some non-standard function by '+', even though their '+'-behaviour is the same throughout a fixed sequence of tests, for he knows how he could go about confirming which category it is to which a given subject belongs. On this view, the dispositionalist must regard as unintelligible the conception of a mistake with exactly one consequence for exactly one type of circumstance, and no other consequences; but that is hardly a damaging limitation.

V

Another difficulty which Kripke challenges the dispositionalist to meet has to do with the 'finiteness' of dispositions. Can there really be a sense in which someone who means addition by '+' is disposed to respond with the sum of x and y when queried with '$x + y$?', for *all* numbers x and y? There are two problems here: one concerns how a dispositional state can have infinitely many consequences, one for each pair (x, y); the other concerns the fact that many numbers x and y are too large for any subject to deal with. However, as regards the first problem, the mathematical case has a deceptive appearance. In fact, for such an observational term as 'red', there are as many consequences of understanding 'red' as there are red things. In standard conditions, when presented first with one, then with another, red thing, a normal subject does one thing: he classifies the presented object as red. But he also does two things; he classifies the *first* object as red, and then the *second*. Similarly, there are as many consequences of understanding addition as there are pairs of numbers.

The second problem is that, because most numbers are too large for people to work with, there is a *prima facie* difficulty for the dispositionalist, which is to explain the difference between two people, one of whom means addition by '+', the other of whom means some non-standard function, but a function which diverges from addition only for pairs of numbers well beyond the capacity of individuals to manipulate. Kripke pours scorn (p. 27) on the suggestion that the difference consists in what each person *would* say if he *were to* comprehend the question and to have the time and mental powers to answer it, on the grounds that we have no idea *what* would occur in circumstances where it is conceivable that people have the required abilities, e.g. 'if my brain had been stuffed with sufficient extra matter to grasp large enough numbers' (p. 27). However, the point of this objection is obscure. We may have no detailed understanding of what humans would have to be like in order to be capable of performing a given computation, but we can surely say that in circumstances in which they are so capable, however realized, then *ceteris paribus,* one man, the one who means addition by '+', will respond with the sum of these numbers, and the other will have a different response, where '*ceteris paribus*' is explained as before. No special problem arises for the thought that there is a distinction in terms of dispositions between two such people, just because we have no idea how we could arrange things so that the difference is manifested.

There is also another line of reply to the second problem about infinitude, to the effect that a fair comparison with non-mathematical cases shows that there is no special difficulty of principle here. Mathematical concepts, like those whose application is *a posteriori,* may be regarded as standing in a hierarchy, at the bottom of which are concepts understanding of which does consist in a disposition to do certain things – we have gone along with Kripke's assumption that addition is one such – while higher up the hierarchy we find concepts for which this is not so, such as that of the derivative of a function. The mathematical hierarchy is therefore analogous to the hierarchy of empirical concepts, with observational ones at the bottom. Now the problem Kripke advances in the mathematical case turns essentially on the fact that there is an inability (perhaps even as a matter of law) to realize the antecedent of the counterfactual said to be true of one subject and false of the other. But Goodmanesque versions of e.g. colour properties give rise to the same difficulty: a man may be hypothesized to understand 'red' to apply to red things except in the case of objects from some distant galaxy, or from some time before which, as a matter of fact, the universe did not exist. This analogy is imperfect: in the mathematical case, the exception condition was given in mathematical terms, so in the experiential, we should try for an exception condition formulable in observational vocabulary, and the difficulty is then to find an exception condition which is sufficiently remote. But if it is just remoteness which is the root of the problem to which Kripke adverts, we should note that the hypothesis about 'red' *can* be tested, since it is only necessary to make the subject *believe* that the object with which he is being presented satisfies the exception condition. Therefore, in the mathematical case, we can distinguish which subject has the non-standard interpretation for '+' by getting each to believe that the numbers he is being presented with, perhaps in a new, super-compact notation to which we have taught him to extend addition, satisfy the hypothesized exception conditions. This procedure would raise new opportunities for misunderstanding, but inductive evidence for some hypotheses rather than others is going to mount up.

It might be objected to this use of belief that the exception conditions in the hypotheses we make about a subject are only intended to specify a possible extension for his concept, and need not reflect the way of thinking about things which constitutes the content of his concept. Indeed, if his concept is supposed to be observational, and the exception condition in question employs non-observational vocabulary, such unfaithfulness to content would be inevitable. And then it may just be beside the point to cause the subject to acquire certain beliefs. But now the hypotheses about non-standard interpretations acquire degrees of implausibility from other sources, specifically from our views about what kinds of concepts a being *could* acquire in circumstances like ours and with sensory routes to the external world like ours; a recognitional capacity activated by objects from distant galaxies is something of a non-starter. In sum, then, the possibility of remoteness in the point at which a certain non-standard interpretation diverges from the standard one seems to raise no new difficulty for the dispositionalist.

VI

Our strategy in reponse to the skeptic about understanding has been to argue that the objections he advances to the dispositionalist view are not very different from objections which could be advanced against a dispositional analysis of water-solubility. However, it might be objected to this strategy that the considerations which justify *ceteris paribus* restrictions on counterfactuals in the latter case do not seem to be available for the former. We argued that certain conceptions of structural states of salt and water, and different ways in which they might causally interact, underlie our grasp of the possibility of salt's disposition to dissolve in water not being manifested on a particular occasion of being in water, and thus justify our idea of interference, and of *ceteris paribus* circumstances being ones in which sources of interference are screened out. But the transfer of this apparatus to the cases under discussion is problematic. We are happy to say that salt is water-soluble *in virtue of* certain physical states of it and water, but then it seems that an analysis of states of understanding as dispositional states requires that there be other states in virtue of which a subject is in a state of understanding; yet no-one would be very happy with the introduction of a mental substance whose states realize the relevant dispositions and which are subject to quasi-mechanical laws analogous to those which obtain for matter, though this would certainly afford the simplest analogy.

Perhaps we can just say that the subject is in a state of understanding in virtue of the nature of certain of his physical states, specifically, his brain states. But this introduces a difference with the inanimate case which may seem significant enough to undermine the strategy of our response to the skeptic, for the states which are relevant to water-solubility are those which *explain* salt's behaviour in water; but physical states do not explain exercises of understanding – they explain at most the physical events in which that exercise is embodied. Explanations of exercises of understanding – exercises of semantic knowledge – are like all explanations of purposive behaviour in being teleological: the explanation works by citing the agent's goal, usually through ascription of an intention or desire (if some goal-directed – Gricean – account of speaker's meaning is correct, ascription of meaning to an utterance or act of inscription is elliptical for ascription of a complex goal and thus explicitly a kind of teleological explanation). However, it seems that this difference with the physical case is not too damaging for the dispositionalist, for along with the idea of the goal-directed goes the conception of the execution of a procedure for goal-achievement, and we have no difficulty with the idea of interference with such a procedure, even in advance of the *a posteriori* details of how such procedures are implemented. If understanding intentional behaviour involves goal-ascription, which is in turn subject to constraints rather different from those involved in understanding the behaviour of salt in water, still it is not difficult to appreciate how attempts to satisfy these constraints should involve ascribing goals not achieved where the failure of achievement is itself explained by independently confirmable states of the subject, such as those of forgetfulness, lack of attention or other intellectual flaws.[6]

6. I wish to thank Mark Sainsbury and Crispin Wright for helpful comments on an earlier version of this paper.

CHAPTER THREE

THE INDIVIDUAL STRIKES BACK

Simon Blackburn

In this paper I address some of the points Saul Kripke makes in his treatment of the 'rule-following considerations' in the later Wittgenstein.[1] There are two different quarries to track down. There is the question of whether Kripke's exegesis of Wittgenstein is correct – whether KW is LW. And there is the distinct question of the real significance of the considerations, as they are put forward by KW. Kripke himself is carefully agnostic about this second issue.[2] KW is not Kripke *in propria persona*. And Kripke is also careful to distinguish the exegetical issue from the question of significance. The two issues only connect like this. If KW's arguments have some property which we are convinced cannot belong to any argument which LW would have used, we shall suppose that KW is not the real LW. And admirers of Wittgenstein will suppose that significance is such a property: if KW's considerations are faulty, then for that reason alone KW cannot be LW. LW would not have used faulty considerations. But without commenting on this optimism, I want to discuss two other properties which might distinguish KW from LW: KW's use of skepticism, and his attitude to facts. Each of these aspects may legitimately raise worries about his identity with LW. And I shall also offer some thoughts about the significance of KW's arguments for our conceptions of meaning.

Our topic is the fact that terms of a language are governed by rules that determine what constitutes correct and incorrect application of them. I intend no particular theoretical implications by talking of rules here. The topic is that there is such a thing as the correct and incorrect application of a term, and to

---

1. Saul A. Kripke, *Wittgenstein on Rules and Private Language* (Oxford: Blackwell, 1982). All page references are to this work. Paragraph references in the text are to the *Philosophical Investigations*.
2. Kripke, p. 5.

say that there is such a thing is no more than to say that there is truth and falsity. I shall talk indifferently of there being correctness and incorrectness, of words being rule-governed, and of their obeying principles of application. Whatever this is, it is the fact that distinguishes the production of terms from mere noise, and turns utterance into assertion – into the making of judgement. It is not seriously open to a philosopher to deny that, in this minimal sense, there is such a thing as correctness and incorrectness.[3] The entire question is the conception of it that we have.

KW pursues this issue by advancing a certain kind of skepticism. As Kripke is well aware, this might provoke immediate protest. Surely LW is consistently scornful of skepticism? But this reaction misunderstands the function of skepticism in a context such as this. The function is not to promote a conclusion about knowledge or certainty, but to force a reconsideration of the metaphysics of the issue. That is, we begin with a common-sense or unrefined conception of some kind of fact. We think we have an understanding of what that kind of fact consists in. The skeptic tries to show that on that conception we would have no way of distinguishing occasions when the fact obtains from those when it does not. Now we might conclude from this that our conception was correct and that there is therefore a definite kind of proposition whose truth value we can never reliably judge. This would be a traditional skeptical conclusion. But we might alternatively conclude that, since we do know the truth about the kind of thing in question, the conception was at fault. The things we know do not have the kind of truth condition we took them to have; the facts are not quite the kind of thing we took them to be. This is a metaphysical conclusion, and the skeptical dialogue is an instrument for reaching it. LW may have had no time for skeptical conclusions. But he may well have had thought processes which can be revealed by using a skeptical instrument to reach a metaphysical conclusion. This is what KW does. So, as far as the issue of using a skeptical weapon goes, KW may well be LW.

It is clear that on this account there are two parts to the business: attacking the old conception, and producing a replacement. The negative part might be successful, although the positive part is not. If LW was successful, then in the positive part he produced a conception on which public rule-following (in some sense of public) is possible, whereas private rule-following is not. I shall be arguing that KW is not successful in doing this. He does not succeed in describing what it is for there to be a rule in force, with the property that this can obtain in a public case, but not in the private case.

---

3. Crispin Wright comes close to denying it in *Wittgenstein on the Foundations of Mathematics*, (London: Duckworth, 1980) e.g., pp. 21–2, where he seems to attribute to Wittgenstein an error theory of determinacy in the correctness of saying anything.

1. SKEPTICAL SOLUTIONS

Kripke describes KW as adopting a 'skeptical solution' to the skeptical considerations, modelled upon Hume's skeptical solution to his own doubts. To assess this idea it is important to separate various strands in Hume's extremely complex position. If KW is understood to be taking over the wrong parts of Hume, he may too easily be rejected as a pretender. I suspect that parts of Kripke's presentation will encourage this – particularly those where he talks of the skeptical solution.

Hume calls Section V of the *First Enquiry* the 'Skeptical Solution of these Doubts'. The doubts in question were introduced in Section IV: they concern operations of the understanding. In particular they concern our ability to reason a priori about what must cause what, and the impossibility of justifying inductive reasoning. The skeptical solution of Section V consists in denying that processes of reasoning have the power and the place hitherto assigned to them. They are replaced by processes of custom. This is why we have a skeptical solution: Hume offers a view of ourselves which in part he shares with traditional skeptics. The shared part is the denial that we can justifiably reason to our beliefs. (Hume differs from tradition in his estimate of the consequences of that.) When Kripke introduces the analogy with Hume, this is what he first mentions. But this is not the aspect of Hume (nor the section of the *Enquiry*) that actually matters. What matters is his reinterpretation of the concept of causation – the topic of Section VII of the *Enquiry*.[4] It is here that Hume has a (fairly) pure example of the process I described: a skeptical argument forcing us to revise our conception of a kind of fact. It is here that he parallels KW. But the reinterpretation does not deserve to be called a 'skeptical solution' to anything, nor did Hume so call it. It is at most a proposal prompted by skeptical problems. But in principle it might have been prompted by other considerations altogether. And in fact Hume's reinterpretation of causation is only partly motivated by skepticism. It is at least as firmly seated in the theory of understanding: problems with our idea of the causal nexus. In this part of Hume, skepticism is subsidiary, even as a tool.

Kripke can rejoin that Hume's reinterpretation of causation is, in itself, deservedly called skeptical for a further reason. It denies that there is a 'fact' whether there is a causal connexion between two events. At least, that is how Kripke takes Hume.[5] But here too there are subtleties in the offing, and they matter to the parallel with KW. This is because LW's attitude about 'facts' is going to be crucial, and crucial to many philosophers' belief that KW differs from him. The philosopher we have described ends up reinterpreting some kind of fact. This leaves various options. The first might be called 'lowering the truth-condition'. This asserts that sentences in the area can only,

---

4. Similarly in the *Treatise*, esp. Bk I, Pt III, section 14.
5. Kripke, pp. 68, 69.

legitimately, be given such-and-such a truth-condition. This can be combined with the view that in our ordinary thought we confusedly attempt to do more, or misunderstand what we are actually doing enough to make mistakes (although there is always a problem about how we can attempt to do more, if we are supposed to have no conception of anything more to do). Lowering the truth condition is then a reforming view, and entails an 'error' theory of ordinary thought. But it can be combined with the view that the lowering really reveals what we meant all along, and we have reductionism. Often it does not matter very much which combination is offered, and indeed, since a decision depends on a fine detection of ordinary meaning, we would expect some degree of indeterminacy.

Quite distinct from lowering the truth-condition, there is the option of denying one altogether. The sentences in question are given some other role than that of asserting that some fact obtains. This option is familiar from expressive theories of moral commitment, or from views that try to see arithmetical theses as rules rather than descriptions or propositions, and so on. Now I say that this option is distinct from lowering the truth-condition, and indeed in its initial stages it certainly is. It is a confusion, for instance, to muddle together expressive theories of ethics with naive subjective theories that give moral commitments a truth-condition, but make it into one about the speaker. Arguments against this latter view often have no force against the former. But Hume is responsible for the very complication that makes it so hard to keep these options properly separated. This is the view that the mind spreads itself on the world: the view I call projectivism. According to projectivism we speak and think 'as if' the world contained a certain kind of fact, whereas the true explanation of what we are doing is that we have certain reactions, habits or sentiments, which we voice and discuss by such talk. Hume was quite clearly a projectivist in moral philosophy, and it is plausible to see his metaphysics of causation as in essence identical.[6]

Like the option of lowering the truth-condition, the option of denying that there is one can be combined with either of two attitudes to our ordinary practice. One would be that it embodies error. Ordinary talk is conducted as if there were facts, when there are no such facts. The talk is 'fraudulent' or 'diseased'. The other option is less familiar, but much more attractive. It holds that there is nothing illegitimate in our ordinary practice and thought. The respects in which we talk as if there are, for instance, moral facts, are legitimate. (I have called this view 'quasi-realism'.)[7] If LW were a projectivist, he would have to be this kind, for it preserves the doctrine that ordinary talk and thought, before we start to philosophize about the nature of our concepts, are in perfect order as they are.

---

6. For typical statements compare Appendix to *Enquiry*, also *Treatise*, p. 167 (Selby Bigge). Projectivism is widely misunderstood even today, and its true resources are not easily recognized.
7. See my 'Truth, Realism and the Regulation of Theory', in French, Uehling and Wettstein (eds), *Midwest Studies in Philosophy*, Vol. V.

Kripke acknowledges the strand in LW which matters here. He also realizes that it goes far – far enough to stop LW from endorsing any such judgement as this: 'there is no fact of the matter whether a term is rule-governed or not'. But KW expresses himself differently: KW believes that there is 'no such fact, no such condition in either the "internal" or the "external" world' (p. 69). This talk will outrage friends of LW. KW denies the existence of a certain kind of fact altogether; LW would never so express himself, *ergo* one is not the other. But now recall that Hume himself says that 'those who deny the reality of moral distinctions may be reckoned amongst the most disingenuous of disputants'.[8] Why? Because insisting on this reality is part of normal thinking. It is part of the way of life, or way of thought or talk, which quasi-realism can protect for us. So there must be room for a different version of LW. This one would abandon his hostility to facts. He should accept that talking of facts is part of our legitimate way of expressing ourselves on the difference between terms which are rule-governed, and terms which are not. He has to do this if he doubles for LW. For recall that the very passage (§137) that begins these considerations is a version of the redundancy theory of truth. And on that theory (whatever else it holds) there is no difference between saying that it is true that p and that p or between saying that it is a fact that p and that p. So anybody prepared to assert that terms are rule-governed – and as I explained initially, that must mean all of us – can equally be heard saying that there are facts, truths, states of affairs of just that kind.

Kripke says something strange about this. On p. 86 he imagines someone saying that it cannot be tolerable to concede to the skeptic that there are no truth-conditions or corresponding facts to make a statement about someone's meaning true: 'Can we not with propriety precede such assertions with "It is a fact that" or "It is not a fact that"?' But Kripke puts this complaint in the mouth of an *objector* to LW. He then reminds us that LW accepts the redundancy theory of truth, and says that this gives him a short way with such objections. The dialectic seems to be the wrong way round. *Because* he accepts the redundancy theory, LW can assent to the locutions of fact and truth. They add nothing to the fact that we judge other people to be following rules, and applying terms in accordance with standards of correctness.

I don't know that the redundancy theory of truth should have this soothing power. It may be that there are explanations of why we make some judgements, and why we apply the calculus of truth-functions to the judgements we make, which still leave us queasy when we consider if there are facts in the case. The quasi-realist construction of ordinary moral discourse is a good example. Even if it protects everything we do, it can still leave us uneasy when we contemplate the question: 'Yes, but are there any moral facts on this account?' I shall not consider that question further in this paper. I just want to note that, on a redundancy theory, it is a bad place to become puzzled, and

---

8. *An Enquiry Concerning the Principles of Morals*, section I.

that LW held a redundancy theory. Hence it seems that there is space for a *persona* who profits from KW's arguments, but draws a rather different conclusion from them. With due humility, I shall call this character BW. He is going to share a great deal of the argumentative strategy of KW. In part his difference is relatively cosmetic: the belief that skepticism is only in play, if at all, as an instrument, and that the eventual conception of rule-following that must emerge does not deserve to be called skeptical. But in part he differs more substantially, because he hopes to preserve the implications of the redundancy theory in LW. And he hopes to cement a more particular relationship between LW and the real Hume, who matters to metaphysics. If he can preserve our right to talk of the fact that words obey principles of application, this may be as much because he forces us to revise our conception of a fact as anything else. Alas, however, BW has one radical flaw. On his philosophy, there is no particular reason to discriminate against the would-be private linguist. But before advertising his intended end-point further, it is necessary to review some of the arguments by which he gets there.

2. THE CRITIQUE OF RULE-FOLLOWING

It may seem outrageous to the touchy friends of LW that anything in Hume could be a model for LW's attitude to rule-following. But perhaps we can stem some of the outrage by reminding ourselves that it is an essentially normative judgement that we are chasing. It is the judgement that something is correct or incorrect. When this fact proves fugitive, as KW shows that it is, its normative nature is largely the problem. So it cannot be that outrageous to apply our best explanations of value judgements to it, and this is what BW hopes to do. But why is the fact fugitive in the first place?

In Kripke's development, we start by considering the understanding I had of some term at some time in the past, which we can arbitrarily call 'yesterday'. Suppose the term is some arithmetical functor, 'plus' or '+'. I understood it by grasping a principle of application. We then consider my position today. When I come to do a calculation, which we suppose I have never done before, I certainly believe myself to follow a principle. I believe myself to be *faithful* to yesterday's rule, by adopting the same procedure or principle in determining answers to problems expressed using the functor. Thus I believe that, if I am faithful to yesterday's principle, I should say '57 + 68 is 125'. Notice that this is not quite the same as claiming that I should say this unconditionally. I may wish to change my allegiances. There is no impropriety in deciding that yesterday's principle of application is not the best one for this term, and to consciously start to use it according to different rules. It is just that, *if* I am faithful, then I ought to give that answer. I most certainly should not say that 57 + 68 is 5. Nor of course should I say that there is more than one answer to that problem, or that the problem is indeterminate, so that there is no answer at all. The skeptical dialogue then commences. The skeptic asks me to point to the fact that I am being faithful to yesterday's rule only by saying one thing, and not these others. And this proves hard to do. For any fact which I tell him about myself seems compatible with the 'bent-rule' hypothesis, as I shall call it: the hypothesis that the rule that was really in force yesterday was a Goodman competitor. In other words, the kinds of fact I am apt to allege are compatible with a story in which I really understood by 'plus' a function with a particular singularity at $x = 57$ and $y = 68$. For example, I might yesterday have meant that we should now express by saying:

$$x + y = \text{the sum of } x, y, \text{ except when } x = 57 \text{ and } y = 68$$
$$\text{and } 5 \text{ otherwise.}$$

This hypothesis is not refuted by my present staunch denial that I had any such thought in mind yesterday, or that if asked I would have used words like these to explain myself. For the skeptic will urge that, as well as having had a bent interpretation of '+' yesterday, I could have had a bent interpretation of these other terms as well. So pointing out that I would have presented no such explanation to myself does not refute the skeptic. It would really be a question of my using another rule to interpret the first (e.g., the rule for interpreting various synonyms for '+' or for interpreting terms that would have occurred in any explanation of the functor that I would have proffered). So the fact that yesterday I would have said, for instance, '$x + y$ is always a number greater than either x or y, with $x = 57$ and $y = 68$ no exception' is consistent with my having been a secret bent rule user. The singularity, by current lights, would have been there in the way I took the words involved in such an affirmation. Perhaps 'exception' meant . . .

This argument (which is much more forcefully and thoroughly presented in Kripke) undoubtedly corresponds to a central negative point of LW's. The point is that taking a term in a certain way is something different from *presenting* anything as an aid to understanding it, or from *accepting* anything as aids to understanding it. He says in §201 that he has shown 'that there is a way of grasping a rule which is *not an interpretation* but which is exhibited in what we call "obeying the rule" and "going against it"'! The negative point, that we gain no approach to the required fact by embarking on a potential regress of interpretations, is quite clear. The more positive claim, that the fact is exhibited in what we call obeying a rule, must wait.

When presenting the skeptical challenge this way, we should not lose sight of the fact that the case can be made without instancing a rival principle of application, a bent rule, at all. A skeptic might just doubt whether there was, yesterday or today, any principle at all behind my application of '+'. Perhaps all that happened was that I would look at things, such as triples of numbers,

PRIVATE CONVICTION IS NOT TRUE. ~~ m

and after a process that was phenomenologically just like one of being guided by a rule, declare '$z = x + y$' or the reverse. I would be in the same case as a lunatic who thinks he is doing sums, when all that is happening is that he is covering pages with symbols. Or, I would be like the man whom Wittgenstein considers at §237 who with great deliberation follows a line with one leg of a pair of dividers, and lets the other leg trace a path, but one whose distance from the original line he varies in an intent but apparently random way. He might think he is tracing a path determined by a rule relating its course to the first line. But his thought that this is what he is doing does not make it true. In some ways this is the primary weapon that LW uses against the private linguist. He forces him back to saying that he has only his own conviction that he is following a rule at all, and this private, phenomenological conviction that one is following a rule is not enough to make it true.

I have followed Kripke in concentrating upon the normative aspect of the fact we are looking for. So I agree with him that the answer to the problem is not going to be given just by talking of dispositions we actually have. However, and crucially for what follows subsequently, I do not think the dispositional account falls to all of Kripke's objections. The analysis he considers (p. 26) says that I mean some function F by my functor if and only if I am disposed, whenever queried about the application of the functor to a pair of numbers, to give the answer that actually is that function, F, of them. Kripke attacks this on the grounds that my dispositions are finite. 'It is not true, for instance, that if queried about the sum of any two numbers, no matter how large, I will reply with their actual sum. For some numbers are simply too large for my mind – or my brain – to grasp' (pp. 26–7). So, according to Kripke, my dispositions fail to make it true that I mean addition by '+' and not quaddition – a function that gives different results just when x and y are so big that I cannot do sums involving them.

There are difficulties here. It is not obvious that dispositions in themselves are either finite or infinite. The brittleness of a glass is a respectable dispositional property. But there is an infinite number of places and times and strikings and surfaces on which it could be displayed. Does this glass have a disposition that covers, for example, the fact that it would break if banged on a rock on Alpha Centauri? What if scientists tell us that this glass couldn't get there, because it would have decayed within the time it takes to be transported there? Perhaps I am not disposed to give the answer faced with huge sums. But perhaps also I have dispositions that fix a sense for the expression 'the answer I would accept'. The answer I would accept is the one that *would* be given by reiterating procedures I *am* disposed to use, a number of times. (The notion is *doubly* dispositional.) The fact that I am not disposed to follow those procedures that number of times seems like the fact that the glass cannot get to Alpha Centauri. Now, a skeptic might maintain that we do not know of a dispositional fact about me that is described in this way. Perhaps I am only disposed to say that '$3 + 5 = 8$' when the calculation is not embedded in really huge calculations. But this is just skepticism about dispositions. It is like supposing that the glass may be not brittle but 'shmittle', where x is shmittle if it breaks when struck except . . . In effect this is inductive skepticism about the concept of a disposition, querying whether we can legitimately take dispositions to cover what would have happened on unobserved occasions. So it cannot be used to argue that, even if we accept the concept, it permits no answer to the problem of huge calculations. A similar complication might answer Kripke's second objection (pp. 28–9). This is that what I mean cannot be read off from what I am disposed to do, since I may be disposed to make mistakes. The dispositionalist would have to read off what I meant from a table of answers I actually give, and this might involve saying that I was computing (correctly) a bent function – 'skaddition' – and not making a mistake in attempting to add. But this seems to ignore surrounding dispositions. Kripke rightly dismisses any view that simply takes for granted a notion of the function it was intended to compute, or which defines user's competence, since it presupposes the ideas we are looking for. But at least it is true that a calculator can have, in addition to dispositions to give answers, dispositions to withdraw them and substitute others. And it is possible that putting the errant disposition into a context of general dispositions of this sort supplies the criterion for which function is meant. The equation would be: By '+' I mean that function F, that accords with my extended dispositions. An answer $z = F(x, y)$ accords with my extended dispositions if and only if (i) it is the answer I am disposed to give and retain after investigation, or (ii) it is the answer I would accept if I repeated a number of times procedures I am disposed to use, this being independent of whether I am disposed to repeat those procedures that number of times.

Kripke's point about mistakes can be illustrated if we consider a calculating machine. There is no physical or dispositional difference between a machine that is 'supposed' to compute addition, but because of a mistake in the hardware computes a bent function, and one that is designed to compute the bent function in the first place. The two may be perfectly identical. This strongly suggests that the notion of correctness, the notion of *the* rule to which we are to be faithful, has to come from outside the thing itself. In the case of the calculator, it certainly does. But this need not entirely destroy a dispositional account, provided it can look for dispositions outside the simple disposition to give answers.

So is it a real truth that the right rule for '+' is in force amongst us? My own answer would be that we do have dispositions that enforce this judgement. They make it the only possible judgement about ourselves, when we describe each other's thoughts. The concealed bent-rule follower is a theoretician's fiction. Whenever we try to fill out the story, of a person or a community that really adopts a bent rule, it turns out that the singularity in the rule (by our lights, of course) must affect the dispositions to behave that the community or individual shows. I have argued this elsewhere in connexion with

Goodman's paradox.[9] The concealed bent-rule follower is often thought of as though nothing about him is different until the occasion of bent application arises. But this is wrong. Someone who has genuinely misunderstood a functor is different, and the difference can be displayed quite apart from occasions of application. Consider, for instance, the bricklayer told to add bricks to a stack two at a time. If this means to him 'add 2 up to 1000, and then 4' his reaction to the foreman may be quite different. Perhaps he cannot carry four bricks at a time.

However, I am not going to pursue this defence of dispositions. I share Kripke's view that whatever dispositions we succeed in identifying they could at most give standards for selection of a function which we mean. They couldn't provide us with an account of what it is to be faithful to a previous rule. It is just that, unlike Kripke, I do not think dispositions are inadequate to the task of providing standards. Indeed, I think they must be. For notice that the problem of finitude applies just as much to any community as to any individual. If the finiteness of an individual's dispositions leaves it indeterminate whether he means one function or another by some functor, then so must the finiteness of community disposition. So although communities induct their members into '+' using practices and go through all the corrections and imitations that constitute community use, still all that is consistent with the 'skaddition' hypothesis too. We don't find communities disposed to calculate numbers which are just too big. But prosecuting this point takes us into BW's divergence from KW.

3. THE COMMUNITY AND THE INDIVIDUAL

The individual has a hard time against Kripke's skeptic. How does the public fare better? The individual couldn't make the skeptic appreciate the kind of fact it was, that he was being faithful to a principle, or rule or previous intention, when he gave some answer. The skeptic charges that there is no fact of the matter whether the bent rule or the natural rule was the one intended, or whether one principle of application or another was in force yesterday. And if there is no fact of the matter of this sort, then there is really no fact of the matter that any principle at all was in force. Any answer to the new sum can be regarded as equally 'right' and that just means that we cannot talk about right. Faced with this impasse the individual thankfully turns to the community. He can point to his inculcation in a public practice, his gradual conformity to patterns of behaviour accepted by others, and his acceptance as a competent operator with '+'.

---

9. *Reason and Prediction* (Cambridge: Cambridge University Press, 1973), Ch. 4; and *Spreading the Word* (Oxford: Oxford University Press, 1984), Ch. 3.

The skeptic might allow all this to make the difference. But he has suddenly gone very soft if he does. He can easily specify bent principles, with points of singularity where neither I nor anybody else used the terms yesterday. If such points worried the individual, then they should equally worry the community. So how does mention of the community give us the determinate rule?

KW's answer is that in a sense it doesn't (see for instance p. 111). The community is as much at a loss to identify the fugitive fact as the individual was. The position is supposed to be no different metaphysically. The difference is that the community endorses or accepts the competent operator. They or 'we' *allow* him to be using '+' to mean addition. He is 'seen' or *dignified* as a rule-follower. We, the community, have justification conditions for doing this. To gain the title, the individual's practice (on the finite number of occasions on which it will have been shown) must accord in some suitable way with the community practice (on the finite number of occasions on which *it* will have been shown).

Now, merely citing the fact that we 'see each other as' obeying the same principle of application makes no headway at all. Remember that the point of the original worries about rule-following was not epistemological. The aim was not to suggest that we cannot provide a foundation of some sort for the judgement that a rule is in force, or that we cannot provide principles for inferring such judgements from others more basic. If this were the aim, then replying that there is no inference and no foundation, but just a basic fact that we make such judgements of each other, 'seeing each other as' following principles, might be relevant – at any rate, as relevant as this move is in other areas of epistemology. But the point does nothing at all to suggest *how* we are seeing each other when we say such a thing. We know well enough what it is to see something as a duck, because we know what ducks are. But we don't know what it is to see someone as obeying a principle of application, unless we know what it is to follow one, and this is the fact of which we still have, so far, no conception. To put it another way, we do not know what a community would be lacking if its members failed to see each other this way, or if they continually saw each other in the light of potential bent-rule followers.

So the skeptic is still liable to feel short-changed. He has pointed out bent rules which might have been in force yesterday, compatibly with all that the individual could point to. He has pointed out that, for all that the individual could show, there might be nothing but his onward illusion that rules are in force, and that his dispositions to respond are correct or incorrect. The individual now links arms with others. The skeptic attempts to point out the same two things to them: for all they can describe about themselves, bent rules (and perhaps differently bent rules) might have been in force, underlying their fortuitous coincidence of behaviour over the finite samples they have come across. Since this means that any answer to a new problem might be as right as any other, the skeptic suggests that again there is just the onward illusion that there is correctness or incorrectness. The community replies that it has a practice of dignifying its members as saying things correctly or incorrectly, and in the light of this practice it says that all its members do mean the same, and that what they mean provides a principle of application of a term.

We can see one way in which this could silence the skeptic. If the mutual support itself provides the standard of correctness, then a community can answer him. To understand this, consider the analogy with an orchestra. Suppose that there is no such thing as an individual playing in accord with instructions coming down from the past, by way of scores or memory. Suppose too that on an individual instrument there is no standard for the way a piece ought to go (all melodies are equally acceptable). Then an individual cannot play well or badly in isolation. Nevertheless, the orchestra may have standards of harmony across instruments. And if at a given time most instruments are playing, say, notes from the chord of C major, then the individual who hits a dissonant C# is incorrect by the standards of the orchestra. They can turn on him. Unfortunately, this provides only a poor analogy for communities and their relations to their own rule-following. For in the orchestra, harmony with others provides a direct standard of correctness. This is just not so with judgement. If my community all suddenly started saying that $57 + 68 = 5$, this fact does not make me wrong when I continue to assert that it is 125. I am correct today in saying that the sun is shining and daffodils are yellow, regardless of what the rest of the world says. Obviously any solution to these problems must avoid the disastrous conclusion that it is part of the truth-condition of any judgement that a community would make it (unless of course the judgement is itself not about the sun and daffodils and so on, but about the community).

If the community cannot turn to the orchestral metaphor then how have they answered the skeptic? And why cannot their answer be taken over by the isolated individual? Remember that there is a distinction between the overall practice of a community, thought of as something defined by principles and rules, and the exposed practice, thought of as only a partial, finite segment of applications. If a community practices addition, meaning one thing and not another by some functor '+', then the exposed practice will cover only a small proportion of the applications whose correctness follows from the overall practice. As the possibility of bent functions is supposed to show, the exposed practice does not logically determine the question of which overall practice is in force. Then we can imagine what we might call a 'thoroughly Goodmanned community' in which people take explanations and exposure to small samples – yesterday's applications – in different ways. The skeptic who won against Kripke's individual will now win against a community, showing that they have no conception of the fact which makes it true that they do not form a thoroughly Goodmanned community.

It may be helpful to think of it like this. The members of a community stand to each other as the momentary time-slices of an individual do. So just as the original skeptic queries what it is for one person-time to be faithful to a rule adopted by a previous person-time, so the public skeptic queries what it is for one person to be faithful to the same rule as that adopted by another. Now if the public skeptic can be by-passed by, in effect, saying that this is what we do – we see each other as mutually understanding the same rule, or dignify or compliment each other as so doing, provided the exposed practice agrees well enough, then the private skeptic can be by-passed in the same way. His doubts admit of the same projective solution. When LW denies that 'we have a model of this superlative fact' (§192) we can, as far as the metaphysics goes, shrug and say that this is how we see ourselves. Then, as I have already explained, the entire problem is to explain how we are seeing ourselves when we go into this mode. In particular we need to cite some *standard* for saying this – and, if LW is to win through, a standard which separates the public from the individual. For when I write the sensation term in my diary I can and will see myself as being faithful to a previous intention to apply it only in a determinate range of circumstances. And, paying me the compliment as it were, you can do so too. It might be different if it somehow came naturally to us to dignify fellow members of the same public with the title of rule followers, and natural to hesitate over any purely private attempt at self-description. But generally speaking there is little difference in naturalness. Until LW supposedly argues that we shouldn't do so, most people would find it quite natural to believe that a putative private linguist might be following or failing to follow previously formed intentions to apply principles of application.

The dilemma so far is this. If the presence or potential presence of a community of persons practising the same way enters as part of the truth-conditions, part of the analysis, of what it is to follow a rule, the skeptic who won against the private individual looks equally set to win against a community which has the benefit of mutual support. But if mention of the community comes as part of a Humean or projective solution, allowing us to by-pass troubles over our conception of the superlative fact, then a similar side-step is in principle available to the individual. To split the individual from the public we need enough understanding of how we are regarding ourselves to be able to specify standards which need to be met by a candidate for rule-following, and we have not yet got this.

The simple move, endorsed by KW and, for instance, by Peacocke, is to say that in the case of the individual there is no distinction between it seeming to him that a rule is in force, and there being a rule in force. The trouble with this is that in any sense in which it is true (see next section), it is equally true that there is no distinction between a community being thoroughly Goodmanned, but seeming to itself to have a unified practice, and its actually having a unified practice. And when the community says 'well, we just see ourselves as agreeing (dignify, compliment ourselves as comprehending the same rule)' the individual just borrows the trick, and compliments himself on his rapport with his previous times. The community needs to say that the compliment is empty in the case of the individual but meaningful in the case of a set of them. How is this to be argued?

4. PUBLIC AND PRIVATE PRACTICE

Peacocke writes:

SUBSTANTIVE ANALOGY B/W BURGE & WITTGENSTEIN IN THIS WAY

> In the end, Wittgenstein holds, the only thing that must be true of someone who is trying to follow a rule, so long as we consider just the individual and not facts about some community, is that he is disposed to think that certain cases fall under the rule and others do not. But this is something which is also true of a person who falsely believes that he is conforming to a rule. His general argument is that only by appealing to the fact that the genuine rule-follower agrees in his reactions to examples with the members of some community can we say what distinguishes him from someone who falsely thinks he is following a rule. [10]

The lynch-pin of this interpretation is the absence of a 'distinction' in the case of an individual, between the case where he believes that there is a rule, when there is none, and where he believes it and there is one. And my question has been: do we think we have yet been given a 'distinction' between a thoroughly Goodmanned community, accidentally agreeing in exposed practice, and a real community of understanding? And then, if the distinction is given using materials from Hume – the projection upon one another of a dignity – I ask what the standards are whereby it takes several people to do this, when one cannot do it to himself. I shall now try to exhibit the force of this question, by considering the individual further. This is to illustrate the gap between anything that has happened in LW, at least as far as §202, and the application to exclude the private linguist.

Let us recall the basic point, that giving an explanation, either in words, or using other aids, such as pictures or models, does not logically determine the rule that governs one's understanding of a term: 'Any interpretation still hangs in the air along with what it interprets, and cannot give it any support' (§198). To avoid the threatening paradox, that nothing can accord nor conflict with a rule, because anything can be made out so to do, LW introduces the positive suggestion that our rules are anchored in practice. In the remainder of this paper I shall assume that this is along the right lines. That is, dignifying each other as rule-following is essentially connected with seeing each other as successfully using techniques or practices. This at least begins to isolate the nature of the judgement. It suggests a direction from which to find standards for making the judgement, and in my view it connects interestingly with pragmatic and coherence aspects of judging. Now, having introduced the notion of a practice or technique, LW immediately goes on to draw two famous

---

10. C. Peacocke, 'Rule Following: The Nature of Wittgenstein's Arguments', in S. Holtzman and S. Leich (eds), *Wittgenstein: To Follow a Rule* (London: Routledge & Kegan Paul, 1981), p. 73.

conclusions – that to think one is obeying a rule is not to do so, and that it is not possible to obey a rule privately. These are not the same, and the second is not warranted. The question is, what kind of thing does a practice have to be, if it is to block the skeptical paradox? Perhaps, for instance, the concept of a practice can include that of someone setting out to describe his mental life, even on a highly private conception of the mental. The basic negative point certainly does not rule that out. To do so we would need further thoughts about what a practice must be, and the connexion it is supposed to need with actual or possible publics. It is therefore a great pity that, with one eye cocked on the later applications, commentators simply assume that by §202 the publicity of practice has been satisfactorily argued (Peacocke for instance just announces that 'by "practice" he here means the practice of a community' (p. 72)). Of course, many believe that the later discussion of sensation S and so on justifies the restriction. But that is another issue; to invoke those is to abandon the hope that the rule-following considerations provide wider, more general thoughts from which the anti-private language conclusion independently emerges. To illustrate the gap we can consider the half-way house (to full privacy) provided by Robinson Crusoe cases.

Consider the example (due to Michael Dummett) of a born Crusoe who finds a Rubik's cube washed onto his island, and learns to solve it. The fact is that he does it. He certainly doesn't solve it randomly, for he can do it on demand. It is natural to say that he follows principles (when there is a last corner left to do . . .). Perhaps he has some rudimentary diagrams or other mnemonics which he consults. With these he can do it, and without them he cannot. Kripke considers what LW's attitude should be to such a case. The attitude he offers, on behalf of KW, is that we can think of Crusoe, in such a case as this, as following rules. But, 'If we think of Crusoe as following rules, we are taking him into our community and applying our criteria for rule following to him.' The skeptical considerations are supposed to show 'not that a *physically isolated* individual cannot be said to follow rules; rather that an individual *considered in isolation* (whether or not he is physically isolated) cannot be said to do so'.[11] Again there is a nice parallel (although not quite the one Kripke makes) with Hume. One conclusion that might be drawn from Hume is not that a pair of events in a universe with no others cannot be related causally (which is how Kripke takes Hume). Rather, if we suppose that they are, we are thinking of them as members of a (potential) family of other regularly related events. We are not considering them in isolation, but, for instance, are thinking of what would happen if there were others like them.

Still, it is not clear what the compromise is. Certainly I, or we, are doing the thought-experiment. I have to consider whether Crusoe is a rule-follower by using the normal, community-wide way I make the judgement. But that would be true of any situation I seek to describe. And then, just as (contra

---

11. Kripke says useful things about this, pp. 90 ff.

42

Berkeley) I might conclude that an island considered in isolation has a tree on it, might I not conclude that Crusoe, considered in isolation, was following a rule? How does the phrase 'considered in isolation' bring the community further into the picture in this case than in the case of the tree? We are apt to retort that Crusoe would have been a rule-follower in this situation whatever I or we or any other community in the world had thought about it – just like the tree. And the reason is that all by himself he had a technique or practice.

Now reconsider the private linguist, meaning someone who believes that he has given an inner state a semantically essential role. Suppose he believes that yesterday, in the presence of the state, he defined for himself a qualitative similarity that other states might bear to it; that he is on the look-out for recurrence, and involved in the practice of judging if such a recurrence takes place. We seek to show that this is not a real practice. Let our private linguist accept the basic point, admitting that the mere offering of words, images and so on does not determine a rule of application, or principle that is really in force. But he does not accept that his candidate practice is unsatisfactory. What has LW got to show him?

'Whatever is going to seem right is right' – there is no distinction between his seeming to himself to follow a rule, and his genuinely doing so. It has often been suggested that this charge is unargued, or, if argued, only supported by overtly verificationist considerations. My endeavour has been to show how difficult it is to release the public from its attack. In the light of this, let us reconsider the projective and naturalistic elements that assisted the public: the point that we naturally and perhaps usefully regard ourselves as mutual possessors of the same understanding. We see ourselves so, and this attitude is, in Humean vein, immune from skeptical destruction. Furthermore, there is no lowering of the truth-condition of this judgement. It sits with its own vocabulary and scorns any 'account' of it in other terms. It is just that if a public failed to see itself in this light, it would mean that it could only see the ongoing patterns of noise and reaction, in which no principle, no genuine judgement, no truth and falsity, is visible.

My criticism of the flat reply to the skeptical problem ('this is how we see ourselves') was, in effect, that it gave no account of what a community would be missing if it failed to see itself in this light. Following LW we have accepted that the clue to what is missing is to come from the notion of a practice. BW therefore uses this thought, and the fact that dispositions provide satisfactory standards for the making of the judgement. Like other judgements with normative elements, there is no attempt to make a lowering of the truth-condition. The judgement can perfectly well be seen in terms of the projection of an attitude (this cannot be uncongenial to LW). But that left us unclear about the standards for applying it. BW therefore accepts most of what emerges from LW, doing less violence to the redundancy theory and to the preparedness to talk of facts, even when the underlying metaphysic is not what that might suggest. But however well BW matches LW, Blackburn insists on asking: is there any reason why the private linguist should not so regard himself? And in that case *whose* is the attitude 'whatever is going to seem right is right'? Not the subject's own, for he dignifies himself as a genuine believer, as having a principle of application and making a judgement with it. In doing so he *allows* the possibility of mistake (it is not something there in the things going on in his head or in his behaviour: it is something arising as a projection from an attitude he takes up to his own projects). It is a component of his attitude that a particular judgement might turn out better regarded as mistaken.

How can this attitude be appropriate? A technique is something that can be followed well or badly; a practice is something in which success *matters*. Now in the usual scenario, the correctness or incorrectness of the private linguist's classification is given no consequence at all. It has no use. He writes in his diary, and so far as we are told, forgets it. So when LW imagines a use made of the report (e.g., to indicate the rise of the manometer) he immediately hypothesizes a public use. He thereby skips the intermediate case where the classification is given a putative private use. It fits into a project – a practice or technique – of ordering the expectation of recurrence of sensation, with an aim at prediction, explanation, systematization, or simple maximizing of desirable sensation. To someone engaged on this project, the attitude that whatever seems right is right is ludicrous. System soon enforces recognition of fallibility.

I conclude then that it is no mistake to see the later sections, from §240 onwards, as integral to the anti-private language polemic. BW simply cannot separate the private from the public with any considerations that are in force earlier on. But I have tried to suggest other things as well. Following through the problem of answering the paradox leads to sympathy with a basically 'anti-metaphysical' conception of rule-following. We simply cannot deliver, in other terms, accounts of what constitutes shared following of a rule, or what the fact of a rule being in force 'consists in'. In my view this invites a projectivist explanation of these kinds of judgement, although also in my view we cannot conclude that it is improper to talk of facts of the case. In any event, we are left searching for standards whereby to make the judgement. It is possible that those standards should exactly separate the public from the private (on some vulnerable conception of the private, of course). But there is no particular reason to expect them to do so. The problems with dispositions, either as giving us the missing kind of fact, or as providing standards for allowing that a rule is in force, failed to separate the public and the individual. So we cannot now simply *demand* from the putative private-linguist an 'account of what the distinction' (between genuinely following a rule, and only seeming to himself to do so) amounts to. He can reply. It amounts to all that it does in the case of the public. Just as a public dignifies itself as producing more than an interminable flood of words and noise, and sees itself as making mutually comprehensible judgements, capable of truth and falsity – so does he. The public doubtless has a purpose in doing this, and is right to do it. When his putative discriminations are part of a practice – so does he.

CHAPTER FOUR

WITTGENSTEIN ON FOLLOWING A RULE[1]

John McDowell

These things are finer spun than crude hands have any inkling of.
(*RFM* VII-57)[2]

1.

I like this guy already

We find it natural to think of meaning and understanding in, as it were, contractual terms.[3] Our idea is that to learn the meaning of a word is to acquire an understanding that obliges us subsequently – if we have occasion to deploy the concept in question – to judge and speak in certain determinate ways, on pain of failure to obey the dictates of the meaning we have grasped; that we are "committed to certain patterns of linguistic usage by the meanings we attach to expressions".[4] According to Crispin Wright, the burden of

---

1. This paper originated in an attempt to respond to Simon Blackburn "Rule-Following and Moral Realism"; I was also stimulated, in writing the first draft, by an unpublished paper of Blackburn's, a revised version of which is Blackburn, "The Individual Strikes Back". I benefited from comments on the first draft from Margaret Gilbert, Susan Hurley, Saul Kripke, David Lewis, Christopher Peacocke, Philip Pettit, David Wiggins, and Crispin Wright, who also kindly let me see a draft of his "Kripke's Wittgenstein", a forerunner of his "Kripke's Account of the Argument against Private Language". [Full bibliographic information is given only for works which do not appear elsewhere in this volume or in the further reading section.]

2. I shall use "*RFM*" for Wittgenstein, *Remarks on the Foundations of Mathematics* (Oxford: Blackwell, 1978).

3. See p.19 of Crispin Wright, *Wittgenstein on the Foundations of Mathematics* (London: Duckworth, 1980).

4. *Ibid.*, p. 21. This idea of commitment to patterns must be treated with care if we are not to falsify the intuition. The most straightforward sort of case, on which it is familiar that Wittgenstein concentrates, is the continuation of a numerical series. Here it is natural to think of the correct expansion of the series as constituting a pattern to which understanding of its principle commits

Wittgenstein's reflections on following a rule, in his later work, is that these natural ideas lack the substance we are inclined to credit them with: "there is in our understanding of a concept no rigid, advance determination of what is to count as its correct application".[5]

If Wittgenstein's conclusion, as Wright interprets it, is allowed to stand, the most striking casualty is a familiar intuitive notion of objectivity. The idea at risk is the idea of things being thus and so anyway, whether or not we choose to investigate the matter in question, and whatever the outcome of any such investigation. That idea requires the conception of how things could correctly be said to be anyway – whatever, if anything, we in fact go on to say about the matter; and this notion of correctness can only be the notion of how the pattern of application that we grasp, when we come to understand the concept in question, extends, independently of the actual outcome of any investigation, to the relevant case. So if the notion of investigation-independent patterns of application is to be discarded, then so is the idea that things are, at least sometimes, thus and so anyway, independently of our ratifying the judgement that that is how they are. It seems fair to describe this extremely radical consequence as a kind of idealism.[6]

We may well hesitate to attribute such a doctrine to the philosopher who wrote:

If one tried to advance *theses* in philosophy, it would never be possible to debate them, because everyone would agree to them.

(*PI* §128)[7]

Notice that the destructive effect of the doctrine goes far beyond Wittgenstein's hostility to the imagery of mathematical platonism, in which

---

one. In the general case, the "pattern" idea is the idea of a series of things that, given the way the world develops, it would be correct to say if one chose to express a given concept; outside the series-expansion case, this idea is obviously metaphorical at best, since what it is correct to say with the use of a given concept, even supposing a determinate state of affairs one aims to describe, depends on what other concepts one chooses to express in the same utterance. (The non-metaphorical kernel is simply the idea that the meaning of what one says is a matter of the conditions under which it would be true.) It is important, also, not to falsify the connection between the patterns and meaningfulness – e.g., by suggesting that the idea is that making sense depends on *conforming* to the appropriate commitments. Tracing out the patterns is what the "pattern" idea takes consistently speaking the truth to be; to make sense (in an affirmation) one needs to do no more than felicitously make as if to be doing what one takes that to require. (See, further, n. 46 below.)

5. *Ibid.*, p. 21. "Rigid" will call for comment; see n. 21 below.
6. Wright does this at p. 252 of "Strict Finitism". See also pp. 246–7 of his "Anti-Realist Semantics: The Role of *Criteria*". Both are reprinted in his *Realism, Meaning, and Truth* (Oxford: Blackwell, 1986).
7. I shall use "*PI*" for Wittgenstein, *Philosophical Investigations*. Stanley Cavell's correction of the usual reading of this passage, at pp. 33–4 of *The Claim of Reason* (Oxford: Clarendon Press, 1979), does not make it any easier to reconcile with Wright's view of Wittgenstein.

mathematics is pictured as "the natural history of mathematical objects" *(RFM* II-40). The remarks about rule-following are not confined to mathematics; on Wright's reading they would undermine our ordinary intuitive conception of natural history, literally so called – the very model on which that suspect platonist picture of mathematics is constructed.

More specific grounds for doubting the attribution might be derived from passages like this *(PI* §195):

> "But I don't mean that what I do now (in grasping a sense) determines the future use *causally* and as a matter of experience, but that in a *queer* way, the use itself is in some sense present."—But of course it is, in *some* sense! Really the only thing wrong with what you say is the expression "in a queer way". The rest is all right . . .[8]

What this suggests is something we might anyway have expected: that Wittgenstein's target is not the very idea that a present state of understanding embodies commitments with respect to the future, but rather a certain seductive misconception of that idea.

Not that Wright merely ignores such passages. His claim is that Wittgenstein seems *almost* to want to deny all substance to the "pattern" idea; what he attributes to Wittgenstein is not an outright abandonment of the idea but a reinterpretation of it.[9] Wright's view is that the intuitive contractual picture of meaning and understanding can be rendered innocuous – purged of the seductive misconception – by discarding the thought that the patterns are independent of our ratification. Later (§§5, 7, 10) I shall suggest that this purged version of the intuitive picture is not recognizable as a picture of meaning and understanding at all, and is not correctly attributed to Wittgenstein. But for the present, let me note only that Wright's reinterpretation, precisely by denying the ratification-independence of the patterns, leaves the intuitive conception of objectivity untenable, in the way I described above. So we are bound to wonder whether the concession that Wright envisages Wittgenstein making to the "pattern" idea can account satisfactorily for Wittgenstein's reassuring tone in his response to the interlocutor of *PI* §195.

MIGHT THE IDEA of PATTERN RECOGNITION HAVE SOME MORE AFTER ALL

2.

In Wright's view, then, the butt of Wittgenstein's reflections on rule-following is the idea that understanding an expression is "grasp of a pattern of

---

8. See also, e.g., *PI* §§187, 692, 693.
9. See *Wittgenstein on the Foundations of Mathematics*, pp. 21, 227.

application, conformity to which requires certain determinate verdicts in so far unconsidered cases". But:

> We have to acknowledge . . . that the "pattern" is, strictly, inaccessible to definitive explanation. For, as Wittgenstein never wearied of reminding himself, no explanation of the use of an expression is proof against misunderstanding; verbal explanations require correct understanding of the vocabulary in which they are couched, and samples are open to an inexhaustible variety of interpretations. So we move towards the idea that understanding an expression is a kind of "cottoning on"; that is, a leap, an inspired guess at the pattern of application which the instructor is trying to get across.
>
> THAT SEEMS RIGHT TO ME   (Wright: 1980, p. 216)

The pictured upshot of this "leap" is something idiolectic. So the suggestion is that the "pattern" idea comes naturally to us, in the first instance, in the shape of "the idea that each of us has some sort of privileged access to the character of his own understanding of an expression; each of us knows of an idiolectic pattern of use, for which there is a strong presumption, when sufficient evidence has accumulated, that it is shared communally" (1980, p. 217).[10]

What is wrong with this idea? Wright's answer is this:

> . . . *whatever* sincere applications I make of a particular expression, when I have paid due heed to the situation, will seem to me to conform with my understanding of it. There is no scope for a distinction here between the fact of an application's seeming to me to conform with the way in which I understand it and the fact of its really doing so.[11]

My PROBLEM w/ THIS IS THAT THERE IS NOTHING ELSE THAT EVER TELLS ANYONE ANYTHING

Now we are naturally inclined to protect the intuitive view that thoughts and utterances make sense by virtue of owing, or purporting to owe, allegiance to conceptual commitments. So, given that idiolectic understanding cannot make room for the "pattern" idea, it is tempting to appeal to communal understanding. But (the argument that Wright ascribes to Wittgenstein continues) this cannot rehabilitate the "pattern" idea. For:

> Suppose that one of us finds himself incorrigibly out of line concerning the description of a new case. We have just seen that he cannot single-handed, as it were, give sense to the idea that he is at

---

10. See also pp. 32, 354.
11. Ibid.; see also p. 36. Compare *PI* §258: "One would like to say: whatever is going to seem right to me is right. And that only means that here we can't talk about 'right'." (See §14 below.)

But as a practical matter, he must do that!

least being faithful to his *own* pattern; that is, that he recognises how he must describe the new case if he is to remain faithful to his own understanding of the relevant expressions. How, then, does his disposition to apply the expression to a new case become, properly speaking, recognition of the continuation of a pattern if it so happens that he is *not* out of line, if it so happens that there is communal agreement? (1980, p. 218)

The trouble is that there is a precise parallel between the community's supposed grasp of the patterns that it has communally committed itself to and the individual's supposed grasp of his idiolectic commitments. Whatever applications of an expression secure communal approval, just those applications will seem to the community to conform with its understanding of the expression.[12] If we regard an individual as aiming to speak a communal language, we take account of the possibility that he may go out of step with his fellows; thus we make room for an application of the notion of error, and so of right and wrong. But it is only going out of step with one's fellows that we make room for; not going out of step with a ratification-independent pattern that they follow. So the notion of right and wrong that we have made room for is at best a thin surrogate for what would be required by the intuitive notion of objectivity. That would require the idea of concepts as authoritative; and the move away from idiolects has not reinstated that idea. In sum:

Exactly! How is it that someone or some group know or are even inclined to believe that someone has gone out of step?

None of us unilaterally can make sense of the idea of correct employment of language save by reference to the authority of securable communal assent on the matter; and for the community itself there is no authority, so no standard to meet. (1980, p. 220)

3.

According to Wright, then, Wittgenstein's reflections are directed, in the first instance, against the idea that a determinate practice can be dictated by a personal understanding – something that owes no allegiance to a communal way of going on. On the surface, at least, there is a point of contact here with Saul Kripke's influential reading of the remarks on rule-following, which I shall now outline.[13]

---

12. One would like to say: whatever is going to seem right to *us* is right. And that only means that here we can't talk about "right".

13. See Kripke, *Wittgenstein on Rules and Private Language* (Oxford: Blackwell, 1982). Wright notes the parallel at p. 249 of "Strict Finitism"; although he takes issue with Kripke in "Kripke's Account of the Argument against Private Language".

Suppose one is asked to perform an addition other than any one has encountered before, either in the training that gave one one's understanding of addition or in subsequently trying to put one's understanding into practice.[14] In confidently giving a particular answer, one will naturally have a thought that is problematic: namely – to put it in terms that bring out the point of contact with Wright's reading – that in returning this answer one is keeping faith with one's understanding of the "plus" sign. To show how this thought is problematic, Kripke introduces a skeptic who questions it. The natural idea is that one's understanding of "plus" dictates the answer one gives. But what could constitute one's being in such a state? Not a disposition: no doubt it is true that answering as one does is an exercise of a disposition that one acquired when one learned arithmetic, but the relation of a disposition to its exercises is in no sense contractual – a disposition is not something to which its exercises are faithful.[15] But nothing else will serve either: for – to quote Kripke's summary of a rich battery of argument – "it seems that no matter what is in my mind at a given time, I am free in the future to interpret it in different ways" (Kripke: 1982, p. 107). That is, whatever piece of mental furniture I cite, acquired by me as a result of my training in arithmetic, it is open to the skeptic to point out that my present performance keeps faith with it only on one interpretation of it, and other interpretations are possible. So it cannot constitute my understanding "plus" in such a way as to dictate the answer I give. Such a state of understanding would require not just the original item but also my having put the right interpretation on it. But what could constitute my having put the right interpretation on some mental item? And now the argument can evidently be repeated.

The upshot of this argument is a "skeptical paradox", which, according to Kripke (1982, pp. 69–71), Wittgenstein accepts: there is no fact that could constitute my having attached one rather than another meaning to the "plus" sign.

It may well seem that if Wittgenstein concedes this much to Kripke's skeptic, he has renounced the right to attribute meaning to expressions at all. According to Kripke, however, Wittgenstein offers a "skeptical solution" to the "skeptical paradox". A "skeptical solution" to a skeptical problem is one that "begins ... by conceding that the skeptic's negative assertions are unanswerable" (1982, p. 66). The essentials of the "skeptical solution" are as follows.

First, we must reform our intuitive conception of meaning, replacing the notion of truth-conditions with some notion like that of justification conditions. Kripke quotes with approval (1982, p. 73) a claim of Michael Dummett's: "The *Investigations* contains implicitly a rejection of the classical

---

14. Where I say "other", Kripke has "larger". This makes the skepticism perhaps more gripping, but the difference is inessential.

15. This is the gist of the excellent discussion at Kripke, *Wittgenstein on Rules and Private Language*, pp. 22–37.

(realist) Frege-*Tractatus* view that the general form of explanation of meaning is a statement of the truth conditions."[16] The "skeptical paradox", which we are to accept, is that there is no fact that could constitute my having attached one rather than another determinate meaning to the "plus" sign. We are inclined to understand this as a concession that I have attached *no* determinate meaning to the "plus" sign: but the suggestion is that this is only because we adhere, naively, to the superseded truth-conditional conception of meaning – applied, in this case, to the claim "I have attached a determinate meaning to the 'plus' sign."

Second, when we consider the justification conditions of the statements in which we express the idea that someone attaches some determinate meaning to an expression (the conditions under which we affirm such statements, and the roles they play in our lives), we see that we can make sense of them in terms of their use to record acceptance of individuals into the linguistic community. (The thesis that we can make sense of the idea of meaning only in that connection is the core of Kripke's interpretation of the Private Language Argument.)

Now there is room for doubt about how successful this "skeptical solution" can be. The exegetical framework within which it is constructed – the Dummettian picture of the transition between the *Tractatus* and the *Investigations* – is not beyond dispute. But without opening that issue (which I shall touch on below: §§10, 11, 14), we can note that when Dummett expresses his doubts about the "realist" (truth-conditional) conception of meaning (which are supposed to be in the spirit of the later Wittgenstein's doubts about the *Tractatus*), it is typically by pressing such questions as this: "What could constitute someone's possession of the sort of understanding of a sentence that 'realism' attributes to him?" The implication is that, failing a satisfactory answer, no one could possess that sort of understanding.[17] It is natural to suppose that if one says "There is no fact that could constitute its being the case that P", one precludes oneself from affirming that P; and this supposition, so far from being a distinctively "realist" one, plays a central role in the standard arguments *against* "realism". Given this supposition, the concession that Kripke says Wittgenstein makes to the skeptic becomes a *denial* that I understand the "plus" sign to mean one thing rather than another. And now – generalizing the denial – we do seem to have fallen into an abyss: "the incredible and self-defeating conclusion, that all language is meaningless" (1982, p. 71). It is quite obscure how we could hope to claw ourselves back by manipulating the notion of accredited membership in a linguistic community.

---

16. "Wittgenstein's Philosophy of Mathematics", p. 348, in his *Truth and Other Enigmas* (London: Duckworth, 1978).
17. See especially Dummett, "What is a Theory of Meaning? (II)", in G. Evans and J. McDowell (eds), *Truth and Meaning* (Oxford: Clarendon Press, 1976).

4.

In any case, Kripke's thesis that Wittgenstein accepts the "skeptical paradox" seems a falsification. Kripke (1982, p. 7) identifies the "skeptical paradox" he attributes to Wittgenstein with the paradox Wittgenstein formulates in the first paragraph of *PI* §201:

> This was our paradox: no course of action could be determined by a rule, because every course of action can be made out to accord with the rule. The answer was: if everything can be made out to accord with the rule, then it can also be made out to conflict with it. And so there would be neither accord nor conflict here.

But §201 goes on with a passage for which Kripke's reading makes no room:

> It can be seen that there is a misunderstanding here from the mere fact that in the course of our argument we give one interpretation after another; as if each one contented us at least for a moment, until we thought of yet another standing behind it. What this shews is that there is a way of grasping a rule which is *not* an *interpretation,* but which is exhibited in what we call "obeying the rule" and "going against it" in actual cases.

What could constitute my understanding, say, the "plus" sign in a way with which only certain answers to given addition problems would accord? Confronted with such questions, we tend to be enticed into looking for a fact that would constitute my having put an appropriate *interpretation* on what I was told and shown when I was instructed in arithmetic. Anything we hit on as satisfying that specification contents us only "for a moment"; then it occurs to us that whatever we have hit on would itself be capable of interpretation in such a way that acting in conformity with it would require something quite different. So we look for something that would constitute my having interpreted the first item in the right way. Anything we come up with as satisfying that specification will in turn content us only "for a moment"; and so on: "any interpretation still hangs in the air along with what it interprets, and cannot give it any support" (*PI* §198). Kripke's reading has Wittgenstein endorsing this reasoning, and consequently willing to abandon the idea that there is anything that constitutes my understanding an expression in some determinate way. But what Wittgenstein clearly claims, in the second paragraph of §201, is that the reasoning is vitiated by "a misunderstanding". The right response to the paradox, Wittgenstein in effect tells us, is not to accept it but to correct the misunderstanding on which it depends: that is, to realize "that there is a way of grasping a rule which is *not* an *interpretation*".

Good Stuff

The paradox of §201 is one horn of a dilemma with which the misunderstanding presents us. Suppose we are not disabused of the misunderstanding – that is, we take it that our problem is to find a fact that constitutes my having given some expression an interpretation with which only certain uses of it would conform. In that case, the attempt to resist the paradox of §201 will drive us to embrace a familiar mythology of meaning and understanding, and this is the second horn of the dilemma. My coming to mean the expression in the way I do (my "grasping the rule") must be my arriving at an interpretation; but it must be an interpretation that is not susceptible to the movement of thought in the skeptical line of reasoning – not such as to content us only until we think of another interpretation standing behind it.

What one wants to say is: "Every sign is capable of interpretation; but the *meaning* mustn't be capable of interpretation. It is the last interpretation."[18]

Understanding an expression, then, must be possessing an interpretation that cannot be interpreted – an interpretation that precisely bridges the gap, exploited in the skeptical argument, between the instruction one received in learning the expression and the use one goes on to make of it. The irresistible upshot of this is that we picture following a rule as the operation of a super-rigid yet (or perhaps we should say "hence") ethereal machine.

> How queer: It looks as if a physical (mechanical) form of guidance could misfire and let in something unforeseen, but not a rule! As if a rule were, so to speak, the only reliable form of guidance.
>
> (*Zettel* §296)[19]

One of Wittgenstein's main concerns is clearly to cast doubt on this mythology. But his attacks on the mythology are not, as Kripke suggests, arguments for acceptance of the "skeptical paradox".[20]

That would be so if the dilemma were compulsory; but the point of the second paragraph of *PI* §201 is precisely that it is not. The mythology is wrung from us, in our need to avoid the paradox of the first paragraph, only because we fall into the misunderstanding; the attack on the mythology is not support for the paradox, but rather constitutes, in conjunction with the fact that the paradox is intolerable, an argument against the misunderstanding.

It is worth noting two points about the second horn of the dilemma that correspond to two aspects of Wright's reading of Wittgenstein.

---

18. Wittgenstein: *Blue Book* (Oxford: Basil Blackwell, 1958), p. 34. Compare *Zettel* §231 (Oxford: Basil Blackwell, 1967).

19. There is a good description of the mythological ideas expressed here, with a wealth of citations of relevant passages, in Gordon Baker, "Following Wittgenstein: Some Signposts for *Philosophical Investigations* §§143–242", in S. Holtzman and C. Leich (eds), *Wittgenstein: To Follow a Rule* (London: Routledge & Kegan Paul, 1981).

20. See *Wittgenstein on Rules and Private Language*, pp. 65, 69: Kripke cannot distinguish rejecting the "superlative fact" of *PI* §192 – rejecting the mythology – from refusing to countenance a fact in which my attaching a determinate meaning to "plus" consists – accepting the paradox.

First, if we picture an interpretation that would precisely bridge the gap between instruction and competent use, it seems that it can only be one that each person hits on for himself – so that it is at best a fortunate contingency if his interpretation coincides with the one arrived at by someone else subjected to the same instruction, or with the one intended by the instructor.

> "But do you really explain to the other person what you yourself understand? Don't you get him to *guess* the essential thing? You give him examples,—but he has to guess their drift, to guess your intention."
> (*PI* §210)

This is clearly the basis in Wittgenstein for Wright's remarks (quoted in §2 above) about "the idea that understanding an expression is a kind of 'cottoning on'; that is, a leap, an inspired guess at the pattern of application which the instructor is trying to get across".

Second, a concomitant of the picture of the super-rigid machine is a picture of the patterns as sets of rails. (See, for instance, *PI* §218.) At each stage, say in the extending of a series, the rule itself determines what comes next, independently of the techniques that we learn in learning to extend it; the point of the learning is to get our practice of judging and speaking in line with the rule's impersonal dictates. (An omniscient God would not need to do mathematics in order to know whether "777" occurs in the decimal expansion of π; see *RFM* VII-41.) Now this conception figures regularly in Wright's formulations of the "pattern" idea:

> ... the pattern extends *of itself* to cases which we have yet to confront. . .
> . . . the investigation-independent truth of statements requires that their truth is settled, *autonomously and without the need for human interference*, by their meanings and the character of the relevant facts.[21]

It is clear, again, that these formulations have a basis in Wittgenstein's polemic against the second horn of the dilemma. A remark like "I give the rule an extension" (*RFM* VI-29) is meant as a corrective of the inclination to say "The rule extends of itself". (And "even God can determine something mathematical only by mathematics": *RFM* VII-41.)

---

21. Wright, *Wittgenstein on the Foundations of Mathematics*, p. 216, and "Strict Finitism", p. 250, both with my emphasis. "Rigid", at *Wittgenstein on the Foundations of Mathematics*, p. 21 (which I quoted in §1 above), is an expression of the same idea – Wright does not mean "rigid" as opposed to, say, "vague" (see Baker, "Following Wittgenstein", pp. 40–1).

5.

[handwritten margin note: COULD MEMORY + DISPOS IT UNMISTA BE TIED TOGETHER?]

In Wright's reading, as I said (§§1 and 2 above), Wittgenstein's point is that the natural contractual conception of understanding should not be discarded, but purged of the idea – which it must incorporate if the intuitive notion of objectivity is to have application – that the patterns to which our concepts oblige us are ratification-independent. I expressed a suspicion (in §1 above) that this purging would not leave a residue recognizable as a conception of meaning and understanding at all, or recognizable as something that Wittgenstein recommends. I want now to begin on an attempt to back up this suspicion.

At *PI* §437 Wittgenstein writes:

> A wish seems already to know what will or would satisfy it; a proposition, a thought, what makes it true—even when that thing is not there at all! Whence this *determining* of what is not yet there? This despotic demand? ("The hardness of the logical must.")

Note the parenthesis: clearly he thinks that the discussion in which this passage occurs – dealing with the relation between wishes or expectations and their fulfilment, and the relation between orders and their execution – raises the same issues as his reflections on the continuation of a series.[22] We can bring out the connection by focusing on the case of orders and their execution: it is natural to say that the execution of an order is faithful to its meaning, and in saying this we clearly express a version of the idea that we express when we say that the competent continuation of a series is faithful to its principle. *[handwritten: Ex: ARMY IS GIVEN ORDERS TO EMPLOY X TYPE of TRAINING]*

What would Wright's reading of Wittgenstein be like, transposed to this case? Something on these lines (compare §2 above). The temptation to say that my execution of an order conforms with my understanding of it arises primarily out of a conception of my understanding as idiolectic – something that cannot be definitively conveyed to someone else, so that it is at best a happy contingency if it coincides with the understanding of the order possessed by the person who issued it. On reflection, however, we should realize that this is an illusion: we cannot make sense of anything that would constitute an essentially personal understanding of an order, but would nevertheless impose genuine constraints on what I did in "execution" of it. For whatever I "sincerely" did would seem to be in conformity with my supposed personal understanding of the order. We naturally want to protect the intuitive notion of an action's fulfiling an order; so we are tempted at this point to appeal to the idea of my membership in a linguistic community. This does make room for my going wrong. But all that my going wrong can

---

22. See Kripke, *Wittgenstein on Rules and Private Language*, pp. 25–6, n.19.

amount to is this: my action does not secure the approval of my fellows, or is not what they would do in attempted fulfilment of such an order. When the community does approve, that is not a matter of its collectively recognizing the conformity of my action to an antecedent communal understanding of the order: for this supposed communal understanding would be in exactly the same position as my supposed idiolectic understanding. We cannot hold, then, that the community "goes right or wrong", by the lights of its understanding, when it awards my action the title "execution of the order"; "rather, it just goes".

Given the correspondence (which I noted in §4 above) between aspects of Wright's reading and aspects of Wittgenstein's polemic against the second horn of the dilemma, it is not surprising that part, at least, of this transposed version of Wright's reading should neatly fit parts of Wittgenstein's discussion. Consider, for instance, *PI* §460:

> Could the justification of an action as fulfilment of an order run like this: "You said 'Bring me a yellow flower', upon which this one gave me a feeling of satisfaction; that is why I have brought it"? Wouldn't one have to reply: "But I didn't set you to bring me the flower which should give you that sort of feeling after what I said!"?

It seems correct and illuminating to understand this as an attack on the idea that the understanding I act on is essentially idiolectic.[23]

Taken as a whole, however, I think this reading gets Wittgenstein completely wrong. I can perhaps begin to explain my disbelief with this remark: it would have been fully in character for Wittgenstein to have written as follows:

> Could the justification of an action as fulfilment of an order run like this: "You said 'Bring me a yellow flower', upon which the one received approval from all the bystanders; that is why I have brought it"? Wouldn't one have to reply: "But I didn't set you to bring the flower which should receive approval from everyone else after what I said!"?

So) Community isn't "right" either

In his later work, Wittgenstein returns again and again to trying to characterize the relation between meaning and consensus. If there is anything that emerges clearly, it is that it would be a serious error, in his view, not to make a radical distinction between the significance of, say, "This is yellow" and the

---

23. That is, the passage is of a piece with the passage from *PI* §258 that I quoted in n. 11 above. This suggestion does not compete with, but rather complements, Kripke's suggestion (1982, pp. 25–6, n. 19) that the passage refers obliquely to Russell's treatment of desire in *The Analysis of Mind* (London: Allen and Unwin, 1921).

[handwritten top margin: IS X PART OF CONCEPT Y WELL I FEEL INCLINED TO SAY YES SO, IN THAT ONE — SAY S BOTH I AM DISPOSED TO RESPOND THUSLY + I FEEL COMPELLED TO RESPOND THUSLY]

significance of, say, "This would be called 'yellow' by (most) speakers of English" (see, for instance, *Zettel* §§428–31). And my transposed version of Wright's reading seems to leave it mysterious, at best, why this distinction should be so important.

It may appear that the answer is both obvious and readily available to Wright: "To say 'This would be called "yellow" by speakers of English' would not be to *call* the object in question 'yellow', and that is what one does when one says 'This is yellow'." But this would merely postpone the serious question: does Wright's reading of Wittgenstein contain the means to make it intelligible that there should so much as *be* such an action as calling an object "yellow"? The picture Wright offers is, at the basic level, a picture of human beings vocalizing in certain ways in response to objects, with this behaviour (no doubt) accompanied by such "inner" phenomena as feelings of constraint, or convictions of the rightness of what they are saying. There are presumably correspondences in the propensities of fellow members of a linguistic community to vocalize, and to feel comfortable in doing so, that are unsurprising in the light of their belonging to a single species, together with similarities in the training that gave them the propensities. But at the basic level there is no question of shared commitments – of the behaviour, and the associated aspects of the streams of consciousness, being subject to the authority of anything outside themselves. ("For the community itself there is no authority, so no standard to meet.") How, then, can we be entitled to view the behaviour as involving, say, calling things "yellow", rather than a mere brute meaning-less sounding off?

The thought that is operative here is one Kripke puts by saying: "The relation of meaning and intention to future action is *normative, not descriptive*" (1982, p. 37). It is a thought Wright aims to respect. This is the point of his aspiration not to discard the contractual conception of meaning, but only to purge it of the idea of ratification-independence. But the purging yields the picture of what I have been calling "the basic level"; and at that level Wright's picture has no room for norms, and hence – given the normativeness of meaning – no room for meaning. Wright hopes to preserve a foothold for a purified form of the normativeness implicit in the contractual conception of meaning, by appealing to the fact that individuals are susceptible to communal correction. It is problematic, however, whether the picture of the basic level, once entertained as such, can be prevented from purporting to contain *the real truth* about linguistic behaviour. In that case its freedom from norms will preclude our attributing any genuine substance to the etiolated normativeness Wright hopes to preserve. The problem for Wright is to distinguish the position he attributes to Wittgenstein from one according to which the possibility of going out of step with our fellows gives us the *illusion* of being subject to norms, and consequently the *illusion* of entertaining and expressing meanings.

[handwritten bottom margin: HOW IS WRIGHT NOT JUST DESCRIBING THE HISTORY OF AN ILLUSION]

6.

Moved by the insight that meaning relates normatively to behaviour, Kripke – like Wright – reads Wittgenstein as concerned to preserve a role for the intuitive contractual conception. But Kripke's Wittgenstein locates that conception only in the context of the "skeptical solution" – a response to a supposedly accepted "skeptical paradox". Applied to the case of orders and their execution, Kripke's "skeptical paradox" will take this form: there is nothing that constitutes my understanding an order in a way with which acting in a certain determinate manner would conform. And, here as before (compare §4 above), it is open to question whether, once that much is conceded to skepticism, a "skeptical solution" can avert the destructive effect that the concession threatens to have.

In any case, this line of interpretation gets off on the wrong foot, when it credits Wittgenstein with acceptance of a "skeptical paradox", so that a "skeptical solution" would be the best that could be hoped for. Just as in the case of the continuation of a series, the reasoning that would lead to this "skeptical paradox" starts with something Wittgenstein aims to show up as a mistake: the assumption, in this case, that the understanding on which I act when I obey an order must be an interpretation. The connection with the thought of *PI* §201 is made clear by this juxtaposition (*RFM* VI-38):

> How can the word "Slab" indicate what I have to do, when after all I can bring any action into accord with any interpretation?

> How can I follow a rule, when after all whatever I do can be interpreted as following it?

The parallel can be extended (see §4 above). If we assume that understanding is always interpretation, then the need to resist the paradox of *PI* §201 drives us into a fantastic picture of how understanding mediates between order and execution. Consider, for instance, *PI* §431:

> "There is a gulf between an order and its execution. It has to be filled by the act of understanding."

> "Only in the act of understanding is it meant that we are to do THIS. The order—why, that is nothing but sounds, ink-marks.—"[24]

The act of understanding, conceived in terms of hitting on an interpretation that completely bridges the gulf between an order and its execution, demands to be pictured as setting up a super-rigid connection between the words and

---

24. Compare the passage from the *Blue Book*, p.34, that I quoted in §4 above.

the subsequent action (hence the allusion, in *PI* §437, to "the hardness of the logical must"). It is this idea that Wittgenstein is mocking in *PI* §461:

> In what sense does an order anticipate its execution? By ordering *just that* which later on is carried out?—But one would have to say "which later on is carried out, or again is not carried out." And that is to say nothing.
>
> "But even if my wish does not determine what is going to be the case, still it does so to speak determine the theme of a fact, whether the fact fulfils the wish or not." We are—as it were—surprised, not at anyone's knowing the future, but at his being able to prophesy at all (right or wrong).
>
> As if the mere prophecy, no matter whether true or false, foreshadowed the future; whereas it knows nothing of the future and cannot know less than nothing.

And the parallel goes further still. When we are tempted to conceive the understanding of an order in this way, what we have in mind is something essentially personal: a guess at the meaning of the person who issued the order. This idea is Wittgenstein's target in, for instance, *PI* §433:

What is diff of interpreting as we interpreting & sceptic of interpreting of sceptic

> When we give an order, it can look as if the ultimate thing sought by the order has to remain unexpressed, as there is always a gulf between an order and its execution. Say I want someone to make a particular movement, say to raise his arm. To make it quite clear, I do the movement. This picture seems unambiguous until we ask: how does he know *he is to make this movement?*—How does he know at all what use he is to make of the signs I give him, whatever they are?—Perhaps I shall now try to supplement the order by means of further signs, by pointing from myself to him, making encouraging gestures, etc. Here it looks as if the order were beginning to stammer.
>
> As if the signs were precariously trying to produce understanding in us.—But if we now understand them, by what token do we understand?

If we read Wittgenstein in Kripke's way, we shall take Wittgenstein's mockery of these ideas as argument in favour of the "skeptical paradox" – the thesis that there is nothing that could constitute my understanding an order in a determinate way. That is what the mockery would amount to if there were no options besides the paradox and the ideas that Wittgenstein mocks. But Wittgenstein's point is that this dilemma seems compulsory only on the assumption that understanding is always interpretation; his aim is not to shift us from one horn of the dilemma to the other, but to persuade us to reject the dilemma by discarding the assumption on which it depends.

7.

Having diagnosed the dilemma as resting on the mistaken idea that grasping a rule is always an interpretation, Wittgenstein goes on, famously, to say (*PI* §202):

> And hence also 'obeying a rule' is a practice. And to *think* one is obeying a rule is not to obey a rule. Hence it not possible to obey a rule 'privately': otherwise thinking one was obeying a rule would be the same thing as obeying it.

The diagnosis prompts the question "How can there be a way of grasping a rule which is not an interpretation?", and I think the thesis that obeying a rule is a practice is meant to constitute the answer to this question. That is, what mediates the inference ("hence also") is this thought: we have to realize that obeying a rule is a practice if we are to find it intelligible that there is a way of grasping a rule which is not an interpretation. (The rest of §202 – the crystallization into two sentences of the Private Language Argument – is offered as a corollary.)

There is another formulation of the same line of thought in *PI* §198:

> "Then can whatever I do be brought into accord with the rule?"—Let me ask this: what has the expression of a rule—say a sign-post—got to do with my actions? What sort of connexion is there here?—Well, perhaps this one: I have been trained to react to this sign in a particular way, and now I do so react to it.
> "But that is only to give a causal connexion: to tell how it has come about that we go by the sign-post; not what this going-by-the-sign really consists in."—On the contrary; I have further indicated that a person goes by a sign-post only in so far as there exists a regular use of sign-posts, a custom.[25]

This passage opens with an expression of the paradox formulated in the first paragraph of §201. Then Wittgenstein introduces the case of sign-posts, in order to adumbrate the diagnosis that he is going to state more explicitly in §201. When I follow a sign-post, the connection between it and my action is not mediated by an interpretation of sign-posts that I acquired when I was trained in their use. I simply act as I have been trained to.[26] This prompts an objection, which might be paraphrased on these lines: "Nothing in what you

---

25. I have ventured to change the punctuation in the second paragraph, in order to make the dialectical structure of the passage clearer.
26. Compare *PI* §506: "The absent-minded man who at the order 'Right turn!' turns left, and then, clutching his forehead, says 'Oh! right turn' and does a right turn.—What has struck him? An interpretation?"

have said shows that what you have described is a case of following a rule; you have only told us how to give a causal explanation of a certain bit of (what might as well be for all that you have said) mere behaviour." The reply – which corresponds to the first sentence of §202 – is that the training in question is initiation into a custom. If it were not that, then the account of the connection between sign-post and action would indeed look like an account of nothing more than brute movement and its causal explanation; our picture would not contain the materials to entitle us to speak of following (going by) a sign-post.[27]

Now how exactly is this to be understood?

Wittgenstein's concern is to exorcize the insidious assumption that there must be an interpretation that mediates between an order, or the expression of a rule given in training, on the one hand, and an action in conformity with it, on the other. In his efforts to achieve this, he is led to say such things as "I obey the rule *blindly*" (PI §219). This is of a piece with his repeated insistence that the agreement that is necessary for the notion of following a rule to be applicable is not agreement in opinions:

> "So you are saying that human agreement decides what is true and what is false?"—It is what human beings *say* that is true and false; and they agree in the *language* they use. That is not agreement in opinions but in form of life. (PI §241)[28]

I take it that at least part of the point of this passage is that an opinion is something for which one may reasonably be asked for a justification; whereas what is at issue here is below that level – "bedrock" where "I have exhausted the justifications" and "my spade is turned" (PI §217). The thought is clear in *RFM* VI-28:

> Someone asks me: What is the colour of this flower? I answer: "red".— Are you absolutely sure? Yes, absolutely sure! But may I not have been deceived and called the wrong colour "red"? No. The certainty with which I call the colour "red" is the rigidity of my measuring-rod, it is the rigidity from which I start. When I give descriptions, *that* is not to be brought into doubt. This simply characterizes what we call describing.
>
> (I may of course even here assume a slip of the tongue, but nothing else.)
>
> Following according to the rule is FUNDAMENTAL to our language-game. It characterizes what we call description.

---

27. Compare *RFM* VI-43.
28. See also *RFM* VI-30, VI-9.

*I think it's
oc you were taught to say Help?*

Again (*RFM* VI-35):

*Dispositional
account*

> How do I know that the colour that I am now seeing is called
> "green"? Well, to confirm it I might ask other people, but if they did
> not agree with me, I should become totally confused and should
> perhaps take them or myself for crazy. That is to say: I should either
> no longer trust myself to judge, or no longer react to what they say as
> to a judgement.
>   If I am drowning and I shout "Help!", how do I know what the
> word Help means? Well, that's how I react in this situation.—Now
> *that* is how I know what "green" means as well and also know how I
> have to follow the rule in the particular case.[29]

What Wittgenstein is trying to describe is a use of language in which what one
does is "to use an expression without a justification" (*PI* §289; compare *RFM*
VII-40). One may be tempted to protest: when I say "This is green", in the
sort of case he envisages, I do have a justification, namely that the thing in
question is green.

But how can I justify the use of an expression by repeating it? It is thoughts
of this sort that lead Wittgenstein to say (*On Certainty* §204):

> Giving grounds, however, justifying the evidence, comes to an end;—
> but the end is not certain propositions' striking us immediately as
> true, i.e. it is not a kind of *seeing* on our part; it is our *acting*, which
> lies at the bottom of the language-game.[30]

Now there is a temptation to understand this on the following lines. At the
level of "bedrock" (where justifications have come to an end), there is nothing
but verbal behaviour and (no doubt) feelings of constraint. Presumably
people's dispositions to behaviour and associated feelings match in interesting
ways; but at this ground-floor level there is no question of shared commitments – everything normative fades out of the picture.

This is the picture of what I called "the basic level" that is yielded, in
Wright's reading, by the rejection of ratification-independence (see §5 above).
I expressed disbelief that a position in which this is how things are at the basic
level can accommodate meaning at all. If it is true that a failure to
accommodate meaning is the upshot of the position, then it can be attributed

---

29. With "Well, that's how I react in this situation", compare *PI* §217: ". . . I am inclined to say: 'This
    is simply what I do.'".
30. (Oxford: Basil Blackwell, 1969). It is worth noting how paradoxical "it is not a kind of seeing"
    can seem in the case of such uses of language as saying that something is green. For an
    illuminating discussion of Wittgenstein's stress on acting as "lying at the bottom of the language-
    game", see Peter Winch, "Im Anfang war die Tat", in I. Block (ed), *Perspectives on the Philosophy
    of Wittgenstein* (Oxford: Basil Blackwell, 1981).

to Wittgenstein only at the price of supposing that he does not succeed in his aims. But we are now equipped to see that the attribution falsifies his intentions. When he describes the "bedrock" use of expressions as "without justification", he nevertheless insists (to complete the quotation from *PI* §289):

> To use an expression without a justification does not mean to use it without right.[31]

And it seems clear that the point of this is precisely to prevent the leaching out of norms from our picture of "bedrock" – from our picture, that is, of how things are at the deepest level at which we may sensibly contemplate the place of language in the world. To quote again from *RFM* VI-28:

> Following according to the rule is FUNDAMENTAL to our language-game.

By Wittgenstein's lights, it is a mistake to think we can dig down to a level at which we no longer have application for normative notions (like "following according to the rule"). Wright's picture of the basic level, so far from capturing Wittgenstein's view, looks like a case of succumbing to a temptation that he is constantly warning against:

> The difficult thing here is not, to dig down to the ground; no, it is to recognize the ground that lies before us as the ground.
>
> (*RFM* VI-31)

Wittgenstein's problem is to steer a course between a Scylla and Charybdis. Scylla is the idea that understanding is always interpretation. This idea is disastrous because embracing it confronts us with the dilemma of §4 above: the choice between the paradox that there is no substance to meaning, on the one hand, and the fantastic mythology of the super-rigid machine, on the other. We can avoid Scylla by stressing that, say, calling something "green" can be like crying "Help!" when one is drowning – simply how one has learned to react to this situation. But then we risk steering on to Charybdis – the picture of a basic level at which there are no norms; if we embrace that, I have suggested, then we cannot prevent meaning from coming to seem an illusion. The point of *PI* §198, and part of the point of §§201–2, is that the key to finding the indispensable middle course is the idea of a custom or practice. How can a performance both be nothing but a "blind" reaction to a situation, not an attempt to act on an interpretation (avoiding Scylla); and be a case of

[margin notes: FASCIST MEANING; MEANING AS ILLUSION]

---

31. On "wrongfully" (*RFM* VII-30). For a discussion of the translation of "zu Unrecht", see Kripke: 1982, p.74, n. 63.

going by a rule (avoiding Charybdis)? The answer is: by belonging to a custom (*PI* §198), practice (*PI* §202), or institution (*RFM* VI-31).

Until more is said about how exactly the appeal to communal practice makes the middle course available, this is only a programme for a solution to Wittgenstein's problem. But even if we were at a loss as to how he might have thought the programme could be executed (and I shall suggest that we need not be: see §§10 and 11 below), this would be no ground for ignoring the clear textual evidence that the programme is Wittgenstein's own.

8.

What I have claimed might be put like this: Wittgenstein's point is that we have to situate our conception of meaning and understanding within a framework of communal practices. Kripke's reading credits Wittgenstein with the thesis that the notion of meaning something by one's words is "inapplicable to a single person considered in isolation" (1982, p. 79). The upshot is similar, then; and it cannot be denied that the insistence on publicity in Kripke's reading corresponds broadly with a Wittgensteinian thought. But it makes a difference how we conceive the requirement of publicity to emerge.

In my reading, it emerges as a condition for the intelligibility of rejecting a premise – the assimilation of understanding to interpretation – that would present us with an intolerable dilemma. So there are three positions in play: the two horns of the dilemma, and the community-oriented conception of meaning that enables us to decline the choice. Kripke conflates two of these, equating the paradox of *PI* §201 – the first horn of the dilemma – with Wittgenstein's conclusion; only so can he take it that when Wittgenstein objects to the "superlative fact" of *PI* §192, he is embracing the paradox of §201.[32] But this is quite wrong. The paradox that Wittgenstein formulates at §201 is not, as Kripke supposes, the mere "paradox" that if we consider an individual in isolation, we do not have the means to make sense of the notion of meaning (something we might hope to disarm by appealing to the idea of a linguistic community). It is the genuine and devastating paradox that meaning is an illusion. Focusing on the individual in isolation from any linguistic community is not the way we fall into this abyss; it is, rather, an aspect of the way we struggle not to, so long as we retain the assumption that generates the dilemma. (See §4 above, on the idiolectic implications of the second horn.) The fundamental trouble is that Kripke makes nothing of Wittgenstein's concern to reject the assimilation of understanding to interpretation; and the nemesis of this oversight is the unconvincingness (see §3 above) of the "skeptical solution" on which Kripke's Wittgenstein must rely.

---

32. See n. 20 above.

9.

Kripke suggests (1982, p. 3) that, in the light of *PI* §202, we should take it that the essentials of the Private Language Argument are contained in the general discussion of rule-following, rather than in the section of the *Investigations* that begins at §243, where it has been usual to look. I cannot accept Kripke's view that the Private Language Argument is a corollary of the "skeptical solution"; but his structural proposal can be detached from that.

Kripke remarks (1982, pp. 79–80) that the lesson of Wittgenstein's reflections on rule-following is particularly counter-intuitive in two areas: mathematics and talk of "inner" facts. This remark is still true after we have corrected Kripke's account of what the lesson is. In the case of mathematics, the difficulty is that we tend to construe the phenomenology of proof as a matter of glimpses of the super-rigid machinery in operation. In the case of talk of "inner" facts, the difficulty lies in the temptation to suppose that one knows what one means from one's own case (*PI* §347). How can one's community have any bearing on the matter – beyond its control over the circumstances in which one gave oneself one's private ostensive definitions? Kripke's illuminating suggestion is that the passages usually regarded as containing the Private Language Argument are not rightly so regarded; the argument is essentially complete by *PI* §202, and the familiar passages (§§258, 265, 293, and so forth) are attempts to dissipate this inclination to cite talk of "inner" facts as a counter-example to its conclusion.

This implies that whether those familiar passages carry conviction is, in a sense, irrelevant to the cogency of Wittgenstein's argument. If the inclination to regard talk of "inner" facts as a counter-example persists through them, that by itself cuts no ice. And we are now in a position to see what would be needed in order to undermine the argument. One would need to show either that one or the other of the horns of the dilemma can be comfortably occupied, or that it is not the case that the assimilation of understanding to interpretation, which poses the dilemma, can be resisted only by locating meaning in a framework of communal practices.

If the target of Wittgenstein's reflections is the assimilation of under-standing to interpretation, we should expect the areas where his conclusion is peculiarly counter-intuitive to be areas where we are strongly inclined to be comfortable with that assimilation. In the mathematical case, we are partic-ularly prone to the assimilation because – as I remarked above – we are especially inclined to accept its natural accompaniment, the picture of the super-rigid machine. What about talk of "inner" facts? We are strongly tempted, in this context, to think there could be a private grasp of a concept – something by which, for all its privacy, it would make sense to think of judgements and utterances as constrained. What Wittgenstein's argument, as I read it, requires is the diagnosis that we are here toying with the picture of an interpretation (placed by us on a private ostensive definition) – that it is

65

only so that we can contrive to conceive the matter in terms of concepts and judgements at all. It is true that this pictured interpretation does not readily succumb to the softening effect of the skeptical reasoning – "one interpretation after another, as if each one contented us at least for a moment, until we thought of yet another standing behind it" (*PI* §201). We imagine that in this case we can picture an interpretation that stays hard – one that comprehensively bridges the gap between the private ostensive definition and the judgements that we picture it as dictating. But there cannot be exceptions to the thesis that no interpretation can bridge the gap between the acquisition of a concept and its subsequent employment. It is this, I think, that Wittgenstein is trying to make vivid for us in the battery of passages of which the following might stand as an epitome:

> Always get rid of the idea of the private object in this way: assume that
> it constantly changes, but that you do not notice the change because
> your memory constantly deceives you. (*PI* §207)[33]

The idea that a private interpretation can be immune to the softening effect must be an illusion. If we conceive such an interpretation as comprehensively filling the gap, whatever the gap turns out to be, we deprive of all substance the hardness that we picture it as having.

It may be tempting to locate a weakness, in the argument I attribute to Wittgenstein, in the claim that we can steer between Scylla and Charybdis only by appealing to the practice of a community. If it is the notion of a practice that does the work, can we not form a conception of the practice of an individual that would do the trick?[34] But if one is tempted by this thought, one must search one's conscience to be sure that what one has in mind is not really, after all, the picture of a private interpretation; in which case one is not, after all, steering between Scylla and Charybdis, but resigning oneself to Scylla, leaving oneself fully vulnerable to the line of argument that I have just sketched.[35]

10.

Wright's reading of Wittgenstein hinges on this conditional: if possession of a concept were correctly conceived as grasp of a (ratification-independent)

---

33. See, e.g., *PI* §§258, 265, 270. See Anthony Kenny, "The Verification Principle and the Private Language Argument", in O. R. Jones (ed.), *The Private Language Argument* (London: Macmillan, 1971).
34. Simon Blackburn presses what is in effect this question, in "The Individual Strikes Back".
35. In this section I have aimed to describe only the *structure* of the Private Language Argument. A fuller account of how it works would require, in addition, discharging the unfinished business noted at the end of §7 above. See especially §11 below.

pattern, then there would be no knowing for sure how someone else understands an expression. This conditional underlies Wright's conviction that, when we entertain the "pattern" idea,

> . . . the kind of reflective grasp of meaning appealed to is essentially *idiolectic*—it is a matter of each of us discerning the character of his own understanding of expressions. There is no temptation to claim a reflective knowledge of features of *others'* understanding of a particular expression—except against the background of the hypothesis that it coincides with one's own.[36]

We can summarize Wright's reading by saying that he takes Wittgenstein to propound a *modus tollens* argument with the conditional as major premise. Thus: the idea of knowledge of idiolectic meaning is an illusion; therefore possession of a concept cannot be correctly conceived as grasp of a (ratification-independent) pattern.

The basis of this argument is, as Wright points out, "the fundamental anti-realist thesis that we have understanding only of concepts of which we can distinctively manifest our understanding" (1980, p. 221). Wright would ground both premises of the *modus tollens* argument on anti-realism. The justification for the minor premise (see §2 above) is that the picture of an idiolectic rule makes no room for a distinction between actually conforming and merely having the impression that one is conforming. In Wright's reading the thought here is an anti-realist one: that in an idiolectic context one could not distinctively manifest – not even with a manifestation to oneself – a difference in one's understanding of "I am actually conforming" and "I have the impression of conforming".[37] What underlies the major premise – the conditional – is the anti-realist conception of what it is to manifest understanding to others.

According to that conception, the behaviour that counts as manifesting understanding to others must be characterizable, in such a way as to display its status as such a manifestation, without benefit of a command of the language in question. Without that proviso, the "manifestation challenge" that anti-realists direct against the truth-conditional conception of meaning would be trivialized.[38] The challenge would hold no fears for the truth-

---

36. Wright, *Wittgenstein on the Foundations of Mathematics*, p. 354. A footnote adds: "Or with one's understanding of another specified expression."

37. This is how Wright thinks the Private Language Argument is to be understood. Note that the requirement of manifestation is not initially imposed, in this line of thought, as a requirement of *public* manifestation. We are supposed to be brought to see that public manifestation is what is required in consequence of an independent (non-question-begging) critique of the idea of idiolectic understanding. On the structure of Wright's reading, see §14 below.

38 For the terminology "manifestation challenge", see Wright, "Realism, Truth-Value Links, Other Minds and the Past", pp. 112–13, in his *Realism, Meaning, and Truth*. For the substance of the challenge, see, e.g., Dummett, *Frege: Philosophy of Language* (London: Duckworth, 1973), p. 467.

conditional conception if one were allowed to count as satisfying the requirement of manifestation by such behaviour as saying – manifestly, at least to someone who understands the language one is speaking – that such-and-such is the case. So the distinctive manifestations allowed by anti-realism consist, rather, in such behaviour as assenting to a sentence in such-and-such circumstances.[39]

Now what – besides itself – could be fully manifested by a piece of behaviour, or a series of pieces of behaviour, described in accordance with the anti-realist requirement?[40] Perhaps the behaviour would license us to attribute a disposition; but how can we extrapolate to a determinate conception of what the disposition is a disposition to do? Our characterization of the manifesting behaviour is not allowed to exploit understanding of the language in question; so even if, in our innocence, we start out by conceiving that as grasp of "a network of determinate patterns",[41] we are debarred from extrapolating along the pathways of the network. It seems clear that within the rules of this game any extrapolation could only be inductive, which means that if we accept the requirement that understanding be fully manifested in behaviour, no extrapolation is licensed at all. The upshot is this: the anti-realist requirement of manifestation precludes any conception of understanding as grasp of a network of patterns. And this is precisely the conclusion Wright draws.[42]

The obstacle to accepting this argument is the normative character of the notion of meaning. As I have granted, Wright aims to accommodate that: he would insist that his conclusion is not that concepts have no normative status, but that the patterns they dictate are not independent of our ratification. But

---

39. It is actually an illusion to think that this kind of characterization of behaviour conforms to the anti-realist requirement: see my "Anti-Realism and the Epistemology of Understanding", in my *Meaning, Knowledge, and Reality* (Cambridge, MA: Harvard University Press, 1998). But in the course of arguing, as I am, that the programme is misconceived in principle, there is no point in jibbing at the details of its purported execution.

40. For "fully" see Dummett, *Frege*, p. 467.

41. Wright, *Wittgenstein on the Foundations of Mathematics*, p. 220.

42. At least in *Wittgenstein on the Foundations of Mathematics*. Contrast "Strawson on Anti-Realism" (reprinted in *Realism, Meaning, and Truth*), p. 81 ". . . suppose [someone] has this knowledge: of every state of affairs criterially warranting the assertion, or denial, of 'John is in pain', he knows in a practical sense both that it has that status and under what conditions it would be brought out that its status was merely criterial; that is, he knows the 'overturn–conditions' of any situation criterially warranting the assertion, or denial, of 'John is in pain'. *No doubt we could not know for sure* that someone had this knowledge; but the stronger our grounds for thinking that he did, the more baffling would be the allegation that he did not grasp the assertoric content of 'John is in pain'." (My emphasis.) Here Wright contemplates maintaining a version (formulated in terms of criteria) of the idea that understanding is grasp of a pattern of use, and accordingly opts – as his overall position indeed requires – for the other horn of this dilemma: the thesis, namely, that one cannot have certain knowledge of the character of someone else's understanding. What is remarkable is Wright's insouciance about this move: it openly flouts the fundamental motivation of anti-realism, which is what Wright is supposed to be defending against Strawson in the passage I have quoted. It seems clear that the contrasting position of *Wittgenstein on the Foundations of Mathematics* is the only one an anti-realist can consistently occupy.

the trouble is (see §§5 and 7) that the denial of ratification-independence, by Wright's own insistence, yields a picture of the relation between the communal language and the world in which norms are obliterated. And once we have this picture, it seems impossible simply to retain alongside it a different picture, in which the openness of an individual to correction by his fellows means that he is subject to norms. The first picture irresistibly claims primacy, leaving our openness to correction by our fellows looking like, at best, an explanation of our propensity to the illusion that we are subject to norms. If this is correct, it turns Wright's argument on its head: a condition for the possibility of finding real application for the notion of meaning at all is that we reject anti-realism. *McDowell's Argument*

I think this transcendental argument against anti-realism is fully cogent. But it is perhaps unlikely to carry conviction unless supplemented with a satisfying account of how anti-realism goes wrong. (Providing this supplementation will help to discharge the unfinished business that I noted at the end of §7.)

Understanding a Rule is a giving an account of one's dispositions & the parts thereof

11.

According to anti-realism, people's sharing a language is constituted by appropriate correspondences in their dispositions to linguistic behaviour, as characterized without drawing on command of the language, and hence not in terms of the contents of their utterances. The motivation for this thesis is admirable: a recoil from the idea that assigning a meaning to an utterance by a speaker of one's language is forming a hypothesis about something concealed behind the surface of his linguistic behaviour. But there are two possible directions in which this recoil might move one. One – the anti-realist direction – is to retain the conception of the surface that makes the idea natural, and resolutely attempt to locate meaning on the surface, so conceived. That this attempt fails is the conclusion of the transcendental argument. The supplementation that the argument needs is to point out the availability of the alternative direction: namely, to reject the conception of the surface that anti-realism shares with the position it recoils from. According to this different view, the outward aspect of linguistic behaviour – what a speaker makes available to others – must be characterized in terms of the contents of utterances (the thoughts they express). Of course such an outward aspect cannot be conceived as made available to just anyone; command of the language is needed in order to put one in direct cognitive contact with that in which someone's meaning consists.[43] (This might seem to represent

---

43. See my "Anti-Realism and the Epistemology of Understanding" reprinted in McDowell, *Meaning, Knowledge, and Reality* (Cambridge, MA: Harvard University Press, 1998) pp. 314–43.

command of the language as a mysterious sort of X-ray vision; but only in the context of the rejected conception of the surface.)

Wittgenstein warns us not to try to dig below "bedrock". But it is difficult, in reading him, to avoid acquiring a sense of what, as it were, lies down there: a web of facts about behaviour and "inner" episodes, describable without using the notion of meaning. One is likely to be struck by the sheer contingency of the resemblances between individuals on which, in this vision, the possibility of meaning seems to depend, and hence impressed by an apparent precariousness in our making sense of one another.[44] There is an authentic insight here, but one that is easily distorted; correcting the distortion will help to bring out what is wrong with the anti-realist construal of Wittgenstein.

The distorted version of the insight can be put as a dilemma, on these lines. Suppose that, in claiming a "reflective knowledge" of the principle of application of some expression, I claim to speak for others as well as myself. In that case my claim (even if restricted to a definitely specified other: say my interlocutor in a particular conversation) is indefinitely vulnerable to the possibility of an unfavourable future. Below "bedrock" there is nothing but contingency; so at any time in the future my interlocutor's use of the expression in question may simply stop conforming to the pattern that I expect. And that would retrospectively undermine my present claim to be able to vouch for the character of his understanding. So I can claim to know his pattern now only "against the background of the hypothesis that it coincides with [my] own".[45] If, then, we retain the conception of understanding as grasp of patterns, the feeling of precariousness becomes the idea that what we think of as a shared language is at best a set of corresponding idiolects, with our grounds for believing in the correspondence no better than inductive. The only alternative – the other horn of the dilemma – is, with Wright, to give up the conception of understanding as grasp of (ratification-independent) patterns. This turns the feeling of precariousness into the idea that I cannot know for sure that my interlocutor and I will continue to march in step. But on this horn my present claim to understand him is not undermined by that concession: my understanding him now is a matter of our being in step now, and does not require a shared pattern extending into the future.

What is wrong with this, in Wittgensteinian terms, is that it conflates propositions at (or above) "bedrock" with propositions about the contingencies that lie below. (See, for instance, *RFM* VI-49.) Its key thought is that, if I claim to know someone else's pattern, I bind myself to a prediction of the uses of language that he will make in various possible future circumstances,

---

44. See *Wittgenstein on Rules and Private Language*, p. 97; compare Cavell, *Must We Mean What We Say?* (New York: Scribners, 1969), p. 52, and my "Noncognitivism and Rule-Following" reprinted in McDowell, *Mind, Value, and Reality* (Cambridge, MA: Harvard University Press, 1998), pp. 198–218.

45. Wright, *Wittgenstein on the Foundations of Mathematics*, p. 354.

with these uses characterized in sub-"bedrock" terms. (That is why coming to see the contingency of the resemblances, at this level, on which meaning rests is supposed to induce appreciation that knowledge of another person's pattern could at best be inductive.) But when I claim understanding of someone else, and construe this as knowledge of the patterns to which his present utterance owes allegiance, what I claim to know is not that in such-and-such circumstances he will do so and so, but rather at most that that is what he will do if he sticks to his patterns.[46] And that is not a prediction at all. (Compare *RFM* VI-15.)

It is true that a certain disorderliness below "bedrock" would undermine the applicability of the notion of rule-following. So the underlying contingencies bear an intimate relation to the notion of rule-following – a relation that Wittgenstein tries to capture by saying "It is as if we had hardened the empirical proposition into a rule" (*RFM* VI-22). But recognizing the intimate relation must not be allowed to obscure the difference of levels.[47] If we respect the difference of levels, what we make of the feeling of precariousness will be as follows. When I understand another person, I know the rules he is going by. My right to claim to understand him is precarious, in that nothing but a tissue of contingencies stands in the way of my losing it. But to envisage its loss is not necessarily to envisage its turning out that I never had the right at all. The difference of levels suffices to drive a wedge between these; contrast the second horn of the above dilemma, on which inserting the wedge requires abandonment of the idea that mutual understanding is mutual knowledge of shared commitments.[48]

---

46. Even this is too much. It passes muster where the "pattern" idea is least metaphorical, namely in the case of continuation of a series. But in the general case, the idea of a corpus of determinate predictions to which a claim of present understanding would commit one is absurd. (See n. 4 above.) The point I am making here is a version of one that Rush Rhees makes, in terms of a distinction between the general practice of linguistic behaviour and the following of rules, at pp. 55–6 of "Can There Be a Private Language?", in his *Discussions of Wittgenstein* (London: Routledge & Kegan Paul, 1970). It disarms, as an objection to Wittgenstein, the insightful remarks of Jerry A. Fodor, *The Language of Thought* (New York: Thomas Y. Crowell, 1975), pp. 71–2.

47. The difference of levels is the subject of Wittgenstein's remarks about "the limits of empiricism": *RFM* III-71, VII-17, VII-21. (The source of the phrase is Russell's paper of that name.) See Wright, *Wittgenstein on the Foundations of Mathematics,* p. 220. I think the point of the remarks is, very roughly, that empiricism can deal only with what is below "bedrock"; the limits of empiricism (which "are not assumptions unguaranteed, or intuitively known to be correct: they are ways in which we make comparisons and in which we act": *RFM* VII-21, compare *On Certainty* §204, quoted in §7 above) lie above it (outside its reach), at "bedrock" level. Wright, by contrast, seems to interpret the passages as if Wittgenstein's view were that for all its limits empiricism contained the truth.

48. Christopher Peacocke, at p. 88 of "Rule-Following: The Nature of Wittgenstein's Arguments" in Holtzman and Leich (eds) *Wittgenstein: To Follow a Rule,* implies that statements about rule-following *supervene,* in Wittgenstein's view, on sub-"bedrock" statements. There may be an acceptable interpretation of this; but on the most natural interpretation, it would make statements about rule-following vulnerable to future loss of mutual intelligibility in just the way I am objecting to.

Anti-realists hold that initiation into a common language consists in acquisition of linguistic propensities describable without use of the notion of meaning. They thereby perpetrate exactly the conflation of levels against which Wittgenstein warns; someone's following a rule, according to anti-realism, is constituted by the obtaining of resemblances, describable in sub-"bedrock" terms, between his behaviour and that of his fellows. Not that anti-realists would put it like that: it is another way of making the same point to say that they locate "bedrock" lower than it is – not accommodating the fact that "following according to the rule is FUNDAMENTAL to our language game" (*RFM* VI-28; see §7 above). If, by contrast, we satisfy the motivation of anti-realism in the different way that I distinguished above, then we refuse to countenance sub-"bedrock" (meaning-free) characterizations of what meaning something by one's words consists in, and thus respect Wittgenstein's distinction of levels.

We make possible, moreover, a radically different conception of what it is to belong to a linguistic community. Anti-realists picture a community as a collection of individuals presenting to one another exteriors that match in certain respects. They hope to humanize this bleak picture by claiming that what meaning consists in lies on those exteriors as they conceive them. But the transcendental argument reveals this hope as vain. A related thought is this: if regularities in the verbal behaviour of an isolated individual, described in norm-free terms, do not add up to meaning, it is quite obscure how it could somehow make all the difference if there are several individuals with matching regularities.[49] The picture of a linguistic community degenerates, then, under anti-realist assumptions, into a picture of a mere aggregate of individuals whom we have no convincing reason not to conceive as opaque to one another. If, on the other hand, we reject the anti-realist restriction on what counts as manifesting one's understanding, we entitle ourselves to this thought: shared membership in a linguistic community is not just a matter of matching in aspects of an exterior that we present to anyone whatever, but equips us to make our minds available to one another, by confronting one another with a different exterior from that which we present to outsiders.

---

49. Blackburn writes ("Rule-Following and Moral Realism", p. 183): "...we can become gripped by what I call a *wooden* picture of the use of language, according to which the only fact of the matter is that in certain situations people use words, perhaps with various feelings like 'that fits', and so on. This wooden picture makes no room for the further fact that in applying or withholding a word people may be conforming to a pre-existent rule. But just because of this, it seems to make no room for the idea that in using their words they are expressing judgements. Wittgenstein must have felt that publicity, the fact that others do the same, was the magic ingredient turning the wooden picture into the full one. It is most obscure to me that it fills this role: a lot of wooden persons with propensities to make noises is just more of whatever one of them is." It will be apparent that I have a great deal of sympathy with this complaint. Where I believe Blackburn goes wrong is in thinking it tells against Wittgenstein himself, as opposed to the position that Wittgenstein has been saddled with by a certain set of interpreters (among whom I did not intend to enrol myself in "Noncognitivism and rule-following", the paper to which Blackburn is responding).

Wittgenstein's problem was to explain how understanding can be other than interpretation (see §7 above). This non-anti-realist conception of a linguistic community gives us a genuine right to the following answer: shared command of a language equips us to know one another's meaning without needing to arrive at that knowledge by interpretation, because it equips us to hear someone else's meaning in his words. Anti-realists would claim this right too, but the claim is rendered void by the merely additive upshot of their picture of what it is to share a language. In the different picture I have described, the response to Wittgenstein's problem works because a linguistic community is conceived as bound together, not by a match in mere externals (facts accessible to just anyone), but by a capacity for a meeting of minds.

When we had no more than an abstract characterization of Wittgenstein's response, as an appeal to the notion of communal practice, there seemed to be justice in this query: if the concept of a communal practice can magic meaning into our picture, should not this power be credited to the concept of a practice as such – so that the practice of an individual might serve just as well? (See §7 above.) But if Wittgenstein's position is the one I have described in this section, it is precisely the notion of a *communal* practice that is needed, and not some notion that could equally be applied outside the context of a community. The essential point is the way in which one person can know another's meaning without interpretation. Contrary to Wright's reading, it is only because we *can* have what Wright calls "a reflective knowledge of features of *others'* understanding of a particular expression"[50] that meaning is possible at all.[51]

12.

Wittgenstein's reflections on rule-following attack a certain familiar picture of facts and truth, which I shall formulate like this. A genuine fact must be a matter of the way things are in themselves, utterly independently of us. So a genuinely true judgement must be, at least potentially, an exercise of pure thought; if human nature is necessarily implicated in the very formation of the judgement, that precludes our thinking of the corresponding fact as properly independent of us, and hence as a proper fact at all.[52]

---

50. *Wittgenstein on the Foundations of Mathematics*, p.354.
51. If I am right to suppose that any merely aggregative conception of a linguistic community falsifies Wittgenstein, then it seems that the parallel Kripke draws with Hume's discussion of causation (independently proposed by Blackburn, "Rule-Following and Moral Realism", pp. 182–3) is misconceived. Wittgenstein's picture of language contains no conception of the individual such as would correspond to the individual cause-effect pair, related only by contiguity and succession, in Hume's picture of causation.
52. The later Wittgenstein may have (perhaps unjustly) found a form of this picture in the *Tractatus*. On the relation between the later work and the *Tractatus,* see Peter Winch, "Introduction: The

We can find this picture of genuine truth compelling only if we either forget that truth-bearers are such only because they are meaningful, or suppose that meanings take care of themselves, needing, as it were, no help from us. This latter supposition is the one that is relevant to our concerns. If we make it, we can let the judging subject, in our picture of true judgement, shrink to a locus of pure thought, while the fact that judging is a human activity fades into insignificance.

Now Wittgenstein's reflections on rule-following undermine this picture by undermining the supposition that meanings take care of themselves. A particular performance, "inner" or overt, can be an application of a concept – a judgement or a meaningful utterance – only if it owes allegiance to constraints that the concept imposes. And being governed by such constraints is not being led, in some occult way, by an autonomous meaning (the super-rigid machinery), but acting within a communal custom. The upshot is that if something matters for one's being a participant in the relevant customs, it matters equally for one's being capable of making any judgements at all. We have to give up that picture of genuine truth, in which the maker of a true judgement can shrink to a point of pure thought, abstracted from anything that might make him distinctively and recognizably one of us.

It seems right to regard that familiar picture as a kind of realism. It takes meaning to be wholly autonomous (one is tempted to say "out there"); this is reminiscent of realism as the term is used in the old debate about universals. And it embraces an extreme form of the thesis that the facts are not up to us; this invites the label "realism" understood in a way characteristic of more recent debates. But if we allow ourselves to describe the recoil from the familiar picture as a recoil from realism, there are two points that we must be careful not to let this obscure.

First: the recoil has nothing to do with rejection of the truth-conditional conception of meaning, properly understood. That conception has no need to camouflage the fact that truth-conditions are necessarily given by us, in a language that we understand. When we say "'Diamonds are hard' is true if and only if diamonds are hard", we are just as much involved on the right-hand side as the reflections on rule-following tell us we are. There is a standing temptation to miss this obvious truth, and to suppose that the right-hand side somehow presents us with a possible fact, pictured as a unconceptualized configuration of things in themselves. But we can find the connection between meaning and truth illuminating without succumbing to that temptation.

Second: the recoil is from an extreme form of the thesis that the facts are not up to us, not from that thesis in any form whatever. What Wittgenstein's polemic against the picture of the super-rigid machine makes untenable is the

---

Unity of Wittgenstein's Philosophy", in P. Winch (ed.) *Studies in the Philosophy of Wittgenstein* (London: Routledge & Kegan Paul, 1969), especially the very illuminating discussion at pp. 9–15.

thesis that possessing a concept is grasping a pattern of application that extends *of itself* to new cases. (See §4 above.) In Wright's reading, that is the same as saying that it deprives us of the conception of grasp of ratification-independent patterns. But rejection of ratification-independence obliterates meaning altogether (see §§5, 7, 10 above). In effect, the transcendental argument shows that there *must* be a middle position. Understanding is grasping patterns that extend to new cases independently of our ratification, as is required for meaning to be other than an illusion (and – not incidentally – for the intuitive notion of objectivity to have a use); but the constraints imposed by our concepts do not have the platonistic autonomy with which they are credited in the picture of the super-rigid machinery.

As before (compare §11 above), what obscures the possibility of this position is the "anti-realist" attempt to get below "bedrock". Wright suggests that the emergence of a consensus on whether, say, to call some newly encountered object "yellow" is subject to no norms. That is indeed how it seems if we allow ourselves to picture the communal language in terms of sub-"bedrock" resemblances in behaviour and phenomenology. But if we respect Wittgenstein's injunction not to dig below the ground, we must say that the community "goes right or wrong" according to whether the object in question is, or is not, *yellow*; and nothing can make its being yellow, or not, dependent on our ratification of the judgement that that is how things are. In Wittgenstein's eyes, as I read him, Wright's claim that "for the community itself there is no authority, so no standard to meet" can be, at very best, an attempt to say something that cannot be said but only shown. It may have some merit, conceived in that light; but attributing it to Wittgenstein as a doctrine can yield only distortion.

Wittgenstein writes, at *RFM* II-61:

> Finitism and behaviourism are quite similar trends. Both say, but surely, all we have here is. . . . Both deny the existence of something, both with a view to escaping from a confusion.[53]

The point about finitism is this. It recoils, rightly, from the mythology of the super-rigid machinery – the patterns that extend of themselves, without limit, beyond any point we take them to. But it equates this recoil with rejecting any conception of patterns that extend, without limit, beyond any such point. This is like the behaviourist idea that in order to escape from the confused idea of the mental as essentially concealed from others behind behaviour, we have to reject the mental altogether. The idealism that Wright reads into Wittgenstein seems to be another similar trend. (Clearly the remark does not applaud the trends it discusses.)

---

53. Kripke discusses this passage at pp. 106–7; but I believe his attribution to Wittgenstein of the "skeptical paradox" and the "skeptical solution" prevents him from fully appreciating its point.

How DO I RECONCILE INTENTIONAL DISPOSITIONALISM WITH GRICIAN IDEA?

13.

In this section I want to mention two sets of passages in Wittgenstein of which we are now placed to make better sense than Wright can.

First: in Wright's reading, the "pattern" idea is inextricably connected with the picture of idiolectic understanding. But this does not seem to be how Wittgenstein sees things. Wittgenstein does not scruple to say that a series "is defined . . . by the training in proceeding according to the rule" (*RFM* VI-16). And at *Zettel* §308 he writes:

> Instead of "and so on" he might have said: "Now you know what I mean." And his explanation would simply be a *definition* of the expression "following the rule + 1". . .

Again, *PI* §208 and the remarks that follow it contain a sustained attack on the idea that successfully putting someone through the sort of training that is meant to "point beyond" the examples given (see §208) is getting him "to *guess* the essential thing" (*PI* §210). For Wright, when these passages reject the picture of a leap to a personal understanding, they should be *eo ipso* rejecting the "pattern" idea. But Wittgenstein combines criticism of the "leap" picture with conceding (§209) how natural it is to think of our understanding as reaching beyond all the examples given. (Wright would construe this concession in terms of his purged version of the "pattern" idea. But we can make sense of what Wittgenstein says without saddling him with the problems generated by denial of ratification-independence.)

Second: Wittgenstein sometimes (for instance at *PI* §151) discusses the idea that one can grasp the principle of a series, or a meaning, "in a flash". Wright suggests that the idea of this "flash" can be nothing but the idea of a leap to a purely personal understanding.[54] But I see no reason to accept that Wittgenstein intends this identification. In fact, the suggestion casts a gratuitous slur on his phenomenological perceptiveness. The idea that the meaning of an expression can be present in an instant is just as tempting about someone else's meaning as it is about one's own; and Wittgenstein is perfectly aware of this:

> When someone says the word "cube" to me, for example, I know what it means. But can the whole *use* of the word come before my mind, when I *understand* it in that way? (*PI* §139; compare §138)

Wright's view must be that the intended answer to this question is "No" – that Wittgenstein intends to show up as an illusion the idea that one can grasp someone else's pattern in a flash. But the only illusion that Wright explains to

---

54. *Wittgenstein on the Foundation of Mathematics*, pp. 30–1.

us in this neighbourhood is the illusion of supposing that one could have an idiolectic grasp of a pattern. So Wright's Wittgenstein owes us something for which we search the writings of the actual Wittgenstein in vain: an explanation of how it is that we not only fall into that illusion but misconceive its character – mistaking what is in fact the supposition that we can guess at someone else's pattern for (what seems on the face of it very different) the supposition that we can hear it in his utterances.

We are now placed to see that this latter supposition is not, in Wittgenstein's view, an illusion at all. "Grasping the whole use in a flash" is not to be dismissed as expressing an incorrigibly confused picture – the picture of a leap to an idiolectic understanding – but to be carefully understood in the light of the thesis that there is a way of grasping a rule which is not an interpretation. In that light, we can see that there is nothing wrong with the idea that one can grasp in a flash the principle of a series one is being taught; and equally that there is nothing wrong with the idea that one can hear someone else's meaning in his words. The "interpretation" prejudice insidiously tempts us to put a fantastic mythological construction on these conceptions; the right response to that is not to abandon the conception but to exorcize the "interpretation" prejudice and so return them to sobriety. ("Really the only thing wrong with what you say is the expression 'in a queer way'": *PI* §195.)

At *PI* §534, Wittgenstein writes:

> Hearing a word in a particular sense. How queer that there should be such a thing!
>
> Phrased *like this*, emphasized like this, heard in this way, this sentence is the first of a series in which a transition is made to *these* sentences, pictures, actions.
>
> (A multitude of familiar paths leads off from these words in every direction.)[55]

What are these "familiar paths"? Presumably, for instance, continuations of the conversation that would make sense: not, then, "patterns" in precisely the sense with which we have been concerned (which would be, as these paths would not, cases of "going on doing the same thing"), but they raise similar issues. Suppose that, in describing a series of utterances that in fact constitutes an intelligible conversation, we conform to the anti-realist account of how meaning must be manifested. We shall have to describe each member of the series without drawing on command of the language in question. Such a description will blot out the relations of meaning between the members of the series, in virtue of which it constitutes an intelligible conversation; what is left

---

55. The last sentence is quoted from *PI* §525. A related passage is *PI* II.xi: the connection between the topics of seeing an aspect and "experiencing the meaning of a word" is drawn explicitly at pp. 214, 215.

will be, at best, a path that one could trace out inductively (whether predicting or retrodicting).[56] Wright's demonstration that anti-realism cannot countenance ratification-independent patterns should work for these "familiar paths" too. An anti-realist cannot extrapolate, from what is done in his presence on an occasion, along paths marked out by meaning; and inductive extrapolation is against the rule that we must restrict ourselves to what is fully manifested in linguistic behaviour. It is obscure to me what interpretation of the passage I have quoted is available to Wright. What seems to be the case is that anti-realism, by, in effect, looking for "bedrock" lower than it is, blocks off the obvious and surely correct reading: that hearing a word in one sense rather than another is hearing it in one position rather than another in the network of possible patterns of making sense that we learn to find ourselves in when we acquire mastery of a language.

I don't see how that excludes private language...

14.

We can centre the issue between Wright's reading and mine on this question: how does Wittgenstein's insistence on publicity emerge? In my reading, the answer is this: it emerges as a condition of the possibility of rejecting the assimilation of understanding to interpretation, which poses an intolerable dilemma. In Wright's reading, the answer is this: it emerges as the only alternative left, after the notion of idiolectic understanding has been scotched by a self-contained argument that is epitomized by this passage (*PI* §258):

> . . . One would like to say: whatever is going to seem right to me is right. And that only means that here we can't talk about "right".

I deny that my personal understanding must be of the sort: "whatever seems right is"

Wright takes the thought here to be an anti-realist one, to the effect that the distinction between being right and seeming right is shown to be empty, in the idiolectic case, by the impossibility of manifesting a grasp of it, even to oneself. (See §10 above.) Given this, I suppose Wright takes it that sheer consistency requires construing the appeal to the community, shown to be obligatory by virtue of being the only remaining possibility, in an anti-realist way.

---

56. At pp. 130–1 of "What Is a Theory of Meaning? (II)", Dummett writes: "We do not expect, nor should we want, to achieve a deterministic theory of meaning for a language, even one which is deterministic only in principle: we should not expect to be able to give a theory from which, together with all other relevant conditions (the physical environment of a speaker, the utterances of other speakers, etc.), we could predict the exact utterances of any one speaker, any more than, by a study of the rules and strategy of a game, we expect to be able to predict actual play." But in the context of the anti-realist restriction, all that this can mean is that we must content ourselves with weaker relations of the same general kind (inductively traceable, not meaning-dependent) as those that would be involved in a theory of the deterministic sort we are to renounce.

Now it is true that the idiolectic conception of understanding is a corollary of the second horn of the dilemma. (See §4 above.) So my reading need not exclude a self-contained argument against that idea, constituting part of the demonstration that the dilemma is intolerable. On such a view, the insistence on publicity would emerge twice over: first as a direct implication of the self-contained argument, and second, indirectly, as required by the rejection of the dilemma. In fact I think this complexity is unnecessary. Wittgenstein has plenty to say against the second horn of the dilemma – the picture of the super-rigid machine – without needing, for his case against it and therefore against accepting the dilemma, the envisaged self-contained argument against this corollary. And I have explained (in §9 above) how passages like the one I quoted above from *PI* §258, which Wright takes as formulations of the self-contained argument, are intelligible in the context of the second, indirect route to the requirement of publicity. But the real flaw in Wright's reading, in my view, is not that it countenances the first route, but that it omits the second. Like Kripke (see §8 above), Wright makes nothing of Wittgenstein's concern – which figures at the centre of my reading – to attack the assimilation of understanding to interpretation.

This oversight shows itself in Wright's willingness to attribute the following line of thought to Wittgenstein:

> . . .the investigation-independent truth of statements requires that their truth is settled, autonomously and without the need of human interference, by their meanings and the character of the relevant facts. For a complex set of reasons, however, no notion of meaning can be legitimised which will play this role. . . the meaning of a statement, if it is to make the relevant autonomous contribution towards determining that statement's truth-value, cannot be thought of as fully determined by previous uses of that statement or, if it is a novel statement, by previous uses of its constituents and by its syntax; for those factors can always be reconciled with the statement's having any truth-value, no matter what the worldly facts are taken to be. The same goes for prior phenomenological episodes—imagery, models— in the minds of the linguistically competent. Nothing, therefore, in the previous use of the statement, or of its constituents, or in the prior streams of consciousness of competent speakers, is, if its meaning is in conjunction with the facts to determine its truth-value, sufficient to fix its meaning. So what does?[57]

---

57. "Strict Finitism", p. 250. Note also *Wittgenstein on the Foundations of Mathematics*, p. 22, where Wright identifies the second speaker in the dialogue of *RFM* I-113 ("However many rules you give me—I give a rule which justifies *my* employment of your rules") with Wittgenstein himself; and p. 216 (a passage I quoted in §2 above), where it is the susceptibility of all explanations to unintended *interpretations* that is said to push us into the idea of understanding as essentially idiolectic.

This is essentially the argument that generates the paradox of *PI* §201; and it can be attributed to Wittgenstein only at the cost of ignoring, like Kripke, that section's second paragraph.

The result of the oversight is that, whereas Wittgenstein's key thought is that the dilemma must be avoided, Wright's reading leaves the dilemma unchallenged. Wittgenstein obviously attacks the second horn of the dilemma – the picture of the super-rigid machinery. The consequence of leaving the dilemma unchallenged is thus to locate Wittgenstein on its first horn – embracing the paradox of §201. This disastrous upshot does not, of course, correspond to Wright's *intentions* in his interpretation of Wittgenstein. (Contrast Kripke, who can be content to attribute acceptance of the paradox of §201 to Wittgenstein because he misses its devastating character.) Nevertheless, it is where his reading leaves us (see §§5, 7, 10 above): a fitting nemesis for its inattention to Wittgenstein's central concern.

The villain of the piece – what makes it impossible for Wright to accommodate Wittgenstein's insistence that understanding need not be interpretation – is the anti-realist conception of our knowledge of others. (See §§ 11 and 12 above. Contrary to what, at the beginning of this section, I took Wright to suppose, the cogency of a passage like *PI* §258, against the picture of idiolectic understanding, is quite unconnected with the anti-realist view of what it is to manifest understanding to others.) From Wright's reading, then, we can learn something important: that there cannot be a position that is both anti-realist and genuinely hospitable to meaning, and that the construal of Wittgenstein as the source of anti-realism, often nowadays taken for granted, is a travesty.

Why to piss away day off anore...

CHAPTER FIVE

WITTGENSTEIN, KRIPKE AND NON-REDUCTIONISM ABOUT MEANING

Colin McGinn

[handwritten annotation: McGinn see representation facts need not be reducible: I say intentional facts need ∅ be reducible]

What is very striking about Kripke's skeptic is an assumption he makes which, once it is brought to light, ought to make us suspicious of his whole way of proceeding; this assumption both is essential to the argument and is itself unargued for. I mean the assumption that if there are semantic facts they will have to be *reducible* to facts specified non-semantically: for the skeptic is in effect demanding an answer to the question 'what does meaning/reference consist in?' which does not just help itself to the notions of meaning and reference. Thus the candidate answers Kripke considers all attempt to say what constitutes a given semantic fact without simply *using* semantic concepts directly (or indeed indirectly) – *viz.* actual application, states of consciousness, dispositions to use. The kind of reply that is being implicitly judged illicit is one that simply uses semantic concepts, as follows: what it consists in to mean/refer to addition by '+' is for the speaker to *mean/refer to* addition by '+' – *this* is the sort of 'fact' that meaning consists in.[1] Remember that Kripke's skeptic is out to show that semantic discourse is not fact-stating; then his implicit assumption is that semantic discourse cannot be regarded as fact-stating *just as it stands*. The skeptic is assuming that unless semantic facts can be captured in non-semantic terms they are not really facts; but why should this assumption be thought compulsory? So the question for Kripke is why we cannot give the truth conditions of 'he means addition by "+"' simply by

---

1. This assumption is implicit from the very beginning of the skeptical challenge (see Kripke, *Wittgenstein on Rules and Private Language* [Oxford: Blackwell, 1982], pp. 11f), but it is concealed by presenting the problem in terms of the 'directions I previously gave myself' in respect of '+': we are invited to consider the actual thoughts I had and computations I performed in the past, and to observe that my past meaning cannot be read off from these. In this way, Kripke's skeptic directs our attention away from the idea that the fact in question may just be an irreducible fact. And he further conceals his reductionist assumption by pretending that 'there are no limitations, in particular, no behaviourist limitations, on the facts that may be cited to answer the skeptic' (p. 14).

re-using that sentence, frankly admitting that no other specification of truth conditions is available – precisely because semantic statements cannot be *reduced* to non-semantic ones.[2] Unless this question can be answered Kripke's skeptic is wide open to the objection that he is mistaking *irreducibility* for non-factuality: he finds that he cannot provide a non-semantic fact to constitute a semantic fact and then concludes that there are *no* semantic facts, when the correct conclusion ought to be that semantic facts cannot be reduced to non-semantic facts. The skeptic thus needs to defend an undefended and undisclosed premise, namely that semantic discourse cannot be regarded as *irreducible*, this premise being tantamount to the claim that semantic discourse is not factual just as it is (without benefit of translation into other terms). For otherwise we can take him to have established in a new way what many have already and independently suspected: that semantic concepts are indeed irreducible to non-semantic concepts.[3]

The dialectical position here can be usefully compared with Quine's attack on the factuality of semantic discourse. Quine explicitly assumes that all genuine facts are physical facts (distributions of elementary particles and their physical properties), and then argues that semantic ascriptions cannot be reduced to statements of physical fact (including behavioural statements); it follows that semantic ascriptions do not state facts. The truth-value of semantic statements is *indeterminate* with respect to the physical facts, so such statements cannot correspond to facts at all.[4] Kripke's skeptic claims that semantic ascriptions are indeterminate with respect to a wider range of facts – including, notably, facts about consciousness – and then concludes that such ascriptions are unfactual. What both Quine and Kripke assume, the former more explicitly than the latter, is that the factuality of semantic ascriptions waits upon their reduction to some favoured class of fact-stating propositions; such ascriptions cannot be taken to be factual *independently* of finding any such reduction. It is thus open to us to take Quine's indeterminacy arguments as showing the hopelessness of a behaviourist or physicalist reduction of semantic discourse; similarly, we may take Kripke's arguments to show that *no* reduction of *any* kind is possible – semantic statements correspond to

---

2. This would be to adopt what Dummett calls a 'naive realist' view of facts about meaning: see his 'Realism', *Synthese* 52 (1982), pp. 78, 105f. Naive realism, as defined by Dummett, is realism about a class of statements combined with an irreducibility thesis in respect of those statements.

3. See, e.g., R. Chisholm, *Perceiving: A Philosophical Study* (Ithaca: Cornell University Press, 1957), ch. 11, for the suggestion that we cannot break out of the circle of intentional notions by explaining these notions in quite other terms.

4. Thus Quine: 'One may accept the Brentano thesis [i.e. the irreducibility of the intentional] either as showing the indispensability of intentional idioms and the importance of an autonomous science of intention, or as showing the baselessness of intentional idioms and the emptiness of a science of intention. My attitude, unlike Brentano's, is the second' (*Word and Object* [Cambridge, MA: MIT Press, 1960], p. 221). It seems that Kripke's skeptic has fundamentally the same attitude as Quine, but he is less forthright in admitting it. (Actually Quine compares his doctrine of indeterminacy of translation with 'Wittgenstein's latter-day remarks on meaning', p. 77, n. 2. Here he seems to be anticipating Kripke's interpretation of Wittgenstein.)

irreducibly *semantic* facts. Kripke's skeptic thus owes us at the least an answer to the question 'why make the reductionist assumption?'.

In fact there is an *ad hominem* point to be made here, namely that Kripke himself has been prominent in resisting reductionist philosophies in general and semantic reductionism in particular. Recall, for example, his antipathy to materialist and functionalist reductions of mental phenomena, and his approving quotation in *Naming and Necessity*[5] of Bishop Butler's dictum 'Everything is what it is and not another thing' (this is actually quoted in the context of urging a general distrust of attempts to explain philosophically central concepts 'in completely different terms' (p. 94)). In the light of these declared views one might have expected Kripke to be the first to seize upon the semantic skeptic's reductionist assumption and to press for a defence of it. And about semantic reductionism in particular Kripke has been no less explicit: discussing his own theory of names, in terms of chains of reference-preserving links, he tells us that he doubts that necessary and sufficient conditions can be found for reference which do not themselves employ the notion of reference; this is indeed why he contents himself with a 'picture' of reference, instead of a *reduction* of it, in which the concept of reference does not ineliminably feature.[6] Is not Kripke's skeptic assuming precisely what Kripke himself elsewhere strongly questions? That the skeptic is doing precisely this becomes more evident when we remember our reformulation of the skeptic's question in terms of the notion of reference and its extension to singular terms such as proper names: for the skeptic is in effect asking for a non-semantic analysis of what it is for a word to refer to a particular object (or property in the case of predicates; compare Kripke on natural kind predicates[7]), and this is precisely the kind of demand Kripke rejects as reductionist in *Naming and Necessity*. So my *ad hominem* point is this: why not take a leaf out of Kripke's (other) book and direct it against his semantic skeptic? Since I myself strongly sympathise with Kripke's anti-reductionism about reference in that other book, this seems to me an entirely reasonable response.

The unmotivated reductionism sustaining Kripke's skeptic is if anything more glaring when we consider concepts. For the *semantic* skeptic at least began with a more or less intuitive and untendentious question about past

---

5. Oxford: Blackwell, 1980. Kripke says: 'I'm always sympathetic to Bishop Butler's "Everything is what it is and not another thing" – in the nontrivial sense that philosophical analyses of some concept like reference, in completely different terms which make no mention of reference, are very apt to fail' (p. 94). This seems a salutary point for Kripke's skeptic to keep in mind.

6. See *Naming and Necessity*, pp. 94–7.

7. *Naming and Necessity*, pp. 135f. It is interesting to compare Kripke's account of what determines the reference of general terms in this work with the treatment he gives to such terms in his book on Wittgenstein: if the skeptic were right about (say) 'table', then Kripke's own earlier account of the semantics of (say) 'tiger' would be undermined, since there would be no fact (in particular, no causal fact) that determines the extension of such a term. And Kripke clearly does not, in the earlier work, suppose that we need to explain the meaning or reference of 'tiger' by means of community assertibility conditions!

meaning and current use, and this question does not in itself commit us to the reductionist presupposition (or at least it need not); but the conceptual skeptic cannot, as I pointed out earlier, proceed in this way – he must make an outright demand for a suitable constitutive fact to make ascriptions of concepts true. And this demand invites the following deflationary retort: the constitutive fact corresponding to the statement 'he possesses/is exercising the concept *cubical*' is precisely the fact that he possesses/is exercising *the concept cubical;* or again, what makes true an ascription to someone of the thought that 5 added to 7 equals 12 is precisely the fact that he has *the thought that 5 added to 7 equals 12.* These truistic replies give expression to the conviction that there is no reduction to be had of the concept of concept or that of a thought having a content; hence the factuality of concept ascription must rest upon nothing other than the existence of irreducibly conceptual facts – facts specified using frankly 'intentional' notions. Why, after all, should we *expect* that the notion of a propositional attitude with a specific conceptual content should be explicable in terms of such notions as actual application, state of consciousness or disposition? Is it not more reasonable to expect that no explication in 'completely different terms' will ever capture what it is to have and exercise a concept?[8] Seeing the matter in this light, we are therefore entitled to ask Kripke's skeptic why he does not take himself to have provided a proof of the irreducibility of concept possession – not of its unfactuality. There is, at any rate, a challenge here that has not been met, nor even properly acknowledged.

It is not only meaning and concepts that resist the kind of reductionism Kripke is tacitly presupposing; there are other psychological concepts which seem not to be capturable by any fact on Kripke's list of candidate constitutive facts. And this being so we have independent confirmation that (psychological) factuality does not require the sorts of grounding Kripke considers: that is, we need to adopt an irreducibility thesis with respect to these other concepts too (or if we do not this is something that has to be *shown*). Consider traits of character: bravery, kindness, irascibility, meanness of spirit, etc. Is it to be supposed that *such* properties of a person can be explained in terms of facts from Kripke's three categories? Well, that does appear rather unlikely: certainly actual behaviour will underdetermine the ascription of character traits, as can be seen by contriving rival skeptical hypotheses about the traits someone has. We ascribe the trait of (say) bravery to someone on the basis of his behaviour in a circumscribed range of situations on a finite number of occasions; but a skeptic might object that this behaviour is (logically) compatible with the ascription of *quavery* to the person, where someone is quave just if he acts bravely in all the kinds of situation hitherto examined but in a cowardly way in other situations (i.e. 'quave' means 'brave up to t and

---

8. To maintain an irreducibility thesis about semantic or intentional facts is not, of course, to rule out the possibility of *any* kind of theory of meaning, or of the possession of concepts; it is rather to say that any such theory will perforce employ irreducibly intentional notions.

cowardly thereafter'). That is to say, the skeptic trades on the acknowledged underdetermination of traits by actual behaviour to define a non-standard ascription of a trait and then challenges us to *show* why the commonsense ascription is the correct one; and whatever we may want to say about the epistemological aspect of this challenge, it is clear that the skeptic is quite right to deny that actual behaviour could *constitute* (or logically determine) bravery. The point here is that character traits, like meaning, have consequences that go beyond their actual manifestations, so that we cannot hope to *define* them simply by reference to their actual manifestations.[9] This kind of skepticism has obvious repercussions for the notion of the *stability* of character traits over time; for it seems that we could mount an argument analogous to Kripke's argument about semantic or conceptual constancy with respect to character-trait constancy: what makes me so sure that my present action issues from the same trait as that which I had yesterday, in view of the fact that I have never in the past performed an action of that kind? Perhaps yesterday I was *quave* and would have fled from the kind of adversary now confronting me – I stand fast now only because I no longer have that trait (suppose my present adversary is red-haired and I have never come across a red-haired adversary in the past). It is clear too that states of consciousness will not serve to constitute the fact of being brave: surely it is not necessary to enjoy any particular kind of experience when one has the trait of bravery (or is acting bravely), and equally surely it is not sufficient – being brave is just not a state in which some experiential item 'comes before the mind'. Concepts of traits of character are not concepts *of* conditions of consciousness; as Wittgenstein might say, states of consciousness do not have the *consequences* of character traits.[10] The dispositional suggestion might appear more hopeful, as it did for the case of meaning; but I doubt that this suggestion will work either, at least if dispositions are construed as Kripke construes them (which is all that is needed for a fair comparison). Let us consider the kinds of counterfactuals that might be supposed to capture the trait we are after: they would presumably be of the form 'if he were in circumstance C, he would do such-and-such'; e.g. 'if he were in circumstances requiring aggressive action, he would act aggressively'. It is I think obvious on reflection that the truth of such counterfactuals is neither necessary nor sufficient for being brave: not necessary because the person may have false beliefs about the kind of situation he is in (he makes a mistake), and not sufficient because it is perfectly

---

9. This point is implicit in Wittgenstein's comparison in *Investigations* §187 of meaning and being disposed to jump in the water if someone had fallen in: Wittgenstein does not here show any concern that such 'dispositions' or traits might not be genuinely factual just because they cannot be explained in terms of their *actual* manifestations; nor does he worry that I never gave myself any 'directions' or 'explicit instructions' about what to do if Smith falls in the water – I need never have considered this possibility and yet the counterfactual will still be true of me.

10. Cf. 'Meaning it is not a process which accompanies a word. For no *process* could have the consequences of meaning' (*Investigations* p. 218).

conceivable that the required aggressive action results from something other than bravery (e.g. some sort of drug).[11] Besides, our concept of bravery is not tied to specific kinds of action in the way envisaged; we allow all *sorts* of actions to count as manifestations of bravery. And then there is the point that the trait of bravery can be modified or overridden by other traits (e.g. prudence) or desires (e.g. an altruistic desire to help the man who is wounded) in such a way that brave action is not forthcoming, though the trait of bravery nevertheless persists. Our concept of bravery is, as it were, much richer than anything that can be delivered by analogues of the kinds of simple dispositions Kripke considers in the case of meaning; and it seems to me highly doubtful that adding counterfactual epicycles will substantially improve the prospects of a dispositional *analysis* of ascriptions of traits. Let us suppose then, if only for the sake of argument, that traits are not identifiable with dispositions, and ask what we should conclude from this: should we conclude that this reductive failure, taken together with the other two failures, shows that there is no *fact of the matter* about what character traits a person has? Should we conclude that 'he is brave' is not made true by any real condition of the person, that our discourse about character traits is in peril of nonfactuality? I venture to suggest that few of us would take that radical conclusion to be entailed; rather we would conclude, perhaps with some surprise, that traits of character are just not reducible to facts of these kinds – and that so far as we can see they are not reducible to facts of any *other* kind either.[12] This would be to conclude, in effect, that 'he is brave' is made true simply by the fact of his being *brave*; there *is* no other way to specify the appropriate constitutive fact – nor is this anything to be especially alarmed about. After all, why do we have a specific vocabulary for character traits if this vocabulary is in principle dispensable in favour of some analytical substitute? It is, at any rate, sufficiently clear that to draw a skeptical conclusion about character traits analogous to Kripke's about meaning would be questionable to say the least: it would be simply to ignore the possibility of an irreducibility thesis. In fact the same sort of question arises with respect to concepts of propositional attitudes – belief, desire, hope, intention, etc. – namely, whether *these* concepts are reducible in the kinds of ways Kripke considers. And it is very far from clear that they are: it is doubtful, for example, that *belief* can be explained in terms of actual behaviour, or conscious states, or dispositions –

11. This claim would need more discussion to be properly substantiated, but I take it that the *sorts* of considerations necessary to establishing it are fairly familiar: in particular, the 'holism of the mental', and the possibility of making the counterfactuals true by means of facts other than those for which the counterfactuals are supposed to provide sufficient conditions. The case of traits would thus parallel that of propositional attitudes, for which dispositional analyses are notoriously problematic.

12. I here disagree with Dummett, who once said that 'only a philosophically quite naive person would adopt a realist view of statements about character' ('Realism', p. 150, in *Truth and Other Enigmas* (London: Duckworth, 1978)): that is to say, an irreducibility thesis about 'brave' would be philosophically naive (it would indeed be a form of 'naive realism': see note 2).

for reasons which should by now be pretty obvious. But such irreducibility is not obviously or uncontroversially a good reason for pressing a claim of non-factuality: perhaps belief too is a *primitive* kind of fact, not capturable in other terms.[13] In the case of propositional attitudes, reductionists have recognised the need to advertise and defend their reductionist presuppositions before an irreducibility result can be converted to a nonfactuality thesis; what I am saying against Kripke's skeptic is that he does not bring this kind of presupposition into the open where it can be seen for what it is.

Kripke formulates his skeptical conclusion as the thesis that there is nothing 'in my mind' that constitutes my meaning one thing rather than another (or having one concept rather than another), or again that there is nothing in my 'mental history' that makes it the case that in the past I meant addition rather than quaddition: if God had access to all the facts concerning my mind, he would not thereby have access to my meaning, since no fact about my mind constitutes my meaning one thing rather than another. Now it might be said, in response to the irreducibility suggestion, that *this* at any rate is still true: maybe meaning (reference) is an irreducible fact but it is not a properly *mental* fact – it is not a fact of a kind to be seen by God when he looks into my mind. And it may be thought that this is still sufficiently para-doxical to warrant a *modified* skeptical thesis, *viz.* meaning is admittedly a fact but not a fact about what is in my mind. However, I think it is clear that even this modified skeptical conclusion is not warranted; it gains what plausibility it has by tacitly assuming a questionable conception of what it is to 'belong to the mind'. This is at bottom the conception that equates 'mental' with 'content of consciousness': finding that meaning (referring) is not a kind of *experience* – something that comes before the mind – the modified skeptic concludes that it is not something mental; but this move can be blocked simply by insisting, I think reasonably, that the realm of the mental is not confined to that of the experiential. The image of God peering into my mind that is invoked by the skeptic is the image of God observing the stream of my conscious experience, and it is true enough that what I mean and understand is not to be found *there;* but it does not follow that it is not, so to speak, in some other part of my mind – the part that houses *non*-experiential mental phenomena.[14] I think, therefore, that we may persist in speaking of meaning and referring and understanding as 'in my mind' and as forming part of my 'mental history'; so the irreducibility suggestion is not after all open to the modified paradox that meaning is not a *mental* fact.

---

13. Or again, suppose that the concept of knowledge persisted in eluding philosophical analysis: should we then conclude that ascriptions of knowledge to people do not state facts – that knowledge 'vanishes into thin air'? How could the results (or lack of them) of philosophical analysis have such power?

14. This is, of course, just a metaphor; its literal purport is as follows: it is not only experiential phenomena ('states of consciousness') that are correctly characterised as 'mental' – there are non-experiential mental phenomena too (e.g. the propositional attitudes).

Kripke does eventually come round to considering some kind of irreducibility thesis about meaning, but I do not find his treatment of it satisfactory. He begins by considering the suggestion that meaning something is a *sui generis* type of experience 'with its own special *quale,* known directly to each of us by introspection' (1982, p. 41), somewhat like seeing yellow or having a headache. This suggestion is quickly and persuasively dispatched: introspection does not in point of fact encounter any such experience, and if it did it would not 'have the consequences of meaning'. But, of course, this is hardly the most favourable version of an irreducibility thesis – think again of an irreducibility thesis concerning character traits; and it is not the form that Kripke's own irreducibility thesis about reference (in *Naming and Necessity*) takes. Rather, the thesis will be that meaning (referring) belongs with the other sorts of mental concept for which an experiential account is inappropriate – belief, intention, bravery, etc. – and it is irreducible in (roughly) the way these are. Kripke does in fact at one point state what is the natural nonreductive view of meaning: 'it is simply a primitive state, not to be assimilated to sensations or headaches or any 'qualitative' states, nor to be assimilated to dispositions, but a state of a unique kind of its own' (1982, p. 51): but I do not think that he gives the view its due. He begins by conceding that 'such a move may in a sense be irrefutable', but then urges that it is 'desperate' and that it leaves the notion of meaning 'completely mysterious' (1982, p. 51). Let me first remark that these accusations of desperation and mysteriousness are not fair as they stand: for it cannot in general be maintained that a claim of primitiveness on behalf of a concept is *eo ipso* desperate or mysterious – as we all know *some* concepts *have* to be taken as primitive.[15] What Kripke needs to show (and doesn't) is that a claim of primitiveness is desperate and mysterious in the present case. His position here resembles that of Quine on the analytic–synthetic distinction: one well-known response to Quine points out that not all concepts are definable by moving outside the family of concepts that are up for explication (consider the family of truth-functions), and that this is not in itself a particularly bad or mysterious thing.[16] Is not Kripke adopting essentially the same attitude here as Quine did to analyticity and synonymy in 'Two Dogmas of Empiricism', alleging mystery when no definition can be found 'in completely different terms'? And, as I observed earlier, does not Kripke himself elsewhere make a claim of primitiveness in respect of the concept of reference, urging that this is not something to get alarmed over if we have a right conception of

---

15. I mean merely that in any system of definitionally related concepts some of these concepts are not themselves defined. This does not imply any great mystery, so long as the undefined concepts are not in some way intrinsically suspect (so we may, for example, take some truth-functional connectives as primitive and define the rest on this primitive basis: there is nothing 'desperate' or 'mysterious' about *this*).
16. See H. P. Grice and P. F. Strawson, 'In Defence of a Dogma', *Philosophical Review* LXV (1956), esp. pp. 147f.

the limitations of reductive philosophical analysis? In fact, since we can formulate Kripke's semantic skepticism in terms of the relation of reference, it seems that he is here in effect accusing his other self of desperate ploys and mystery-mongering; but I myself would say that this self-criticism is unjust.

Kripke follows up his accusation by trying to spell out just what the alleged mystery consists in. His first point is that meaning something 'is not supposed to be an introspectible state, yet we are supposedly aware of it with some fair degree of certainty whenever it occurs' (1982, p. 51) – and that this in itself is mysterious. It is not easy to see just what Kripke's point is here, but I think it is something like the following: once we abandon the idea that meaning is an irreducible *experiential* state we have no account of the nature of our first-person knowledge of meaning – we have no conception of how the non-experiential primitive state of meaning something is an object of distinctively first-person knowledge.[17] This point is surely misguided; for one thing it proves far too much. For we do not generally suppose that first-person knowledge of psychological states – the kind of knowledge one has just if the state actually obtains – is always of a 'qualitative' state of consciousness: consider the knowledge we have of our beliefs, thoughts, intentions, hopes, etc. – knowledge which displays a first-person/third-person asymmetry but which is not of anything *experiential* in character.[18] That is to say, there is a legitimate notion of 'introspection' which does not involve what Kripke describes as 'attending to the qualitative character of our own experiences' (1982, p. 41): it is the kind of 'introspection' we employ when coming to know what we intend, believe and mean (we do not of course need to say that this faculty is absolutely infallible). How to give a philosophical *theory* of this kind of knowledge is of course a difficult and substantive question, but the lack of a theory of a phenomenon is not in itself a good reason to doubt the *existence* of the phenomenon. I therefore see no mystery-mongering in the claim that there are primitive non-experiential mental states which display a distinctive first-person epistemology. Why, indeed, should this be found any *more* mysterious on reflection than our capacity to know about our *sensations* whenever they occur? This too raises genuine and difficult philosophical questions, but Kripke

---

17. All we would achieve by *(per impossibile)* reducing meaning to an experiential state would be to assimilate one kind of introspective knowledge (first-person avowal) to another; we would not thereby have answered the question how we come to know our own mental states at all (make such avowals). And does the skeptical solution make the problem of accounting for our first-person knowledge of meaning any *more* tractable?

18. Here I am disagreeing with Wittgenstein's well-known remark: 'It can't be said of me at all (except perhaps as a joke) that I *know* I am in pain' (*Investigations* §246). This remark is, in fact, crucially ambiguous between: it would be literally *false* to say this, and: it would be odd or misleading or humorous to say this. I would agree with Wittgenstein under the second interpretation, but resist (for familiar reasons) the inference to the first interpretation. Of course, if we interpret Wittgenstein merely as warning us not to assimilate this kind of knowledge with other kinds (e.g. of the material world), then again I think he is quite right – but then he is putting the point needlessly hyperbolically.

does not say that the existence of the states known about is therefore in doubt, or that a claim of primitiveness (irreducibility) for sensations leads to insoluble epistemological mysteries.[19] Our first-person knowledge of sensations seems to me to be no more pellucid and unproblematic than our first-person knowledge of our intentions – and of our meanings and concepts.

Kripke's second objection to the idea of a primitive non-experiential state of meaning is harder to evaluate because it raises some difficult questions about infinity and how we grasp it. This is the objection that there is a 'logical difficulty' in the very idea of a state of meaning addition by ' + ' because 'such a state would have to be a finite object, contained in our finite minds' (1982, p. 52), and 'it remains mysterious exactly how the existence of *any* finite past state of my mind could entail that, if I wish to accord with it, and remember the state, and do not miscalculate, I must give a determinate answer to an arbitrarily large addition problem' (1982, p. 53). Kripke's point here, insofar as I have a firm grasp on it, is a point about a sort of conceptual collision between the fact that our minds are 'finite' and the infinity of the objects we seem capable of referring to or meaning; thus he speaks of 'the problem of how our finite minds can give rules that are supposed to apply to an infinity of cases' (1982, p. 54).[20] Now I have no wish to deny that our possession of infinitary concepts raises philosophical difficulties – notably how an infinite object such as the number series can be represented by a finite object (the mind or brain) – but I think that this is not a problem on which Kripke can legitimately rest his case; for this is a *special* problem about *mathematical* language and concepts, not a *general* problem about meaning as such – most words, after all, do not have (like ' + ') infinite extensions! Kripke's original paradox was intended to apply to *any* word or concept, and it concerned the normative hold of present meaning over future use; the paradox would be of a quite different character if it came to rest upon the question how a finite mind represents an infinite object. This latter problem is a specific problem about *infinity;* it is not a general problem about the notion of *meaning.* It is true, of course, that the meaning of any word will have 'indefinitely many' consequences for use in future and counterfactual situations, and that the primitive state of meaning something by the word (or referring to something) will have in some way to 'generate' these consequences; but I cannot see that

---

19. In assuming that first-person knowledge of meaning, construed as primitive state, must derive from 'attending to the "qualitative" character of our own experience', Kripke is able to charge that such a state, like experiences in general, could never determine a unique meaning (1982, pp. 41–2); but this consideration lapses if we refuse so to characterise the primitive state of meaning something.

20. Such (seeming) problems have encouraged views such as intuitionism and finitism – views which deny that we can have concepts capable of comprehending an actual infinity of objects. But these views are distant from those recommended by Kripke's skeptic. What he chiefly relies upon is the claim that any finite state could be interpreted in a nonstandard way. But if the state is specified simply as (e.g.) meaning addition by ' + ', then this is not so, since this specification just *does* determine a unique meaning (with infinitely many normative consequences); *it* is not susceptible of nonstandard interpretation.

this raises any irresoluble 'logical difficulty' – at least none that could justify abandoning the notion of meaning altogether. For consider, by way of analogy, our beliefs and desires: do not they have 'indefinitely many' (normative and causal) consequences for action in different circumstances? A given desire may interact with any of a great many different beliefs to produce different actions in different circumstances, but this 'productive power' does not seem especially problematic or mysterious. Indeed, ordinary non-psychological states, dispositions and capacities (powers) appear to give rise to essentially the same kind of productivity: the same state or disposition placed in different circumstances at different times will produce 'indefinitely many' effects (token events); but is there really a 'logical difficulty' in the idea that (say) solubility is a property which can be manifested on 'indefinitely many' occasions, both future and counterfactual?[21] What happens in each of these cases is that the property in question – meaning, desire, solubility – *interacts* with the circumstances in which it is present in such a way as to determine a range of effects of certain kinds; we do not have to suppose that in some 'queer way' these effects are already present in the state in some shadowy form.[22] When a dog acquires the habit of extending a paw on demand it presumably comes to instantiate some 'finite state' which is the (causal) basis of its behaviour in 'indefinitely many' future and counterfactual situations: it acquires a 'disposition' to perform actions of a certain type in appropriate circumstances, and there seems no special problem about how the finite state underlying the disposition can have this kind of productivity. Somewhat similarly, according to Wittgenstein's conception of meaning, it is our natural propensities that underlie our meaning, and these propensities have the capacity to generate linguistic behaviour in 'indefinitely many' situations.[23] It seems to me, then, that Kripke has no cogent objection to the primitive state suggestion, i.e. to the idea that meaning or referring is an irreducible property of a person; and if I am right in this, then we have at least one solid line of resistance to the constitutive semantic skeptic.

---

21. In the case of physical dispositions, the productivity is purely causal – there is no normative aspect to it; but this does not affect the point I am making. When a state has intentional content its causal productivity is coupled with a normative aspect which determines whether an event (say an utterance) is correct or incorrect. If it be asked how this normativity works, then the answer (according to the irreducibility thesis) is that it is simply in the nature of meaning to have normative consequences (as it is in the nature of moral values to determine what is right conduct).

22. A concrete example might help here. Suppose I refer to Smith with 'Smith'; then there will be indefinitely many occasions on which this semantic fact determines what would be a correct use of 'Smith', e.g. occasions on which Smith is presented to me and I recognise him as Smith, and hence call him 'Smith'. Similarly for the recognitional application of predicates. Here we have semantic properties that interact with occasions of recognition and dictate correctness of use.

23. See again *Investigations* §187 in which (in effect) semantic productivity is compared with counterfactuals about what someone would have done in virtue of possessing a trait of character. What ground the counterfactuals associated with meaning, according to Wittgenstein, are our spontaneous and natural ways of reacting, as these are fixed by our 'form of life'. These seem to me adequate materials for providing the requisite productivity.

CHAPTER SIX

KRIPKE ON WITTGENSTEIN ON RULES*

Warren Goldfarb

[handwritten annotation] ⟶ NO RESPONSE TO THE "⊕" EXAMPLE IN KRIPKE

There is no doubt that Ludwig Wittgenstein thought the topic of rule-following to be important; nearly forty sections of the *Philosophical Investigations* are devoted to it, as are large swatches of the manuscripts published as *Remarks on the Foundations of Mathematics*.[1] Its relevance to Wittgenstein's philosophy of mathematics was emphasized early on by Michael Dummett;[2] but only recently has it received significant attention in the less specialized context of the *Investigations,* that is, with respect to questions of meaning and intentionality. This recent attention has, to a large extent, been engendered by Saul Kripke's exposition of Wittgenstein, first presented publicly at the 1976 Wittgenstein Colloquium in London, Ontario, and laid out more expansively in his book, *Wittgenstein on Rules and Private Language*.[3] Kripke reads Wittgenstein to be mounting a skeptical challenge to the notion of following a rule and, thereby, also to the notion of meaning a word in a particular way; and then to be providing a solution to the challenge that accedes to much of the skepticism in it. This solution, it turns out, has direct and far-reaching consequences, including the impossibility of a private language and the refutation of many traditional theories of meaning. So construed, Wittgenstein's remarks on rule-following become the central and basic argument of the *Investigations;* indeed, they form, in an almost deductive sense, the foundation of Wittgenstein's later philosophy.

---

* I am grateful to Burton Dreben, Paul Hoffman, Peter Hylton, Edward Minar, and, especially, Thomas Ricketts, for helpful comments and discussions.

1. *Philosophical Investigations* (New York: Macmillan, 1953), hereafter cited as *PI*; *Remarks on the Foundations of Mathematics,* rev. ed. (Cambridge, MA: MIT Press, 1978), hereafter cited as *RFM*.
2. "Wittgenstein's Philosophy of Mathematics," *Philosophical Review,* LXIX, 3 (1959): pp. 324–48.
3. Cambridge, MA: Harvard University Press, 1982. Parenthetical page references to Kripke will be to this book.

Kripke's reading is, unquestionably, a tour de force. It is sharply and forcefully drawn, couched in terms readily accessible to a wide philosophical audience, and executed with great brio. Nonetheless, there are important questions to be raised about both its accuracy to Wittgenstein and its success as an independent argument.

Suspicions on the former score may arise from Kripke's view of the structure of the *Investigations*. On that view, the 184 sections that precede the remarks on rule-following must be taken as mere ground clearing. These sections include the discussions of meaning and reference, family resemblance and universals, and understanding; Kripke's characterization of these markedly underestimates their intent and force.[4] Moreover, given the strength Kripke imputes to his central argument, it is unclear that any ground clearing should even be required. Further suspicions come from Kripke's lack of detailed exegesis of the sections devoted to rule-following. Much is based on a handful of them, specifically around §200. Others are cited, but often with no attention to the contexts in which they appear. Little is made, for example, of §§203–42, which treat relations among the notions of rule, compulsion, agreement, identity, and logic.

To a considerable extent, however, an assessment of Kripke's accuracy to Wittgenstein will rest on the attractiveness of the whole package Kripke presents, on whether at least vaguely Wittgensteinian themes are clarified and woven into a compelling argument. Hence I shall largely be concerned to examine Kripke's skeptical challenge and solution on their own. I hope to raise some doubts about Kripke's argument and about the distinction it claims to provide between language and what Kripke calls "private language." These doubts do, to my mind, undermine Kripke's claim to represent Wittgenstein[5]; on the positive side, though, they may suggest a direction in Wittgenstein's thought rather different from that exhibited in Kripke's reading.

I

Kripke sees Wittgenstein as raising a skeptical challenge to our assertions that a person means some word in a certain way. The challenge arises from the fact

---

4. Even the first few sections of the *PI* do far more philosophical work than "ground clearing," as I have argued in "I Want You to Bring Me a Slab," *Synthese* LVI, 3 (September 1983): pp. 265–82. The crucial role of those sections has long been urged by Stanley Cavell, in lectures on the *PI* at Harvard University over the last fifteen years. In looking over what I wrote about those sections in that paper, I now realize that I had almost forgotten how heavily what I said draws on Cavell's lectures.

5. Although Kripke admits that his formulations probably "are done in a way Wittgenstein would not himself approve" (p. 5), in general he does claim the stance of an exegete. He says, "The present work is intended to expound my understanding of Wittgenstein's position" (pp. 30–1), and he talks of not wanting to "abandon the role of advocate and expositor" (p. 146).

that everything about the person's previous utterances and performances is compatible with different ascriptions of meaning. Thus, my taking Walter Cronkite to mean chair by 'chair' is challenged by alleging that he might mean something else, something that would have led him to use 'chair' as if he meant chair in the past but would lead him to use 'chair' differently in the future. This possibility is elaborated by the proposal of bizarre alternative ascriptions, of a Goodmanesque "grue"-like nature. In short, the finitely many uses of the word made to date do not fix what is meant; nor would verbal elaborations help, since they themselves would be subject to the same sort of question.

So far, it is hard to see any force in the challenge. The ascription of meaning with which we start is supposed to be jeopardised by noting a possibility that it might turn out mistaken. Yet that there is such a possibility is less evident than Kripke assumes. For it is far from clear that *any* odd behaviour that Cronkite might suddenly start exhibiting would show that in, say, July 1984 he did not mean chair by 'chair'. The point is just Austin's, about the alleged "predictive" nature of factual statements;[6] and I suspect Wittgenstein would agree.

Even if we grant that there are possible future responses that would undo the current ascription, all Kripke offers is a bare possibility. As such, it provides no reason to think that it is in any *real* sense possible that Cronkite does not mean chair by 'chair' and, hence, no reason to doubt that he does. We do, after all, engage in elaborate and articulated practices of ascribing meanings to people; we can and do justify our ascriptions when the need arises, we clear up obscurities, and so on. This is our position at the start. To have force, any challenge to our ascriptions must have weight enough to move us from our present, ordinary, position. A serious skeptic must accept a burden of proof and provide some ground from which the attack proceeds. The situation here is no different from that with skepticism of more familiar kinds: a skeptical problem cannot be assumed to arise just from the logical possibility of error. To take it that skepticism about meaning can so arise is to agree to a jejune global skepticism about all our knowledge and, perhaps, all our concepts. In any case, nothing has as yet been invoked that is special about ascriptions of meaning.

To be sure, more is forthcoming from Kripke. His challenge constantly takes the form of asking what *fact* it is about Walter Cronkite that *constitutes* his meaning chair by 'chair'. This formulation shows that the skeptical challenge is not intended to operate epistemologically (despite Kripke's tendency to slip into the language of epistemological skepticism). Rather, it rests on ontological considerations. It questions whether, if everything there is were laid out before us, we could read off the correct ascriptions of meaning to people. That is why Kripke is content with raising bare possibilities of

---

6. See, for example, *Sense and Sensibilia* (New York: Oxford University Press, 1963), ch. 10.

deviant ascriptions. If nothing in the world settles an issue between one or another possibility, then we may conclude that there is nothing to be settled; issues of whether there are any particular grounds for doubting an ascription simply do not enter. Thus, it is the notion of fact, of "everything there is," that is to provide the ground of the challenge.

The weight that this notion must bear may perhaps be clarified by a brief reflection on how the challenge would appear to Gottlob Frege. Frege holds that we have no notion of objective fact apart from our ability to reason, our mastery of logic. It is only against the backdrop of logic that questions of any kind can be intelligibly raised. Now, our mastery of logic presupposes our understanding of language, or, as Frege terms it, our immediate access to the realm of sense. Consequently, we can never be in a position to question generally whether our words and statements have sense. Frege's notion of fact, in short, precludes any perspective from which to challenge our immediate access to the realm of sense, that is, to challenge the existence of semantic facts. Obviously, I do not intend here to assess the cogency of Frege's metaphysics and the view of logic undergirding it;[7] I wish only to note how this conception of fact serves to turn aside Kripke's challenge.

The closest Kripke comes to treating Frege's position is in his dismissal of "irreducible meaning facts" (p. 43; cf. 54). This dismissal is philosophically tendentious and has no force against Frege. For Kripke's characterization of "irreducible meaning facts" rests on a particular conception of the factual. His exposition says nothing about how this conception is given us. It turns out, though, that the conception Kripke exploits is basically physicalistic; he talks of overt behaviour, brain states, and the like, and makes full use of causal notions. The physicalism is modified by the admission of introspectible raw feels and their felt qualities. Given this conception or, perhaps, given whatever implicit views give rise to it, Kripke urges that irreducible meaning facts can only be mental meaning facts that have quasi-sensory introspectible semantic qualities. Naturally, such curious items are easy to dismiss. Indeed, Frege himself, in his polemics against psychologism in the *Foundations of Arithmetic* and elsewhere, emphatically rejects any notion of introspectible meaning fact. But all this shows is that the modified physicalistic conception of fact underlying Kripke's characterization, and subsequent dismissal, of "irreducible meaning facts" is – for better or worse – quite different from Frege's identification of the realm of objective fact with the judgeable, that is, with what is subject to logic.

The lack of confrontation between Kripke's challenge and Frege indicates sharply that the challenge is not what Wittgenstein means to exploit. First, I take it as clear that Wittgenstein *was* deeply concerned to undermine the

---

7. For an elaboration of the understanding of Frege's logical and metaphysical views that is expressed here, see Thomas Ricketts, "Objectivity and Objecthood: Frege's Metaphysics of Judgment," in J. Hintikka and L. Taiminen, eds, *Synthesizing Frege* (Boston: Reidel, 1989).

positions of early analytic philosophy, positions that (to him) led inexorably to the *Tractatus*. Second, the contrast with Frege shows that Kripke's conception of fact must provide the ground of his challenge. In the end, one does not need to accept the Fregean metaphysic to turn the challenge aside. For the stance from which the challenge is launched bespeaks its own picture of what the facts are, of what "everything there is" comes to. If we start, as Wittgenstein would urge us to, from the ordinary, then the challenge cannot arise;[8] one cannot lay out everything there is about a person without specifying the language the person speaks.

Thus Kripke's is not a purely skeptical challenge, in the sense that it does not operate by pushing on ordinary conceptions from within. Rather, it proceeds from a sophisticated notion of the limits of the objective world, and so relies on a substantial assumption. Wittgenstein would, I believe, claim that such an assumption already involves a piece of philosophical sleight of hand. Nonetheless, since the (modified) physicalistic notion of fact that Kripke exploits, or something close to it, is widely shared among philosophers today, it may be worth while to accede to it and follow the challenge out.[9]

Kripke begins by arguing that ascriptions of meaning cannot be identified with ascriptions of dispositions to respond in certain ways, because people simply do not have the appropriate dispositions. The point is familiar from Noam Chomsky's criticisms of behaviourism,[10] and rests on human limitations and the consequent need for *ceteris paribus* clauses. That is, if, following W. V. Quine, we take a disposition to be a physical state that causally yields a certain response under a particular stimulus, then anyone possessing such a disposition must invariably have that response under that stimulus. Yet people have finite capacities, and are prone to error, lapses of attention, apathy, and so on. No one will always exhibit the correct verbal behaviour; hence no one has a disposition (in the Quinean sense) to respond correctly.

Kripke's challenge to any putative physicalistic reduction of meaning extends this line of thought. The argument just given shows that meaning a word in a certain way cannot be identified with a physical state that causally yields all the future responses that are determined as correct by that meaning. The problem for the reductionist, it seems then, is to specify a physical state that allows the right exceptions. Kripke argues that there can be no delineation of these exceptions, since which cases are to be adjudged errors

---

8. The notion of the ordinary, and its importance to Wittgenstein, has been stressed by Stanley Cavell. See, for example, his *Claim of Reason* (New York: Oxford University Press, 1979), chs. 1–4.

9. Since Kripke's admission of introspectibilia affects nothing in what follows, I shall henceforth omit the qualifier 'modified', and refer to his notion of fact simply as "physicalistic." Similarly, I shall speak of reductions of meaning to physical states, even though Kripke would allow introspectible mental states of a sensory character as well.

10. See Chomsky's review of B. F. Skinner's *Verbal Behaviour, Language*, xxxv (1959): pp. 26–58, and his "Quine's Empirical Assumptions," in D. Davidson and J. Hintikka, eds, *Words and Objections* (Boston: Reidel, 1969), pp. 53–68.

or other allowable violations of "ideal" responses cannot be specified in noncircular fashion. The required *ceteris paribus* clauses cannot be delimited physicalistically.

The argument rests, in the end, on the enormous intricacy of our practices surrounding ascriptions of meaning, particularly those of ascription of error rather than change of meaning or vice versa. Kripke's point is that the characterization of those practices and, hence, of the relation of behaviour to meaning, already requires the use of meaning notions. Consequently, there is no purely physicalistic way of specifying a physical state that is identifiable with meaning a word in a certain way. Kripke is thus charging that reductionists illicitly assume as known what the conditions are on a physical state that would allow it to be identified with meaning. This is a powerful consideration. In deserves further elaboration, and any reductionist should be concerned to provide the details of his program that would answer it.[11]

At the level of generality at which Kripke operates, however, the point is inconclusive. A reductionist could claim, for example, that future physiological psychology might reveal two mechanisms, separable on scientific grounds. States of the first amount to a person's linguistic competence, and would, if untrammeled, always cause correct responses; states of the second are identifiable with interfering features, which explain why on particular occasions the first mechanism does not issue in an appropriate response (and the person errs). Of course, in the empirical work that leads to these identifications we must use our ordinary meaning ascriptions and practices of ascribing error. In the end, though, we can identify the physical states of the first mechanism as constituting meaning words in certain ways. To be sure, this is speculative; but nothing Kripke adduces rules it out in principle.[12]

Kripke would, apparently, claim that this speculation underestimates the extent of the issue raised by error, the issue of what he calls "normativity." To identify meaning and a physical state, he says, "would be to give a descriptive account of the relation [between one's meaning the word and one's future use of the word], but the relation of meaning and intention to future action is *normative*, not descriptive" (p. 37). As he elaborates, one's meaning does not determine how one will use the word, but rather how one should use it. Kripke connects this with justification: "any candidate for a fact [of meaning] must in some sense show how I am justified" in going on to use the word in a certain way (p. 11; cf. p. 37).

---

11. Note that the problem Kripke raises is different from that of holism. W. V. Quine has argued that there is no way to demarcate the responses that are determined as correct by the meanings of the words, as opposed to those which are correct given the meanings and the way the world is. Kripke, in contrast, grants a set of purely "meaning-determined" responses, and then asks, given the inevitable discrepancies between those responses and actual behaviour, what relation the physical state allegedly identical with meaning the words in the particular way has to those responses.

12. This reply by the reductionist is canvassed in Paul Horwich's critical notice of Kripke's book in *Philosophy of Science*, LI, **1** (1984): pp. 163–71.

The reductionist imagined above does have an answer. If we do find physical states that can, on internal grounds, be distinguished as competency states, as well as other states that are interfering mechanisms, then clearly that will be enough to ground the notion of how the person would ideally respond, as different from how the person actually responds. In the difference, the normative force of an ascription of meaning can be lodged.

To be sure, on this account, the true justifications of our judgements of correctness of responses are hidden; they are matters of facts deep in the brain. Now Kripke, in saying the "fact must show how I am justified," does seem to mean that the justifications must in some sense be transparent (pp. 27, 37). Yet I see no reason for the reductionist to accept this. Indeed, there is a standard reductionist response on this issue: of course these physical states are not what we consciously reflect upon in our ordinary ascriptions of meaning, and it does not *feel* as if we are making physiological hypotheses, that is, talking about hidden physical states; but that is exactly what we are doing, just as we are talking about molecular constitution when we say the glass is filled with water.

Yet it can be urged that meaning *is*, so to speak, transparent. We operate fluently with the notion; we are ordinarily quite certain in our ascriptions; when doubt arises we know how to proceed – and our procedures do not include physiological investigation. These practices reflect conceptual features of our notion of meaning. No reduction to hidden physical facts can carry these conceptual features with it; in that sense, meaning is not conceptually constituted by physical states. This seems crucial to Kripke's conclusion that there are no facts of meaning.

A re-examination of an earlier step in Kripke's argument supports the point. Surely some reductionists would reject Kripke's demand that a physical state identifiable with meaning have a reasonably tight (although not necessarily exceptionless) causal relation to the potential infinity of future correct responses. For example, one could propose to identify meaning table by 'table' with a physical state which is caused by a certain linguistic training involving tables and which causes assent and dissent, as appropriate, in a few paradigmatic confrontations with objects that are or are not tables.[13] Such an identification is neither gratuitous nor extensionally faulty, since if a person receives such training and voices a few correct responses (so that we can be sure the training has taken), then as a matter of fact that person *will* mean table by 'table'. Kripke's noting that it is *possible* that someone receive this training and voice those responses, yet not mean table by 'table', would be dismissed by this reductionist, who takes as irrelevant any concern but for the *actual* world. The weight of Kripke's objection, then, has to lie in the

---

13. A more refined proposal to the same end could be made by a proponent of a causal theory of meaning. Kripke's neglect of that theory is puzzling. Perhaps he thinks that to discuss it he would have to "abandon the role of advocate and expositor for that of critic."

insistence that the fact of meaning determine, in a direct way, what the correct responses are in cases beyond the paradigmatic cases used in this reduction. This turns out to be the punch of "normativity." Yet our reductionist here would deny such a responsibility, admitting that there is much about the (intuitive) notion of meaning that a physical reduction does not capture. How much a reduction should be required to capture, we may surmise, is a debatable issue; but clearly Kripke's conclusion is justified only if a heavy burden of conceptual adequacy is put on the identification of a fact of meaning.

The idea that the isolation of a fact of meaning does bear some such burden is not entirely foreign to Wittgenstein. Wittgenstein does, apparently, argue that an examination of our practices of ascribing meaning, intending, and understanding will undercut the notion that meaning and the rest are to be analyzed as underlying states. It is a subtle matter to render Wittgenstein convincing here (much depends on how 'to be analyzed' is taken). It is, I think, even harder to do so with Kripke. For in giving us the physicalist picture of fact, Kripke may well be providing the wherewithal to deny that the conceptual burden need be borne. Even by itself the conceptual burden Kripke exploits is difficult to assess. His challenge marries the idea that our ordinary practices exhibit conceptual features that must be preserved (transparency, normativity) to the idea that those practices do not yield true justifications of our ascriptions, since they do not fend off bizarre Goodmanesque possibilities. These two ideas pull in opposite directions; it is no wonder that nothing can meet the demands imposed by the two in tandem.

In sum, Kripke's concern is with physicalist reductions of meaning notions, a concern that is narrower than Wittgenstein's and arises on a different basis; and Kripke's challenge relies on a highly problematic mixture of demands imposed on reductions. Thus it does not appear that Kripke has provided the means to illuminate Wittgenstein's views on the nature of meaning, or the ways in which the rule-following considerations are to support them.

With respect to reductionism, though, Kripke's argument does raise important issues. His emphasis on the role of meaning ascriptions in discourse elicits difficulties in formulating the criteria for identifying any particular physical state with meaning. In the face of these difficulties, the question of how candidates for physical meaning states are to be located cannot be answered by vague allusions to the causal effects of the physical states or to a simple notion of concomitance. The issue has, I think, been taken to be better understood and more settled than in fact it is. Kripke has forcefully presented considerations that destroy this complacency and suggest the clarificatory progress that needs to be made.

II

Whatever flaws there may be in Kripke's challenge do not render it pointless to examine what he offers as a solution. That solution is meant to do more than overcome the paradox Kripke takes his challenge to present; it is claimed to yield a distinction between language and "private language" through which the latter notion is shown to be incoherent. As such, it might well be illuminating, and illuminating of Wittgenstein.

It should be noted that Kripke's use of "private language" differs from Wittgenstein's. Wittgenstein characterizes the notion thus:

> The individual words of this language are to refer to what can only be known to the person speaking, to his immediate private sensations. So another person cannot understand the language (*PI* §243).

What Kripke imagines is rather a language the constitution of which depends on properties of each speaker taken in isolation. There is no notion of private object, and no mention of necessary unintelligibility to others. Hence I shall call Kripke's notion that of a *solitary language*. Evidently, it is a more general notion than Wittgenstein's; so the impossibility of a solitary language would yield *a fortiori* that of a private language in Wittgenstein's sense.

Kripke's solution starts by accepting the conclusion of his challenge, that there are no (physical) facts with which meaning a certain word in a certain way can be identified. For this reason, Kripke calls his solution a "skeptical solution." Kripke then claims than, given this lack of facts, to legitimize ascriptions of meaning we must be able to specify the conditions under which it is licensed to make such ascriptions, and the conditions under which it is licensed to assert that a speaker's response is in accord with what the speaker meant in the past (pp. 73, 78). The requirement that we be able to provide such "assertibility conditions" is meant to be relatively weak; only a rough specification is needed, and there is no demand for comprehensiveness or any sort of hierarchical ordering. In this way, Kripke distinguishes his requirement from a commitment to a theory that identifies the *content* of a sentence with its assertibility conditions. Kripke's requirement is thus pretty much unexceptionable, and, to some extent, plausibly found in Wittgenstein's practice.[14]

Kripke then considers the case of solitary language. Here we are to imagine that the conditions for licensed ascription of a certain meaning (or ascription of adherence to a certain rule) to a person invoke only properties of the

---

14. Kripke adds a second requirement, namely, that there be an account of the role and utility in our lives of the practice of ascribing meaning (p. 73). This requirement is troublesome. It is hard to see any content in a general notion of "role and utility in our lives;" what does it rule out? Textual support in Wittgenstein is tenuous, at best. However, Kripke does not exploit such a general requirement in his argument.

person in isolation. Kripke argues that such conditions will imply that it is licensed to ascribe that meaning (or ascribe adherence to that rule) if the person responds as he is inclined to respond. The point is meant to explicate Wittgenstein's remark that, in some such case, "thinking one was obeying the rule would be the same thing as obeying it" (*PI* §202).

I shall question Kripke's conclusion later, but, if it is correct, then clearly the ascription of meaning is empty. As Kripke says, "the notion of a rule [or a meaning] as guiding the person who adopts it can have *no* substantive content" (p. 89). In that case, we cannot be said to be talking of a language here, and the incoherence of solitary language is shown.

In the case of public language, Kripke does find assertibility conditions that yield "substantive content" to the notion of a person's meaning a word in a certain way and, hence, speaking a language. Those conditions, however, explicitly bring in the person's relation to a community of speakers and thus go beyond the individual in isolation. They do this by relying on agreement; the conditions for licensed ascription of meaning are that the person's responses agree with those of the rest of the community. Kripke says, "Smith will judge Jones to mean addition by 'plus' only if he judges that Jones's answers agree with those *he* intended to give" (p. 91); and "if the individual no longer conforms to what the community would do in these circumstances, the community can no longer attribute the concept to him" (p. 95). Thus Kripke sees the community as providing what is needed for a distinction between how a person is inclined to respond and what is demanded by a licensed ascription of meaning. The consequence obtained in the solitary case, that anything a person takes to be correct is correct, is blocked.

Kripke emphasizes the limited role of his assertibility conditions. They are not conditions for the correctness of ascriptions of meaning or for the correctness of future responses of a speaker given an ascription. They are merely the conditions that speakers, in fact, obey in their ascriptions and their assessments of responses; they describe the circumstances under which it is taken to be appropriate to ascribe and to approve a response. Given this limited role, no Kripkean challenge can be raised against the account of meaning ascription they provide. The insufficiency of responses to date is granted, but harmless; questions of the ultimate grounds for decisions between competing meaning hypotheses are irrelevant. The normativity of ascriptions of meaning is in part captured by the distinction between what the community agrees on and an individual's momentary inclinations. For the rest, that is, insofar as ascriptions of meaning might previously have been thought to provide justifications for the correctness of future responses, normativity is jettisoned.

Now an objection might be raised, broadly, to the use of assertibility conditions at all. One might argue, on Kripkean grounds, that nothing fixes the meanings of the words used in the conditions, and hence the project fails. This objection mistakes the nature of Kripke's solution. The assertibility conditions are descriptive; they are not intended to show how, from a standpoint of a world without meaning, meaning is constituted. That task was scrapped as a result of Kripke's challenge. Consequently, as Kripke says, it is no objection that the description is couched in language (146).

However, if we accept this characterization of the assertibility conditions, as merely descriptive conditions in the formulation of which we may take language for granted, then a different problem arises. For consider the following proposal:

(*) It is licensed to assert that a person means addition by '+' when that person has responded with the sum in every case so far attempted.

As a description of our practices, (*) is roughly correct, that is, correct up to the room needed for ascription of error and the like. But Kripke's conditions that invoke agreement are equally rough. Whatever level of precision in describing exceptions, the greater importance of simple cases, and so on, that is to be attained by amplifying Kripke's conditions can be attained here as well. Moreover, (*) does concern matters of Kripkean fact; Kripke would not claim that there is no fact as to what numbers sum to what. Hence (*) cannot be thought deficient for want of factuality. Despite all this, Kripke cannot accept (*), for it is tied to the individual in isolation. To accept it would be to renounce the point that any substantive assertibility conditions must allude to a community of speakers.

Of course, an individual cannot judge that he fulfills the condition for licensed ascription given by (*) in any better sense than that it appears to him that he fulfills it. But that was not Kripke's objection to a solitary language – that would, after all, apply to any conditions, communal or solitary. Kripke's objection was that, in the solitary case, there would be no difference between an individual's *actually* fulfilling a condition and its appearing to him that he fulfills it. Clearly, however, with respect to (*) there is a difference.

In short, descriptively adequate assertibility conditions can be framed using (not mentioning) what is ascribed as being meant, that is, notions like addition, table, green, and so on. Such conditions invoke neither a community nor agreement. Yet they do yield a distinction between an individual's fulfilling a condition and the individual's taking himself to fulfill it, and they do provide a basis for distinguishing between responses that are in accord with a previously ascribed meaning and responses an individual is simply inclined to make. Thus Kripke's central claim, that his solution shows how public language is possible but solitary language is not, collapses.

To avoid this collapse, Kripke must argue for some restriction on assertibility conditions which excludes those like (*) but allows those invoking agreement. Such a restriction could be grounded only by putting a burden on the conditions beyond that of descriptive adequacy. It is unclear what Kripke would offer here; but the emphases in his exposition suggest that he would focus on the manner in which the distinction between appropriate future responses and a speaker's inclinations is secured. If we are to *apply* conditions like (*) for that end, we must make full use of our grasp of 'addition', 'table', and so on; we thus rely on *our* knowledge of the correct continuations according to various rules. Perhaps, then, assertibility conditions should be so restricted as to exclude those whose application involves such reliance. The problem, however, is that such a restriction seems to rule out too much. It may even be that the application of any assertibility condition whatsoever requires knowledge of the sort that is excluded. More specifically, as I shall now argue, it does not appear that Kripke's conditions that involve agreement will satisfy the restriction.

The notion of agreement rests on the notion of sameness of response. To say that two utterances or signs are the same response to a question (of the sum of two numbers, for example) is to say that the utterances or signs are tokens of the same type. We cannot identify or differentiate responses except by invoking the relation of token to type. But the relation of token to type is a case of the relation between the continuation of a series and the rule governing the series. To apply a condition that invokes sameness of response thus requires knowledge of the correct continuations according to a rule, and so would be ruled out by the restriction suggested above.[15]

Hence the notion of agreement allowed by the restriction is extremely limited. *At best* it can draw on actual, face-to-face occasions of acquiescence of persons to each other. One occasion of my giving a certain sum and another of yours cannot be taken to be relevant to each other; nor can one occasion of acquiescence be linked with another, since that would invoke the sameness of what the acquiescence is acquiescence to. This weak notion of agreement does not support the characterizations Kripke often gives of his assertibility conditions, like "conforming to what the community would do." (Indeed, all subjunctive conditionals would seem ruled out.) Assertibility conditions restricted to this weak notion can amount to little more than that it is licensed to ascribe a certain meaning to a person, or adherence to a previous meaning, if his utterance receives acquiescence. It is hard to imagine any conditions of this sort that would be correct descriptions of our practices. In any case, since only actual occurrences of acquiescence can be invoked, and then only one by one, in does not appear than the conditions obtainable will have any substantive content.

In sum, to save his claim Kripke must provide a constraint on assertibility conditions which rules out those like (*). The constraint most consonant with his argument bars any conditions the application of which relies on substantial knowledge of correct continuations according to rules. But then the constraint

---

15. The point in this paragraph is due to Paul Hoffman; it is elaborated in his "Kripke on Private Language," *Philosophical Studies*, XLVII, 1 (1985): pp. 23–8. The criticism of Kripke that he bases on it is different from that given here.

also bars use of the notion of sameness of response. Assertibility conditions limited to the resulting thin notion of agreement, if they can be accurate at all, cannot sustain enough of a distinction between inclination and justified ascription to make out the difference between public and solitary language.

III

I've argued that Kripke's solution founders as a result of its need to disallow assertibility conditions that would be perfectly respectable in a purely descriptive context. That need bespeaks a foundational element in Kripke's project; for Kripke, agreement among speakers is, in some sense, to ground ascriptions of meaning or adherence to a rule. Wittgenstein, however, puts no such onus on agreement, I believe. Agreement is exhibited in rule-following, but does not ground it.

> The word "agreement" and the word "rule" are *related* to one another; they are cousins. If I teach anyone the use of one word, he learns the use of the other with it (*PI* §224).

That a particular difficulty for Kripke emerges with respect to the notion of sameness of response should not, then, be surprising. Wittgenstein emphasizes that any problem we find in rule-following will arise even with respect to what counts as the same.

> If you have to have an intuition in order to develop the series 1 2 3 4 . . . then you must also have one to develop the series 2 2 2 . . . (*PI* §214; cf. §225).

All this suggests that Wittgenstein's concerns are different from Kripke's. To begin to clarify them, it is helpful to return to the passage with which Wittgenstein begins his treatment of rule-following. In *Investigations* §185, Wittgenstein presents the scenario of a wayward child, who writes the +2 series correctly until 1000 but then writes 1004, 1008, . . . , and who is resistant to correction. The point of the scenario should seem extremely puzzling. Many commentators, including Kripke, take Wittgenstein to be using the scenario to argue that nothing determines how to go on with the series. Yet the scenario doesn't show anything like that. In presents a case in which we might have thought the child understood, but we find out he didn't. The child's resistance to correction is bizarre; but if we cannot get him to see what we mean by going on the same way, then the conclusion, naturally, is that he is incapable of understanding what we mean. To be sure, nothing *forces* him to continue that way. Nonetheless, how to go on is certainly *determined*, in

104

the sense that if he is to continue the series we asked him to continue, then he must go on to write 1002, 1004, 1006.

Such a response is just plain sense. Thus it hardly seems that any issue is raised by the scenario. I suspect, though, that it is introduced in order to provoke a further response. We are tempted to elaborate: now of course there always is a question whether someone understands, since all a person can do is exhibit a finite amount of behaviour, and all I can do in trying to instruct is to exhibit a finite amount of behaviour myself. Hence there is a gap between what the pupil and I do, on the one hand, and the understanding, on the other.

This elaboration can seem ineluctable; it is certainly familiar. In saying that Wittgenstein means to provoke it, however, I do not mean that he finds it acceptable. In fact, I believe he wishes to depict it as the first, and fatal, misstep, the decisive move in the conjuring trick. Consider how it begins: "Of course, there is always a question as to whether someone understands." That is a step, for in ordinary life there isn't always a question. Most often, there's no question about it. To think that there is always a question is to take it that there is something particular that understanding must accomplish, which provides the standard against which any behaviour is to be measured.

That is, the scenario elicits the following. We give a rule, some examples of its application, and perhaps some further explanations. Yet, for all that, a person "could" go on in different ways and take himself to be going on the same. This seems to indicate that what we give is insufficient to tell, or to justify, how to go on; and we demand something more. The demand is not for that which in fact succeeds in showing a person, in particular circumstances, how to go on. It is rather for that which picks out the correct continuation in some unconditioned way, by giving that in which going on the same really consists. It is this demand that Wittgenstein wishes to attack.

> I can train someone in a *uniform* activity . . . Now I ask myself, what is it that I want him to do, then? The answer is: He is always to go on as I have shown him. And what do I really mean by: he is always to go on in that way? The best answer to this that I can give myself is an example like the one I have just given.
>
> I would use this example in order to show him, and *also* to show myself, what I mean by uniform (*RFM* VI, §20).

By "best answer" Wittgenstein does not mean *faute de mieux*. The answer – that is, the example – does not work by pointing to something beyond itself that is really at stake. It is, simply, the answer to the question of what is really meant, for it works as an answer. Wittgenstein concludes, "We talk and act. That is already presupposed in everything that I am saying."[16]

---

16. The formulation of the preceding two paragraphs owe much to Cora Diamond, "Realism and the Realistic Spirit", in her *The Realistic Spirit: Wittgenstein, Philosophy and the Mind* (Cambridge, MA: MIT Press, 1991).

The theme is repeated in *PI* §§208ff. Some of Wittgenstein's remarks, like that just cited, are exhortations. Some of them seek to unearth views that lie behind and animate our dissatisfaction with the explanations we actually give, and the consequent search for something more. Prominent among these is a view of justification as "reaching through logical space," as having to settle any conceivable doubt, and as thus removed from actual doubts and our practices of settling them (§§213, 217). Such views are what Wittgenstein would call "pictures," and in these sections he urges that our ordinary conceptions, if thoroughly examined, can be seen not to force them on us. The intended effect is to break the hold of the demand for that in which "going on the same" consists and of the feeling that if it is not satisfied then how we go on is ungrounded.

The earlier part of the rule-following considerations, *PI* §§185–202, deals more directly with the substance of the demand, that is, with the search for that which unconditionally fixes the correct continuation according to a rule. The scenario of §185 immediately engenders the proposal in §186, that how the rule is meant is what does this. Wittgenstein then points out that if we are not to take for granted what we (unofficially) know, namely, what follows from the rule, then no way of characterizing what is meant will settle what to call agreement of any continuation with it.

Now there are circumstances in which we do say that how we mean a rule determines what the continuation should be. But the plain sense in which we speak of such determination is the sense in which the explanations and examples we actually give are the best answers to the question of what going on in the same way consists in.

> It may now be said: "The way the formula is meant determines which steps are to be taken." We say, for instance, to someone who uses a sign unknown to us: "If by $x!2$ you mean x^2, then you will get *this* value for y; if you mean $2x$, *that* one." Now ask yourself: how does one *mean* the one thing or the other . . . *That* will be how meaning it can determine the steps in advance (*PI* §190).

There is nothing mysterious here, for this is a notion of fixing the correct continuation that operates *for us,* given the background our language provides, our practices, and our understandings of each other.

The demand, however, is for a fixing of the correct continuation that does not rely upon us or take for granted anything about us, at all. What Wittgenstein principally wants to suggest is that we do not have any real conception of what this comes to. We have, as Wittgenstein is wont to say, "no model of it."

This, in part at least, is what is on Wittgenstein's mind in *PI* §201:

> This was our paradox: no course of action could be determined by a rule, because every course of action can be made out to accord with

the rule. The answer was: if everything can be made out to accord with the rule, then it can also be made out to conflict with it. And so there would be neither accord nor conflict here.

In believing that anything can be brought into agreement – in believing, for example, that there is something we could do that would make 1000, 1004 in agreement with the rule "add 2" – the paradox monger has assumed some notion of accord with a rule, but has divested it of the ways we go about taking things to be in accord or not. That is why the answer to the paradox is that there is no sense of accord here at all. Interpretations of a rule make sense only given a conception of agreement with a rule. To take variant interpretations to pose a problem about the functioning of rules is to ignore what goes into our having that conception, namely, the background that our practices provide.

Of course, far more can be got out of (or read into) this section of the *Investigations* and its forerunner, §198. But it is clear that Wittgenstein is not proposing his "paradox" full voice; it arises only for those who accede to the terms of the demand for that in which following a rule really consists.

On the approach to Wittgenstein's rule-following considerations which I have sketched, the points they bring to bear are far less conclusive than Kripke claims. I think this is accurate to Wittgenstein's intentions. In particular, the private-language argument is not given in §202, and does not fall directly out of the rule-following considerations. That argument can be joined only by an examination of what is supposed to provide a notion of fixing correctness in its case. Such an examination, I take it, is the task of the fourteen sections between Wittgenstein's proposal of the idea of a "private language" in §243 and the section containing the private-language argument proper, §258.[17]

Similarly, the rule-following considerations are not meant to yield a conclusive refutation of one or another sophisticated philosophy of language. Rather, they operate by examining what frames the first steps of a search for an account of meaning; and they are effective only insofar as what Wittgenstein provides, starting in §185, is a convincing portrayal of how such a project comes to have a hold on us. A better understanding of Wittgenstein's position thus requires far more clarity than we currently have about the sources of the inchoate demands we put on the notion of meaning and about the role such demands play in philosophical theorizing.

---

17. The textual importance of those fourteen sections has been argued, on independent grounds, by Barry Stroud, in his "On Wittgenstein's 'Treatment' of the Quest for 'a Language which Describes My Inner Experiences and which Only I Myself Can Understand'," *Proceedings of the Seventh International Wittgenstein Symposium,* 1982. Stroud's reading of those sections, I think, supports the general approach to the rule-following sections I have suggested.

CHAPTER SEVEN

CRITICAL NOTICE OF COLIN McGINN'S *WITTGENSTEIN ON MEANING*

Crispin Wright

Colin McGinn's book belongs to the reaction to, and against Saul Kripke's *Wittgenstein on Rules and Private Language.*[1] The book is in four chapters. The first and third are respectively devoted to exegesis of Wittgenstein's ideas on rule-following and understanding, and to criticism of them. The second attacks Kripke's famous tandem of Skeptical Argument and Skeptical Solution as an interpretation of Wittgenstein; and the fourth criticizes Kripke's dialectic on its own terms.

McGinn's book is not straightforward to appraise. Certainly, there is much in it to admire, and much with which to agree. One must admire, in particular, – though with one very major qualification to be developed below – the lucid and well-organized presentation of a number of the most fundamental themes concerning meaning and understanding in Wittgenstein's later philosophy; McGinn's first chapter will surely become a standard reference in the reading lists for undergraduate courses on Wittgenstein for some considerable time. And one must agree – though perhaps with more reluctance than McGinn can be credited with – that Kripke does misrepresent, in significant respects, the overall gist of the discussion of rules and rule-following which Wittgenstein's later writings contain. In particular, as commentators on Kripke's book have pointed out almost without exception, Wittgenstein does not accept the paradox – it is another question whether it is the same as Kripke's Skeptical Paradox – with which *Investigations* §§198–201 are concerned.

Because the view is so widely received that Kripke's book fails as strict exegesis of Wittgenstein, and because there has been so much independent discussion of its Skeptical Argument and Solution, I shall here mainly concentrate on McGinn's own interpretation of Wittgenstein and his criticisms of the views which he finds. But I shall begin, in part I, by noting

---

1. Oxford: Basil Blackwell, 1982.

three respects, in increasing order of seriousness, in which McGinn seems to misrepresent the structure of the train of argument which Kripke's Wittgenstein is riding, or to underrate its power and resources. In particular, I shall suggest that McGinn's principal point of response to Kripke is, in a sense, facile, and that he is encouraged in this response by a reading of the *Investigations* which is, in certain crucial respects, superficial.

Parts II and III will be concerned with the account of Wittgenstein which McGinn wishes to oppose to Kripke's. I shall give grounds for rejecting certain of McGinn's criticisms of Wittgenstein. But my principal complaint will be that, despite his careful rehearsal of central Wittgensteinian themes, McGinn never brings Wittgenstein's most basic concerns in the discussions of rule-following into a proper perspective. The result is that Wittgenstein's most important legacy to contemporary philosophy, and Kripke's contribution to our ability to receive it, both go unrecognized in McGinn's book.

I

First, there are passages[2] where it seems that McGinn is seriously unclear about the role of epistemological considerations in the development of the Skeptical Paradox. He writes

I have so far expounded Kripke's skeptical paradox as a constitutive or metaphysical claim . . . But Kripke also presents an epistemological thesis, to the effect that I cannot now justify my present linguistic inclinations . . .

and goes on to stress that a solution to either problem might in principle be independent of a solution to the other. The fact is, however, that there is no distinct epistemological problem. To think that there is is to miss the sense in which Kripke's Skeptic is a device. It is an *idealized* subject who, purportedly, loses the debate with the Skeptic: a subject who knows all there is to know about his or her former mental life and behaviour.[3] Granted the assumption that it is within those provinces, if anywhere, that states of affairs constitutive of the subject's former meanings have to be found, it follows that there cannot be any such constitutive states of affairs. Whether or not there are specific points in McGinn's criticisms of Kripke which are undermined by this apparent oversight, it does not inspire confidence to find the broad structure of the Skeptical Argument misrepresented in so fundamental a way.

---

2. McGinn, pp. 149–50.
3. Kripke, 1982, p. 21 is completely explicit.

Second, some of the things which McGinn says raise a doubt whether he has really taken the point of the constraint, imposed by the Skeptic, that whatever constitutes the meaning of an expression must discharge the *normative* role of meaning. It is for its failure to meet this constraint that Kripke dismisses the Dispositional response to the Skeptical Argument. McGinn seems to accept this criticism of the Dispositional response.[4] But later he canvasses a 'straight solution' to the Paradox, which he evidently believes is not vulnerable to the same difficulty, in terms of the idea of a *capacity* to mean, for instance, green by 'green' is to have, not a disposition, but a capacity of a certain kind. He writes[5]

> Does the capacity suggestion account for normativeness? . . . We have an account of this normativeness when we have two things: (a) an account of what it is to mean something at a given time and (b) an account of what it is to mean the *same* thing at two different times . . . Put in these terms, it is easy to supply what we require: to mean addition by '+' at t is to associate with '+' the capacity to add at t, and to mean the same by '+' at t^* is to associate with '+' the *same capacity* at t^* as at t.

But a transposition of *this* construal of the normativity constraint could have saved the dispositional account! Simply replace the occurrences of 'capacity' in the last part of the quoted passage by occurrences of 'disposition'.[6]

What is the normativity constraint which McGinn, apparently, misunderstands? The basic problem posed by the normativity of meaning for the Dispositional response is that, whereas how I understand an expression contributes towards determining how I *ought* to use it, all that apparently can be recovered from a description of the way in which I am disposed to use it are claims about how I habitually do, will, or would use it. A solution to the problem would accordingly be to show how suitably circumscribed facts about how one does, will, or would use a particular expression actually constitute facts about how one ought to use it. This would call, clearly, for an account which non-arbitrarily idealized certain elements in a subject's actual dispositions of use. One will accordingly be inclined to accept, or dismiss, Kripke's criticism of the Dispositional response depending on whether one believes that such an idealizing account can satisfactorily be accomplished.[7]

---

4. McGinn, pp. 172 and following.

5. *Ibid.*, p. 74.

6. This is pointed out by Paul A. Boghossian in his review of McGinn, *Philosophical Review* (1989). pp. 91.

7. For sympathy with a defence of the dispositional response along these lines, see Simon Blackburn, 'The Individual Strikes Back', *Synthese*, (1984), pp. 281–301 (this volume Ch. 3), and Graeme Forbes, 'Skepticism and Semantic Knowledge', *Proceedings of the Aristotelian Society*, (1983–4), pp. 221–37 (this volume Ch. 2).

Whether one believes that or not, it is hard to see any prospect of an advantage to be gained, in respect of the normativity constraint, by dropping dispositions in favour of capacities. If we ask, *what* capacity is constitutively associated with an understanding of 'green'?, the natural answer is: the capacity to use the word correctly. And here 'correctly' means, roughly: in ways which are appropriately sensitive to its meaning. This answer is, precisely, an intuitive expression of the normativity of meaning. But a proponent of McGinn's 'straight solution' would have to dismiss it as misleading or, at any rate, non-fundamental. For it apparently sets the meaning of 'green' up as an *independent* constraint to which a capacity for using the word must conform if it is to constitute a correct understanding of it. And that cannot be the right criterion for the capacity in question if it is to be in terms of possessing it that a proper understanding of 'green', and thence the meaning of 'green', are to be philosophically constituted, as it were. Rather, the line must be, understanding 'green' just is possessing a particular capacity of use of it, not to be identified – or only in a non-fundamental sense to be identified – as the capacity to suit one's use of the word to its meaning.

Well, what then is the capacity, allegedly constitutive of an understanding of 'green', a capacity, most fundamentally, to *do*? McGinn's discussion contains, so far as I have been able to see, no clear suggestion about how a proponent of his 'straight solution' should respond to this question, nor any clear perception of its importance. Capacities may *seem* better adapted than dispositions to cope with problems of normativity because we typically invoke the notion of capacity where there is some connotation of discharging a role, accomplishing an objective, or meeting a constraint. But just for that reason the use of the notion creates an obligation to characterize the relevant role, objective, or constraint. To be sure, we cannot assume, without question-begging against McGinn, that meeting this obligation in the present case would involve thinking of the proper use of 'green' as determined quite independently of anyone's capacities of use, and of those capacities as qualifying as understanding only insofar as they are capacities to track that pattern of proper use. But it remains that the relevant capacities have to be singled out somehow, and the problem is structurally reminiscent of – indeed, in no way interestingly different from or more promising in outcome than – the problem, confronted by the Dispositional response, of saying what puts a particular disposition in the idealized, meaning-constituting class which it is obliged to define.

McGinn's apparently imperfect understanding of the role of the normativity of meaning in Kripke's dialectic does not prevent him from isolating its most vulnerable point. This is that there is an unsupported reductionism involved at the stage at which the Skeptic challenges his opponent to cite some feature of his previous mental life which could constitute his having formerly meant green by 'green', for instance. It will not do, it seems, if the opponent attempts to cite that very fact. Rather the challenge is implicitly taken to recall some state of affairs characterized in such a way as not simply to assume that there are states of affairs of the disputed species. And it then has to be *argued* of the state of affairs so characterized that it has the properties requisite to constitute meaning. So the ground-rules of Kripke's debate have the effect of restricting the search to phenomena of consciousness which are not simply characterized as having a recollectable content. States having content are somehow to be constituted out of materials whose description, at the point where they are introduced into the debate with the Skeptic, does not presuppose their contentfulness.

The implicit assumption here will not strike any philosopher as uncongenial who accepts the traditional Quinean idea that the hygiene of semantic or, more generally, intentional states depends on their reducibility to something extensional, or physical, or wherever the thick ice is thought to be. But the route from such a presupposition to skepticism about meaning can in that case be rather more direct than the one provided by the Skeptical Argument, which now emerges as merely an implicit prejudice against the idea that we may and usually do non-inferentially know of our current meanings and intentions, and may and often do non-inferentially recall them later.[8]

Even here, however, where he seems to me entirely right, McGinn's discussion is unsatisfying. He notes[9] Kripke's stigmatization of such a response as 'desperate' and 'completely mysterious', but is content with rejoinders which, by their preoccupation with finessing the letter of Kripke's text, mask rather than clarify the genuine problems in the vicinity. For genuine problems there surely are. McGinn attributes to Kripke the thought that

> ... once we abandon the idea that meaning is an irreducible *experiential* state, we have no account of the nature of our first-person knowledge of meaning – we have no conception of how the primitive, non-experiential state of meaning something is an object of distinctively first-person knowledge.[10]

And against this he is content to set the ordinary idea of first-person authority for psychological states like – believing, thinking, intending, etc. – which, unlike sensations, may be associated with no individuative affective phenomenology. He acknowledges that 'How to give a philosophical *theory* of this

---

8. Cf. pp. 771 onwards of my 'Kripke's Account of the Argument against Private Language', *Journal of Philosophy*, (1984), pp. 759–78, and pp. 395–403 of my 'On Making Up One's Mind: Wittgenstein on Intention', *Logic, Philosophy of Science and Epistemology: Proceedings of the XIth International Wittgenstein Symposium*, eds, P. Weingartner and G. Schurz (Vienna: Holder-Pichler-Temsky, 1987), pp. 391–404.
9. McGinn, p. 160.
10. *Ibid.*, pp.160–61.

kind of knowledge is of course a difficult and substantive question, . . .' but rejoins that 'Lack of a theory of a phenomenon is not in itself a good reason to doubt the *existence* of the phenomenon. . .'[11] This is about as flagrant an instance of philosophical stone-kicking as one could wish for. For, surely, the relevant feature of the concepts in question – the combination of first-person avowability with disposition-like connections to behaviour in circumstances which the avower need not have envisaged – is no sooner marked than anyone of genuine philosophical curiosity will feel his intellectual conscience pricked. How is it possible to be, for the most part, effortlessly and reliably authoritative about, say, one's intentions if the identity of an intention is fugitive when sought in occurrent consciousness, as McGinn grants that Kripke's Skeptic has shown, and the having of an intention is thought of as a disposition-like state? There are plenty of dispositions – courage, patience, intellectual honesty – the self-ascription of which is warranted only on grounds which any third party could employ. If, notwithstanding points of disanalogy generated for example by the holism of the mental, content-bearing psychological states like belief, intention, and hope *resemble* dispositions in the manner in which they have to answer to an indefinitely circumscribed range of behavioural manifestations, how is the institution of non-inferential first-person authority with respect to such states not simply a *solecism* – evidence of the permeation through into ordinary discourse of a discredited Cartesian typology of the mental which takes sensation as its paradigm?

The matter is, of course, a central preoccupation of the *Investigations* and Wittgenstein's other later writings on the philosophy of psychology. The examples vary – Wittgenstein moves between meaning, understanding, expecting, wishing, fearing, hoping, and others. But the central problem is the same in each case. It is posed by the way these concepts seem to hover, puzzlingly and unstably, between two paradigms. One is constituted by states like pain, tickles, the experience of a red after-image, and ringing in the ears, which may enjoy a definitely dated onset and departure, which may be interrupted by breaks in consciousness, and whose occurrence makes no demands upon the conceptual equipment of the subject. Such states are authoritatively avowable, and it comes easily to us to think we understand why. The subject is authoritative about such states because, since they are events in his consciousness, he is in the nature of the case conscious of them. Further, because such states are essentially *of* a consciousness, they can presumably bear only causal relations to their outward and behavioural expressions. For these are states (or events, or processes) which are not essentially of a consciousness and are therefore ontologically independent of things which are. So the relation, we conceive, of for example pain to its expression can only be that of antecedent state to symptom or trace. By

---

11. *Ibid.*, p. 161.

contrast, in the case of the other paradigm – that of the dispositional psycho-logical state – the connection with behavioural display is not symptomatic but constitutive. And – or so one would think – subjects can generally know that they themselves possess such a state only insofar as and in the same way that others can know that they do. If Cartesian psychology was dominated by the first paradigm, the Rylean reaction imperialized on behalf of the second. But neither is adequate for the class of psychological concepts with which Wittgenstein was most concerned.

While it is fair to say, then, that the Skeptical Argument, as far as Kripke explicitly takes it, is open to the charge of relying upon an unargued reductionism, and may be rebutted by the adduction of ordinary features of the epistemology of intention, meaning, etc., it would be a very short step to continue the argument by pressing questions which the actual Wittgenstein was intensely concerned with, and to which I do not think that philosophy has yet disclosed satisfactory answers. To repeat: how is it possible to be effort-lessly, non-inferentially, and generally reliably authoritative about psychologi-cal states which have no distinctive occurrent phenomenology and which have to answer, after the fashion of dispositions, to what one says and does in situations so far unconsidered? Perhaps Kripke's use of 'desperate' in response to the idea of meaning, etc., as *sui generis* states was uncalled-for. But the characterization, 'mysterious', it seems to me, was not. And the problem is, to stress, one of Wittgenstein's own central preoccupations in the *Investigations*.

That McGinn's principal point of response to Kripke should bring us, in this way, to one of Wittgenstein's own principal quarries is striking in two respects. First, it is striking that the matter goes unremarked in McGinn's book, in which the comparison of Wittgenstein with Kripke is an overriding concern. Second, the thought now suggests itself that, despite the shortcomings tabled by McGinn of Kripke's book as textual exegesis, the Skeptical Argument of Kripke's Wittgenstein may yet correspond to something real and central in the *Investigations* – a powerful and expanded development of a train of thought tersely prefigured there, which brings home the hopelessness of a Cartesian conception of intentional states and, at the same time, teaches how vital – and problematical – the ordinary epistemological 'grammar' of these states is. One way or another we have to answer, or undermine, the question: how is first-person authority for intentional states possible? Until we do, we have not answered the Skeptical Argument. Wittgenstein thought the question could be answered by attention to detail – to the surroundings and everyday phenomenology of ascriptions of intention, expectation, and hope. However that may be, Kripke should at least be granted that the Skeptical Argument takes us, in the way I have described, to the heart of the Wittgensteinian agenda.

II

McGinn finds four principal themes, three negative and one positive, in Wittgenstein's treatment of meaning and understanding. Summarized early in his book,[12] they are:

(i) To mean something by a sign is not to be the subject of an inner state or process.
(ii) To understand a sign is not to interpret it in a particular way.
(iii) Using a sign in accordance with a rule is not founded upon reasons.
(iv) To understand a sign is to have mastery of a technique or custom of using it.

The ascription of these lines of thought to Wittgenstein is hardly controversial. But it is nevertheless very useful to have the patient and effective assembly of source material, interspersed with some of the clearest commentary on Wittgenstein to be found anywhere, which McGinn provides.

McGinn, for his part, is largely content to record his agreement with the four theses, as he amplifies them, although with two important exceptions. One is that, in his view, Wittgenstein habitually overstates thesis (i), and that there is no real objection to thinking of understanding or meaning something by a sign as an inner state or process provided we are clear that it is not an occurrent or episodic state of consciousness. Wittgenstein's stronger formulations should be viewed, he believes, as '. . . misplaced linguistic legislation in the interests of philosophical prophylaxis'.[13] I think the issue here is partly verbal, but partly substantial and difficult. First, is Wittgenstein's objection to 'state' or to 'inner'? McGinn, somewhat tentatively, suggests the latter,[14] but the footnote to page 59 of the *Investigations* – which McGinn cites – seems to be quite definite in his favour. Baker and Hacker[15] regard the footnote as aberrant, and claim that the notion that meaning something is *any* sort of state is clearly repudiated in *Brown Book* 66 (p. 117). In fact, though, Wittgenstein is there speaking of *abilities* in general; he nowhere says that understanding, meaning, etc., simply *are* abilities, and there is no clear repudiation. Rather he writes that

> . . . we are strongly inclined to use the *metaphor* [my italics] of something being in a peculiar state for saying that something can behave in a certain way. And this . . . metaphor is embodied in the expressions 'He is capable of . . .', 'He is able to multiply large

12. *Ibid.*, p. 3.
13. *Ibid.*, p. 117.
14. *Ibid.*, p. 166.
15. G. P. Baker and P. M. S. Hacker, *An Analytical Commentary on Wittgenstein's Philosophical Investigations*, paperback edition (Oxford: Basil Blackwell, 1983), p. 284.

numbers in his head', 'He can play chess': in these sentences the verb is used in the *present tense,* suggesting that the phrases are descriptions of states which exist at the moment when we speak.

The same tendency shows itself in our calling the ability to solve a mathematical problem, the ability to enjoy a piece of music, etc., certain states of mind; we don't mean by this expression 'conscious mental phenomena'. Rather a state of the mind in this sense is the state of a hypothetical mechanism, a mind model meant to explain the conscious mental phenomena. . . . Note also how sure people are that to the ability to add or to multiply or to say a poem by heart, etc., there *must* correspond a peculiar state of the person's brain, although . . . they know next to nothing about such psycho-physiological correspondences.

This suggests that Wittgenstein has points to make about both 'inner' or 'mental' *and* 'state'. The point about 'inner' is the one with which McGinn agrees and which he thinks Wittgenstein overstates. And there we can surely say what we like provided we acknowledge Wittgenstein's point. The point about 'state' is that its application to abilities and ability-like items, including perhaps understanding and meaning so-and-so by such-and-such an expression, is merely a metaphor – an optional 'form of representation' – rather than anything imposed by the nature of these items. On this account, it would not be *wrong,* in Wittgenstein's view, to describe understanding as a mental state; but it might encourage either of two errors.

But is the second an error? Perhaps we would not now be tempted by the idea that a state of a *mental* mechanism must underlie the ability to add, but *doesn't* there have to be a brain state? Notoriously, Wittgenstein explicitly and forcefully denies that there does in *Zettel* 608–10. Wittgenstein does not express himself in such terms – to a denial of the *supervenience* of the psychological on the physiological: there may be psychological differences to which no physiological differences correspond. McGinn discusses the matter in some detail[16] but I do not think he takes the measure of Wittgenstein's view. His counter-argument[17] is that if understanding, for instance, does not supervene upon a person's physical constitution – and if differences in understanding must issue, as presumably on Wittgenstein's view is so, in differences in use, ergo in *behaviour* – then

> . . . there are events which differ physically but which have no differentiating physical explanation. . . . This is tantamount to the admission or claim that some physical events have no physical explanation.

16. McGinn, pp. 112–16.
17. *Ibid.*, p. 113.

One could reproach McGinn's resort to the indicative here: denying the supervenience claim would not commit Wittgenstein to the *actuality* of what McGinn describes. It would involve at most that nothing precludes its possibility. But in fact even that does not follow. What follows is only that, *for all the concept of understanding has to say about the matter,* there could be behavioural, ergo physical events whose explanation was not to be found in the *internal* physical state of the behaving subject. That may seem bizarre. But it falls well short of the claim that such events would be physically inexplicable. Nothing in physics rules out the idea that the movements of a body be explained not in terms of any internal change in it but as a direct result of external influences, for instance. And, to stress: Wittgenstein's claim is one about what is compatible with our concepts of the psychological, not about what is possible *tout court.* Maybe it is profoundly in error, But if so, the reasons do not emerge from McGinn's discussion.

McGinn's other major point of disagreement with his Wittgenstein concerns thesis (iv). He has no quarrel with what he regards as its principal burden: the conception of understanding as a practical capacity, with which he attempted a 'straight' rejoinder to Kripke's Skeptic. But he does take issue with the associated 'multiple application thesis' which Wittgenstein expresses like this:

> It is not possible that there should have been only one occasion on which someone obeyed a rule. It is not possible that there should have been only one occasion on which a report was made, an order given or understood; and so on. To obey a rule, to make a report, to give an order, to play a game of chess, are *customs* (uses, institutions).[18]

Some of McGinn's criticism of what he takes such passages to be advancing is based on saddling Wittgenstein with an idea for which there is simply no warrant in the texts. This is that all is well provided there has been *more* than one occasion! Thus the 'subtraction argument', which McGinn finds telling, runs:

> . . . consider a possible situation in which . . . actually followed rules are not obeyed. Imagine we carry out this thought-experiment one rule at a time gradually whittling the applications away. Wittgenstein in effect allows that we can carry out this procedure very extensively: in fact, the thought-experiment is deemed coherent until we get to the final rule grasped by the subject . . . at which point, he thinks, we must call a halt to our supposings. We can also, he allows, remove large segments of the actual application made of *the final rule,* but we must leave intact at least *two* applications of this rule. . . . The

---

18. *Investigations* §199.

problem is to see why what seems such a small change in the actual situation – *viz*. deleting the penultimate surviving application of the final rule could have such momentous consequences . . .[19]

But Wittgenstein said nothing to lay himself open to this. His claim was that the very existence of any rules depends on some rules actually being applied; and that one rule being applied only once would not be enough. No claim was made about what would be enough – still less was anything said about a definite numerical threshold.

McGinn's antipathy to the multiple application thesis is led by the physicalism for which, he believes, Wittgenstein's thesis (i) – the repudiation of understanding as an inner state or process – must be made to make room. For if understanding an expression is a capacity – a state of readiness for appropriate use, as it were – and if any such state must ultimately be constituted in the condition of the body and central nervous system then there seems to be no conceptual barrier to piling up such states within a 'totally indolent' subject, as McGinn puts it, nor to imagining that all actual subjects are indeed totally indolent. Isn't it just like imagining leopards which never hunt, or swim, or mate, or climb trees, but which *can* do all these things?

The real issue here, however, is not physicalism but normativity. Let us grant, for the sake of argument, that, for any capacity I have, there must be some state of my physiological constitution in which my possession of that capacity consists *as matters stand*. The qualification is, of course, essential. I can swim; but the physiological condition which makes that true does so courtesy of a co-operative physical environment. Constituted as I am, I would not, for instance, be able to swim if suddenly subjected to massively increased gravitational forces. Likewise, I can add; but the physiological condition which – by the terms of our assumption – makes that true does so courtesy of a co-operative *institutional* environment. There has to *be* such a thing as adding correctly before any physiological condition can constitute the ability to add. And Wittgenstein's contention is precisely that, with the demise of platonism, there can be such a thing as adding correctly – such a thing as a determinate requirement imposed by the rules of addition – only within a framework of extensive institutional activity and agreement in the judgements which participation in those institutions involves us in making. The very existence of our concepts depends on such *activity*.

The proper interpretation and appraisal of the multiple application thesis raises issues of the greatest difficulty. The passages in which Wittgenstein gives it expression go right to the heart of his ideas on rules and rule-following. The thesis is not an aberrant dangler alongside the basically sound capacitive conception of understanding, as McGinn would have us believe – another example where, for reasons which remain obscure, Wittgenstein has

---

19. McGinn, p. 131.

overcooked a simple insight. Rather it belongs with his attempt to point to an alternative account of normativity to the 'rules-as-rails' imagery of platonism, to explain how there can be stable middle ground between the hypostatiz-ation of rules and the denial of their existence. The thesis is believed by Wittgenstein, it is fair to assume, to be a *consequence* of the proper account of the middle ground and is therefore a vital clue to the character of Wittgenstein's view. In any case, its assessment has to be set in the context of the issues to do with objectivity to which the platonistic conception of rules and rule-following is a response in the first place, and which is Wittgenstein's principal concern in the passages of which McGinn is so keen to controvert Kripke's account. McGinn fails to set the question in the appropriate context, and his disagreement with this aspect of Wittgenstein's thought is miscon-ceived in consequence.

There are a number of other points of detail in McGinn's discussions of Wittgenstein – on the interpretation of *Investigations* §202, for instance, and its relation to the private language argument – which deserve extended discussion but which I have here no space to engage. The question which has to be paramount is: how does Wittgenstein come out of McGinn's book? What estimate could somebody properly form of Wittgenstein as a philoso-pher who knew of him only through McGinn's presentation? The answer would have to be that he was a philosopher who mixed a number of insights that were important in their historical context with as many obscure or obscurely motivated themes. Wittgenstein would emerge as a philosopher who contributed greatly to the slow post-Cartesian revolution in our thinking about the psychological. But the judgement would be hard to resist that, by the mid-1970s say, his most distinctive ideas had been thoroughly absorbed into the general philosophical consciousness, his writings assuming the status merely of pedagogically important tracts – a philosophical mine whose viable ores had largely been extracted.

The contrast with Kripke's book is thus very marked. The Wittgenstein who emerges there is a contemporary philosophical antagonist, the inventor of a startling and unignorable paradox, and an ingenious if flawed resolution of it, bearing in a profound way on our thinking about almost everything but about logic, mathematics, and the mental in particular.

Which Wittgenstein should we believe in? Has the study of the *Investiga-tions* nothing substantive to teach us now? Or are there still unexploded philosophical bombs, which we have failed to trigger only by digging insufficiently close?

I have already indicated one respect in which, as it seems to me, McGinn missed a chance to explore a genuine Wittgensteinian concern: the first-person epistemology of intentional states, and the task of achieving an understanding of how it is reconciled with their disposition-like theoreticity. That is an example of a theme which McGinn overlooks, or underplays, because his primary purpose is to controvert Kripke, and Kripke himself makes nothing of it. But the real failing of the parts of McGinn's book that are concerned with Wittgenstein is less a matter of overlooking, or playing down, Wittgensteinian themes of importance, than of failing to grasp the choreographic role of ideas he is aware of or even actually highlights. It is for this reason that there is no focused attention in McGinn's book on perhaps the most profound of all the concerns in Wittgenstein's later philosophy: the exposure of certain bogus ideas to which we are inclined concerning what the objectivity of a linguistic practice can consist in, and the relations of those ideas to misconceptions concerning the nature of language-mastery and the conditions for its existence. In this respect, because it places such matters in the forefront and makes Wittgenstein speak to them in clear, if highly controversial ways, Kripke's book, whatever its shortcomings as philosophical scholarship, seems to me to be superior as philosophical interpretation.

III

Let me conclude, then, with an indication of some of the choreography: a way of arranging some of the themes which McGinn highlights, together with others to which he gives less prominence, in such a way that we are led directly to the cluster of concerns which I have claimed to be fundamental to Wittgenstein's later work. I shall stay, for the most part, within the bounds of sections 185–219 of the *Investigations* and paragraphs 23–47 of part VI of the *Remarks on the Foundations of Mathematics*.

It needs to be stressed that the characteristic concerns of these passages have, *pace* Kripke, nothing to do with the *reality* of rules, but are epistemological. Wittgenstein is concerned to examine the idea that a rule can be genuinely an object of intellection, something whose requirements we keep track of by grace of some intuitive or interpretative ability. Undoubtedly the tone of the passages is negative. The working assumption is that we tend badly to misunderstand the nature of the accomplishment involved in competent rule-following, and that our misunderstandings lead us to a mythology of the character of the constraint imposed by a rule, and of what successfully following it actually consists in. But there is nowhere to be found any explicit denial of the existence of such constraints, or any consequential rejection of the very notion of accomplishment in this context.

Following McGinn's example, we can usefully highlight four themes. The third and fourth collectively encompass McGinn's main theses (ii)–(iv); the second is briefly glossed by McGinn[20] as part of his thesis (iii); and that, I believe, is how he would view the first, which he does not explicitly advert to, if asked to locate it in his scheme of interpretation. The first is:

---

20. *Ibid.*, pp. 21–2.

One's own understanding of a rule does not exceed what one can explain. *(Investigations* §§209–10; *RFM* VI, 23)

The temptation to think otherwise arises from the reflection that the explanation of a rule must eventually culminate in, or anyway ultimately be founded upon the giving of illustrations of its application; and that any such illustrations are finite, and hence open in principle to an indefinite variety of interpretations. Yet explanations do usually, or so we suppose, secure mutual understanding. So somehow more is got across – the thought continues – than the pursuit of explanations can ever make completely explicit. Correct uptake of an explanation is having the *right* 'something' come into one's mind as a result of the explanation; and the resulting informational state, though it is expressed in one's subsequent practice with the concept concerned, essentially transcends it.

Now, it is essential to recognize that this notion of what is involved in successfully giving and receiving explanations is a consequence of another notion, elaborated in the 'rules-as-rails' imagery of *Investigations* §§218–19. This is the idea that, as Wittgenstein characterizes it at *RFM* VI, 31:

'Once you have got hold of the rule, you have the route traced for you.'

Suppose the rule governing a particular arithmetical series, for example, really was somehow able to determine its every nth place quite independently of any judgement or reaction of ours. Then since any feasible illustration of the rule will sustain alternative interpretations generating conflicting verdicts about what happens at nth places which were not explicitly illustrated, the every-nth-place-determining 'something' which someone who correctly receives the illustrations somehow comes to have in mind, the 'essential thing' which we 'have to get him to *guess*',[21] is clearly at best imperfectly conveyable by illustration. Of course, we can maybe say in other words what the rule is. But that will help only if the recipient is already a master of the vocabulary used in the alternative formulation. And such mastery cannot always be the product of explicit definition; sooner or later, we have to hit concepts acquired by witness of illustrative practice.

The upshot is, then, that the picture of rules as rails forces us to think of our ability to follow them, to know in a potential infinity of cases what moves are in accord with them, as owing to a kind of hyper-cognitive felicity. Explanations come to be viewed not so much as communicating understanding as *triggering* the jump to an informational state by which the accord or clash with the rule of any proposed move is settled. Every competent rule-

---

21. *Investigations* §210.

follower is the beneficiary of such informational states – and each of them packs in more than explanations ever made explicit to him or he can ever make explicit to others. When Wittgenstein sets himself against this idea, as when he writes

> If you use a rule to give a description, you yourself do not know more than you say . . . If you say 'and so on', you yourself do not know more than 'and so on',[22]

his concern is, of course, to challenge a mistaken epistemological picture; but he *thereby* challenges the parent rules-as-rails imagery which is simply a figurative expression of platonism.

The second theme I want to highlight might be expressed like this:

> It might be preferable, in describing our most basic rule-governed responses, to think of them not as informed by an *intuition* (of the requirements of the rule) but as a kind of *decision.*
> *(Investigations* §§186 and 213; *RFM* VI, 24; *Brown Book* 5)

The point of the contrast between 'intuition' and 'decision'[23] is that the former implies and the latter repudiates the suggestion that – even in the most basic cases, where one can say nothing by way of justification for one's particular way of proceeding – rule-following is a cognitive accomplishment, success in tracking an independently constituted requirement. 'Intuition' suggests an unarticulated *ur-cognition,* a form of knowledge too basic to admit of any further account. But this very primitiveness has the effect that there can be no further story to be told about how the relevant sort of intuitive faculty might accomplish the harmony, which it would supposedly generate, between the real requirements of a rule and a subject's impression of them. For that reason, it is wide open to skeptical assault:

> If intuition is an inner voice – how do I know *how* I am to obey it? And how do I know that it doesn't mislead me? For if it can guide me right, it can also guide me wrong. (Intuition an unnecessary shuffle.)
> *(Investigations* §213)

There is no response to this skeptical assault because nothing can be done by way of *filling out* the thought that, in the most primitive cases of rule-following, when everything seems immediate and beyond further account, we nevertheless track a set of independent requirements. The fact is, though, that neither the skeptical thought, nor the intuitional epistemology which it

---

22. *RFM* IV, 8.
23. *Intuition* and *Entscheidung.*

challenges, are really intelligible. We have no accountable idea of what would constitute the direction taken by the rule off its own bat, as it were, if the deliverances of our intuitive faculties were to take us collectively off track – 'no model of this superlative fact'(*Investigations* §192). And that is just to say that we have no model of what constitutes the direction taken by a rule, period – once the direction is conceived, after the fashion of platonism, as determined autonomously, and our performance, whether communal or solitary, as merely an exercise in tracking. That is why it 'would almost be more correct to say' that decision rather than intuition is involved (*Investigations* §186). Such a way of putting the matter would have disadvantages of its own, not least its connotation of a felt absence of constraint. But at least it would be free of the cognitive pretentiousness of platonism.

The third theme is complementary to the second, and elaborates Wittgenstein's critique of a 'tracking' epistemology of rule-following:

> Supposing that grasping a rule were a matter of coming to have something 'in mind', how would one thereby be enabled to recognize, step by step, what its requirements were?
> (*Investigations* §§198, 209–13, *RFM* VI, 38, 47)

It is in the context of this theme that the 'paradox' is presented which Kripke has celebrated:

> 'But how can a rule show me what I have to do at *this* point? Whatever I do is, on some interpretation, in accord with the rule.' – That is not what we ought to say, but rather: any interpretation still hangs in the air along with what it interprets, and cannot give it any support. Interpretations by themselves do not determine meaning.
> (*Investigations* §198)

Suppose I undergo some process of explanation – for instance, a substantial initial segment of some arithmetical series is written out for me and as a result I come to have the right rule 'in mind'. How, when it comes to the crunch – at an nth place which lies beyond the demonstrated initial segment, and which I have previously never thought about – does having the rule 'in mind' help? Well, with such an example one tends to think of having the rule 'in mind' on the model of imagining a formula, or something of that sort. And so it is natural to respond by conceding that, strictly, merely having the rule in mind *is* no help. For I can have a formula in mind without knowing what it means. So – the response continues – it is necessary in addition to *interpret* the rule. But then we immediately get the 'paradox' which Wittgenstein's interlocutor blunders into in *Investigations* §198. *Any* selection for the nth place can be reconciled, on *some* interpretation, with the rule. An interpretation is of help to me, therefore, in my predicament at the nth place only if it is *correct*. But to invoke the idea of correctness at this point makes the play with interpretation nugatory. To describe someone as 'knowing the correct interpretation of the rule for the nth place' becomes just a piece of patter equivalent to saying that he knows how to *apply* the rule at the nth place. And then we might just as well have put the initial question in the form: how am I to know what interpretation of the rule for the nth place *is* correct?

It should be reasonably evident how these three themes interrelate. Suppose that what I take up from an episode of explanation, if it is successful, does indeed transcend that explanation and any other that I might give in turn. I come to have the right rule in mind but might, save for a kind of felicity, equally well have arrived at a wrong one, despite having missed no overt feature of the explanation. This idea, explicitly challenged by the first theme, connects with the second and third in that they jointly confront it with a dilemma. How does the explanation-transcendent rule which I supposedly have 'in mind' tell me what to do in novel cases? How does the rule, once grasped, help – what is the epistemology of acting on it? If it requires interpretation, that could be done in lots of ways. So how do I tell which interpretation is correct? Does that, for instance, call for a *further* rule – a rule for determining correct interpretation of the original – and if so, why does it not raise the same difficulty again, thereby generating a regress? If, on the other hand, it is not necessary to interpret the original rule, then the only possible answer appears to be that I have some unmediated, intuitional contact with its requirements, and this is the thought challenged by the second theme.

So the overall structure is this. It comes naturally to us to think, with the platonist, of the objectivity of many of our practices – including *par excellence* logic and mathematics – as residing in our following rules-as-rails, rules which somehow reach ahead of us and determine of themselves their every actual and counterfactual proper application. But if we have the capacity to keep track of rules when so conceived, we must be capable of somehow getting them 'in mind', notwithstanding the necessarily imperfect character of explanations – ultimately illustrations – of their application. The grasp of such a rule is thus the internalization of an open-ended set of pre-ordained requirements, an informational state accessible, as Wittgenstein had his interlocutor put it, only by a kind of guesswork. Well, let it be so. Wittgenstein's question is then: what does the deployment of this 'informational state' consist in: *how* does it inform the actual practice of following the rule? Thinking of the rule as literally an object of consciousness – as a formula, or whatever – either raises the regress-of-interpretations paradox, or requires construal of the rule as 'self-interpreting', as it were; which is to say that the epistemology of it is conceived as intuitional, too primitive to allow of an account, and hence as vulnerable to the simple skeptical thought – not, of course, that of Kripke's Skeptic – of *Investigations* §213. If however – as is perhaps likely if autobiography is any guide – one is thinking of the way in which the rule allegedly informs one's ongoing practice not in terms of something which is literally an object of consciousness – like a formula, or picture, or whispered instructions in the car[24] – but just in terms of a kind of inner confidence or sense of directedness, the epistemology of the step-by-step judgements involved in applying the rule remains irremediably intuitional, and thus vulnerable to the same skeptical attack. In short: think of the objectivity of rule-following on the model of the rules-as-rails picture, and you will be completely beggared for any satisfactory account of our ability to stay on track.

I do not present this, as it seems to me, powerful and vivid train of thought as the spine, so to speak, of the 'rule-following considerations'. I claim for it only that it is one very important development contained in the relevant passages in Wittgenstein's writings, and that it brings out the fundamental preoccupation that I advertised at the conclusion of the preceding section. Its connection with platonism in the philosophy of mathematics is perhaps obvious enough,[25] but I would suggest that a bearing on the private language argument is also evident. For what does the would-be private linguist do except *platonize* his baptismal intention? If you think that, just by concentrating inwardly upon a sensation and labelling it 'E', you can thereby create – in advance of your own response to the cases as and when they occur – indefinitely many truths about the proper use of 'E' on subsequent occasions, then you are thinking of your original intention in a way which is going to give rise to exactly similar – and similarly hopeless – epistemological problems.

How do the ideas which I have adumbrated relate to those developed by Kripke? One point of difference between Kripke's Wittgenstein and Wittgenstein which has not been generally noted is that the regress-of-interpretations paradox of *Investigations* §§198–201 diverges in focus from Kripke's Skeptical Paradox. Kripke's Skeptic challenges his adversary to substantiate a claim to know what rule he formerly followed – the problem is to describe aspects of his former behaviour and/or mental life which take us *to* an identification of the former rule. The regress-of-interpretations paradox, by contrast, focuses on a particular conception of the path *from* a rule to a judgement about its proper application in a new case. The rule is assumed from the outset to be in place – 'in mind' – and the issue is, how does it help to have it there? Further, the problem is conceived as arising as a result

---

24. *Investigations* §223.

25. Though one should not lose sight of the consideration that the aspect of mathematical platonism targeted is not the ontology of abstract objects but something which platonism shares with the sort of structuralist conception of the subject matter of number theory, e.g., famously advocated by Benacerraf in 'What Numbers Could Not Be', *Philosophical Review* (1965), pp. 47–73. This is the notion that we can somehow pack more into our mathematical concepts and rules than need ever be elicitable by proof and that proof is accordingly a mere cognitive auxiliary whereby finite minds may unlock implications of the understanding of mathematical notions to which they subscribe.

of a certain specific (mis)conception of what rules are, one which pictures the relation between receiving an illustration of a practice and going on to participate in it successfully as essentially mediated by cognition of the requirements of something which has been interiorized. So not merely do the two paradoxes focus on different – though of course connected – kinds of question concerning rules, namely:

How is it possible to know which rule I (used to) follow?

vs.

How is it possible to know what the rule which I grasp requires of me here?

In addition, while Kripke's Skeptic directs his Paradox at the very existence of rules and rule-following, Wittgenstein's 'paradox' is directed, in intention at least, at what he regards as a misunderstanding of the nature and epistemology of rule-following – something which it should be possible to correct without calling into question the reality of rules.

Well, that may have been Wittgenstein's intention. The question is: did he succeed in carrying it through? For to stress: if the interiorized, explanation-transcendent rule, with all its hopeless epistemological difficulties, is merely the upshot of a platonist conception of the autonomy of rules, then that has to be a casualty too. So the distinguishability of his view from that of Kripke's Skeptic is totally dependent on Wittgenstein's ability to dislodge the thought that rules are *nothing* if not autonomous in that way. Unless that thought is dislodged, then while Kripke's account of the route in, as it were, may have involved somewhat free play with Wittgenstein's text, the terminus of the train of thought which I have described and that of Kripke's Skeptic will be the same.

Dislodging that thought requires indicating an alternative: a conception of rules and rule-governed practices which allows a sufficient gap between the requirements of a rule and a subject's reaction in any particular case to make space for something worth regarding as normativity, yet abrogates the spurious autonomy which gave rise to the difficulties. It is clear enough what Wittgenstein regards as the *sort* of considerations which should point us towards the right perspective on the matter. They are the considerations which constitute the fourth theme which I wish to highlight:

> Language, and all rule-governed institutions, are founded not in our internalization of the same strongly autonomous, explanation-transcendent rules, whose requirements we then succeed, more or less, in collectively tracking, but in *primitive* dispositions of agreement in judgement and action.
>
> (*Investigations* §§211, 217, 242; *RFM* VI, 39)

There is no essential inner epistemology of rule-following. To express the matter dangerously, we have nothing 'in mind'. The connection between the training and explanations which we receive and our subsequent practices is no doubt effected in ways which could only be sustained by conscious, thinking beings; but it is not mediated by the internalization of explanation-transcendent rules that, in our training, we (something like) guessed at. It is, for epistemological purposes, a *basic* fact about us that ordinary forms of explanation and training do succeed in perpetuating practices of various kinds – that there is a shared uptake, a disposition to concur in novel judgements involving the concepts in question. The rules-as-rails mythology attempts an explanation of this fact. But the truth is the other way round: it is the basic agreement which sustains all rules and rule-governed institutions. The requirements which our rules impose upon us would not be violated if there were not this basic agreement; they would not so much as exist.

This aspect of Wittgenstein's thought is very familiar and, as the familiar often does, it can seem quite clear. But it is not clear at all. The great difficulty is to stabilize it against a drift to a fatal simplification: the idea that the requirements of a rule, in any particular case, are simply *whatever we take them to be*. For if the requirements of the rule are not constituted, as the platonist thought, independently of our reaction to the case, what is there available to constitute them *but* our reaction? But that idea effectively surrenders the notion of a requirement altogether. And Wittgenstein in any case explicitly cautions against it as a misreading of his text.[26] In which case how do matters stand? Wittgenstein tells us that the requirements of rules exist only within the framework of institutional activities which depend upon basic human propensities to agree in judgement; but he reminds us that such requirements are also, in any particular case, independent of our judgements, supplying standards in terms of which it may be right to regard those judgements, even if they enjoy consensus, as incorrect. So we have been told what does *not* constitute the requirement of a rule in any particular case: it is *not* constituted by our agreement about the particular case, and it is *not* constituted autonomously, by a rule-as-rail, our ability to follow which would be epistemologically unaccountable. But we have not been told what *does* constitute it; all we have been told is that there would simply be no such requirement – the rule could not so much as exist – but for the phenomenon of actual, widespread human agreement in judgement.

I fear that it is probably vain to search Wittgenstein's own texts for a more concrete positive suggestion about the constitutive question. His later conception of philosophical method seems to be conditioned by a mistrust of such constitutive questions. Consensus cannot constitute the requirements of a rule because we do, on occasion, actually *make use* of the notion of a consensus based on ignorance or a mistake. That is a distinction to which our

---

26. *Investigations* §241; cf. *RFM* VII, 40.

ordinary practices give content. The thing to guard against is the tendency to erect a mythological picture of its content, the myth about rule-following challenged by the first three themes. The myth is active in the platonist philosophy of mathematics, and in the Cartesian philosophy of inner experience. So it is important to expose it. But, once exposed, it does not need to be supplanted:

> Our mistake is to look for an explanation where we ought to look at what happens as a 'proto-phenomenon'. That is, where we ought to have said: *this language-game is played*.

No further *account* of the distinction is necessary. Enough has been done when we have pre-empted philosophical misunderstandings of our linguistic practices in a way that avoids misdescription of their details.

I mean that to be recognizable as an 'official' Wittgensteinian line. I do not know whether it is really Wittgenstein's own; and in so far as it may be, I suspect that he did not succeed in clearly representing to himself a sound theoretical basis for declining rather than – perhaps quixotically – rising to the challenge posed by his own thought which I have tried to describe. In any case, *we* now confront a challenge: make out the constitutive answer which Wittgenstein's fourth theme does not deliver, though it imposes constraints upon it; or make out the necessary theoretical basis for the analytical quietism which, 'officially', he himself adopted.

Three things are worth stressing. First, these are not issues from a mined-out corpus, but remain of the greatest contemporary interest and importance. Second, Kripke's Skeptic continues to loom over them: it is still to be shown that the ideas of Wittgenstein which I have described can be prevented – quite contrary to his intentions, no doubt – from spiralling into some kind of incoherent irrealism about meaning. Third, this agenda which Wittgenstein has bequeathed us – this whole clutch of issues concerning meaning, intention, content, truth, and objectivity – comprises some of the most exciting and profound questions which engage contemporary philosophers. The agenda is, of course, broader than the Wittgensteinian legacy: there has been important imput from Quine, Putnam, and indeed Kripke, in Wittgenstein's name. But, though often tantalisingly within range, these matters are never in focus in McGinn's book. So hardly any of the excitement comes through.

CHAPTER EIGHT

MEANING AND INTENTION
AS JUDGEMENT DEPENDENT

Crispin Wright

I want to canvass a third possibility: an account of the central insight of Wittgenstein's discussion of rule-following which is neither Kripkean nor 'official'. It may be that the 'official' view is exegetically correct, and that I do here part company with the intentions of the actual, historical Wittgenstein. But it seems to me that it is an important methodological precept that we do not despair of giving answers to constitutive questions too soon; if the accomplishments of analysis in philosophy often seem meagre, that may be because it is difficult, not impossible.

The rule-following considerations attack the idea that judgements about the requirements of a rule on a particular occasion have a 'tracking' epistemology, answer to states of affairs constituted altogether independently of our inclination to make those judgements. How can judgements lack a substantial epistemology in this way, and yet still be *objective* – still have to answer to something distinct from our actual dispositions of judgement?

A good example of a broadly parallel problem is provided by secondary qualities of material objects – qualities of colour, taste, smell, palpable texture, audible sound, and so on. It is an old idea that, in our judgements concerning such qualities, we respond more to aspects of our own affective phenomenology than to anything real in nature, and there is a corresponding perennial temptation towards an irrealist construal of such judgements.[1] But the irrealist response is, in this case, an overreaction. What may be true, I believe, is that (a large class of) judgements of colour, for instance, fail what I have elsewhere called the *order-of-determination* test.[2] Judgements of shape, by contrast, to take the most often discussed example of a Lockian primary quality, arguably

---

1. Famously succumbed to by Locke, of course, and recently by the late John Mackie (*Problems From Locke* (Oxford: Clarendon Press, 1976), pp. 17–20).
2. In my 'Realism: the Contemporary Debate – Whither Now?' in J. Haldane and C. Wright (eds) *Reality, Representation, and Projection* (Oxford: Oxford University Press, 1993).

129

ORDER OF DET JUDGEMENTS [handwritten]

pass the test. The order-of-determination test concerns the relation between *best* judgements – judgements made in what are, with respect to their particular subject-matter, *cognitively ideal* conditions of both judge and circumstance – and truth. Passing the test requires that there be some content to the idea of best judgements *tracking* the truth – the determinants of a judgement's being true and of its being best have to be somehow independent. Truth, for judgements which pass the test, is a standard constituted independently of any considerations concerning cognitive pedigree. For judgements which fail the test, by contrast, there is no distance between being true and being best; truth, for such judgements, is constitutively what we judge to be true when we operate under cognitively ideal conditions.

confusing [handwritten]

The contrast, then, is between judgements among which our best opinions *determine* the extension of the truth-predicate, and those among which they at most reflect an extension determined independently – henceforward *extension-determining* and *extension-reflecting* judgements respectively. So expressed, it is an intuitive and inchoate contrast, which can doubtless be elaborated and refined in a variety of ways. To fix ideas, let us look a bit more closely at the way matters might proceed first in the cases of (primary) colour and (visually appraisable, three-dimensional) shape; and then in the case of psychological characteristics.

① vs. ② / perhaps intuitions vs. concepts [handwritten marginalia]

Consider a plane surface one foot square. What conditions on a judge and circumstances of judgement should we impose in order to ensure that his/her (visual) judgement will be that the surface is, say, uniformly royal blue only if it is? Well, the surface must be in full view, and in good light, relatively stationary, and not too far away; and the subject must know which object is in question, must observe it attentively, must be possessed of normal visual equipment and be otherwise cognitively lucid, and must be competent with the concept *blue*. In addition, the subject must be free of doubt about the satisfaction of any of these conditions – for a doubt might lead to an unwillingness to make any judgement, or even to the making of some bizarre, compensatory judgement, in circumstances which were otherwise ideal for the appraisal of colour.

Now, it is presumably necessary, in order for our judgements, appropriately constrained (partially)[3] to *determine* the extension of some concept, that

---

3. 'Partially' because we are, in effect, considering something of the form:

If S judges under conditions C, then (P if and only if S believes P),

which says nothing at all about the truth-conditions of P-type propositions under non- C-conditions. But we cannot plausibly consider, for present purposes, the stronger *basic equation* (to use Mark Johnston's term), namely,

P if and only if (if S judges under conditions C, S believes P)

unless we can foreclose on the possibility that bringing about conditions C might materially affect the truth-status of P. And that cannot be done with colour, or any characteristic sustained by a causally active and acted-upon base. Cf. note 26 in C. Wright, "Moral Values, Projection, and Secondary Qualities", *Proceedings of the Aristotelian Soceity*, supp. vol. 62, 1988.

it be *a priori* true that the concept applies when, so constrained, we judge that it does. And it is, I suggest, *a priori* true that when all the foregoing conditions are met, the fact of the object's colour – at least at the level of refinement captured by a predicate like 'blue' – and the subject's judgement of the fact will, as it were, covary.[4] It is another question whether such *a priori* covariance is sufficient for the judgements to enjoy extension-determining status. But there are, in this case, three supplementary considerations which, if correct, arguably confer such sufficiency.

First, a priority in such a claim – a claim that, under certain conditions, C, a subject will hold a certain belief if and only if it is true (henceforward, a *provisional equation*) – may be the product of a certain triviality, consequent on the conditions' receiving no substantial specification but being described purely in terms of 'suitability', 'conduciveness', or, generally, as whatever-it-takes to appraise judgements of the relevant sort correctly. Clearly, we would have made no case for regarding best opinion as *determining* the extension of the truth-predicate among a given class of judgements if, although we had constructed an appropriate kind of provisional equation whose instances held *a priori* true, their *a priority* was owing to this kind of trivial specification of the C-conditions. For it is an *a priori* truth of *any* kind of judgement whatever that, if I operate under conditions which have everything it takes to ensure the correctness of my opinion, then it will be the case that P if and only if I take it to be so. But the conditions listed above for the appraisal of colour allow, it is plausible, substantial, non-trivial elaboration in a manner conservative of the *a priori* connection between their satisfaction and the correctness of the subject's opinion. We can, for instance, specify normal visual equipment on

---

4. Two possible doubts about the sufficiency of the listed conditions would need to be addressed before this claim could be finally sustained.

(I) Might a subject not be possessed of eccentric background beliefs – for instance, that there are no blue things at all! – which would prevent his formation of the appropriate belief about the object's colour, even though he met the conditions as stated? (I am here indebted to Paul Boghossian.) It is not clear. If the object is blue, it will look blue to him under the stated conditions; and then, if he believes that

Blue things look blue to *normally visually equipped* subjects in *good light*,

he is going to be constrained by the eccentric belief – if cognitively lucid – to doubt whether both those conditions are met. So he will violate the extremal condition, of being free of doubt, etc. But if he doesn't believe the principle connecting blueness and blue appearance, does he count as appropriately competent with the concept, *blue*? Still, that is just one kind of eccentric belief.

(II) Background colour affects colour appearance: a cream circle, for instance, may look pink, or eau-de-Nil, even in normal light, depending on the colour of the surface behind it. May we not need to strengthen the C-conditions to contain some stipulation of an appropriately coloured background? There would be great difficulties with the important independence condition, see text p. 132 if so. But does the phenomenon affect *royal blue, scarlet, emerald green, lemon yellow* to any extent which might result in a subject's erroneously judging (or withholding the judgement) that an object meets one of those descriptions? And would it anyway be absurd to think of colour as involving an element of situation-relativity – so that the judgements about, e.g., the cream circle are all correct?

the part of the subject as: equipment which is actually statistically usual among human beings. Likewise, good lighting conditions can be specified as: conditions like those which actually typically obtain out-of-doors and out-of-shadow at noon on a cloudy summer's day.[5]

The second supplementary consideration is that the question whether the C-conditions, substantially specified, are satisfied in a particular case is logically independent of any truths concerning the details of the extension of colour concepts. If this were not so, it would be open to question whether subjects' opinions, formed under these C-conditions, could be extension-determining; for satisfaction of the C-conditions would always presuppose some anterior constitution of colour facts. It is here that one disanalogy opens up with the case of shape, as we shall see in a moment.

The final supplementary consideration is that there is to hand no other account of what does determine the extension of the truth-predicate among simple judgements of colour, of which the *a priority* of provisional equations of the kind in question, whose C-conditions are substantially specified and, in the requisite way, free of logical presupposition about the extension of colour concepts, would be a derivable consequence. So there is, to put the matter another way, no *explaining away* the case which the other considerations supply for saying the judgements formed under the conditions in question are extension-determining rather than extension-reflecting.

The suggestion, in summary, is that there is at least a strong *prima facie* case for regarding a base class[6] of our best judgements about colour as extension-determining. The case consists in the circumstances (i) that we can construct

---

5. The occurrences of 'actually' in these two specifications are to be understood as securing rigidity of reference to the status quo. So counterfactual situations in which other things are statistically usual are not C-conditions as specified.

6. A base class, rather than merely a proper subclass, because our beliefs about objects' colours under non-C-conditions are variously constrained by the characteristics of colours as determined by C-conditioned judgements. It is, for instance, conclusive justification for the belief that something is blue in the dark to justify the claims (i) that we would judge it to be blue if we saw it in good light and under the other C-conditions; and (ii) that bringing these conditions about would effect no changes in any determinable (contrast: determinate) aspect of the object which would need to be mentioned in an explanation of the form which our C-conditioned response would assume.

A connected point, which may help to forestall possible confusion, is that the relationship between the characteristic, being-judged-to-be-blue-under-C-conditions, and being blue is not to be compared to that between the characteristic marks of the instance of a natural kind and being an instance of that kind. It is true that the marks of gold, e.g. – its colour, lustre, heaviness, resistance to corrosion, etc. – are in some sense *a priori*; we do not learn what gold is and then discover that it has these characteristics. But in the case of genuine natural kinds we are (a) open to the discovery that some things which have the marks whereby we succeeded in identifying the kind are not actually instances of the kind; and (b) open to the discovery that actually no genuine kind of thing *is* individuated by those marks. By contrast, if what I have been suggesting about colour is correct, we are not open to the discovery that some objects judged to be blue under C-conditions are not blue; nor open to the discovery – should the microphysics of blue things prove bizarrely heterogeneous – that there is no such thing as an object's being blue.

a priori true provisional equations for such judgements; (ii) that the C-conditions in these equations can be substantially specified, in a manner free of the triviality associated with whatever-it-takes formulations; (iii) that the satisfaction of the C-conditions is, in any particular case, logically independent of the details of the extensions of colour concepts; (iv) that no other account is available of what else might determine the extension of the truth-predicate among judgements of colour, of which the satisfaction by the relevant provisional equations of conditions (i)–(iii) would be a consequence.[7]

Contrast now the situation of shape. Suppose x is some nearby middle-sized object, and consider the judgement, 'x is pear-shaped'. We will want to characterise the conditions which are cognitively ideal for the visual appraisal of x's shape in terms very similar to those suggested for the case of colour. But there are differences. One, relatively unimportant, is that the lighting conditions do not have to be as good; sodium street-lighting, for instance, is suitable enough for recognising shapes. But a second, much more important, consideration is that a single subject's *best* opinion about three-dimensional shape, if visually grounded, must needs be the product of *several* observations, from a suitable variety of spatial positions. And in order for it to be *a priori* true that, subject to whatever other conditions we wish to impose, such a subject's opinion about the shape of x will be correct, we need to ensure that no *change* in x's shape takes place through the period of these several observations. But that calls for some ingredient in the C-conditions of which it is an *a priori* consequence that whatever it is true to say of x's shape at any time during the subject's observations is also true at any other time within the relevant period. Some independent determinant is therefore called for of what it *is* true to say about x's shape during that period – independent, that is, of the opinion formed by the subject. There is accordingly, it seems, no immediate prospect of a provisional equation for 'x is pear-shaped' meeting both conditions (i) and (iii) above.

A natural response is that there is no reason why a particular kind of subject-matter might not dictate that the formation of a best opinion required *teamwork*. What if we discharge the single observer and consider instead the opinion concerning x's shape which would be arrived at cooperatively by a number of strategically positioned subjects who observed x at the same time? That should filter out the problem of instability. But there is a deeper problem

---

7. It is not inconsistent with thinking of best judgements about colour as being extension-determining simultaneously to hold that the extensions of colour concepts are determined by microphysical characteristics of objects – supposing that the physics *doesn't* prove bizarrely heterogeneous. For it will be best judgements about colour which determine *which* microphysical characteristics are fit to play a (supplementary) extension-determining role. And no obstacle to colour's satisfying condition (iv) is posed by this view of the relationship between colour and the microphysical, since the microphysical account of the determinants of the extension of 'blue' e.g., will not, presumably, entail that appropriate provisional equations can be formulated satisfying conditions (i)–(iii).

[Handwritten marginal annotations:]

Top of page: MY AIM IS NOT NECESSARILY TO SAY DEFINITIVELY HOW WE FOLLOW RULES, BUT RATHER TO SHOW THAT THERE MIGHT IN FACT BE SOME JUSTIFICATION FOR OUR PRACTICE (THOUGH...

Right margin: ME THIS IS IRRELEVANT. IF WE DO NOT GO ABOUT FOLLOWING RULES IN THE MANNER I STATE, ONE INTEREST. QUESTION WOULD BE WHETHER IT IS AT ALL NECESSARY FOR OUR PRACTICE TO BE SUBSTANTIVE IN ORDER TO FUNCTION. SORT OF NATURALISM & THE SKEPTICISM. SOLUTION SAY NO.

which brings out, I think, the real point of disanalogy between shape and colour. The application of shape predicates, even ones as rough and ready as 'pear-shaped', is answerable to a variety of considerations besides visual appearance. For instance, a solid is pear-shaped only if any maximal two-dimensional section of it describes two contiguous circles of substantially different sizes. But it cannot be an *a priori* truth that conditions of the kind which we regard as optimal for the visual detection of shape are adequate for the reliable visual appraisal of characteristics which are in this way answerable to such operational considerations. The operational criteria dominate the visual – that is why the Müller-Lyer illusion is a *visual* illusion. And we can well enough imagine starting out again, as if at the dawn of man's intellectual history, armed with the concepts which we have now but with no experience of the world, and finding that the cost of maintaining the thesis that reliable visual appraisals of shape are generally possible would be a disorderly plague of hypotheses about changes in shape, forced on us by the need to reconcile our visual appraisals with operational ones. It is an *a posteriori* courtesy of experience that the world in which we actually live is not of this awkward kind. And if that is right, then no kind of true provisional equation for visual judgements of shape, even if it invokes teamwork and thereby meets the independence condition (iii), can be both *a priori* and substantial.[8]

I am not, of course, presenting these remarks as establishing conclusively that (a base class of) judgements of colour fail the order-of-determination test, while judgements of shape pass it.[9] Nor is it clear that the considerations advanced, even as far as they go, will generalise to other instances of the primary/secondary distinction. My purpose is, rather, to indicate one framework for the discussion and development of the test; to give credence to the thought that there is a distinction here – perhaps a number of distinctions – and an explanatory programme of great potential importance.

Nevertheless, if the gist of the foregoing is correct, visual judgements of colour will emerge as an interesting mix of subjectivity and objectivity. They should not, at least in a basic class of cases, when appropriate C-conditions are met, be regarded as responsive to states of affairs which are constituted

---

8. This train of thought is elaborated somewhat in Wright, "Moral Values, Projection, and Secondary Qualities", pp. 19–20.

9. Various interesting further questions have to be negotiated which I cannot go into here. For instance, might best *operationally-determined* (contrast: visually determined) beliefs about shape arguably play an extension-determining role, or are even such beliefs at most extension-reflecting? One germane consideration would be that very many shape concepts – 'pear-shaped' is an example – are, while operationally constrained, subject to no obvious operational, as opposed to tactuo-visual, criteria of application. Another would be that we would expect to need stability provisos in the appropriate lists of C-conditions for operationally determined beliefs, since proper execution of the appropriate kinds of operation is essentially subject to invalidation by instability. It would be pleasant if that consideration were decisive, but I do not think that it is. For it may perhaps be mitigated by some play with the *positive-presumptiveness* of assumptions of stability, along the lines illustrated in the next section of the text for the role of lack of self-deception in the C-conditions for appraisal of one's own intentions.

independently – our best opinions about colour do not, in that sense, *track* colour. But neither is it the case that there is no standard to meet, that whatever we say about colour goes or – what comes to the same thing – that there is no such thing as an object's real colour. Rather, it is a perfectly objective question what, in a particular case, the deliverance of best opinion would be; and that deliverance is something with which a majority, or even a whole community, may for some reason be out of accord.

* * *

I pass now to the second set of potential examples which I want to air: that of self-ascriptions of psychological states like sensation, emotion, mood, belief, desire, and intention – the traditional category of *avowals*. The proposal that such judgements are extension-determining is an extremely attractive one. The traditional Cartesian epistemology attempts to construe avowals in general on the model of a certain conception of what is involved in competent self-ascription of *sensation* – a model which draws heavily on a comparison with perception of material objects, but with the crucial differences that the sensation, *qua* 'inner' object, is accessible only to the subject, whose gaze is conceived as all-seeing and error-proof. As a picture of knowledge of one's own sensations, this generates problems enough, principally by its presupposition of the operability of private schemes of classification – 'private languages'. But, even if we let the Cartesian account of sensation pass, it provides only the most feeble basis for an account of the self-ascription of other kinds of psychological states. For there are no plausible introspectible processes or states which are candidates to be, for instance, beliefs and intentions. And besides – and more important – to think of, for example, intention as an introspectible episode in consciousness generates no end of difficulties and contortions when we try to make sense of the necessarily holistic character of the scheme of beliefs, desires, and intentions by reference to which we explain subjects' behaviour, and of the notion of *fit* between an intention and the behaviour which implements it. One of the most central themes in Wittgenstein's later philosophy of mind is the idea that Cartesianism is based on a *grammatical* misunderstanding, a misinterpretation of the language-game of self- and other-ascription of mental states. The Cartesian takes the authority of avowals as a symptom of, as it were, a superlatively sure genre of detection. We should accomplish a very sharp perspective on the sense in which this is a 'grammatical' misunderstanding if it could be shown that avowals fail the order-of-determination test – in other words, that subjects' best opinions determine, rather than reflect, what it is true to say about their intentional states, with the consequence that the notion of detection or 'inner tracking', as it were, is inappropriate. (Naturally, it would have to be part of a satisfying development in this direction that best opinions turned out to be relatively easily accomplished; otherwise, the authority of avowals would be unaccounted for.)

Can we, then, provide a set of conditions whose satisfaction will ensure, *a priori*, that subjects will believe themselves to have, for example, certain particular intentions if and only if they do? Well, how might a subject who had the conceptual resources to form a belief appropriate to the presence, or absence, of a certain intention, nevertheless fail to do so? Self-deception is one possibility, whatever the correct account of that puzzling idea. A subject may, as many people think, be simply unable to bring to consciousness the real intentions which inform certain of his courses of action. Conversely, we are familiar with the kind of weak-mindedness which can lead subjects into deceiving themselves that they have formed certain intentions – typically ones which are desirable but difficult of implementation – when in truth they have not done so.

In both these kinds of case, we typically regard the self-deceptive (lack of) belief as *motivated*. But in certain other circumstances it would be better to think of it as having a primarily physiological – perhaps a pharmacological – explanation. The cause of a subject's mistaken belief about his/her intentions need not reside in other aspects of his/her intentional psychology. Anyway, one way or another, an appropriate set of C-conditions will have to ensure that nothing of this kind is operative. And in addition, we need only include, it seems, a condition to the effect that the subject be appropriately attentive to the question what his/her intentions are. However, nothing in what follows will depend on whether these three conditions – grasp of the appropriate concepts, lack of any material self-deception or anything relevantly similar, and appropriate attentiveness – do indeed suffice.

The most salient difficulty, for our purposes, with the provisional biconditional which will emerge from these suggestions is that of making a case that it meets condition (ii) – the condition that the C-conditions be substantially specified. The motive for condition (ii) was not a distaste for triviality as such, it will be remembered, but rather for the particular kind of triviality involved in whatever-it-takes formulations. Such formulations are always possible and, by prejudicially representing matters in terms of the jargon of tracking, leave us with no way of getting at the distinction which it is the point of the order-of-determination test to reflect. And on the face of it, unfortunately, we are some considerable distance from a formulation of the no-self-deception condition which can count as non-trivial in the relevant sense. The problem is, first, that 'self-deception' covers, for the purposes of the biconditional, *any* motivated condition which might lead to a subject's ignorance or error concerning his or her intentions; and, second, we need, as noted, to allow for the possibility of unmotivated conditions – chemically induced ones, or whatever – with the same effect. So we seem to be perilously close to writing in a condition to the effect that the subject be 'free of any condition which might somehow impede his ability reliably to certify his own intentions'. And that, of course, is just the sort of insubstantial, whatever-it-takes formulation which condition (ii) was meant to exclude.

Perhaps it is possible to do better, to produce some description which excludes the relevant class of states but does so non-trivially. But none comes to mind, and it would of course be pointless to wait on the deliverance of empirical science if one is hoping for vindication of an extension-determining view of the beliefs expressed by avowals, and so requires something which will subserve the *a priority* of the resulting biconditional. So how to proceed?

We have, I think, to depart somewhat from the approach which emerged in the case of colour. But a possible variant of it is suggested by the reflection that the troublesome no-self-deception condition is *positive-presumptive*. By that I mean that, such is the 'grammar' of ascriptions of intention, one is entitled to assume that a subject is *not* materially self-deceived, or unmotivatedly similarly afflicted, unless one possesses determinate evidence to the contrary. Positive-presumptiveness ensures that, in all circumstances in which one has no countervailing evidence, one is *a priori* justified in holding that the no-self-deception condition is satisfied, its trivial specification notwithstanding. Suppose, then, that we succeed in constructing an *a priori* true provisional biconditional:

C (Jones) → (Jones believes he intends to φ ↔ Jones intends to φ),

where C includes the (trivial) no-self-deception condition but no other trivially formulated conditions. Then if – lacking evidence to the contrary – we are *a priori* justified in holding the no-self-deception condition to be met, we are also *a priori* justified in believing the result of deleting that condition from the provisional biconditional in question. Likewise for any other positive-presumptive conditions listed under C. In this way we can eventually arrive at a restricted provisional biconditional in which all the C-conditions are substantially specified and which, in the absence of any information bearing on whether the conditions are satisfied which we have deleted from it, it is *a priori reasonable* to believe.

It is true that we are now dealing with something *a priori* credible rather than *a priori* true. But the question still arises: what is the *explanation* of the *a priori* credibility, in the relevant kind of circumstances of ignorance, of the restricted version if what determines the fact of Jones's intention, under the residual C-conditions, is something quite detached from his or her belief? The explanation cannot be that the C-conditions are trivially formulated, for they are all, by hypothesis, substantial.

Suppose that the three conditions suggested above – possession of the appropriate concepts, attentiveness, and lack of self-deception – do indeed suffice *a priori* for Jones's opinion about his or her intention to covary with the facts. But suppose also that possession of the relevant concepts and attentiveness raise, unlike lack of self-deception, no problems of triviality. Then the matter for explanation is: why is it *a priori* reasonable to believe that, provided Jones has the relevant concepts and is attentive to the matter, he will believe that he intends to φ if and only if he does? The key thought of the variant approach will be that the matter will be nicely explained if the concept of intention works in such a way that Jones's opinions, formed under the restricted set of C-conditions, play a *defeasible* extension-determining role, with defeat conditional on the emergence of evidence that one or more of the background, positive-presumptive, conditions are not in fact met.

To elaborate a little, there are, in contrast to the case argued for colour, no conditions which can be characterised non-trivially but independently – in the sense of condition (iii) above – whose satisfaction *a priori* ensures covariance of a subject's beliefs about his intentions and the facts. But there are such non-trivially, independently specifiable conditions whose satisfaction ensures, courtesy of no *a posteriori* background beliefs, that, failing any other relevant information, a subject's opinions about his or her intentions should be accepted. And the proposed strategy of explanation is, roughly, as follows. What determines the distribution of truth-values among ascriptions of intention to a subject who has the conceptual resources to understand those ascriptions and is attentive to them are, in the first instance, nothing but the details of the subject's self-conception in relevant respects. If the assignment of truth-values, so effected, generates behavioural singularities – the subject's behaviour clashes with ingredients in his/her self-conception, or seems to call for the inclusion of ingredients which he/she is unwilling to include – then the self-deception proviso, broadly interpreted as above, may be invoked, and the subject's opinion, or lack of it, overridden. But that is not because something is shown, by the discordant behaviour, about the character of some *independently constituted* system of intentions which the subject's opinions at best reflect. When possession of a certain intention is an aspect of a self-conception that coheres well enough both internally and with the subject's behaviour, there is nothing *else* that makes it true that the intention is indeed possessed.

The view proposed is minimalist. Nothing leaner has any prospect, so far as I can see, of accommodating both the avowability and the theoreticity of intention. To be sure, explaining the *a priori* reliability of a subject's C-conditioned beliefs about his intentions will do nothing to explain the reliability of his avowals – even assuming our right to regard him as honest – unless the C-conditions in question are likely to be met. But there seems no cause to anticipate problems on that score. Attentiveness – however precisely it should be elaborated – is presumably, like lack of self-deception, a positive-presumptive condition; and a subject's possession of the appropriate concepts is prerequisite for their being able to effect the avowal in the first place. So there is every promise of a straightforward kind of explanation of the authority which avowals of intention, *qua* avowals, typically carry.

Suppose, by contrast, that subjects' best opinions about their intentions are at most extension-reflecting. Then the *a priori* reasonableness, when nothing else relevant is known, of the restricted provisional biconditional needs another explanation. And providing one will require explaining how it coheres with the view that subjects' best opinions track independently constituted states of affairs to suppose it *a priori* reasonable to think, failing evidence to the contrary, that some of the conditions on an opinion's being best are satisfied. Why, in the absence of germane evidence, is *agnosticism* about the satisfaction of, for example, the self-deception condition not a preferable stance? The three conditions collectively formulate, on this view, what it takes to ensure a certain kind of cognitive accomplishment, a feat of detection. Why is it *a priori* warranted to assume, failing information to the contrary, that a subject satisfies any such conditions?

To avoid misunderstanding, I do not mean to present the question as rhetorical. There are various ways in which it might be approached by an opponent of the extension-determining view. Perhaps it could be made out that the warrant somehow flows from the subject's nature, *qua* subject, or from the nature of the states of affairs – the intentions in question are *his* or *hers*, after all – of which the conditions ensure his or her detection. Alternatively, perhaps other examples can be produced where best opinions are extension-reflecting and yet certain of the conditions on their being best are likewise positive-presumptive, for general reasons which might be argued to apply to the present case. But it is fair to say, I think, that the onus is now on someone who prefers to think that one's best opinions about one's own intentions, etc. are extension-reflecting. Why are we, apparently, so cavalierly optimistic about our general fitness for such detection? And what, fundamentally, when we succeed in holding best opinions, *does* determine the extension of the truth-predicate among the class of judgements in question, if not those opinions themselves?

My purpose in introducing the psychological was only the limited one of canvassing a second shape which the attempt to refine and apply the order-of-determination test might assume. Perhaps enough has been said to accomplish that. But note a prospective corollary, if the extension-determining character of subjects' best opinions about their intentions and similar states, and the authority typically carried by avowals of such states, can indeed be accounted for along the lines proposed. Earlier, I criticised responses to Kripke's Skeptical Argument which – like the dispositional conception, or Chomsky's own proposal – locates the called-for meaning-constitutive facts only at the cost of obscuring subjects' non-inferential knowledge of their own meanings.[10] It would be appropriate to level a similar complaint against dispositional or theoretical construals of the notion of intention. But no such complaint is appropriate against an account of self-

---

10. [A crude version of this might go as follows. We have (sometimes) non-inferential knowledge of what we mean by an expression; but we don't have non-inferential knowledge of facts about how we are disposed to use that expression. So how can what I mean by an expression be constituted by facts about how I am disposed to use it? See p. 236 of the original version of this article. – Eds]

knowledge of intention further developed along the lines canvassed; one according to which subjects' best opinions about their intentions, *both past and present,* are properly conceived as provisionally extension-determining, and which explains how and why the opinions which they typically hold are indeed best. It will be, similarly, a perfect answer to Kripke's Skeptic to explain how judgements concerning one's own meanings, both past and present, are likewise provisionally extension-determining in the most ordinary circumstances. Challenged to justify the claim that I formerly meant addition by 'plus', it will not be necessary to locate some meaning-constitutive fact in my former behaviour or mental life. A sufficient answer need only advert to my present opinion, that addition is what I formerly meant, and still mean, and to the *a priori* reasonableness of the supposition, failing evidence to the contrary, that this opinion is best.

Responding to Kripke's Skeptic in this way does not require construal of meaning as a kind of intention; it is enough that the concepts are relevantly similar – that both sustain authoritative first-person avowals,[11] and that this circumstance is to be explained in terms of failure of the order-of-determination test. However, I can go no further into the matter here except to record the view that it is indeed with the conception of meanings as items which our best opinions may *reflect,* rather than with their reality *tout court,* that the Skeptical Argument engages.[12]

---

11. Note that the most likely reservation about the claim that they do – the thought that certain elements *of convention,* which have no counterpart in the case of intending in general, sustain my ability to mean anything in particular by a word – will undercut the Skeptic's strategy in any case, since restricting the search for facts about my former meanings to aspects of my former behaviour and conscious mental states will precisely exclude the relevant conventional (presumably social) elements. I am here indebted to Bob Hale.

12. For further discussion, see C. Wright, "On Making Up One's Mind: Wittgenstein on Intention", in P. Weingartner and G. Schurz (eds), *Logic, Philosophy of Science and Epistemology: Proceedings of the XIth International Wittgenstein Symposium, Kirchberg* (Vienna: Holder-Pichler-Temsky, 1987), pp. 391–404.

CHAPTER NINE

THE RULE-FOLLOWING CONSIDERATIONS[1]

Paul A. Boghossian

INTRODUCTION

1.

Recent years have witnessed a great resurgence of interest in the writings of the later Wittgenstein, especially with those passages – roughly, *Philosophical Investigations* §§138–242 and *Remarks on the Foundations of Mathematics*, section VI – that are concerned with the topic of rules. Much of the credit for all this excitement, unparalleled since the heyday of Wittgenstein scholarship in the early 1960s, must go to Saul Kripke's *Wittgenstein on Rules and Private Language*.[2] It is easy to explain why.

To begin with, the dialectic Kripke uncovered from Wittgenstein's discussion is enormously exciting on its own terms. On Kripke's reading, the passages on rule-following are concerned with some of the weightiest questions in the theory of meaning, questions – involving the reality, reducibility, and privacy of meaning – that occupy centre-stage in contemporary philosophy. Furthermore, Kripke represented Wittgenstein as defending a set of unified and extremely provocative claims concerning these questions. And, finally, he argued for these claims with power and clarity. The ensuing flood of articles and books on the subject of rule-following was both predictable and warranted.

1. I am grateful to many people for helpful discussion of the issues covered in this paper, including Mark Johnston, John Burgess, Jerry Fodor, Barry Loewer, Richard Rorty, Barry Allen, Larry Sklar, Crispin Wright, Saul Kripke, Neil Tennant, Steve Yablo, Nick White, and participants in various seminars at the University of Michigan. Special thanks are due to Paul Benacerraf, Jennifer Church, and David Velleman.
2. Cambridge, MA: Harvard University Press, 1982. Henceforth, 'K'.

The present paper is the result of an invitation to survey this literature. It could have been about exegetical matters, on what the recent discussions have had to teach us about the historical Wittgenstein's philosophical views. In the event, however, it is almost entirely concerned with a retrospective assessment of the *philosophical* contributions. Limitations of space dictated that a choice be made; and the philosophical assessment seemed the more fruitful thing to do.[3] Despite a lot of discussion, there is room for an improved understanding of the precise nature of Kripke's arguments, of their ultimate cogency, and of their relation to the wider discussion of meaning in contemporary philosophy of mind and language. Pulling on the thread that is Kripke's argument leads quite naturally to a discussion of many of the most significant issues occupying philosophers today; in that lies the main impetus behind the present essay.

I proceed as follows. In parts I and II, I lay out the essentials of Kripke's argument. In subsequent parts, I offer an extended critique of the dialectic it presents, considered on its own terms and independently of exegetical concerns. A discussion of the critical literature will be woven in as appropriate. The moral will not be recognizably Wittgensteinian: I shall argue that, *pace* Kripke's intent, the conception of meaning that emerges is a realist, non-reductionist, and judgement-independent conception, one which, moreover, sustains no obvious animus against private language.

I KRIPKE ON MEANING AND THE SKEPTICAL PROBLEM

THE SKEPTICAL PROBLEM

2.

As Kripke sees it, the burden of the rule-following considerations is that it cannot literally be true of any symbol that it expresses some particular concept or meaning. This is the now-famous 'skeptical conclusion' he attributes to Wittgenstein:

> [T]here is no fact about me that distinguishes between my meaning a definite function by '+' . . . and my meaning nothing at all.[4]

How is such a radical thesis to be supported? Kripke argues, in effect, by elimination: all the available facts potentially relevant to fixing the meaning of a symbol in a given speaker's repertoire – facts about how the speaker has

---

3. The main reason is that I have actually come to despair of a satisfactory interpretation of Wittgenstein's views.

4. K, p. 21.

actually used the expression, facts about how he is disposed to use it, and facts about his qualitative mental history – are canvassed, and found wanting. Adequate reflection on what it is for an expression to possess a meaning would betray, so Kripke invites us to believe, that that fact could not be constituted by any of *those*.

The claim is, of course, indisputable in connection with facts about actual use and qualitative phenomena; it is a familiar and well-assimilated lesson of, precisely, Wittgenstein's *Investigations*, that neither of those species of fact could, either in isolation or in combination, capture what it is for a symbol to possess a meaning. Much more important and controversial, however, is Kripke's rejection of a *dispositional* account of meaning facts. Why are facts about how a speaker is disposed to use an expression held to be insufficient to determine its meaning?

Kripke develops two sorts of consideration. First, the idea of meaning ①
something by a word is an idea with an infinitary character – if I mean *plus* by '+', then there are literally no end of truths about how I ought to apply the term, namely to just the members of this set of triples and not to others, if I am to use it in accord with its meaning. This is not merely an artefact of the arithmetical example; it holds for any concept. If I mean *horse* by 'horse', then there are literally no end of truths about how it would be correct for me to apply the term – to horses on Alpha Centauri, to horses in Imperial Armenia, and so on, but not to cows or cats wherever they may be – if I am to use it in accord with its meaning. But, Kripke argues, the totality of my dispositions is finite, being the dispositions of a finite being that exists for a finite time. And so, facts about dispositions cannot capture what it is for me to mean addition by '+'. ②

The second objection to a dispositional theory stems from the so-called 'normativity' of meaning. This objection is somewhat harder to state, but a rough formulation will do for now. The point is that, if I mean something by an expression, then the potential infinity of truths that are generated as a result are *normative* truths: they are truths about how I *ought* to apply the expression, if I am to apply it in accord with its meaning, not truths about how I *will* apply it. My meaning something by an expression, it appears, does not guarantee that I *will apply* it correctly; it guarantees only that there will be a fact of the matter about whether my use of it is correct. Now, this observation may be converted into a condition of adequacy on theories of meaning: any proposed candidate for being the property in virtue of which an expression has meaning must be such as to ground the normativity of meaning – it ought to be possible to read off from any alleged meaning-constituting property of a word what is the correct use of that word. And this is a requirement, Kripke maintains, that a dispositional theory cannot pass: one cannot read off a speaker's disposition to use an expression in a certain way what is the *correct* use of that expression, for to be disposed to use an expression in a certain way implies at most that one will, not that one should.

143

THE CONTENTS OF THOUGHTS

3.

But what about thoughts, intentions, and other content-bearing mental states? How do they figure in the skeptical argument? More specifically: is the skeptical thesis directed against them as well, or is it confined solely to *linguistic* representation?

It is hard to see how a convincing meaning skepticism could be confined purely to the linguistic domain, given the intimate relation between thought and language. Philosophers divide, of course, on the precise nature of this relation and, in particular, on the question of priority: Do the semantic properties of language derive from the representational properties of thought, or is it the other way round?[5] Whatever the correct answer, however, there would appear to be no plausible way to promote a *language-specific* meaning skepticism. On the former (Gricean) picture, one cannot threaten linguistic meaning without threatening thought content, since it is from thought that linguistic meaning is held to derive; and on the latter (Sellarsian) picture, one cannot threaten linguistic meaning without *thereby* threatening thought content, since it is from linguistic meaning that thought content is held to derive. Either way, content and meaning must stand or fall together.

If a skeptical thesis about linguistic meaning is to have any prospect of succeeding, then, it must also threaten the possibility of mental meaning (or content). Of course, on a Sellarsian view, that result is automatic, given a demonstration that nothing *non-mental* fixes linguistic meaning. But on a Gricean view matters are not so simple. Since the Gricean holds that linguistic items acquire their meaning from the *antecedently* fixed content of mental states, an argument to the effect that nothing non-mental fixes linguistic meaning would leave the Gricean unmoved; he needs to be given a *separate* argument against the possibility of mental content. Does Kripke see this need and does he show how it is to be met?

Colin McGinn has argued that the answer to both questions is 'no':

---

5. In the United States, it is the Gricean view, that linguistic expressions acquire their semantic properties by virtue of being used with certain intentions, beliefs, and desires, that is most influential; whereas in Britain it appears to be the Sellarsian (Wittgensteinian?) view that thinking is a form of internalized speaking – speech *in foro interno*, as Sellars likes to put it – that tends to predominate.

   For the Gricean view see H. P. Grice, 'Meaning', *Philosophical Review* (1957); and related papers. See also S. Schiffer, *Meaning* (Oxford: Clarendon Press, 1972). For the Sellarsian view see his 'Empiricism and the Philosophy of Mind', in his *Science, Perception and Reality* (London: Routledge & Kegan Paul, 1963). For a debate on the priority question see 'The Chisholm–Sellars Correspondence', in *Intentionality, Mind, and Language,* ed. A. Marras (Urbana: University of Illinois Press, 1972).

My third point . . . points up a real lacuna in Kripke's presentation of his paradox. The point is that it is necessary for Kripke to apply his paradox at the level of *concepts*; that is, he has to argue that the notion of possessing a determinate concept is likewise devoid of factual foundation . . . It cannot be said, however, that Kripke explains how this need is to be met, how this extension of the paradox to the level of concepts is to be carried out; and brief reflection shows that the exercise is by no means trivial.[6]

I think McGinn is wrong on both counts; it will be worthwhile to see why.

In fact, the suggestion that some appropriately general thought or intention constitutes the sought after meaning-determining fact comes up early in Kripke's presentation, *before* the dispositional account of meaning is considered and found wanting:

> This set of directions, I may suppose, I explicitly gave myself at some earlier time. It is engraved on my mind as on a slate. It is incompatible with the hypothesis that I meant quus. It is this set of directions, not the finite list of particular additions that I performed in the past, that justifies and determines my present response.[7]

And his response to it seems clear (pp. 16ff). The idea is that thoughts that someone may have had concerning how he is prepared to use a certain expression will help determine a meaning for that expression only if their correct interpretation is presupposed. But this is equivalent to assuming, Kripke suggests, that the skeptical challenge has been met with respect to the *expressions that figure in those thoughts*. But how was *their* meaning fixed? Not by facts about their actual or counterfactual history of use (if the argument against a dispositional account of meaning is to be believed); and not by facts concerning associated experiential episodes. Hence – on the assumption that no other sort of fact is relevant to the fixation of meaning – by nothing.

The strategy seems clear; but is it not problematic? The trouble is that it seems to depend on the assumption that thought contents are the properties of syntactically identifiable bearers – properties, that is, of expressions belonging to a 'language of thought'. And although there may be much to recommend this view, still, does Kripke really wish to rest the skeptical conclusion on so contestable a premiss?

Fortunately for the skeptical strategy, we will see below that, although a contestable premiss about thought is involved, it is nothing so rich as a language of thought hypothesis. But we will be in a position to appreciate this

---

6. Colin McGinn, *Wittgenstein on Meaning* (Oxford: Basil Blackwell, 1984), pp. 144–6.
7. K, pp. 15–16.

properly only after we have examined McGinn's claim that, even granted a linguistic model of thinking, it is still impossible to run a Kripke-style skeptical argument against thought.

THE NORMATIVITY OF MEANING

4.

McGinn writes:

> The issue of normativeness, the crucial issue for Kripke, has no clear content in application to the language of thought: what does it mean to ask whether my current employment of a word in my language of thought (i.e. the exercise of a particular concept) is *correct* in the light of my earlier employment of that word? What kind of linguistic mistake is envisaged here? . . . There is just no analogue here for the idea of linguistic incorrectness (as opposed to the *falsity* of a thought): linguistic incorrectness (of the kind we are concerned with) is using the same word with a different meaning from that originally intended (and doing so in ignorance of the change), but we cannot in this way make sense of employing a concept with a different content from that originally intended – it would just be a *different concept*.[8]

The idea of mental content cannot be threatened by Kripke, McGinn argues, because the principal requirement by which putative reconstructions of that notion are to be dispatched – the normativity requirement – has no cogent application to the language of thought. The claim calls for a somewhat more searching articulation of the normativity thesis than we have attempted so far. In what does the normativity of meaning consist?

McGinn offers the following characterization:

> The notion of normativeness Kripke wants captured is a trans-temporal notion . . . . We have an account of this normativeness when we have two things: (a) an account of what it is to mean something at a given time and (b) an account of what it is to mean the *same* thing at different times – since (Kripkean) normativeness is a matter of meaning now what one meant earlier.[9]

---

8. McGinn, 1984, p.147.
9. *Ibid.*, p. 174.

So, the later use of the expression is 'correct', according to McGinn, if it then expresses the same meaning as it did earlier; 'incorrect' if, without intending to introduce a change of meaning by explicit stipulation, it expresses a different meaning. It is in such facts as this that the normativity of meaning is said to consist.

Supposing this were the right understanding of normativity, how would it affect mental content skepticism? McGinn says that the problem is that we cannot make sense of employing a concept with a different content from that originally intended – it would just be a different concept. But although that is certainly true, it is also irrelevant: what we need to make sense of is not employing a *concept* with a different content from that originally intended, but employing an *expression in the language of thought* with a different content from that originally intended, which is a rather different matter.

As it happens, however, it is an idea that is equally problematic. The difficulty is that we do not have the sort of access to the expressions of our language of thought that an attribution to us of semantic intentions in respect of them would appear to presuppose. You cannot intend that some expression have a certain meaning unless you are able to refer to that expression independently of its semantic properties. But we have no such independent access to the expressions of our language of thought; we do not, for instance, know what they look like. So we cannot have semantic intentions in respect of them and, hence, cannot make sense of using them correctly or incorrectly in the sense defined by McGinn.

If McGinn's understanding of normativity were the correct one, then, it would indeed be difficult to see how it could operate at the level of thought (though not quite for the reasons he gives). It ought to be clear, however, that the 'normativity' requirement defined by McGinn has nothing much to do with the concept of meaning *per se* and is not the requirement that Kripke is operating with.

We may appreciate this point by observing that the requirement defined by McGinn could hardly act as a substantive constraint on theories of meaning, even where these are theories solely of *linguistic* meaning. *Any* theory of meaning that provided an account of what speakers mean by their expressions at arbitrary times – however crazy that theory may otherwise be – would satisfy McGinn's constraint. In particular, the main theory alleged by Kripke to founder on the normativity requirement would easily pass it on McGinn's reading: since there are perfectly determinate facts about what dispositions are associated with a given expression at a given time – or, rather, since it is no part of Kripke's intent to deny that there are – it is always possible to ask whether an expression has the same or a different meaning on a dispositional theory, thus satisfying McGinn's requirement. How to explain, then, Kripke's claim that a dispositional theory founders precisely on the normativity requirement?

5.

The answer is that the normativity requirement is not the thesis McGinn outlines. What is it then?

Suppose the expression 'green' means *green*. It follows immediately that the expression 'green' applies *correctly* only to *these* things (the green ones) and not to *those* (the non-greens). The fact that the expression means something implies, that is, a whole set of *normative* truths about my behaviour with that expression: namely, that my use of it is correct in application to certain objects and not in application to others. This is not, as McGinn would have it, a relation between meaning something by an expression at one time and meaning something by it at some later time; it is rather, a relation between meaning something by it at some time and its *use at that time*.

The normativity of meaning turns out to be, in other words, simply a new name for the familiar fact that, regardless of whether one thinks of meaning in truth-theoretic or assertion-theoretic terms, meaningful expressions possess conditions of *correct use*. (On the one construal, correctness consists in *true* use, on the other, in *warranted* use.) Kripke's insight was to realize that this observation may be converted into a condition of adequacy on theories of the determination of meaning: any proposed candidate for the property in virtue of which an expression has meaning must be such as to ground the 'normativity' of meaning – it ought to be possible to read off from any alleged meaning-constituting property of a word what is the correct use of that word. It is easy to see how, on this understanding of the requirement in question, a dispositional theory might appear to fail it: for, it would seem, one cannot read off a disposition to use a word in a certain way what is the correct use of that word, for to be disposed to use a word in a certain way implies at most that one *will,* not that one *should* (one can have dispositions to use words *incorrectly*).[10]

6.

With this clarification of the normativity thesis in place we are finally in a position to settle the question: can Kripke develop the same sort of meaning-skeptical argument against a language of thought as he develops against public language? And the answer is: clearly, yes. For: what fixes the meaning of expressions in the language of thought? Not other thoughts, on pain of vicious regress. Not facts about the actual tokening of such expressions or

---

10. As we shall see below, however, the question whether dispositional accounts of meaning really do succumb to the normativity objection is much more complicated than this. I am not here trying to assess the objection, but merely to state it.

WE CANNOT BOTH BE RIGHT DOING TWO DIFF THINGS

facts about associated qualitative episodes, for familiar reasons. And not dispositional facts about the tokening of such expressions, for, since meaningful expressions of mentalese possess conditions of correct use in precisely the same sense as public language expressions do, because correctness cannot be reconstructed dispositionally. So, nothing fixes their meaning.

Indeed, we are also now in a position to see, as promised, that nothing so rich as a language of thought hypothesis is strictly needed. A language of thought model is composed out of two theses: (a) that thinking the thought that *p* involves tokening an item – a representation – that means that *p*; and (b) that the representation whose tokening is so involved possesses a combinatorial syntactic and semantic structure. In other words, according to a language of thought hypothesis, thought contents are the semantic properties of syntactically and semantically *structured bearers*. But it should be quite clear that nothing in the skeptical argument depends on the assumption of *structure*: even if the representation were to possess no internal syntax, we could still ask, in proper Kripkean fashion, what its correctness conditions are and in virtue of what they are determined.

It would appear, however, that the skeptical argument's strategy does presuppose that content properties have *some* sort of bearer (even if not necessarily a structured one). For, otherwise, there will he no natural way to formulate a dispositional theory of thought content, and no natural way to bring the normativity requirement to bear against it. There has to be *something* – a state, event, or particular, it need not matter which – whose disposition to get tokened under certain circumstances constitutes, on a dispositional theory, its possession of a certain content. And although this commitment is, I suppose, strictly speaking contestable, it is also very natural and plausible. After all, contents do not figure in a mental life except as subtended by a particular *mode* – belief, desire, judgement, wish – and, hence, are naturally understood as the properties of the states or events that instantiate those modes.

And so we see that the skeptical argument must, can, and does (in intent, anyway) include mental content within the scope of the skepticism it aims to promote.[11]

THE CONSTITUTIVE NATURE OF THE SKEPTICAL PROBLEM

7.

Having a meaning is essentially a matter of possessing a correctness condition. And the skeptical challenge is to explain how anything could possess *that*.

---

11. Since nothing will hang on it, and since it will ease exposition, I shall henceforth write as if a language of thought hypothesis were true.

Notice, by the way, that I have stated the skeptical problem about meaning without once mentioning Kripke's notorious skeptic. That character, as everyone knows, proceeds by inviting his interlocutor to defend a claim about what he previously meant by the expression '+'. The interlocutor innocently assumes himself to have meant addition; but the skeptic challenges him to prove that the concept in question was not in fact *quaddition*, where quaddition is just like addition, except for a singularity at a point not previously encountered in the interlocutor's arithmetical practice.

It may seem, then, that the skeptical problem I have described could not be Kripke's. For Kripke's problem appears to be essentially *epistemological* in character – it concerns a speaker's ability to defend a particular meaning ascription; whereas the problem I have outlined is *constitutive*, not epistemological – its topic is the *possibility* of meaning, not our knowledge of it.

In fact, however, the two problems are the same; Kripke merely chooses to present the constitutive problem in an epistemological guise. Epistemological skepticism about a given class of judgements is the view that our actual cognitive capacities are incapable of delivering justified opinions concerning judgements in that class. Kripke's skeptic is not after a thesis of that sort. This is evident from the fact that his interlocutor, in being challenged to justify his claim that he meant addition by '+', is permitted *complete and omniscient* access to all the facts about his previous behavioural, mental, and physical history; he is not restricted to the sort of knowledge that an ordinary creature, equipped with ordinary cognitive powers, would be expected to possess.[12] Kripke's skeptical scenario is, thus, completely unsuited to promoting an epistemological skepticism. What it *is* suited for is the promotion of a constitutive skepticism. For if his skeptic is able to show that, even with the benefit of access to all the relevant facts, his interlocutor is still unable to justify any particular claim about what he meant, that would leave us no choice but to conclude that there are no facts about meaning.[13]

Pace many of Kripke's readers, then, the problem is not – not even in part – epistemological skepticism about meaning.[14] But, of course, one may agree

---

12. McGinn's failure to note this leads him to wonder how the constitutive and epistemological aspects of Kripke's discussion are related, 'for the epistemological claim is clearly distinct from the metaphysical claim' (McGinn, 1984, p. 149).

13. This point is made very nicely by Crispin Wright in his 'Kripke's Account of the Argument Against Private Language', *Journal of Philosophy* (1984), pp. 761–2. Wright, however, discerns another sort of epistemological dimension to the skeptical problem. I will discuss that below.

14. For example, McGinn, 1984, pp. 140–50; G. Baker and P. Hacker, 'On Misunderstanding Wittgenstein: Kripke's Private Language Argument', *Synthese* (1984), pp. 409–10. Neil Tennant has complained that Kripke's skeptic does not ultimately supply a convincing bent-rule reinterpretation of his interlocutor's words. See his *The Taming of the True*, Ch. 4. Tennant may well be right about this. But here again, I think the perception that this affects the force of the skeptical problem about meaning is a result of taking the dialogic setting too seriously. The constitutive problem about meaning – how could there be so much as a correctness condition – can be stated quite forcefully without the actual provision of a convincing global reinterpretation of a person's words.

that the problem is constitutive in character, and yet believe it to have an epistemological dimension. According to Crispin Wright, for example, Kripke is not interested in the mere possibility of correctness conditions; he is interested in the possibility of correctness conditions that may be, at least in one's own case, *known non-inferentially*.[15] The problem is essentially constitutive in character; but acceptable answers to it are to be subject to an epistemic constraint.

I do not wish to argue about this at length. It does seem to me that, once we have corrected for the distortions induced by the dialogic setting, there ought not to be any residual temptation to think that epistemological considerations are playing a critical role in Kripke's argument. In any case, whatever intention Kripke may have had, the considerations he adduces on behalf of the skeptical conclusion appear to owe nothing to epistemological constraints and can be stated without their help.[16] That, anyway, is how I shall present them.

THE 'RULE-FOLLOWING' CONSIDERATIONS?

8.

It would not be inappropriate to wonder at this point what all this has to do with the topic of *rule-following?* Where, precisely, is the connection between the concepts of meaning and content, on the one hand, and the concept of following a rule, on the other, forged? I shall argue that, in an important sense, the answer is 'nowhere', and hence that 'the rule-following considerations' is, strictly speaking, a misnomer for the discussion on offer.

Many writers seem to assume that the connection is straightforward; they may be represented as reasoning as follows. Expressions come to have correctness conditions as a result of people following rules in respect of them; hence, exploring the possibility of correctness is tantamount to exploring the possibility of rule-following.

But, at least on the ordinary understanding of the concept of following a rule, it cannot be true of *all* expressions – in particular, it cannot be true of *mental* expressions – that they come to have correctness conditions as a result of people following rules in respect of them. The point is that the ordinary concept of following a rule – as opposed to that of merely conforming to one – is the concept of an *intentional* act: it involves the intentional attempt to bring one's behaviour in line with the dictates of some grasped rule. Crispin Wright has described this intuitive conception very clearly:

---

15. See Wright, 1984, pp. 772–5.
16. With one relatively minor exception to be noted below.

Correctly applying a rule to a new case will, it is natural to think, typically involve a double success: it is necessary both to apprehend relevant features of the presented situation and to know what, in the light of those apprehended features, will fit or fail to fit the rule. Correctly castling in the course of a game of chess, for instance, will depend both on apprehension of the configuration of chessmen at the time of the move, and on a knowledge of whether that configuration (and the previous course of the game) permits castling at that point.[17]

As such, however, the ordinary concept of following a rule is the concept of an act among whose causal antecendents lie contentful mental states; consequently, it is a concept that *presupposes* the idea of a correctness condition, not one that can, in full generality, help explain it. Since it makes essential play with the idea of a propositional attitude, which in turn makes essential play with the idea of content, rule-following in this sense presupposes that *mental expressions* have conditions of correct application. On pain of regress, then, it cannot be true that mental expressions themselves acquire meaning as a result of anyone following rules in respect of them.

What Kripke's discussion is concerned with is the possibility of correctness; so long as we keep that clearly in mind, talk of 'rule-following' is harmless. Simon Blackburn has captured this perspective very well:

> I intend no particular theoretical implications by talking of rules here. The topic is that there is such a thing as the correct and incorrect application of a term, and to say that there is such a thing is no more than to say that there is truth and falsity. I shall talk indifferently of there being correctness and incorrectness, of words being rule-governed, and of their obeying principles of application. Whatever this is, it is the fact that distinguishes the production of a term from mere noise, and turns utterance into assertion – into the making of judgement.[18]

---

17. Crispin Wright: 'Wittgenstein's Rule-Following Considerations and the Central Project of Theoretical Linguistics', in *Reflections on Chomsky*, ed. A. George (Oxford: Basil Blackwell, 1989), p. 255.
18. Simon Blackburn, 'The Individual Strikes Back', *Synthese*, (1984), pp. 281–2 (this volume Ch. 3). My only disagreement with this passage concerns its identification of correctness conditions with truth conditions. Truth conditions are simply one species of a correctness condition; proof conditions or justification conditions supply further instances.

II THE SKEPTICAL SOLUTION

A NON-FACTUALIST CONCEPTION OF MEANING

9.

Having established to his satisfaction that no word could have the property of expressing a certain meaning, Kripke turns to asking how this conclusion is to be accommodated. The question is urgent, in his view, because the conclusion threatens to be not merely shocking but paradoxical. The trouble is that we would ordinarily take a remark to the effect that there could not be any such thing as the fact that I mean something by the '+' sign to entail that there is nothing I could mean by the use of that sign. Applied quite generally, across all signs and all people, the claim becomes the seemingly paradoxical and self-refuting thesis that no one could mean anything by their use of linguistic expressions.

A skepticism about meaning facts would appear to be, then, prima facie anyway, an unstable position. Sustaining it requires showing that what it asserts does not ultimately lapse into a form of pragmatic incoherence. What is called for, in other words, is a rehabilitation of our ordinary practice of attributing content to our thoughts and utterances, which nevertheless conserves the skeptical thesis that there are no facts for such attributions to answer to. That is what the 'skeptical solution' is designed to do. It is alleged to have the following startling consequence: the idea of a language whose meanings are constituted solely out of an individual's speaker's properties, considered 'completely in isolation from any wider community to which he may belong', is incoherent.[19]

The skeptical solution has two parts that are usefully distinguished. The first consists in the suggestion that we replace the notion of truth conditions, in our intuitive picture of sentence meaning, by that of *assertibility* conditions. The second consists in a *description* of the assertibility conditions for meaning-attributing sentences, in the course of which it is argued that it is essential to such sentences that their assertibility conditions advert to the actions or dispositions of a community.

The adjustment recommended in the first part is supposed to help because

---

19. Following Goldfarb, we may call this the concept of a 'solitary language'. See his 'Kripke on Wittgenstein on Rules', *Journal of Philosophy,* 1985. Goldfarb goes on to say that the idea of a solitary language is more general than that of a Wittgensteinian 'private language', for the latter essentially involves the idea of *necessary unintelligibility* to another. It is hard to assess this, because it is hard to know how to interpret 'necessary unintelligibility'. Surely it cannot mean: a language to whose predicates no two people *could* attach the same descriptive conditions. And it is not clear what it is to mean, if not that. For useful discussion see C. Wright, 'Does *Philosophical Investigations* 258–60 Suggest a Cogent Argument Against Private Language?', in *Subject, Thought and Context,* ed. P. Pettit and J. McDowell (Oxford: Clarendon Press, 1986).

if we suppose that facts or truth conditions are of the essence of meaningful assertion, it will follow from the skeptical conclusion that assertions that anyone ever means anything are meaningless. On the other hand, if we apply to these assertions the tests suggested . . . no such conclusion follows. All that is needed to legitimize assertions that someone means something is that there be roughly specifiable circumstances under which they are legitimately assertible, and that the game of asserting them has a role in our lives. No supposition that 'facts correspond' to those assertions is needed.[20]

The proposed account is, in effect, a *global* non-factualism: sentence significance is construed quite generally in assertion-theoretic terms and no invidious distinction is drawn between the sort of significance possessed by meaning-attributing sentences and that possessed by sentences of other types.

THE ARGUMENT AGAINST SOLITARY LANGUAGE

10.

The argument against 'solitary language' emerges, according to Kripke, from the observation that, so long as a speaker is considered in isolation we can assign no assertibility conditions to judgements to the effect that he has misapplied a symbol in his repertoire:

> [I]f we confine ourselves to looking at one person alone, this is as far as we can go . . . There are no circumstances under which we can say that, even if he inclines to say '125', he should have said '5', or *vice-versa* . . . Under what circumstances can he be wrong? No one else by looking at his mind or behavior alone can say something like, 'He is wrong if he does not accord with his own intention'; the whole point of the skeptical argument was that there are no facts about him in virtue of which he accords with his intentions or not.[21]

The possibility of error, however, is essential to our ordinary concept of meaning, and can only be accommodated if we widen our gaze and take into consideration the interaction between our imagined rule-follower and a linguistic community. Were we to do so, Kripke continues, we could introduce assertibility conditions for judgements about error in terms of the agreement, or lack of it, between a given speaker's propensities in the use of a term and

---

20. K, pp. 77–8.
21. *Ibid.*, p. 88.

the community's. Since, however, this would appear to be the *only* way to give substance to the correlative notions of error and correctness, no one considered wholly in isolation from other speakers could be said to mean anything. And so a solitary language is impossible.

Let us turn now to an assessment of the various central aspects of Kripke's argument.

III ASSESSMENT OF THE ARGUMENT AGAINST SOLITARY LANGUAGE

CONSTITUTIVE ACCOUNTS AND SOLITARY LANGUAGE

11.

Kripke is very clear about the limited, wholly descriptive nature of the skeptical solution, at least in his 'official' explications of the view:

> We have to see under what circumstances attributions of meaning are made and what role these attributions play in our lives. Following Wittgenstein's exhortation not to think but to look, we will not reason *a priori* about the role such statements *ought* to play; rather we will find out what circumstances *actually* license such assertions and what role this license *actually* plays. It is important to realize that we are *not* looking for necessary and sufficient conditions (truth conditions) for following a rule, or an analysis of what such rule-following 'consists in'. Indeed such conditions would constitute a 'straight' solution to the skeptical problem, and have been rejected.[22]

It is important to see that the counselled modesty – we will not reason a priori about the role such statements ought to play – is compulsory. The assertibility conditions may not be understood to provide the content (or truth conditions) of the meaning-attributing sentences, on pain of falling prey to the accepted skeptical considerations. (That is why the solution on offer has to be *skeptical*: it has already been conceded that nothing could cogently amount to the fact that a meaning sentence reports.) It would appear to follow from this, however, that the skeptical solution can do no more than record the conditions under which speakers in fact consider the attribution of a certain concept warranted and the endorsement of a particular response appropriate. The Wittgensteinian exhortation 'not to think but to look' is not merely (as it may be) good advice; the modesty it counsels is enforced by the fact that truth conditions for these sentences has been jettisoned. For how, in

---

22. *Ibid.*, pp. 86–7.

the absence of a conception of the truth conditions of meaning attributing sentences, could the project of providing an account of their assertion conditions aspire to anything more than descriptive adequacy? Were we equipped with an account of their truth conditions, of course, we might be able to reason a priori about what their assertion conditions *ought* to be and, hence, potentially, to revise the conditions for assertion *actually* accepted for them. But without the benefit of such an account there is no scope for a more ambitious project: a descriptively adequate account of the *actual* assertion conditions for such sentences is the most one may cogently aim for.

If this is correct, however, we ought to be puzzled about how the skeptical solution is going to deliver a conclusion against solitary language of the requisite modal force: namely, that there *could not* be such a language. For even if it were true that our *actual* assertibility conditions for meaning-attributing sentences advert to the dispositions of a community, the most that would license saying is that *our* language is not solitary. And this would be a lot less than the result we were promised: namely, that any *possible* language has to be communal.

[handwritten: He shows public lang. to be possible]

COMMUNAL ASSERTIBILITY CONDITIONS?

12.

Putting this worry to one side, let us ask whether it is in fact true that, if we accept the skeptical conclusion, we cannot introduce substantive assertibility conditions for meaning-attributions that do not advert to the dispositions of a community of speakers? It appears, on the contrary, that not only can we introduce such conditions, but have actually done so.[23] Consider the following:

(A) It is warranted to assert of Jones that he means addition by '+', provided he has responded with the *sum* in reply to most arithmetical queries posed thus far.

As a description of our practice, (A) is, of course, quite rough: room has to be made for the importance of systematic deviations, the greater importance attaching to simple cases, and many other such factors. But all these refinements may be safely ignored for the purpose of raising the following critical question: what in the skeptical conclusion rules out attributions of form (A)? It had better rule them out, of course, if the argument against solitary language is to be sustained, for (A) adverts to no one other than the

---

23. This sort of rejoinder is canvassed both in Goldfarb, 1985, and in McGinn, 1984.

individual. But as Goldfarb points out, there appears to be nothing in the skeptical conclusion that will rule it out.[24] It can hardly be objected that the interpretation of 'sum' is being presupposed in the statement of the condition, for the skeptical solution is not meant to be a *straight* solution to the problem about meaning; as Kripke himself says, in fending off a similar imagined objection to his own account of the assertibility conditions:

> What Wittgenstein is doing is describing the utility in our lives of a certain practice. Necessarily he must give this description in our own language. As in the case of any such use of our language, a participant in another form of life might apply various terms in the description (such as 'agreement') in a non-standard 'quus-like' way. . . . This cannot be an objection to Wittgenstein's solution unless he is to be prohibited from any use of language at all.[25]

Nor is there any problem in the assumption that it is a genuinely factual matter what any two numbers sum to; as Kripke himself repeatedly emphasizes, the skeptical argument does not threaten the existence of *mathematical* facts. But how, then, is (A) to be ruled out, and the argument against solitary language preserved?

13.

Could it perhaps be argued that (A) is permissible though *parasitic* on the communal assertibility conditions Kripke outlines? As a matter of fact, just the opposite seems true.[26]

Kripke's communitarian account of meaning-attributions runs as follows:

> Smith will judge Jones to mean addition by 'plus' only if he judges that Jones's answers to particular addition problems agree with those he is inclined to give. . . . If Jones consistently fails to give responses in agreement. . . with Smith's, Smith will judge that he does not mean addition by 'plus'. Even if Jones did mean it in the past, the present deviation will justify Smith in judging that he has lapsed.[27]

According to this account, then, I will judge that Jones means addition by 'plus' only if Jones uses 'plus' enough times in the same way I am inclined to use it. As a rough description of our practice, and many important

---

24. *Ibid.*
25. K, p. 146.
26. This is argued in McGinn, 1984, pp. 185–7, from which this point is derived.
27. K, p. 91.

refinements aside, this seems acceptable enough. One of the refinements that is called for, however, exposes the fact that Kripke's communitarian conditions are parasitic on the solitary conditions, and not the other way round.

It would be absurd for me, under conditions where I had good reason to believe that I had become prone to making arithmetical mistakes – perhaps owing to intoxication or senility or whatever – to insist on agreement with me as a precondition for crediting Jones with mastery of the concept of addition. And this would appear to show that, at a minimum, Kripke's communitarian account must be modified to read:

(B) It is warranted to assert of Jones that he means addition by '+', provided he agrees with my responses to arithmetical queries, *under conditions where I have been a reliable computer of sums.*

But this modification would seem immediately to reveal that the reference to 'my own responses' is idle, and that the basic assertion condition I accept is just (A):

It is warranted to assert of Jones that he means addition by '+', provided he has responded with the *sum* in reply to most arithmetical queries posed thus far.

It would appear, in other words, that the acceptability of the communitarian conditions is strongly parasitic on the acceptability of the solitary ones, and not the other way around.

In sum: both because it is difficult (impossible?) to generate constitutive results out of non-constitutive accounts, and because our actual assertibility conditions for meaning ascriptions appear not to be communitarian, I conclude that the skeptical solution does not yield a convincing argument against solitary language.

IV IRREALIST CONCEPTIONS OF MEANING

14.

The argument against solitary language was supposed to flow from the adjusted understanding of sentence significance forced by the skeptical conclusion. The skeptical conclusion has it that it cannot literally be true of any symbol that it expresses a particular meaning: there is no appropriate fact for a meaning-attributing sentence to report. The skeptical solution's recommendation is that we blunt the force of this result by refusing to think of sentence significance in terms of possession of truth conditions, or a capacity to state facts. We should think of it, rather, in terms of possession of assertibility conditions. But is this solution forced? Are there not, perhaps, other ways of accommodating the skeptical conclusion?

The solution on offer is bound to strike one as an overreaction, at least at first blush, in two possible respects. First, in that it opts for a form of *non-factualism*, as opposed to an *error* theory; and second, in that the recommended non-factualism is *global*, rather than restricted solely to the region of discourse – meaning talk – that is directly affected by the skeptical result it seeks to accommodate.

Semantically speaking, the most conservative reaction to the news that nothing has the property of being a witch is not to adopt a non-factualist conception of witch talk, it is to offer an *error* conception of such talk. An error conception of a given region of discourse conserves the region's semantical appearances – predicates are still understood to express properties, declarative sentences to possess truth conditions; the ontological discovery is taken to exhibit – merely – the systematic falsity of the region's (positive, atomic) sentences.[28] *So MEANING EXPRESSIONS ARE MERELY FALSE?*

Could not the moral of the skeptical argument be understood to consist in an error conception of meaning discourse? It could not, for an error conception of such discourse, in contrast with error conceptions of other regions, is of doubtful coherence. The view in question would consist in the claim that all meaning-attributions are false:

(1) For any S: ⌜S means that p⌝ is false.

But the disquotational properties of the truth predicate guarantee that (1) entails *A BIT TO QUICK*

(2) For any S: ⌜S⌝ has no meaning.

(1) implies, that is, that no sentence whatever possesses a meaning. Since, however, a sentence cannot be *false* unless it is meaningful to begin with, this in turn implies that (1) cannot be true: for what (1) says is that some sentences – namely meaning-attributing sentences – are false.[29]

So it appears that Kripke was right to avoid an error conception of meaning discourse. But does his *non-factualist* conception fare any better?

---

28. See John Mackie, *Ethics: Inventing Right and Wrong* (London: Penguin, 1977) for such a conception of moral discourse.

29. An error conception of meaning has been advocated by Paul Churchland; see his 'Eliminative Materialism and the Propositional Attitudes', *Journal of Philosophy* (1981). This argument is elaborated and defended in my 'The Status of Content', *Philosophical Review* (April 1990).

15.

The canonical formulation of a non-factualist view – and the one that Kripke himself favours – has it that some targeted declarative sentence is not genuinely truth-conditional. A non-factualism about meaning consists, that is, in the view that

(3) For any S, p: ⌜S means that p⌝ is not truth-conditional.

As I noted above, however, the projectivism recommended by the skeptical solution is intended to apply globally: it is not confined solely to meaning-attributing sentences. Thus,

(4) For any S: ⌜S⌝ is not truth conditional.

Why does Kripke adopt so extreme a view? Why does he not suggest merely that we abandon a truth-conditional model for *semantic* discourse, while preserving it, as seems natural, for at least *some* regions of the rest of language? Kripke does not say. But it may be that he glimpsed that the global character of the projectivism is in fact *forced* in the present case.[30] For consider a non-factualism solely about meaning – the view that, since there is no such property as a word's meaning something, and hence no such fact, no meaning-attributing sentence can be truth-conditional. Since the truth-condition of any sentence S is (in part, anyway) a function of its meaning, a non-factualism about meaning will enjoin a non-factualism about truth-conditions: what truth-condition S possesses could hardly be a factual matter if that in virtue of which it has a particular truth-condition is not itself a factual matter. And so we have it that (3) entails:

(5) For all S, p: ⌜S has truth-condition p⌝ is not truth-conditional.

However, since courtesy of the disquotational properties of the truth predicate, a sentence of the form ⌜S has truth-condition p⌝ is true if and only if S has truth-condition p, and since (5) has it that ⌜S has truth-condition p⌝ is never simply true, it follows that

(4) For any S: ⌜S⌝ is not truth-conditional

just as predicted.

It is, then, a fascinating consequence of a non-factualism about meaning that it entails a *global* non-factualism; in this respect, if no other, a non-factualism about meaning distinguishes itself from a similar thesis about *any*

---

30. Somewhat different arguments are given for this both in Crispin Wright's 'Kripke's Account', 1984, pp. 769–70 and in my 'Meaning, Content and Rules', in Part I of my PhD dissertation 'Essays on Meaning and Belief', Princeton University, 1986.

other subject matter. Crispin Wright has suggested that it also renders it irremediably problematic:

> it is doubtful that it is coherent to suppose that projectivist views could be applied quite globally. For, however exactly the distinction be drawn between fact-stating and non-fact-stating discourse, the projectivist will presumably want it to come by way of a *discovery* that certain statements fail to qualify for the former class; a statement of the conclusion of the skeptical argument, for instance, is not *itself* to be projective.[31]

It is hard not to sympathize with Wright's suggestion that there must be something unstable about a projectivist thesis that is itself within the scope of the projectivism it recommends. But it is also not entirely clear to me in what the instability consists. To be sure, a global projectivism would have to admit that it is no more than *assertible* that no sentence possesses a truth condition. But what is wrong with that? If there is an instability here, it is not a transparent one.

16.

In fact, however, I do believe that a non-factualism about meaning is unstable, but not because of its global character. Rather, the reasons have to do with the clash between what you have to suppose about truth in order to frame a non-factualist thesis about anything, and what you have to suppose about truth as a result of accepting a non-factualism about meaning. I have developed the argument for this in some detail elsewhere;[32] here I have space only to sketch its outlines.

Consider a non-factualist thesis about, say, the good:

(7) All sentences of the form ⌜x is good⌝ are not truth-conditional.

The point that needs to be kept in focus is that the sentence of which truth conditions are being denied is a significant *declarative* sentence. For this fact immediately implies that the concept of truth in terms of which the non-factualist thesis is framed cannot be the *deflationary* concept that A. J. Ayer succinctly described as follows:

> ... to say that *p* is true is simply a way of asserting *p*. . . . The traditional conception of truth as a 'real quality' or a 'real relation' is

---

31. *Ibid.*, p. 770.
32. In 'The Status of Content', 1990.

due, like most philosophical mistakes, to a failure to analyze sentences correctly . . . . There are sentences in which the word 'truth' seems to stand for something real . . . [but] our analysis has shown that the word 'truth' does not stand for anything.[33]

If the concept of truth were, as Ayer claims in this passage, merely the concept of a device for semantic ascent, and not the concept of some genuine property – some 'real relation' – that a sentence (or thought) may enjoy, then non-factualism is nowhere a coherent option. For on a deflationary understanding of truth, a sentence will be truth-conditional provided only that it is apt for semantic ascent; and it will be apt for semantic ascent provided only that it is a significant, declarative sentence. But it is constitutive of a non-factualist thesis precisely that it denies, of some targeted, significant, declarative sentence, that it is truth-conditional. It follows, therefore, that a non-factualism about any subject matter presupposes a conception of truth richer than the deflationary: it is committed to holding that the predicate 'true' stands for some sort of language-independent property, eligibility for which will not be certified purely by the fact that a sentence is declarative and significant. Otherwise, there will be no understanding its claim that a significant sentence, declarative in form, fails to possess truth-conditions.

So we have it that any non-factualist thesis presupposes that truth is, as I shall henceforth put it, *robust*. But, now, notice that judgements about whether an object possesses a robust property could hardly fail to be factual. If P is some genuinely robust property, then it is hard to see how there could fail to be a fact of the matter about whether an object has P. It does not matter if P is subjective or otherwise dependent upon our responses. So long as it is a genuine, language-independent property, judgements about it will have to be factual, will have to be possessed of robust truth-conditions. In particular, if *truth* is a robust property, then judgements about a sentence's truth value must themselves be factual. But we saw earlier – see (5) above – that a non-factualist thesis about meaning implies that judgements about a sentence's truth cannot be factual: whether a certain sentence is true cannot be a factual matter if its meaning is not. And this exposes the contradiction we have been stalking: a non-factualism about meaning implies both that truth is robust and that it is not.

17.

It is hard to do justice to the issues involved within the confines of the present essay.[34] I do hope, however, that the preceding discussion has succeeded in

---

33. A. J. Ayer, *Language, Truth and Logic* (New York: Dover, 1952), p. 89.
34. Again, for a more detailed account, see 'The Status of Content', 1990.

sowing some doubts about the cogency of irrealist conceptions of meaning – whether in the form of a non-factualism about meaning, as in the skeptical solution, or an error theory, as suggested, for instance, by Churchland.

The uncompromising strength of the claim is bound to arouse suspicion. Irrealist conceptions of other domains may not be particularly appealing or plausible, but they are not incoherent. Why should matters stand differently with meaning discourse?

The source of the asymmetry is actually not that hard to track down. It consists in the fact that error and non-factualist theories about *any* subject matter presuppose certain claims about truth and truth-conditions, that an error or non-factualist conception directed precisely at our talk of meaning itself ends up denying. Not surprisingly the ensuing result is unstable.

Thus, an error thesis about any subject matter presupposes that the target sentences are truth-conditional. But an error thesis directed precisely at our talk about meaning entails the denial of that presupposition. Thus, also, a non-factualism about any subject matter presupposes a robust conception of truth. But a non-factualism directed precisely at our talk about meaning entails the denial of that presupposition.

If these considerations are correct, then, they would show that the skeptical conclusion cannot be sustained: there appears to be no stable way of accommodating the claim that there are no truths about meaning. Something must be wrong, therefore, with the argument that appeared to lead us to it. What could it be?

V REDUCTIVE ACCOUNTS OF MEANING

18.

The skeptical argument has been faulted on a number of grounds, the most important being:

- That its arguments against dispositional accounts of meaning do not work.
- That it neglects to consider all the available naturalistic facts.
- That its conclusion depends on an unargued reductionism.

The first two objections issue from a naturalistic perspective: they claim that the skeptical argument fails to establish its thesis, even granted a restriction to *naturalistic* facts and properties. The final objection concedes the failure of naturalism, but charges that the skeptical argument is powerless against an appropriately anti-reductionist construal of meaning. In this part I shall examine the naturalistic objections, and in the next the anti-reductionist suggestion.

I should say at the outset, however, that I see no merit to objections of the second kind and will not discuss them in any detail here. All the suggestions that I have seen to the effect that Kripke ignores various viable reduction bases for meaning facts seem to me to rest on misunderstanding. Colin McGinn, for example, claims that Kripke neglects to consider the possibility that possession of a concept might consist in possession of a certain sort of capacity. Capacities, McGinn explains, are distinct from dispositions and are better suited to meet the normativity constraint.[35] This rests on the misunderstanding of normativity outlined above. Warren Goldfarb charges that Kripke neglects to consider causal/informational accounts of the determination of meaning.[36] This derives from a failure to see that, in all essential respects, a causal theory of meaning is simply one species of a dispositional theory of meaning, an account that is, of course, extensively discussed by Kripke. It is unfortunate that this connection is obscured in Kripke's discussion. Because Kripke illustrates the skeptical problem through the use of an *arithmetical* example, he tends, understandably, to focus on *conceptual role* versions of a dispositional account of meaning, rather than on causal/informational versions. This has given rise to the impression that his discussion of dispositionalism does not cover causal theories. But the impression is misleading. For the root form of a causal/informational theory may be given by the following basic formula:

O means (property) P by predicate S iff (it is a counterfactual supporting generalization that) O is disposed to apply S to P.

DISPOSITIONS AND MEANING: FINITUDE

19.

The single most important strand in the skeptical argument consists in the considerations against dispositional theories of meaning. It would be hard to exaggerate the importance of such theories for contemporary philosophy of mind and semantics: as I have just indicated, the most influential contemporary theories of content-determination – 'informational' theories and 'conceptual-role' theories – are both forms of a dispositional account.[37] In my discussion I shall tend to concentrate, for the sake of concreteness, on

---

35. See McGinn, 1984, pp. 168–74.
36. See Goldfarb, 1985, n. 13.
37. For correlational theories see: F. Dretske, *Knowledge and the Flow of Information* (Cambridge, MA: MIT Press, 1981); D. Stampe, 'Towards a Causal Theory of Linguistic Representation', *Midwest Studies in Philosophy*, vol. 2 (Minneapolis: University of Minnesota Press, 1977); Jerry Fodor, *Psychosemantics* (Cambridge, MA: MIT Press, 1987). For conceptual role theories see:

informational theories of the content of *mental* symbols; but the issues that arise are general and apply to any dispositional theory whatever!?

The root form of an information-style dispositional theory is this:

> My mental symbol 'horse' expresses whatever property I am disposed to apply it to.

Kripke's first objection amounts, in effect, to suggesting that there will always be a serious *indeterminacy in what my dispositions are,* thus rendering dispositional properties an inappropriate reduction base for meaning properties. For, Kripke argues, if it is indeed the property *horse* that I am disposed to apply the term to, then I should be disposed to apply it to *all* horses, including horses so far away and so far in the past that it would be nonsense to suppose I could ever get into causal contact with them. Otherwise, what is to say that my disposition is not a disposition to apply the term to the property *nearby horse,* or some such? But no one can have a disposition to call all horses 'horse', for no one can have a disposition with respect to inaccessible objects.

The argument does not convince. Of course, the *counterfactual*

> If I were now to go to Alpha Centauri, I would call the horses there 'horse'

is false. If I were now to go to Alpha Centauri, I probably would not be in any position to call anything by any name, for I would probably die before I got there. But that by itself need not pose an insuperable obstacle to ascribing the disposition to me. *All* dispositional properties are such that their exercise – the holding of the relevant counterfactual truth – is contingent on the absence of interfering conditions, or equivalently, on the presence of ideal conditions. And it certainly seems conceivable that a suitable idealization of my biological properties will render the counterfactual about my behaviour on Alpha Centauri true. Kripke considers such a response and complains:

> But how can we have any confidence in this? How in the world can I tell what would happen if my brain were stuffed with extra brain matter? . . . Surely such speculation should be left to science fiction writers and futurologists.[38]

If the point is supposed to be, however, that one can have no reason for accepting a generalization defined over ideal conditions unless one knows

---

H. Field, 'Logic, Meaning and Conceptual Role', *Journal of Philosophy*, (1977); Ned Block, 'Advertisement for a Semantics for Psychology', *Midwest Studies in Philosophy*, vol. 10 (Minneapolis: University of Minnesota Press, 1986).

38. K, p. 27.

exactly which counterfactuals would be true if the ideal conditions obtained, then, as Jerry Fodor has pointed out, it seems completely unacceptable.[39] For example, no one can claim to know all of what would be true if molecules and containers actually satisfied the conditions over which the ideal gas laws are defined; but that does not prevent us from claiming to know that, if there were ideal gases, their volume would vary inversely with the pressure on them. Similarly, no one can claim to know all of what would be true if I were so modified as to survive a trip to Alpha Centauri; but that need not prevent us from claiming to know that, if I were to survive such a trip, I would call the horses there 'horse'.[40]

Still, it is one thing to dispel an objection to a thesis, it is another to prove the thesis true. And we are certainly in no position now to show that we do have infinitary dispositions. The trouble is that *not every* true counterfactual of the form

If conditions were ideal, then, if C, S would do A

can be used to attribute to S the disposition to do A in C. For example, one can hardly credit a tortoise with the ability to overtake a hare, by pointing out that if conditions were ideal for the tortoise – if, for example, it were much bigger and faster – then it would overtake it. Obviously, only certain idealizations are permissible; and also obviously, we do not now know which idealizations those are. The set of permissible counterfactuals is constrained by criteria of which we currently lack a systematic account. In the absence of such an account, we cannot be completely confident that ascriptions of infinitary dispositions are acceptable, because we cannot be completely confident that the idealized counterfactuals needed to support such ascriptions are licit. But I think it is fair to say that the burden of proof here lies squarely on Kripke's shoulders: it is up to him to show that the relevant idealizations would be of the impermissible variety. And this he has not done.

DISPOSITIONS AND MEANING: NORMATIVITY

20.

Few aspects of Kripke's argument have been more widely misunderstood than his discussion of the 'normativity' of meaning and his associated criticism of dispositional theories. This is unsurprising given the difficulty and delicacy of

---

39. See 'A Theory of Content, Part II' in *A Theory of Content and Other Essays* (Cambridge, MA: MIT Press, 1990).
40. For a related criticism of Kripke on this score, see Blackburn, 'The Individual Strikes Back'.

the issues involved. In what sense is meaning a normative notion? Kripke writes:

> Suppose I do mean addition by '+'. What is the relation of this supposition to the question how I will respond to the problem '68 + 57'? The dispositionalist gives a *descriptive* account of this relation: if '+' meant addition, then I will answer '125'. But this is not the right account of the relation, which is normative, not descriptive. The point is not that, if I meant addition by '+', I will answer '125', but that, if I intend to accord with my past meaning of '+', I *should* answer '125'. Computational error, finiteness of my capacity, and other disturbing factors may lead me not to be disposed to respond as I should, but if so, I have not acted in accordance with my intentions. The relation of meaning and intention to future action is *normative,* not *descriptive.*[41]

The fact that I mean something by an expression, Kripke says, implies truths about how I *ought* to use that expression, truths about how it would be *correct* for me to use it. This much, of course, is incontestable. The fact that 'horse' means *horse* implies that 'horse' is correctly applied to all and only horses: the notion of the extension of an expression just is the notion of what it is correct to apply the expression to. It is also true that to say that a given expression has a given extension is not to make any sort of *simple* descriptive remark about it. In particular, of course, it is not to say that, as a matter of fact, the expression *will* be applied only to those things which are in its extension. Kripke seems to think, however, that these observations by themselves ought to be enough to show that no dispositional theory of meaning can work. And here matters are not so straightforward.

Let us begin with the very crude dispositional theory mentioned above: 'horse' means whatever property I am disposed to apply it to. This is a hopeless theory, of course, but the reasons are instructive. There are two of them, and they are closely related. The first difficulty is that the theory is bound to get the extension of 'horse' wrong. Suppose I mean *horse* by it. Then, presumably, I have a disposition to call horses 'horse'. But it will also be true that there are certain circumstances – sufficiently dark nights – and certain cows – sufficiently horsey looking ones – such that, I am disposed, under those circumstances, to call those cows 'horse' too. Intuitively, this is a disposition to make a mistake, that is, to apply the expression to something not in its extension. But our crude dispositional theory, given that it identifies *the property I mean by an expression* with *the property I am disposed to apply the expression to,* lacks the resources by which to effect the requisite distinction between correct and incorrect dispositions. If what I mean by an

---

41. K, p. 37.

expression is identified with whatever I am disposed to apply the expression to, then everything I am disposed to apply the expression to is, *ipso facto,* in the extension of that expression. But this leads to the unacceptable conclusion that 'horse' does not express the property *horse* but rather the disjunctive property *horse or cow.*

There is a related conceptual difficulty. Any theory which, like the crude dispositional theory currently under consideration, simply equates how it would be correct for me to use a certain expression with how I am disposed to use it, would have ruled out, as a matter of definition, the very possibility of error. And as Wittgenstein was fond of remarking, if the idea of correctness is to make sense at all, then it cannot be that whatever seems right to me is (by definition) right.

One would have thought these points too crucial to miss; but it is surprising how little they are appreciated. In a recent, comprehensive treatment of conceptual role theories, Ned Block has written

> of a choice that must be made by [conceptual role semantics] theorists, one that has had no discussion (as far as I know): namely, should conceptual role be understood in ideal or normative terms, or should it be tied to what people actually do? . . . I prefer not to comment on this matter . . . because I'm not sure what to say...[42]

This ought to seem odd. If conceptual role is supposed to determine meaning, then there can be no question, on pain of falling prey to Kripke's objection, of identifying an expression's conceptual role with a subject's actual dispositions with respect to that expression.

21.

The objections from normativity show, then, that no dispositional theory that assumes the simple form of identifying *the property I mean by 'horse'* with *the property I am disposed to call 'horse',* can hope to succeed. But what if a dispositional theory did not assume this simple form? What if, instead of identifying what I mean by 'horse' with the *entire* range of my dispositions in respect of 'horse', it identified it only with certain select dispositions. Provided the theory specified a principle of selection that picked out only the extension-tracking dispositions; and provided also that it specified that principle in terms that did not presuppose the notion of meaning or extension, would it not then be true that the objections from normativity had been disarmed?

---

42. Ned Block, 1986, p. 631.

Let us try to put matters a little more precisely. If a dispositional theory is to have any prospect of succeeding, it must select from among the dispositions I have for 'horse', those dispositions which are *meaning-determining*. In other words, it must characterize, in non-intentional and non-semantic terms, a property M such that: possession of M is necessary and sufficient for being a disposition to apply an expression in accord with its correctness conditions.[43] Given such a property, however, could we not then safely equate meaning something by an expression with: *the set of dispositions with respect to that expression that possess M*? For, since dispositions with that property will be guaranteed to be dispositions to apply the expression correctly, both of the objections from normativity canvassed so far would appear to have been met. There will be no fear that the equation will issue in false verdicts about what the expression means. And, since it is only M-dispositions that are guaranteed to be correct, it will no longer follow that *whatever* seems right is right: those dispositions not possessing M will not be dispositions to apply the expression to what it means and will be free, therefore, to constitute dispositions to apply the expression falsely.

At this point two questions arise. First, is there really such a property M? And, second, supposing there were, is there really no more to capturing the normativity of meaning than specifying such a property?

Now, Kripke is clearly skeptical about the existence of an appropriate M-property. I will consider that question below. But more than this, Kripke seems to think that even if there were a suitably selected disposition that captured the extension of an expression accurately, that disposition could still not be identified with the fact of meaning, because it still remains true that the concept of a disposition is descriptive whereas the concept of meaning is not. In other words, according to Kripke, even if there were a dispositional predicate that logically covaried with a meaning predicate, the one fact could still not be identified with the other, for they are facts of distinct sorts. A number of writers have been inclined to follow him in this. Simon Blackburn, for instance, has written:

> I share Kripke's view that whatever dispositions we succeed in identifying they could at most give us standards for selection of a function which we mean. They couldn't provide us with an account of what it is to be faithful to a previous rule. It is just that, unlike

---

43. It is occasionally suggested that it would be enough if possession of M were *sufficient* for the disposition's correctness. But that is not right. If only sufficiency were required we would not know, simply by virtue of a definition of M, the expression's meaning. For although we would know what properties were definitely part of the expression's meaning we would not know if we had them all. And so we would not have even a sufficient condition for the expression's possessing a given meaning.

> Kripke, I do not think dispositions are inadequate to the task of providing standards. Indeed, I think they must be.[44]

Blackburn here is explicitly envisaging the successful, substantive specification of dispositions that mirror the extensions of expressions correctly. But he cites the normative character of facts about meaning as grounds for denying a dispositional *reduction*. But what precisely has been left over, once the extensions have been specified correctly?

One might have a thought like this. A proper reduction of the meaning of an expression would not merely specify its extension correctly, it would also reveal that what it is specifying is an *extension* – namely, a *correctness* condition. And this is what a dispositional theory cannot do. There might be dispositions that logically covary with the extensions of expressions; so that one could read off the dispositions in question the expressions' correctness conditions. But the dispositional fact does not amount to the meaning fact, because it never follows from the mere attribution of any disposition, however selectively specified, that there are facts concerning *correct* use; whereas this does follow from the attribution of an extension. To be told that 'horse' means *horse* implies that a speaker ought to be motivated to apply the expression only to horses; whereas to be told, for instance, that there are certain select circumstances under which a speaker is disposed to apply the expression only to horses, seems to carry no such implication.

It is not clear that this is in general true. Perhaps the *M*-dispositions are those dispositions that a person would have when his cognitive mechanisms are in a certain state; and perhaps it can be non-question-beggingly certified that that state corresponds to a state of the *proper* functioning of those mechanisms. If so, it is conceivable that that would amount to a non-circular specification of how the person would *ideally* respond, as compared with how he actually responds; and, hence, that it would suffice for capturing the normative force of an ascription of meaning.

There is clearly no way to settle the matter in advance of the consideration of particular dispositional proposals. What we are in a position to do, however, is state conditions on an adequate dispositional theory. First, any such theory must specify, without presupposing any semantic or intentional materials, property *M*. This would ensure the theory's extensional correctness. Second, it must show how possession of an *M*-disposition could amount to something that deserves to be called a *correctness* condition, something we would be inherently motivated to satisfy. This would ensure the intensional equivalence of the two properties in question, thus paving the way for an outright reduction of meaning to dispositions.

---

44. 'The Individual Strikes Back', pp. 289–91 (this volume Ch. 3). Similar concessions are made by Wright in his 'Kripke's Account', pp. 771–2; and by John McDowell, 'Wittgenstein on Following a Rule', *Synthese*, (1984), p. 329 (this volume Ch. 4).

What property might M be? There are, in effect, two sorts of proposal: one, long associated with Wittgenstein himself, seeks to specify M by exploiting the notion of a community; the other, of more recent provenance, attempts to define M in terms of the notion of an optimality condition. I shall begin with the communitarian account.

[handwritten: ONLY IF SOMEONE EMPLOYS THE EXACT SAME PROCEDURE AS I DO IT DOES NOT SEEM AS IF THEY ARE WRONG OTHERWISE THEY ARE USING A FN WHICH]

THE COMMUNITARIAN ACCOUNT

22.

The idea that correctness consists in agreement with one's fellows has a distinguished history in the study of Wittgenstein. Even before the current concern with a 'rule-following problem', many commentators – whether rightly or wrongly – identified communitarianism as a central thesis of the later writings. As a response to the problem about meaning, it found its most sustained treatment in Wright's *Wittgenstein on the Foundations of Mathe- matics*.[45] Which of the many dispositions a speaker may have with respect to a given expression determine its meaning? Or, equivalently, which of the many dispositions a speaker may have with respect to an expression are dispositions to use it correctly? Wright's communitarian account furnishes the following answer:

[handwritten margin right: IS DIFF ? I HAVE NO MEANS TO REJECT THAT]

> ... it is a community of assent which supplies the essential background against which alone it makes sense to think of individuals' responses as correct or incorrect .... None of us can unilaterally make sense of correct employment of language save by reference to the authority of communal assent on the matter; and for the community itself there is no authority, so no standard to meet.[46]

[handwritten: "NOT FAITHFUL TO THEIR OWN DISPOSITION]

It is important to understand that, according to the proposal on offer, the correct application of a term is determined by the *totality* of the community's *actual* dispositions in respect of that term. The theory does not attempt, in specifying the communal dispositions that are to serve as the constitutive arbiters of correctness, to select from among the community's actual dispositions a privileged subset. There is a reason for this. Communitarianism is a response to the perceived inability to define a distinction, at the level of the individual, between correct and incorrect dispositions. The suggestion that

---

45. Cambridge, MA: Harvard University Press, 1980. (His more recent writings suggest that Wright no longer holds this view.) See also Christopher Peacocke, 'Reply: Rule-Following: The Nature of Wittgenstein's Arguments', in *Wittgenstein on Following a Rule*, ed. S. Holtzman and C. Leich, (London: Routledge & Kegan Paul, 1981).
46. *Ibid.*, pp. 219–20.

correctness consists in agreement with the dispositions of one's community is designed to meet this need. The proposal will not serve its purpose, however, if the problem at the level of the individual is now merely to be replayed at the level of the community. A communitarian does not want it to be a *further* question whether a given actual communal disposition is itself correct. The proposal must be understood, therefore, as offering the following characterization of M: M is the *property of agreeing with the actual dispositions of the community*.

How does the proposal fare with respect to the outlined adequacy conditions on dispositional theories?

Consider first the 'intensional' requirement, that possession of the favoured M-property appears intuitively to resemble possession of a correctness condition. Does *communal consensus* command the sort of response characteristic of truth?

A number of critics have complained against communitarianism that communal consensus is simply not the same property as truth, that there is no incoherence in the suggestion that all the members of a linguistic community have gone collectively, but non-collusively, off-track in the application of a given predicate.[47] This is, of course, undeniable. But the communitarian is not best read as offering an *analysis* of the ordinary notion of truth, but a *displacement* of it. His thought is that the emaciated notion of truth yielded by communitarianism is the best we can hope to expect in light of the rule-following considerations. The crucial question, then, is not whether communitarianism captures our ordinary notion of truth, for it quite clearly does not; it is, rather, whether communitarianism offers *any* concept deserving of that name.

This is a large question on which I do not propose to spend a lot of time.[48] Although there are subtle questions about how much of logic will be recoverable from such a view, and whether it can be suitably nonreductively articulated (can 'non-collusive agreement' be defined without the use of intentional materials?), I am prepared to grant, for the sake of argument, that the proposal does not fare all that badly in connection with the 'intensional' requirement. Non-collusive communal agreement on a judgement does usually provide one with some sort of reason for embracing the judgement (even if, unlike truth, not with a decisive one); it thus mimics to some degree the sort of response that is essential to truth. Where communitarianism fails, it seems to me, is not so much here as with the extensional requirement.

Consider the term 'horse'. What dispositions do I have in respect of this expression? To be sure, I have a disposition to apply it to horses. But I also have a disposition, on sufficiently dark nights, to apply it to deceptively

---

47. See Blackburn, 'Individual Strikes Back'.
48. For a more extensive discussion see my *Essays on Meaning and Belief*; see also Blackburn, *Spreading the Word* (Oxford: Oxford University Press, 1984), pp. 82ff.

Handwritten annotations at top: TRY BURGE'S THOUGHT EXPERIMENT on 'PLUS' AND 'HORSE' TO SHOW THAT NO ONE KNOWS ENOUGH TO CONSTITUTE A RULE

horsey looking cows. Intuitively, the facts are clear. 'Horse' means *horse* and my disposition to apply it to cows on dark nights is mistaken. The problem is to come up with a theory that delivers this result systematically and in purely dispositional terms. The communitarian's idea is that the correct dispositions are constitutively those which agree with the community's. What, then, are the community's dispositions likely to be?

The community, I submit, however exactly specified, is bound to exhibit precisely the same duality of dispositions that I do: it too will be disposed to call both horses and deceptively horsey looking cows on dark nights 'horse'. After all, if *I* can be taken in by a deceptively horsey looking cow on a dark night, what is to prevent 17,000 people just like me from being taken in by the same, admittedly effective, impostor? The point is that many of the mistakes we make are *systematic:* they arise because of the presence of features – bad lighting, effective disguises, and so forth – that have a generalizable and predictable effect on creatures with similar cognitive endowments. (This is presumably what makes 'magicians' possible.) But, then, any of my dispositions that are in this sense systematically mistaken, are bound to be duplicated at the level of the community. The communitarian, however, cannot call them *mistakes,* for they are the community's dispositions. He must insist, then, firm conviction to the contrary notwithstanding, that 'horse' means not *horse* but, rather, *horse or cow.*

The problem, of course, is general. There are countless possible impostors under countless possible conditions; and there is nothing special about the term 'horse'. The upshot would appear to be that, according to communitarianism, none of our predicates have the extensions we take them to have, but mean something wildly disjunctive instead. Which is to say that communitarianism is bound to issue in false verdicts about the meanings of most expressions, thus failing the first requirement on an adequate dispositional theory.

Handwritten margin note: HE MUST CLAIM THAT 'HORSE' ACTUALLY MEANS 'HORSE & deceptively HORSEY COW AT NIGHT'

It seems to me that we have no option but to reject a pure communitarianism. If we are to have any prospect of identifying the extensions of our expressions correctly, it will simply not do to identify truth with communal consensus. Even from among the *community's* dispositions, we have to select those which may be considered meaning-determining, if we are to have a plausible theory of meaning. Which is to say that we are still lacking what communitarianism was supposed to provide: the specification of a property *M* such that, possession of *M* by a disposition is necessary and sufficient for that disposition's correctness.

Of course, once we have abandoned communitarianism, we lack any motive for defining *M* over *communal* dispositions; nothing – at least nothing obvious – tells against defining *M* directly over an *individual's* dispositions. Which is precisely the way the voluminous literature on this topic approaches the problem and to a discussion of which I now propose to turn.

OPTIMAL DISPOSITIONS

[handwritten annotation: What if you took optimary conditions 23 AND applied them to ordinary meaning]

The literature supplies what is, in effect, a set of variations on a basic theme: M is the property of: being a disposition to apply (an expression) *in a certain type of situation.*[49] The idea behind such proposals is that there is a certain set of circumstances – call them 'optimality conditions' – under which subjects are, for one or another reason, incapable of mistaken judgements; hence, we may equate what they mean by a given (mental) expression with the properties they are disposed to apply the expression to, under optimal conditions. Different proposals provide different characterizations of the conditions that are supposed to be optimal in this sense. Fred Dretske, for example, holds that optimal conditions are the conditions under which the meaning of the expression was first acquired. A number of other writers subscribe to some form or other of a *teleological* proposal: optimality conditions are those conditions – defined by evolutionary biology – under which our cognitive mechanisms are functioning just as they are supposed to.[50]

Now, Kripke is very short with such possible elaborations of a dispositional theory. He briefly considers the suggestion that we attempt to define idealized dispositions and says that 'a little experimentation will reveal the futility of such an effort'.[51] But, surely, this underestimates the complexity of the problems involved and fails to do justice to the influence that such proposals currently exert. What Kripke needs, if his rejection of dispositional accounts is to succeed, but does not really provide, is a set of principled considerations against the existence of non-semantically, non-intentionally specifiable optimality conditions. What I would like to do in the remainder of this section is to begin to sketch an argument for that conclusion. Several specific problems for specific versions of an optimality theory have received discussion in the literature.[52] Here, however, I want to attempt an argument with a more general sweep: I want to argue that we have reason to believe that there could not be naturalistically specifiable conditions under which a subject will be

---

49. There is one exception to this generalization: Jerry Fodor's recent proposal has it that S's meaning-determining dispositions are those that serve as an 'asymmetric dependence base' for S's other dispositions. See his 'A Theory of Content, Part II'. In 'Naturalizing Content', in *Meaning in Mind: Essays on the Work Jerry Fodor* (Oxford: Basil Blackwell, 1992) I argue that this theory is subject to the same difficulties as confront standard optimality versions.

50. For theories of this form see: David Papineau, *Reality and Representation* (Oxford: Basil Blackwell, 1987); J. Fodor: 'Psychosemantics', MS, MIT, 1984. I shy away from saying whether R. Millikan, *Language, Thought and Other Biological Categories* (Cambridge, MA: MIT Press, 1987) presents a theory of this form.

51. K, p. 32.

52. Against Dretske see Fodor, 'Psychosemantics'; against teleological theories see my *Essays on Meaning and Belief* and Fodor, 'A Theory of Content Part I'.

disposed to apply an expression only to what it means; and, hence, that no attempt at specifying such conditions can hope to succeed.[53]

24.

It will be worthwhile to lay the problem out with some care. Consider Neil and a particular expression, say, 'horse', in Neil's mental repertoire, And suppose that Neil is disposed to token that expression 'in the belief mode' both in respect of horses and in respect of deceptively horsey looking cows on dark nights. Let it be clear, furthermore, that 'horse' for Neil means *horse,* and that on those occasions when he applies 'horse' to cows, this amounts to his *mistaking* a cow for a horse. Now, the thought behind an optimality version of a dispositional theory is that there is a set of naturalistically specifiable conditions under which Neil cannot make mistakes in the identification of presented items.[54] Under those conditions, then, he would believe that there is a horse in front of him only if there is one. But that in turn implies that, under those conditions, 'horse' will get tokened (in the belief mode) only in respect of the property it expresses. So, to figure out what any expression means: look at the properties Neil is disposed to apply the expression to, when conditions are in this sense optimal. The end result is a dispositional reconstruction of meaning facts: for Neil to mean horse by 'horse' is for Neil to be disposed to call only horses 'horse', when conditions are optimal. Clearly, two conditions must be satisfied: (i) the specified conditions must really be such as to preclude the possibility of error – otherwise, it will be false that under those conditions 'horse' will get applied only to what it means; (ii) the conditions must be specified purely naturalistically, without the use of any semantic or intentional materials – otherwise, the theory will have assumed the very properties it was supposed to provide a reconstruction of.

What I propose to argue is that it is impossible to satisfy both of these conditions simultaneously.

---

53. This amounts to saying that such theories cannot meet the extensional requirement; so I shall not even consider whether they meet the intensional one.
54. This restriction to perceptually fixed beliefs stems partly from a desire to simplify exposition and partly from a desire to consider such theories at their strongest.

OPTIMAL DISPOSITIONS AND OBJECTIVE CONTENTS

25.

The dispositionalist is after a non-semantically, non-intentionally specifiable set of conditions O, which will be such as to yield true, a priori *optimality equations* of the form:

(8) For any subject S and concept R: $O \rightarrow (S$ judges $Rx \rightarrow Rx)$.

Could there be such a set of conditions?

Notice, to begin with, that where R is the concept of an *objective* property, we ought not to expect optimality equations for R, even if O were not required to meet the rather stiff constraints imposed by a reductive dispositionalism – namely specification in non-semantic and non-intentional terms. For, intuitively, the very idea of a wholly objective property (or object or relation) is the idea of a property (object, relation) whose nature is independent of any given person's abilities or judgements: for such a property, in other words, there is no necessary function from a given person's abilities and judgements to truths about that property.[55] The contrast is with a class of contents for which there does exist a range of circumstances such that appropriate subjects are necessarily authoritative about those contents under those circumstances. Philosophers disagree, of course, about what contents fall where, but it is typical to think of judgements about shape as wholly objective and of judgements about pain as representing an extreme example of the contrasting class. Let us call this a distinction between *accessible* versus *inaccessible* contents.[56]

We are now in a position to see, however, that a dispositional theory of meaning, by virtue of being committed to the existence of optimality equations for every concept, is committed thereby to treating every concept as if it were accessible. It is thus committed to obliterating the distinction between accessible and inaccessible contents.

Of course, this objection will not impress anyone reluctant to countenance wholly objective, inaccessible contents in the first place. I turn, therefore, to arguing against the dispositional theory on neutral ground: for any concept, subjective or objective, it is impossible to satisfy dispositionalism's basic requirement: the specification of a set of conditions O, *in non-semantic, and*

---

55. See, for example, Tyler Burge, 'Cartesian Error and the Objectivity of Perception', in *Subject, Thought and Context,* ed. J. McDowell and P. Pettit (Oxford: Clarendon Press, 1986), p. 125, for a similar formulation of the concept of an objective property.

56. It is important to appreciate that this is an *epistemological* distinction, not a constitutive one. It does not follow from the fact that a content is accessible, that it is therefore constituted by our best judgements about it. (I take it no one is tempted to conclude from the fact that we are authoritative about our pains that pains are *constituted* by the judgements we make about them.) We shall have occasion to discuss constitutive claims of this sort later on in the paper.

non-intentional terms, such that, under O, subjects are immune from error about judgements involving that concept.

OPTIMAL DISPOSITIONS AND BELIEF HOLISM

26.

The basic difficulty derives from the holistic character of the processes which fix belief. The point is that, under normal circumstances, belief fixation is typically mediated by background theory – what contents a thinker is prepared to judge will depend upon what other contents he is prepared to judge. And this dependence is, again typically, arbitrarily robust: just about any stimulus can cause just about any belief, given a suitably mediating set of background assumptions. Thus, Neil may come to believe *Lo, a magpie,* as a result of seeing a currawong, because of his further belief that that is just what magpies look like; or because of his belief that the only birds in the immediate vicinity are magpies; or because of his belief that whatever the Pope says goes and his belief that the Pope says that this presented currawong is a magpie. And so on. The thought that something is a magpie can get triggered by a currawong in any of an indefinite number of ways, corresponding to the potentially indefinite number of background beliefs which could mediate the transition. Now, how does all this bear on the prospects for a dispositional theory of meaning?

A dispositional theorist has to specify, without use of semantic or intentional materials, a situation in which a thinker will be disposed to think, *Lo, a magpie* only in respect of magpies. But the observation that beliefs are fixed holistically implies that a thinker will be disposed to think *Lo, a magpie* in respect of an indefinite number of *non-magpies,* provided only that the appropriate background beliefs are present. Specifying an optimality condition for 'magpie', therefore, will involve, at a minimum, specifying a situation characterized by the absence of *all* the beliefs which could potentially mediate the transition from non-magpies to *magpie* beliefs. Since, however, there looks to be a potential infinity of such mediating background clusters of belief, a non-semantically, non-intentionally specified optimality situation is a non-semantically, non-intentionally specified situation in which it is guaranteed that none of this potential infinity of background clusters of belief is present. But how is such a situation to be specified? What is needed is precisely what a dispositional theory was supposed to provide: namely, a set of naturalistic necessary and sufficient conditions for being a belief with a certain content. But, of course, if we had *that* we would already have a reductive theory of meaning – we would not need a dispositional theory! Which is to say that, if there is to be any sort of reductive story about meaning at all, it cannot take the form of a dispositional theory.

VI ANTI-REDUCTIONIST CONCEPTIONS OF MEANING

AN ARGUMENT FROM QUEERNESS?

27.

If these considerations are correct, there would appear to be plenty of reason to doubt the reducibility of content properties to naturalistic properties. But Kripke's skeptic does not merely draw an anti-reductionist conclusion; he concludes, far more radically, that there simply could not *be* any content properties. Suppose we grant the anti-reductionism; what justifies the content *skepticism?* Not, of course, the anti-reductionism by itself. At a minimum one of two further things is needed. Either an independent argument to the effect that only naturalistic properties are real. Or, failing that, a frontal assault on the irreducible property in question, showing that it is, in Mackie's phrase, somehow inherently 'queer'.

The single greatest weakness in Kripke's skeptical argument is that he fails to bring off either requirement. He does not even try to defend a reductionist principle about the intentional; and his brief attempt at a 'queerness' argument is half-hearted and unconvincing:

> Perhaps we may try to recoup, by arguing that meaning addition by 'plus' is a state even more sui generis than we have argued before. Perhaps it is simply a primitive state, not to be assimilated to sensations or headaches or any 'qualitative' states, nor to be assimilated to dispositions, but a state of a unique kind of its own.
>
> Such a move may in a sense be irrefutable, and if it is taken in an appropriate way Wittgenstein may even accept it. But it seems desperate: it leaves the nature of this postulated primitive state – the primitive state of 'meaning addition by "plus"' – completely mysterious. It is not supposed to be an introspectible state, yet we supposedly are aware of it with some fair degree of certainty whenever it occurs. For how else can each of us be confident that he does, at present, mean addition by 'plus'? Even more important is the logical difficulty implicit in Wittgenstein's skeptical argument. I think that Wittgenstein argues, not merely as we have said hitherto, that introspection shows that the alleged 'qualitative' state of understanding is a chimera, but also that it is logically impossible (or at least that there is a considerable logical difficulty) for there to be a state of 'meaning addition by "plus"' at all.
>
> Such a state would have to be a finite object, contained in our finite minds. It does not consist in my explicitly thinking of each case of the addition table . . .. Can we conceive of a finite state which *could* not be interpreted in a quus-like way? How could that be?[57]

---

57. K, pp. 51–2.

There are several problems with this passage. In the first place, it miscon-strues the appropriate anti-reductionist suggestion. I take it that it really is not plausible that there are 'primitive states' of meaning *public language* expres-sions in certain ways, one state per expression. The process by which the inscriptions and vocables of a public language acquire meaning is a manifestly complex process – involving an enormous array of appropriate propositional attitudes – the outlines of which may arguably be found in the writings of Paul Grice and others.[58] A plausible anti-reductionism about meaning would not wish to deny that there is an interesting story to be told about the relation between *linguistic content and mental content;* what it maintains, rather, is that there is no interesting reduction of *mental content properties* to *physical/ functional properties*. According to anti-reductionism, in other words, at some appropriate level mental content properties must simply be taken for granted, without prospect of identification with properties otherwise described.

Does Kripke manage to create a difficulty for *this* suggestion? The passage contains a couple of considerations that may be so construed.

The first charge is that we would have no idea how to explain our ability to know our thoughts, if we endorsed a non-reductionist conception of their content. Now, no one who has contemplated the problem of self-knowledge can fail to be impressed by its difficulty.[59] But I think that we would be forgiven if, before we allowed this to drive us to a dubiously coherent irreal-ism about content, we required something on the order of a *proof* that no satisfactory epistemology was ultimately to be had.

Kripke, however, provides no such proof. He merely notes that the non-phenomenal character of contentful states precludes an introspective account of their epistemology. And this is problematic for two reasons. First, because there may be non-introspective accounts of self-knowledge.[60] And second, because it does not obviously follow from the fact that a mental state lacks an individuative phenomenology that it is not introspectible.[61]

Kripke's second objection to the anti-reductionist suggestion is that it is utterly mysterious how there could be a finite state, realized in a finite mind,

---

58. See the papers cited under n. 5 above.

59. For discussion of some of the difficulties, see my 'Content and Self-Knowledge', *Philosophical Topics*, Spring 1989.

60. See, for example, Tyler Burge, 'Individualism and Self-Knowledge', *Journal of Philosophy*, November 1988, and D. Davidson, 'Knowing One's Own Mind', *Proceedings of the APA*, January 1987.

61. It is interesting to note, incidentally, that one of the more striking examples of the introspective discernment of a non-qualitative mental feature is provided by, of all things, an experiential phenomenon. I have in mind the phenomenon, much discussed by Wittgenstein himself, of seeing-as. We see the duck-rabbit now as a duck, now as a rabbit; we see the Necker cube now with one face forward, now with another. And we know immediately precisely how we are seeing these objects as, when we see them now in one way, now in the other. But this change of 'aspect', although manifestly introspectible, is nevertheless not a change in something qualitative, for the qualitative character of the visual experience remains the same even as the aspect changes.

that nevertheless contains information about the correct applicability of a sign in literally no end of distinct situations. But, again, this amounts merely to insisting that we find the idea of a contentful state problematic, without adducing any independent reason why we should. We *know* that mental states with general contents are states with infinitary normative characters; it is precisely with that observation that the entire discussion began. What Kripke needs, if he is to pull off an argument from queerness, is some substantive argument, distinct from his anti-reductionist considerations, why we should not countenance such states. But this he does not provide.

None of this should be understood as suggesting that an anti-reductionism about content is unproblematic, for it is far from it. There are, for example, familiar, and serious, difficulties reconciling an anti-reductionism about content properties with a satisfying conception of their causal efficacy.[62] But in the context of Kripke's dialectic, the anti-reductionist suggestion emerges as a stable response to the skeptical conclusion that is seemingly untouched by all the considerations adduced in the latter's favour.

MCDOWELL ON PRIVACY AND COMMUNITY

28.

If we endorse a non-reductionist conception of meaning, does that mean that the rule-following considerations disturb nothing in our ordinary conception of that notion? A number of writers who have found an anti-reductionist suggestion attractive have certainly not thought so; they have discerned in those considerations important lessons for the correct understanding of the possibility of meaning, while rejecting substantive reductive answers to the constitutive question: in virtue of what do expressions possess meaning?

John McDowell, for example, has written that:

> By Wittgenstein's lights, it is a mistake to think we can dig down to a level at which we no longer have application for normative notions (like 'following according to the rule').[63]

We have to resist the temptation, according to McDowell's Wittgenstein, to form a picture of 'bedrock' – 'of how things are at the deepest level at which we may sensibly contemplate the place of [meaning] in the world' – which does not already employ the idea of the correct (or incorrect) use of an expression.

---

62. See below.
63. 'Wittgenstein on Following a Rule', p. 341.

Oddly, however, McDowell does not take this to commit him to a *quietism* about meaning, a position from which no substantive results about the conditions for the possibility of meaning can be gleaned. On the contrary, he claims that it is the discernible moral of the rule-following considerations that correctness, and hence meaning, can exist only in the context of a *communal practice*, thus precluding the possibility of a private language. He writes:

> Wittgenstein warns us not to try to dig below 'bedrock'. But it is difficult, in reading him, to avoid acquiring a sense of what, as it were, lies down there: a web of facts about behavior and 'inner' episodes, describable without using the notion of meaning. One is likely to be struck by the sheer contingency of the resemblances between individuals on which, in this vision, the possibility of meaning seems to depend . . ..[64]

And:

> It is true that a certain disorderliness below 'bedrock' would undermine the applicability of the notion of rule-following. So the underlying contingencies bear an intimate relation to the notion of rule-following . . ..[65]

This is, of course, McDowell's characterization of the familiar Wittgensteinian claim that a certain measure of agreement in communal responses is a precondition for meaning. But how is such a thesis to be motivated? How, in light of the rejection of substantive answers to the constitutive question, is it to be argued for? The claim that communal practice is necessary for meaning is a *surprising* claim; mere reflection on the concept of meaning does not reveal it. And what, short of a substantive constitutive account, could conceivably ground it?

Consider the contrast with the communitarian view considered above. That view engages the constitutive question, offers a substantive answer to it, and generates, thereby, a straightforward argument for the necessity of a communal practice: since correctness is said to *consist* in conformity with one's fellows, correctness, and with it meaning, are possible only where there are others with whom one may conform. But McDowell, rightly in my view, rejects the suggestion that correct application might be analysed in terms of communal dispositions. Indeed, as I have already noted, he rejects the very demand for a substantive account of correctness: norms are part of the 'bedrock', beneath which we must not dig. But if we are simply to be allowed to take the idea of correctness for granted, unreduced and without any

---

64. *Ibid.*, p. 348.
65. *Ibid.*, p. 349.

prospect of reconstruction in terms of, say, actual and counterfactual truths about communal use, how is the necessity of an 'orderly communal' practice to be defended? From what does the demand for orderliness flow? And from what the demand for community? McDowell's paper contains no helpful answers.[66]

WRIGHT ON THE JUDGEMENT-DEPENDENCE OF MEANING

29.

Crispin Wright has written about the anti-reductionist conception that:

> [t]his somewhat flat-footed response to Kripke's Skeptic may seem to provide a good example of 'loss of problems.' . . . In fact, though, and on the contrary, I think the real problem posed by the Skeptical Argument is acute, and *is* one of Wittgenstein's fundamental concerns. But the problem is not that of *answering* the Argument. The problem is that of seeing how and why the correct answer given can *be* correct.[67]

Wright's intriguing suggestion is that there are important constitutive results to be gleaned from the epistemological question we shelved some pages back: namely, how, if content properties are simply to be taken for granted, without prospect of reconstruction either in experiential or dispositional terms, can they be known? As we saw, Kripke attempted to use this question to embarrass his anti-reductionist opponent. Wright, however, has a more constructive project in mind. Pressing the epistemological question will reveal, so he claims, that facts about content are essentially 'judgement-dependent'.

What does it mean for a class of facts to be judgement-dependent? Wright's explanation is framed in terms of a failure to pass the 'order-of-determination test':

---

66. Though see his remarks – which I am afraid I do not understand – on a 'linguistic community [that] is conceived as bound together, not by a match in mere externals (accessible to just anyone), but by a meeting of minds'. McDowell's problems here echo, I think, Wittgenstein's own. The main difficulty confronting a would-be interpreter of Wittgenstein is how to reconcile his rejection of substantive constitutive accounts – especially of meaning, see *Zettel* §16: 'The mistake is to say that meaning something consists' – with the obvious constitutive and transcendental pretensions of the rule-following considerations. It is fashionable to soft-pedal the rejection of constitutive questions, representing it as displaying a mere 'distrust' on Wittgenstein's part. But this ignores the fact that the rejection of analyses and necessary and sufficient conditions is tied to extremely important first-order theses about meaning, including, most centrally, the family-resemblance view of concepts.
67. 'Wittgenstein's Rule-Following Considerations and the Central Project of Theoretical Linguistics', p. 237.

The order-of-determination test concerns the relation between *best* judgements – judgements made in what are, with respect to their particular subject matter, *cognitively ideal* conditions of both judger and circumstance – and truth . . .. Truth, for judgements which pass the test, is a standard constituted independently of any considerations concerning cognitive pedigree. For judgements which fail the test, by contrast, there is no distance between being true and being best; truth, for such judgements, is constitutively what we judge to be true when we operate under cognitively ideal conditions.[68]

We may explain the contrast Wright has in mind here by recurring to the idea of an accessible content (see above). An accessible content is one about which subjects are necessarily authoritative under cognitively optimal circumstances. Now, a question may be raised about the correct explanation for this authority: is it that, under those optimal circumstances, subjects are exceptionally well-equipped to *track* the relevant, independently constituted facts? or is it, rather, that judgements under those circumstances simply *constitute* the facts in question? A fact is judgement-independent if the former, judgement-dependent if the latter.

The contrast, then, is between facts which are constituted independently of our judgements, however optimal, and facts which are constituted precisely by the judgements we would form under cognitively ideal circumstances. And the claim is that facts about content have to be construed on the latter model. *Pace* Kripke, the target of the rule-following considerations is not the reality of content facts, but, rather, a judgement-independent (or *Platonist*, if you think these come to the same thing) conception of their *constitution*. Best judgements constitutively determine the truth-value of sentences ascribing content to mental states; they do not *track* independently constituted states of affairs which confer truth or falsity upon them.

Wright argues for this 'judgement-dependent' conception of content by attacking the epistemologies available on the alternative model. Drawing extensively on Wittgenstein's actual text, Wright reconstructs an interesting set of considerations against both *introspective* and *inferential* conceptions of self-knowledge, thus, presumably, exhausting the epistemologies available to his opponent. So long as facts about our mental states are construed as independent of, and, hence, as tracked by our self-regarding judgements, we can have no satisfactory explanation of our ability to know them. On the assumption, then, that Kripke's unstable content irrealism is to be avoided at all costs, that leaves the judgement-dependent conception as the only contender. So goes Wright's argument.

Wright's discussion raises a number of interesting and difficult questions. Is it really true that Wittgenstein's discussion destroys all 'cognitive

---

68. *Ibid.*, p. 246.

accomplishment' theories of self-knowledge? Supposing it does, does this inevitably drive us to a judgement-dependent conception of content? Are there not other conceptions that would equally accommodate the rejection of a tracking epistemology? Unfortunately, none of these questions can be adequately addressed within the confines of the present essay. Here I have to settle for raising a question about whether a judgement-dependent conception of *content* could *ever* be the cogent moral of any argument.

So, WE MEAN SOMETHING IN VIRTUE OF A SPECIFIC EXAMPLE, THEN WE FORGET THE EXAMPLE AND WE THEN 30. MEAN SOMETHING IN A VERY GENERAL WAY

The suggestion is that we must not construe facts concerning mental content as genuine objects of cognition, and that this is to be accomplished by regarding them as constituted by truths concerning our best judgements about mental content. Well what does this amount to? For illustrative purposes, Wright offers the case of colour. What would have to be true, if facts about colour are judgement-dependent? We would need, first and foremost, to secure the *accessibility* of colour facts, and so a biconditional of the following form:

if C: S would judge x to be blue $\leftrightarrow$ x is blue

But not just any biconditional of this form will serve to secure the accessibility of colour. For example, unless restrictions are placed on the permissible specifications of C, *every* property will turn out to be accessible; just let C be: conditions under which S is infallible about colour. So, it must be further required that C be specified in substantial terms, avoiding a 'whatever-it-takes' formulation.

Now, what would it take to ground not merely the accessibility of colour facts, but their *judgement-dependence*? What is needed, as Wright points out, is that

the question whether the C-conditions, so substantially specified, are satisfied in a particular case is logically independent of any truths concerning the details of the extension of colour concepts.[69]

This seems right. For unless the specification of the C-conditions, or, indeed, of anything else on the left-hand-side, is precluded from presupposing facts about the colours of objects, it will remain entirely open whether subjects' judgements, formed under the relevant C-conditions, really did determine facts about colour. For satisfaction of the conditions described on the left-

69. *Ibid.*, pp. 247–8.

hand-side would always presuppose some antecedently fixed constitution of colour facts, thus undermining the claim that it is precisely truths about best judgement that fix those facts.

No doubt, other requirements are in order as well.[70] But it is, I trust, already clear that there is a serious difficulty seeing how facts about mental content could conceivably satisfy the stated requirements on judgement-dependence. For it is inconceivable, given what *judgement-dependence* amounts to, that the biconditionals in the case of mental content should satisfy the requirement that their left-hand-sides be free of any assumptions about mental content. For, at a minimum, the *content of the judgements* said to fix the facts about mental content have to be presupposed. And that means that any such biconditional will always presuppose a constitution of mental content quite independent of constitution by best judgement.

In a way, an intuitive difficulty should have been clear from the start. A 'judgement-dependent' conception of a given fact is, by definition, a conception of that fact according to which it is *constituted* by our *judgements*. The idea is clearly appropriate in connection with facts about the *chic* or the *fashionable;* familiar, though less clearly appropriate, in connection with facts about colour or sound; and, it would appear, impossible as a conception of facts about mental content. For it cannot in general be true that facts about content are constituted by our judgements about content: facts about content, constituted independently of the judgements, are presupposed by the model itself.

CONCLUSION: ROBUST REALISM – PROBLEMS AND PROSPECTS

31.

Let *robust realism* designate the view that judgements about meaning are factual, irreducible, and judgement-independent. Then the moral of this paper – if it has one – is that the major alternatives to robust realism are beset by very serious difficulties.

Irrealism – the view, advocated by Kripke's Wittgenstein, that judgements about meaning are non-factual – appears not even to be a coherent option. (An error-theoretic variant, as promoted, for example, by Paul Churchland, seems no better.)

Reductionist versions of realism appear to be false. The proposal that judgements about meaning concern communal dispositions is unsatisfactory not merely because, implausibly, it precludes the possibility of communal

---

70. For a very illuminating discussion of the conditions that would have to be met, see *ibid.*, pp. 246–54.

error, but because it appears bound to misconstrue the meaning of every expression in the language. The rather more promising (and rather more popular) proposal, that judgements about meaning concern a certain sort of *idealized* disposition, also appears to confront serious difficulties: it is hard to see how the idealizations are to be specified in a non-question-begging way.

And, finally, *a judgement-dependent* conception of meaning seems not to be a stable option, because the very idea of constitution by best judgement appears to presuppose a *judgement-independent* conception of meaning.

It is sometimes said that an anti-reductionist conception is too facile a response to the problem about meaning. It is hard not to sympathize with this sentiment. But if the considerations canvassed against the alternatives are correct, and if it is true that the 'rule-following' considerations leave an anti-reductionist conception untouched, it is hard, ultimately, also to agree with it. Meaning properties appear to be neither eliminable, nor reducible. Perhaps it is time that we learned to live with that fact.

I do not pretend that this will be easy. Robust realism harbours some unanswered questions, the solutions to which appear not to be trivial. There are three main difficulties. First: what sort of room is left for *theorizing* about meaning, if reductionist programs are eschewed? Second: how are we to reconcile an anti-reductionism about meaning properties with a satisfying conception of their causal or explanatory efficacy? And, finally: how are we to explain our (first-person) knowledge of them?

I cannot, of course, hope to address any of these questions adequately here. A few brief remarks will have to suffice.

To begin with the last question first, I cannot see that an anti-reductionist conception of content has a *special* problem about self-knowledge. As far as I am concerned, no one has a satisfactory explanation of our ability to know our own thoughts.[71] But I do not see that the anti-reductionist need feel any special embarrassment about this. If anything, it seems to me, the prospects are better for him than for his opponent. A reductionist would have it that meanings are fixed by certain kinds of dispositional fact, the sort of fact that could hardly be known observationally. It would appear to follow that the reductionist is committed, if he is to have a substantial epistemology of self-knowledge, to an inferential conception – a conception that may be, as I have argued elsewhere, worse than implausible.[72] The anti-reductionist labours under no comparable burden.

As for the charge that there would be nothing left for a theory of meaning to be, if reductionism is eschewed, it seems to me simply false. Let me here mention just a few of the questions that survive the rejection of reductionist programmes. For one thing, as I have stressed, a nonreductionism about meaning is best understood as a thesis about *mental* meaning, not about

---

71. See my 'Content and Self-Knowledge'.
72. Again see my *ibid*.

linguistic meaning. So anti-reductionism, as I understand it, is not only consistent with, but positively invites, a theory about the relation between thought and language. How do public language symbols come to acquire meaning and what role does thought play in that process? Secondly, anti-reductionism in my sense is consistent with wanting a general account of the principles by which we interpret other people. The important work of Quine, Davidson, Lewis, Grandy, and others on the theory of radical interpretation neither needs, nor is best understood in terms of, reductionist aspirations. Its proper goal is the articulation of the principles we evidently successfully employ in interpreting the speech and minds of others. And, finally, an anti-reductionism about mental content is perfectly consistent both with substantive theories of the nature of the propositional *attitudes* – that is, of what makes a given mental state a *belief,* as opposed to a wish or a desire – and with the claim that the grasping of certain mental contents depends on the grasping of others, and so with theories of the *compositional structure* of mental content.

There is hardly any fear, then, that we shall run out of things to do, if we forego reductionist programmes in the theory of mental content.

Finally, though, there is the question of mental causation: how are we to reconcile an anti-reductionism about content properties with a satisfying conception of their causal efficacy? It is a view long associated with Wittgenstein himself, of course, that propositional attitude explanations are not causal explanations. But, whether or not the view was Wittgenstein's, it has justifiably few adherents today. As Davidson showed, if propositional attitude explanations are to rationalize behaviour at all, then they must do so by causing it.[73] But propositional attitudes rationalize partly by virtue of their content – it is partly because Neil's belief is *that there is wine in his glass* that he reaches for it; so, propositional attitude explanations commit us to holding that content properties have a genuine causal role in the explanation of intentional action. But, now, how is an anti-reductionist about content properties to accord them a genuine causal role without committing himself, implausibly, to the essential incompleteness of physics?

This is, I believe, the single greatest difficulty for an anti-reductionist conception of content. It may be that it will eventually prove its undoing. But the subject is relatively unexplored, and much interesting work remains to be done.[74]

---

73. See 'Actions, Reasons, and Causes', in his *Essays on Actions and Events* (Oxford: Oxford University Press, 1980).
74. For some recent papers see E. LePore and B. Loewer, 'Mind Matters', *Journal of Philosophy*, 1987, and Jerry Fodor, 'Making Mind Matter More', *Philosophical Topics*, Spring 1989.

CHAPTER TEN

THE REALITY OF RULE-FOLLOWING

Philip Pettit

Drawing on Wittgensteinian materials, Saul Kripke has raised a problem for anyone who thinks that we follow rules, say rules of meaning, in the ordinary sense of that phrase: the sense in which it suggests that rules are entities we can identify at a time and form the intention of trying to honour thereafter.[1] He has presented a skeptical challenge to the idea of rule-following, elaborating – if not wholly endorsing – arguments which purport to show that the idea is rooted in illusion.

I believe that this challenge is of the greatest importance in the philosophy of mind, though many practitioners seem to think that they can ignore it. I argue that the challenge can be met and the reality of rule-following vindicated. But I show that, in order to meet it in this way, some quite dramatic shifts have to be made in the ways of conceiving mentality that have become standard among philosophers and psychologists.

The paper is in five parts. In the first I give a characterization of rules and rule-following, trying to show how central they are in our everyday thought about ourselves. In the second I present the skeptical challenge, drawing heavily on Kripke's work; I exercise some license here, since I do not aspire to be an exegete either of Kripke or of Wittgenstein. In the third section I offer my response to the challenge, outlining a non-skeptical conception of rules and rule-following. In the fourth section I look at three corollaries of the response. And then in the last section I buttress the response, showing how the non-skeptical conception can be extended to encompass public as well as private rules.

One word of warning, in case too much is expected. I formulate the problem of rule-following, and I propose a solution, on the assumption that

---

1. Saul Kripke, *Wittgenstein on Rules and Private Language* (Oxford: Basil Blackwell, 1982); henceforth, *WRPL*. See also Robert Fogelin, *Wittgenstein,* 2nd edn (London: Routledge, 1987).

a creature which does not follow rules in my sense, and is not therefore a speaker or thinker – see section 1 – may yet be capable of having beliefs, desires, and intentions, including beliefs, desires, and intentions directed to others of its kind: it may yet be an intentional and even social subject. Those who want to ascribe intentionality only to speakers or thinkers will quarrel with this assumption but they will probably endorse a variant that would serve my purposes equally well: they will recognize the possibility that creatures who do not follow rules may yet display a suitably complex range of recognitional, behavioural, and information-processing skills. The important point is that rule-following, as I understand it, does not encompass the full leap from protoplasm to personhood, only the transition from, as it were, sub-personal to personal mentality.[2]

1. RULES AND RULE-FOLLOWING

What the skeptical challenge puts in doubt is the fact, as it appears to us, that we follow rules. The notion of following a rule, as it is conceived here, involves an important element over and beyond that of conforming to a rule. The conformity must be intentional, being something that is achieved, at least in part, on the basis of belief and desire. To follow a rule is to conform to it but the act of conforming, or at least the act of trying to conform – if that is distinct – must be intentional. It must be explicable, in the appropriate way, by the agent's beliefs and desires.

But more than this is required to understand the appearance of rule-following which the skeptical challenge questions. We need to understand not just what following involves, but also what sorts of things the rules followed are supposed to be. From the viewpoint of the skeptical challenge, there are four important elements in the notion of rules; a further element will be identified later when we move to the discussion of public rules. I make no pretence at analysing the everyday notion of rules in distinguishing these elements. My analysis, which is influenced in great part by Kripke's discussion, is offered as a stipulative account.

The first and main element in the definition of rules is the stipulation that rules are normative constraints, in particular normative constraints which are relevant in an indefinitely large number of decision-types. That something is a normative constraint in a decision means that it identifies one option – or perhaps one subset of options – as more appropriate in some way than the

---

2. I defend the assumption mentioned in this paragraph in *The Common Mind: From Folk Psychology to Social and Political Theory* (Oxford: Oxford University Press, 1993). I also mark the distinction there between the problem of rule-following and the problem of content that arises for unthinking intentional subjects.

others. The option may be the most polite, as with a rule of etiquette; the most becoming, as with a rule of fashion; the most just, as with a rule of fairness; or whatever. That a normative constraint is relevant in an indefinitely large number of decision-types means that the decisions which it is capable of constraining are not limited to sorts of situations which the rule-follower can use an effective procedure to specify independently in advance. Most familiar rules involve normative constraints which are relevant in an indefinitely large number of decision-types. There is no suitable specification of the types of situation where most rules of etiquette or ethics apply and certainly no such specification of the circumstances where the rules governing normal word-usage apply; the point is made vivid, if that is necessary, by Wittgenstein on family resemblance.

This first element in our definition means that a rule is a function which can take an indefinite variety of decision-types as inputs and deliver in each case one option – or set of options – as output: this is the option that is identified as the most appropriate in some way. Consistently with meeting this condition a rule may be a total function over all decision-types – a function yielding an output in each case – or a partial function that only yields an outcome in some cases. An example of a suitable function would be the indefinitely large set of pairs, one for every decision-type, which each involve, first, a relevant decision-type and then the option appropriate for that type. We might refer to such a set as the rule-in-extension. Another example of a suitable function would be the abstract object which is conceived as having the property of identifying the appropriate option for every relevant decision-type to which it is applied. We call this the rule-in-intension, though it might be more familiar under a name like 'universal' or 'concept' or 'property'.

The other three elements in the definition of a rule can be derived from this first element, together with the assumption that the rule is capable of being followed. They are requirements that an indefinitely normative constraint – a rule in the objective sense – must satisfy, if it is to make sense for finite subjects like you and me to try to conform to it.

The first of the additional elements is the requirement that not only should a rule be normative over an indefinite variety of applications, it should be determinable or identifiable by a finite subject independently of any particular application: the prospective rule-follower should be in a position to identify the rule in such a manner that he can sensibly try to be faithful to it in any application. If the rule were identified by reference in part to how the subject responded in a given case, then the subject could not see the rule as something to which he should try to be faithful in that case.

He could not see it as a normative constraint for him to try to respect there.

The other two additional elements in our account of rules require respectively that a rule must be directly readable and fallibly readable. That a rule is directly readable means that the competent rule-follower can tell straight-away what it apparently requires or, if he tells what it requires by applying

190

[handwritten: ① ISN'T THIS WHAT KRIPKE'S SKEPTIC IS POINTING TO?]

other rules, that these are ultimately rules whose apparent requirements he can tell straightaway. That a rule is fallibly readable means that no matter how directly the rule speaks to him, no matter how quickly he can tell what it apparently requires, that fact alone does not provide the rule-follower with an epistemic guarantee that he has got the requirement of the rule right. He can understand properly the situation on hand, seeing clearly the options before him, and yet for all that shows, fail to read the rule properly. Thus, in one sense at least, he is not an infallible authority; there is an epistemic possibility of his going wrong.[3]

[handwritten: ARE THERE ANY DEFINITE CONDITIONS UNDER WHICH THIS OCCURS? OR HOW IS IT TOO SKETCHY!]

It is clear that an infinitely normative constraint must be identifiable independently of any application, if it is to make sense for a finite subject to try intentionally to conform to it. But the fulfilment of that condition also requires that the rule be directly and fallibly readable. The rule-follower must be able to tell straight off what the rule apparently requires or to tell what it requires by applying rules such that ultimately he tells straight off what they apparently require. How else could he intentionally try to conform? And the rule-follower must be able to tell only fallibly what a rule requires. Otherwise the notion of intentional action, in particular the notion of trying, would be out of place.

[handwritten: HMMM... MIGHT 'TRYING' NOT RELATE MORE TO ONE'S DISPOSITION THAN ANY NORMATIVE UNDERSTANDING?]

This account of rules suffices, I hope, to give some sense of the apparent fact about ourselves which the skeptical challenge is designed to put in doubt. The fact under challenge is that we intentionally try to conform to rules: that we intentionally try to conform to indefinitely normative constraints that are independently determinable, directly and fallibly readable. Before going to the skeptical challenge however it will be useful to consider two respects in which we are required, it seems, to be capable of following rules: first, so far as we are speakers, and secondly – this is more contentious – so far as we are thinkers.

The case of speech is the one that is most commonly mentioned. The situation, as acknowledged on all sides, is that when I grasp the meaning of a word, say by examples of its usage, I put myself in touch with a rule which I am then in a position to intend to honour in future cases. The meaning normatively constrains usage over an indefinite variety of cases. It is determinable independently of any particular case. And from the point of view of someone like me who has just grasped it, the meaning is directly but fallibly readable. Thus consider the case on which Kripke focuses, in which a few examples of addition enable me, or so I feel assured, to grasp the meaning of 'plus'. 'I feel confident that there is something in my mind – the meaning I attach to the "plus" sign – that instructs me what I ought to do in all future cases. I do not *predict* what I *will* do . . . but instruct myself what I ought to do to conform to the meaning.'[4]

---

3. In another sense he may be: he may be designed so that he always reads the rule right as a matter of fact.

4. Kripke, *WRPL*, p. 22.

[handwritten: A FACT: COOPERATIONAL PRINCIPLE IS ACTIVE IN BOTH PARTICIPANTS IN A RULE]

Although it is generally conceded that we are required to be able to follow rules so far as we speak, it is not always recognized that we also seem required to be able to follow rules if we are to think.[5] Thinking requires more than just the having of intentional attitudes: attitudes, as most people are prepared to describe them, of belief and desire. A system has such attitudes, I am prepared to say, so far as its behaviour is non-redundantly explained by their presence.[6] The behaviour is intentional, being produced in each case – and produced in the right way – by the desire for a certain state of affairs and the belief that doing this or that offers the best promise of desire-satisfaction. But a system that is intentional in this sense need not be cogitative or thoughtful.

Thinking involves not just having intentional attitudes, but intentionally shaping those attitudes: say, shaping them with a view to having beliefs that are adequate for certain projects, or beliefs that are true. The thinker must be able to wonder whether something is so, to institute tests to see whether it is so or not, to accept in the light of those tests that it probably is, and so on. He may or may not conduct these activities very explicitly of course and the only sign that he is thoughtful, one to which Donald Davidson draws attention in another context, may be that he shows surprise at the appearance of this or that piece of evidence.[7] That a subject shows such surprise means, plausibly, that he had a belief whose content was that the potential content of another belief is likely to be true, is supported by the evidence so far, or whatever; previously he believed that it is likely that *p* and he is surprised because it turns out that not *p*.[8] If a subject has beliefs about contents in this way, as distinct just from beliefs with contents, then he is able to wonder about whether such contents – such propositions – are true, able to desire that he have beliefs with contents that are true, and the like. In short he is able, in our sense, to think. He is a cogitative system, not just an intentional one.

Thinking in the sense involved here seems to require, like speech, the capacity to follow rules. This is not surprising, since in this sense thinking conforms to the shape of what has traditionally been regarded as inner speech, discourse with oneself. The thinker who wonders what is the sum of two numbers is in exactly the position of the speaker who sets out to apply the word 'plus' properly. He is required, it seems, to have identified something that serves as a normative constraint in the determination of this, and an indefinite variety of other sums; something determinable in advance of any particular application; and something that he can directly, if only fallibly,

---

5. But see Colin McGinn, *Wittgenstein on Meaning* (Oxford: Basil Blackwell, 1984), pp. 144–6.
6. See Frank Jackson and Philip Pettit 'Functionalism and Broad Content', *Mind*, 1987, pp. 381–400 and 'In defence of Folk Psychology', *Philosophical Studies* 57, 1990, pp. 7–30.
7. 'Rational Animals', in Ernest Le Pore and Brian McLaughlin (eds), *Action and Events* (Oxford: Basil Blackwell, 1985). Davidson wishes to make the possibility of surprise a criterion, not of thought, but of belief.
8. If surprise at evidence does not require such a belief about '*p*', then of course it is not a sign of the capacity to think.

read. His problem is to identify in the case on hand the answer that is fixed by the concept of addition; that concept constitutes a rule and his problem is to remain faithful to it in performing the computation.

If speech and thought involve rule-following, then the magnitude of the challenge discussed in the next section can hardly be overstated. Deny that there are such things as rules, deny that there is anything that counts strictly as rule-following, and you put in jeopardy some of our most central notions about ourselves. More than that, you also put in jeopardy our notion of the world as requiring us, given our words and concepts, to describe it this way rather than that; you undermine our conception of objective characterization. There is no extant philosophical challenge that compares on the scale of iconoclasm with the skeptical challenge to rule-following.

2. THE SKEPTICAL CHALLENGE

I can be brief in stating the skeptical challenge to rules and rule-following, since the challenge has been well elaborated by Kripke.[9] Only a difference in emphasis separates my version of the challenge from his. He tends to ask after what fact about a person could constitute his following a rule whereas I shall ask after what sort of thing could constitute a rule that the person might follow.[10] But this shift of emphasis does not beg the question against any possible resolution of Kripke's problem; thus I remain open to the possibility that there is something to constitute rule-following without there being anything to constitute a rule. The shift of emphasis is designed to link up smoothly with our discussion in the last section.

Among the elements invoked in the definition of a rule, there is a salient distinction between the first element and the other three. The first tells us about what objectively, so to speak, a rule is. It is a constraint that is normative over an indefinite variety of cases; in effect, or so it would seem, it is a rule-in-extension or rule-in-intension. The other three elements tell us what an objective rule must be to engage subjectively with potential followers. It must be identifiable independently of any particular application, it must be directly readable, and it must be fallibly readable.

The skeptical challenge to rules is best presented as a challenge to identify anything that could simultaneously satisfy the objective and subjective elements in the definition of a rule. What sort of thing could be indefinitely normative and engage in the manner required with finite minds like ours? Putting the question the other way around, among the things that engage

---

9. Kripke, *WRPL*, ch. 2.
10. We may, in doing this, be sticking more closely to Wittgenstein. See Marie McGinn, 'Kripke on Wittgenstein's Skeptical Problem', *Ratio*, 1984, pp. 19–32.

[handwritten: Rule-in-extension seems to be the rule is defined by its results, so in the case of addition it is impossible.]

appropriately with our minds, what sort could serve as an indefinitely normative constraint?

Take the sorts of entities which we know to satisfy the objective condition: the rule-in-extension and the rule-in-intension. The rule-in-extension does not seem capable of satisfying the subjective conditions because it is liable, as in the case of 'plus', to be an infinitely large set. 'The infinitely many cases of the table are not in my mind for my future self to consult.'[11] There is no way that I could get in touch appropriately with such an infinite object. Or so it certainly seems.

What of the rule-in-intension? What, for example, of the addition function, as Frege would conceive of it, which determines the correct option in any decision about the sum of two numbers?[12] What is there against the idea that this abstract object might be able to satisfy the subjective conditions, engaging our minds appropriately? Here the problem is to explain how we are able to get in contact with such an abstract object. It does not affect our senses like a physical object and so we are not causally connected with it in the ordinary way. So how then does it become present to our minds? The obvious sort of answer is to say, like Frege, that it does so via an idea – or some such entity – that we can contemplate. But then the suggestion boils down to one that we consider in a moment and find wanting.[13]

[handwritten: Rule in intension is rule as abstract object?]

Moving from the entities which can clearly satisfy the objective condition on a rule to entities that look more likely to be able to satisfy the subjective conditions, the question here is whether such entities can be objectively satisfactory: whether they can serve as normative constraints over an indefinite variety of cases. Kripke mentions two main candidates for entities of this kind: first, actual or possible examples of the application of the rule in question, such as examples of addition; and secondly, introspectible states of consciousness, as for instance the sort of *quale* that might be thought to be associated with adding numbers together. There is a special problem with the second candidate, which is that often no plausible *quale* is available.[14] But, more importantly, there is an objection that applies equally to both candidates, so Kripke argues, and indeed to any finite object that is proposed for the role in question.[15]

The objection, and this is clearly derived from Wittgensteinian materials, is that no finite object contemplated by the mind can unambiguously identify a constraint that is normative over an indefinite variety of cases. Consider a series of examples of addition: $1 + 1 = 2, 1 + 2 = 3, 2 + 2 = 4$, and the like. For all that any such finite object can determine, the right way to go with a novel case remains open. 'Plus', as we understand it, forces us to say that

[handwritten in left margin: Objection concerns objects in observation?]

---

11. Kripke, *WRPL*, p. 22.
12. *Ibid.*, p. 53.
13. *Ibid.*, p. 54.
14. *Ibid.*, p. 43.
15. *Ibid.*, p. 43.

[handwritten annotation at top: THERE IS A CORRE.FNT, IN THE FORM OF A GRICEAN ASSUMPTION THAT DOES DETERMINE MY MEANING.]

$68 + 57 = 125$ but the examples given do nothing to identify the plus-rule as distinct from, say, the quus-rule, where this says that the answer in the case of 68 and 57 is 5. The fact is that any finite set of examples, mathematical or otherwise, can be extrapolated in an infinite number of ways; equivalently, any finite set of examples instantiates an infinite number of rules.

It appears then that I cannot be put in touch with a particular rule just on the basis of finite examples.

> When I respond one way rather than another to such a problem as '68 + 57', I can have no justification for one response rather than another. Since the skeptic who supposes that I meant quus cannot be answered, there is no fact about me that distinguishes between my meaning plus and my meaning quus. Indeed, there is no fact about me that distinguishes between my meaning a definite function by 'plus' (which determines my responses in new cases) and my meaning nothing at all.[16]

[handwritten annotation: How DOES GRICE TELL ME how TO APPLY RULE IN FUTURE CASES?]

The problem raised extends to *qualia*. 'No internal impression, with a *quale*, could possibly tell me in itself how it is to be applied in future cases.'[17] If the impression has a bearing on future cases, say on the application of 'plus', it will be capable of being extrapolated in any of an infinite number of ways. How then am I supposed to grasp a particular rule in contemplating the impression? How is the impression supposed to make salient just one of the infinite number of rules that it might be held to illustrate? The question extends from qualitative impressions to all mental objects of contemplation, including the sort of idea postulated by Frege. 'The idea in my mind is a finite object: can it not be interpreted as determining a quus function, rather than a plus function?'[18]

The upshot of these considerations is that rules are, at the least, extremely mysterious. They are required to satisfy two sets of conditions, objective and subjective, which no familiar sort of entity seems to be capable of simultaneously satisfying. A number of responses are possible at this point. One is to go skeptical and deny that there are rules. A second is to go dogmatic and, insisting that of course there are rules, argue that they are *sui generis*.[19] Such responses are not attractive however and so we shall look again in the next section for some way around the challenge.

But before leaving this section we must mention the response to his challenge on which Kripke spends most time. This response says nothing on

---

16. *Ibid.*, p. 21.
17. *Ibid.*, p. 43.
18. *Ibid.*, p. 54.
19. See, for example, Warren Goldfarb, 'Kripke on Wittgenstein on Rules', *Journal of Philosophy*, 1985. A third response, to which Peter Menzies has drawn my attention, would be to argue that there are two distinct conceptions of rules corresponding to the two sorts of conditions.

what rules are but still insists that there is such a thing as rule-following. It identifies following a rule with displaying a disposition to go on after a certain pattern, say a pattern in applying the word 'plus' to new cases. I will not delay over this theory since, while it attracts a variety of criticisms from Kripke, the basic flaw is already crippling. The theory does nothing to explain how in following a rule I am directly but fallibly guided by something which determines the right response in advance. A disposition may determine what I do but it cannot provide this sort of guidance. 'As a candidate for a "fact" that determines what I mean, it fails to satisfy the basic condition on such a candidate, . . . that it should *tell* me what I ought to do in each new instance. Ultimately, almost all objections to these dispositional accounts boil down to this one.'[20]

3. A NON-SKEPTICAL RESPONSE

Any non-skeptical response to the challenge about rules has to vindicate the idea that we intentionally try to conform to entities that satisfy the objective condition: constraints that are normative over an indefinite variety of cases. Let us assume then that if we follow a rule we are indeed put in touch with an entity of this kind. We can think of it as a rule-in-extension or a rule-in-intension.

The question that arises under this assumption is how a rule-in-extension or rule-in-intension – henceforth I shall simply say, a rule – can satisfy the subjective conditions, being independently identifiable, directly readable, and fallibly readable. This is a question, at base, about how a rule can be suitably represented to a human subject, since there is no possibility of a rule presenting itself immediately: there is no possibility of the subject's 'mainlining' the rule. Let us concentrate then on this representational issue. In exploring the issue, we shall have in mind rules of a kind that can be identified and read without the application of other rules. If the issue can be solved for such simple rules, as we may call them, it can be solved for more complex ones.[21]

What material, directly accessible to the human subject, could serve to represent a rule, in particular a simple rule? The outstanding candidate is: examples of its application. The plus rule might be represented then as the (1, 1, 2) – (1, 2, 3) – (2, 2, 4) rule, the rule for chair as the (X) – (Y) – (Z) rule, where X, Y, and Z are all chairs, and so on. It appears however that this candidate has already been ruled out. Any finite set of examples instantiates

---

20. Kripke, *WRPL*, p. 24.
21. I do not assume that the simple–complex distinction is invariant across persons or for a single person across times. Division of linguistic labour argues against the first sort of invariance, conceptual development against the second.

an indefinite number of rules, as we saw in the last section. And does not that mean that no set of examples can represent a determinate rule for an agent?

The first step towards the proposal I wish to develop here is to recognize that no, it does not necessarily mean this. Instantiation is a two-place relationship between a set of examples and a rule and it certainly has the feature of being a one–many relationship: one finite set of examples instantiates many rules. But the relationship that is of concern to us when we ask whether a finite set of examples can represent a determinate rule is not instantiation but exemplification. Exemplification is a three-place relationship, not a two-place one: it involves not just a set of examples and a rule but also a person for whom the examples are supposed to exemplify the rule.[22] Although any finite set of examples instantiates an indefinite number of rules, for a particular agent the set may exemplify just one rule. Nothing has been said at least to disallow this possibility.

The second step in developing the proposal I wish to defend is to see how that possibility might be realized. Suppose that on being presented with a set of examples, an agent develops an independent disposition or inclination to extrapolate in a certain way to other cases: an inclination of which he may or may not be aware. That set of examples will continue to instantiate many rules but the rule it will then exemplify for the agent will certainly be a rule associated suitably – we come back to this in the next step – with the inclination generated by the examples. If she uses the examples to pick out a rule for herself – if she refers to that rule, the one that goes (1, 1, 2), (1, 2, 3), (2, 2, 4), and so on – she will certainly have in mind that rule among the rules instantiated by the examples which her inclination makes salient. We know of course, and indeed we recognized this in the last section, that human agents who claim to pick up rules by ostension, by the use of examples, certainly develop independent inclinations to carry on in a particular way when they are exposed to such examples. Thus we now see that there really is a possibility that a finite set of examples can exemplify a determinate rule for a human agent: it can exemplify the rule that is suitably associated with the inclination generated by the examples.

It is commonly recognized that the inclination involved in following any rule plays a role in prompting the agent's case by case responses. I do not reject that observation, though I did argue in the last section that following a rule must involve more than just indulging such a disposition: otherwise there would be no question of taking one's guidance directly but fallibly from something that determines the right response in advance. What we have now been led to see however is that the inclination involved in following a rule may have a dual function, serving not only to prompt the agent's responses, but also to make salient the rule she intends to follow: the rule which, given

---

22. See Nelson Goodman, *Languages of Art* (Oxford: Oxford University Press, 1969).

the inclination they engender, a certain set of examples can exemplify.

But it is important to stress one aspect of the proposal. This is that it does not require a rule-follower to have any awareness of the inclination generated by the examples that exemplify a rule, let alone to attend to that inclination in herself. I speak of the inclination making salient one of the rules instantiated by the examples, and of the agent representing the rule – via the examples – on the basis of the inclination. But none of this is meant to suggest that the rule-follower focuses on the inclination. She will focus simply on the examples and – in them, as it were – on the rule they manifest to her. The inclination explains how the examples exemplify or manifest a particular rule but it does this without having to feature in consciousness.

Perhaps the best way of casting the proposal is with the help of a familiar analogy. When I look at a physical object, all that is in one sense presented to me is a sequence of profiles: now this profile, now that, as I move around the object. Yet in experiencing those profiles I see the object itself in the perfectly ordinary sense of that verb. I see it, as we might say, *in* the profiles. Indeed I scarcely notice the profiles, focusing as I do on the object they manifest to me. What explains how the profiles manifest *this* sort of object, conforming to the ordinary image of the middle-sized spatio-temporal continuant: *this* object, rather than any of the many ontological inventions that are strictly consistent with the sequence of profiles? Presumably something about my psychology, a disposition that I share with others of my species. This disposition may lend itself to psychological investigation but it will not be something of which I am necessarily aware.

The relevance of the analogy should be clear. As I see a particular sort of object in these profiles, so I see a particular rule manifested in such and such examples. As the profiles efface themselves in my attention, yielding centre stage to the object, so the examples command less attention than the rule they exemplify. And as the disposition which explains why I see a certain sort of object is something of which I may not be aware, so the inclination which explains why I am directed to a particular rule need not figure in my consciousness either. This analogy may be the best way of grasping the sort of proposal I am trying to develop.

We are now in a position to move to the third and most crucial step in developing the proposal. We have to identify a relationship between an inclination and a rule which would serve to save the appearance of rule-following, vindicating the claim that a finite set of examples can exemplify a determinate rule for an agent and can put her in a position to read the rule directly but fallibly. What relationship would be suitable? In order to approach an answer, notice that the sort of inclination in question serves like a description of the rule, so far as it gives putative information about the rule: the putative information that the rule requires those responses, those ways of going on, which the inclination supports. Given that the inclination has the status of a description, we can taxonomize the salient ways in which it may

198

relate to the rule. It may or may not be a priori true to the rule. And it may or may not be necessarily true to the rule.

The inclination will be a priori true to the rule, if the rule is this: whatever rule dictates the responses which the inclination supports. But if inclination and rule are related in this way, then the proposal must fail. Rule-following will become a matter of intentionally trying to conform to that rule, whatever it is, which is revealed by my inclination, instance by instance. It will become an enterprise in which I cannot fail, and cannot see myself as failing, contrary to the assumption that rules are fallibly readable. The question then is whether there is a suitably a posteriori relationship that might be postulated between inclination and rule. Happily there is.

If the inclination is a priori connected with the rule, then it correlates with that rule which fits it exactly: the rule correctly applied in the responses it supports. If the inclination is to be a posteriori connected, then it must connect with a rule which is related to it in some other way, a rule which may not exactly fit it. What other way is there for a rule to relate to my inclination? It can only relate as that rule which fits my inclination but only so far as certain favourable conditions are fulfilled: in particular favourable conditions such that I can discover that in some cases they are not fulfilled, and that I got the rule wrong. The rule associated with the inclination will be that rule, the one that satisfies this inclination, provided the inclination fires under the conditions identified.

It is important to be clear about what exactly this proposal means for the first person point of view. As emphasized before, there is no suggestion that I as rule-follower am reflective about the inclination generated by the cases exemplifying the rule: I may scarcely have recognized that I have such an inclination. All that I need be aware of is that here are some examples that, so far as I am concerned, exemplify a particular rule. Which rule? *That* rule, I say, gesturing at the original examples and perhaps some others. The rule is fixed by what goes in favourable conditions with my inclination but I do not think of it in that way. So how then do favourable conditions enter my consciousness? In this way: that I will be able to admit that I may have got the rule wrong in a particular application, so far as I find that conditions were not favourable there.

In order to see that this suggestion may have something going for it, we need to recognize that the favourable conditions required do not have to be identified in advance by the subject. If they had to be, then that would make the suggestion implausible from the start. All that is necessary however is that I be in a position such that I may have to recognize after following the inclination in a given case that the response was vitiated by some perturbing conditions and was not in conformity with the rule which I represent to myself on the basis of the inclination. If I am in such a position then the inclination can serve to represent a rule with which it is associated other than by invariably supporting responses that conform to the rule.

We are pushed on by this observation to ask about how I might come to occupy a position of this kind. One obvious way, and perhaps the only conceivable way, is this. I might be committed to the principle that intertemporal or interpersonal differences in how the inclination generated by certain examples goes are a sign that perturbing influences are at play and I might generally be able to identify such influences and provide an *ex post* explanation of any difference. The inclination on the basis of which I represent a rule to myself leads me at one time to respond in one way to a certain type of decision, at another time in another.[23] Or the inclination leads me to respond in one way, while the counterpart inclination – associated with the same generative examples – leads you to respond in another. Happily however I am able to explain the difference – I am able to find it intelligible – recognizing that a factor which is generally explanatory of differences – say, intoxication or inattention –affected me at one of the times in question, or affected one of the two of us in the interpersonal case.

Let us suppose then, in developing our proposal, that the inclination involved in rule-following connects in this a posteriori fashion to the rule it enables the agent to identify. The other question, given that the inclination has the status of a description, is whether it connects with it necessarily or contingently. It will connect necessarily if the rule is the rule which the inclination corresponds with in favourable conditions, whatever the possible world in question. In this case there will be no possibility that the inclination could fail under favourable conditions to correspond to the rule. The inclination will connect contingently with the rule on the other hand if the rule is that which the inclination corresponds with under favourable conditions in the actual world. This will allow for the possibility of inclination and rule coming apart, even under such conditions. There will be possible worlds where the inclination corresponds with quite different rules from that involved in the actual world.

This question is not as pressing as the issue about a priori and a posteriori status. There is no conflict between either reading of the inclination-rule relationship and the constraints on rules. But I prefer the contingent reading to the necessary one, at least in the general case. Consider that possible world where our counterparts are led by a counterpart inclination to claim that $68 + 57 = 5$. We would hardly want to say that they were being faithful to the plus-rule and yet that is what the necessity reading would entail. Under the contingent reading there is no such problem. Our counterparts are not faithful to the rule with which the inclination corresponds in the actual world and so they are simply miscounting. There may be cases where the necessary

---

23. See Simon Blackburn, 'The Individual Strikes Back', *Synthese*, 1984, p. 294 (this volume Ch. 3), and following on this intrapersonal case. For a critical perspective see Crispin Wright, 'Does PI 258 Suggest a Cogent Argument against Private Language?', in Philip Pettit and John McDowell (eds), *Subject, Thought and Context* (Oxford: Oxford University Press, 1986).

reading is less implausible, for example with colour-rules. We might accept that counterparts whose inclination led them to group green things with red were not misclassifying those things. But even here there is an intuition that after all that may be the least Pickwickian thing to say. Hence I shall generally assume that inclination relates contingently to rule, the rule being that rule with which the inclination corresponds under favourable circumstances in the actual world.

We have taken three steps in developing our response to Kripke's challenge. We have argued, firstly, that the fact that any finite set of examples instantiates an indefinite number of rules does not mean that it cannot exemplify a determinate rule for a given agent; secondly, that the set of examples can exemplify such a rule if the examples generate an inclination in the agent to go on in a certain way: the rule exemplified will be one which is suitably associated with the inclination; and thirdly, that a suitable association between inclination and rule is this: that the rule is that rule to which the inclination corresponds in the actual world, provided the inclination operates under favourable conditions.

We know that, in picking up rules from examples, human beings develop inclinations of the kind which this proposal requires. Thus the materials required for the proposal are certainly available and there is nothing to be said against the claim that it may be sound. But whether we assert that it is sound or not will depend on whether it has explanatory value: on whether, in particular, it can explain how human beings can identify a determinate rule independently of any particular application and can then read the rule directly but fallibly.

A rule will be identifiable independently of any particular application provided two conditions are fulfilled. The first, and it is surely plausible, is that no particular application has to figure among the instances that exemplify the rule for the agent. The second, which requires a little more commentary, is that there is only one rule exemplified by such examples. This will be fulfilled so long as the inclination generated by those examples is associated suitably, after standardization for favourable circumstances, with just one rule. I hold that this condition too is plausible.

The inclination invoked in any case is a currently determinate object, however standardized by the reference to favourable conditions, and it can serve in principle therefore to make it determinate which rule is the one identified by the individual subject. The rule is that which, other things being equal, the standardized inclination would identify, instance by instance.[24] True,

---

24. Does the inclination stretch to an infinite number of instances? Under idealization, yes. *Pace* WRPL, p. 27, it is not necessary to have a story about what in fact would happen if we had the unbounded memory required. Jerry Fodor makes a related point in 'A Theory of Content, Part 2', in *A Theory of Content and Other Essays* (Cambridge, MA: MIT Press, 1990). See also Simon Blackburn 'The Individual Strikes Back', pp. 289–91 (this volume Ch. 3).

we have to wait on the operation of the standardized inclination to see how the rule goes in new instances. But that means only that at any time we may be uncertain as to what the rule requires in new cases, not that there is an objective indeterminacy about the requirement before the case comes up for resolution. So far as there is no objective indeterminacy, the inclination enables the individual to identify a particular rule in advance of any particular application.

The other subjective conditions on a rule are that it should be directly and fallibly readable. If the rule is identified by inclination then of course there is no difficulty about how it can be directly readable. The inclination serves on our proposal, not just to identify the rule, but also to prompt the agent's responses: it has a dual function. The individual will read off the requirement of the rule in a new case by letting her inclination lead her, as with the simple rule, or by applying other rules whose requirements she ultimately reads off in that way. No mode of reading a rule could be more direct. But if the rule is read under the assumption that conditions are favourable, then equally there is no difficulty, even with a simple rule, about how it comes to be fallibly readable. The individual will have to recognize in any instance of reading the rule that for all she knows she may be forced *ex post* to judge that she got it wrong.[25]

The upshot is a cheering one. It begins to seem that the skeptical challenge can be met after all. I can intentionally conform my behaviour to a rule exemplified for me by certain examples, given that those examples generate a certain inclination in me. I can identify such a rule independently of any particular application; I can read off what it requires directly; and yet in any instance of applying the rule I have to admit that I may be mistaken. The phenomenology of rule-following, as it is described in the first section, can be saved.

In conclusion, a methodological comment. Kripke is sometimes accused of putting a tendentious challenge: the challenge to identify rule-following reductively with this or that independent and familiar sort of psychological fact.[26] This challenge would be tendentious, so far as it assumes that rule-following is not a *sui generis* psychological fact. In responding however to the challenge posed in section 2, I have assumed that it takes a different form. I have taken the challenge to be that of explaining in familiar psychological terms how rule-following is possible, given the different and apparently conflicting constraints, objective and subjective, on rules. To explain rule-following in this sense need not be to identify it reductively with any independent psychological fact; it need not be to analyse rule-following in some other terms.[27]

---

25. The account also makes room for a different sort of fallibility: not fallibility in applying a rule but fallibility in picking it up. Circumstances may miscue me so that I judge later that I went wrong about the rule which certain examples exemplified.

26. See Goldfarb, 'Kripke on Wittgenstein on Rules' (this volume Ch. 6).

27. See Huw Price, *Facts and the Function of Truth* (Oxford: Blackwell, 1989), for the distinction between explanation and analysis.

I could provide that link.

A noteworthy feature of the account offered here is that while it seeks to explain how rule-following is possible, it does nothing to identify or analyse rule-following in reductive terms. Rule-following is possible, I argue, under two conditions. The first is that on being presented with certain examples the rule-follower develops an inclination to carry on in a particular fashion, an inclination in virtue of which the examples exemplify a particular rule for the agent. The second condition is that the agent is able to explain any inter-temporal or interpersonal discrepancies in spontaneous application by appeal to perturbing factors, so that the rule exemplified – though she will not think of it this way – is the rule which dictates those responses that the corrected or standardized inclination supports, not the inclination neat. This explanation of how rule-following is possible – of how the objective and subjective constraints on rules can be simultaneously satisfied – nowhere says what rule-following is, reductively characterized. It tells a story about how rule-following might get going; it offers a genealogy of rule-following on a par with Hume's genealogy of causal talk or, more notoriously, Nietzsche's genealogy of morals. But it does not analyse in reductive terms what it means to say that this or that is a rule, that this or that is what it means for a rule to require something, and so on. That the agent follows such and such a rule will be supervenient in a suitable way on the facts about her inclination and context but it will not be identifiable with any such fact.

This abstention from analysis has one important result that we should mention in particular. The proposal which Kripke spends most time in demolishing, the proposal that rule-following reduces to indulging a disposition to go on in a certain way, is open to the following criticism: that the disposition mentioned in this analysis must be subject to the qualification of operating in the right way and that there is no reductive way of expressing this; to operate in the right way is just to operate in accord with the rule.[28] Our proposal, by contrast, is not vulnerable to this style of criticism. Since we do not try to analyse rule-following in reductive terms, we face no such problems. We attempt to give an explanation of how a rule-follower may see herself as having made a mistake and an explanation therefore of how we may see her inclination as having misfired. But this does not involve an assumption that there is a reductive account available of what it is for the inclination to fire correctly or incorrectly.

4. SOME COROLLARIES

Some philosophers will not be enthusiastic about the picture we have developed. While it saves the phenomenology of rule-following, the

---

28. Kripke, *WRPL*, p. 28.

picture has corollaries which they will find repugnant. I shall mention three.

A first corollary we may describe as the precariousness of rule-following. Suppose that for some relevant decision-type, the standardized inclination goes awry; now it dictates this response, now that, without any evidence of perturbing influences. In that case I will have to conclude that the decision-type is not relevant or that there never was a unique rule on which I was targeted. The latter possibility is the threatening one and it remains ever present, so far as I cannot at any time be sure that there will not be a future breakdown of the kind envisaged. In order to aspire to follow a rule I must assume that the standardized inclination picks out a unique rule for me to follow. But I can never redeem that assumption fully. The enterprise of rule-following, and all that goes with it, then, is precarious. It rests on the contingency that certain responses can be corrected so as reliably to yield convergence.[29]

A second corollary of our story is that not only is rule-following precarious, it is also in a certain sense interactive. It requires that the rule-following subject be in a position to interact with other bearers of the inclination – or a counterpart – at work in her: her self at later times or other persons. Without such interaction there cannot be a relationship between the inclination and the rule other than one of exact fit: specifically, there cannot be a suitable relationship of fit under favourable conditions. The subject would not be in a position to identify favourable conditions, even *ex post*. This means that the isolated *doppelgänger* of a rule-follower at any time *t*, the *doppelgänger* without history or company, cannot itself follow a rule. It may avail itself of certain inclinations to refer to *this* or *that* rule, as exemplified by certain examples, but it will not be fallible with respect to any rule identified and so it will not follow such a rule. Rule-following, like keeping your balance, is essentially an interactive enterprise. It makes requirements on the context of the rule-follower as well as on what happens in her head.

A third corollary, besides the precariousness of rule-following and its interactive character, is the relativity of rules. The story we have told means that it is a priori that if under favourable conditions there is appropriate convergence on response *r* in situation *s,* then the rule in question requires that *r* in *s.* This is not to say that the person or even the total community can ever be certain – infallibly certain – that *r* is the correct response, for they can never rule out the possibility that later divergence will reveal that the conditions did in fact involve perturbations; they can never be sure that existing conditions are indeed favourable. Still, even if the a priori connection does not raise the spectre of infallibility, it does introduce a relativity to our

---

29. On this topic see John McDowell, 'Wittgenstein on Rule-Following', *Synthese*, 1984, pp. 326–63.

species, perhaps even our culture, which many philosophers will find repugnant. It means that while I may struggle fallibly to be faithful to an objective rule in the enterprise of rule-following, which rule I am tracking is determined in a certain sense by my nature. Someone who lacked that nature, someone who lacked a suitable counterpart to the inclination operative in me, would have no capacity to tell what rule I was following or even that I was following a rule.

Of the three corollaries this last one will probably be found the most troubling. Consider how it bears on properties. Properties are rules-in-intension, so far as they normatively constrain predications over an indefinite variety of cases; they are thought of as determinable independently of any particular predication; and they are regarded generally as directly and fallibly accessible. The third corollary means that properties are in a certain sense relative to our kind. Each property may be independent of us, in the sense of being something in the world to which we each have only fallible access. But the extension of any property we engage with is determined in such a way that only someone who shares our inclinations can identify it.

This means, it will be said, that on our approach all the properties with which we engage fit a condition which many think of as a mark of secondary properties only. I agree but insist that a number of qualifications should be borne in mind. First, the secondary properties in any area are all of equal stature – for example properties of colour – whereas on our account some properties may well be identifiable only via other properties. Secondly, secondary properties have the characteristic that they are primarily associated with one sense only, whereas the inclination that goes by our account with any sort of property may operate on the basis of information from a number of senses. Thirdly, and perhaps most significantly, if I agree that secondary properties typify properties generally, that is only as far as I endorse a distinctively objectivist understanding of such properties. On that understanding the secondary property is realized in things perceived and is subjective only in the sense that which property is discerned in any perception is fixed relative to our kind: it is that property which is picked out in the actual world by such and such a sensation – and the associated inclination to go on – provided that conditions are favourable.[30]

Since the last corollary will still be found troubling, here is one further remark which may help to reconcile people to it. Where a property P is associated with human responses, such as judgements that it applies here or there, the following question picks up an important issue of objectivity: is something P because it is judged to be so or is it judged to be so because it is

---

30. We assume that favourable conditions cannot be identified in advance here any more than elsewhere. If they could be so identified, the secondary properties would cease altogether to be typical. See Crispin Wright, 'Moral Values, Projection and Secondary Qualities', *Proceedings of the Aristotelian Society*, 1988, pp. 1–22, for the sort of view I assume false.

$P.$[31] The interesting feature of the account of properties inherent in our story about rules is that on that account this question naturally attracts the objectivist answer. Something is judged to be P because it is P; something commands a convergence in the P-response because of how it is, not because of collusion or whatever. Its being P is not exhausted then by its being subject to suitable judgements. Its being P ensures that under favourable conditions it will elicit suitable judgements.[32]

5. PUBLIC RULES

There is a condition that is commonly imposed on the notion of a rule, other than the five distinguished in section 1. This is that the rule should be public in roughly the Wittgensteinian sense. 'Grasp of a rule must be manifest in what is interpersonally accessible – i.e. to others as well as to oneself – so that there can be no such thing as intrinsically *unknowable* (by another) rule-following.'[33] The question which we raise in this final section is whether this extra condition would force us to tell a more specific story about rule-following than that which is offered in the last section. I argue that it does, in particular that it requires rule-following to be interpersonally interactive. This means that any rule that it is possible for another to know someone is following is a rule identified by reference, not just to that person's own responses, but also to the responses of certain actual other people.

---

31. This is like the *Euthyphro* question as to whether something is right because the gods will it or whether the gods will it because it is right. It is akin to what Wright calls the order of determination test in 'Moral Values, Projection and Secondary Qualities'. For a similar test applied to truth and consensus see Philip Pettit, 'Habermas on Truth and Justice', in G. H. R. Parkinson, *Marx and Marxisms* (Cambridge: Cambridge University Press, 1982).
32. Thus its being P will explain why it is judged to be P. The sort of explanation relevant is the program style of explanation distinguished in Frank Jackson and Philip Pettit, 'Functionalism and Broad Content' *Mind*, 1988, pp. 381–400. It is important with the Euthyphro question to distinguish the causal – strictly, the causally programmatic – sense of 'because' from the evidential. An eraser bends because (causal) it is elastic, yet it is elastic because (evidential) it bends. Consistently with thinking that something is judged to be P because (causal) it is P, a theorist may think it is P because (evidential) it is judged to be P – by suitable subjects in suitable cirumstances. Indeed the theorist may even think that the evidential claim has a certain a priori support. In maintaining the causal claim as well as the evidential, the theorist will be distinguishing the property of being P from pseudo-properties like that of being 'U' rather than 'non-U' (where saying 'lavatory' is 'U', saying 'toilet' is 'non-U' and so on). For a different perspective – and for the useful idea of a response-dependent concept – see Mark Johnston, 'Dispositional Theories of Value', *Proceedings of the Aristotelian Society*, supp. vol. 63, 1989, especially the last section. I read Johnston's paper while my own was going to press.
33. Colin McGinn, *Wittgenstein on Meaning*, p. 192. See too Crispin Wright, 'Does PI 258 Suggest a Cogent Argument against Private Language?', in Philip Pettit and John McDowell (eds), *Subject, Thought and Context*, pp. 209–10.

Suppose I believe that another person has identified a particular rule. Under the story of the last section, that means that I must take him to be representing the rule by certain examples. He will be doing this on the basis of an inclination that is intertemporally or interpersonally standardized: it is that rule which fits the inclination under favourable conditions, favourable conditions being judged on the basis of the assumption that intertemporal or interpersonal differences are explicable by perturbations. But suppose that the person identifies the rule on the basis of an inclination that is only intertemporally standardized; he has no expectation that others will display convergent responses. In such a circumstance it turns out that while I may *believe* that the person has identified such and such a rule – a rule I represent to myself via my intertemporally standardized inclination – I am not in a position to *know* that he has done so.

I am in no position to know what rule he has identified, because I do not meet a weak condition on knowledge. I cannot reliably tell that he is following one rule rather than any other. I have no reliable means of telling that the rule he is representing by such and such examples is the rule which requires this rather than that response on an example hitherto unencountered. Were our responses to come apart, he might remain quite content with his own response to the example. Using myself as a prosthetic device I may guess that it is this rule rather than that which he is following. But that is all I can do: guess. For all I know in any strict sense, his inclination may differ in a manner which means that he has a quite divergent rule in mind.[34]

This negative result means that it is only if the person identifies the rule on the basis of an interpersonally as well as intertemporally standardized inclination that I can know which rule he is following. But of course it remains to establish the corresponding positive result, showing that the fulfilment of this extra condition is probably sufficient as well as necessary to make such knowledge available to me. Suppose that I regard the person, and regard him rightly, as following a rule such that he expects convergence between us; he represents the rule on the basis of an intertemporally and interpersonally standardized inclination. Suppose that I get in step with him, developing the appropriately generated counterpart inclination: both of us survey some examples and we each develop the inclination to go on with which the rule is associated. The question is whether I am then in a position to know what rule he is following.

I am, for the following reasons. If there is a rule he is intentionally following, it is a rule exemplified in certain examples on the basis of an inclination we share. If there is a rule exemplified in certain examples on the basis of an

---

34. If Donald Davidson is right then, on pain of dismissing the hypothesis that he is a rule-follower, I will have to interpret him as following rules familiar to me at some level. See his 'On the Very Idea of a Conceptual Scheme', reprinted in his *Truth and Interpretation* (Oxford: Oxford University Press, 1984). But interpretation in this sense may still be just guesswork.

inclination we share, then I am in a position to know what it is; I may actually get it wrong but I have at hand materials for reliably identifying the rule. Therefore if there is a rule he is intentionally following, I am in a position to know what it is. The condition under which I do not know what rule he is following – where our responses come irremediably apart – is a condition under which the rule he aspires to follow – the rule represented by the intertemporally and interpersonally standardized inclination – is an illusion; there is no such rule there to be identified.

There remains an assumption which has to be redeemed. This is the assumption that the other person follows a rule such that he expects convergence between us: a rule represented by an interpersonally standardized inclination. How can I – or we as analysts – have reason to think this and so to claim that I can know what rule he follows? The only way is *ambulando,* by finding in practice that the assumption works out, fitting with a disposition in the person to seek out an explanation of any difference between us. In that practice, as Wittgenstein would say, we hit bedrock. Here is where our spade turns.[35]

The upshot is that if rule-following is to be public then the rule-followers must interact with one another as well as with their earlier and later selves. Here we see a sort of vindication for the allegedly Wittgensteinian view that rule-following is possible only in a communal context. Rule-following as such requires interaction, or so the story of the last section has it. But that interaction can be provided in principle by oneself at other times as well as by other persons. Interaction with other persons only gets to be required if the rule is to be public: if it is to be a rule which another person can know you follow.[36]

---

35. See Edward Craig's discussion of the assumption of uniformity in 'Meaning, Use, and Privacy', *Mind*, 1982, pp. 341–64.

36. I am greatly indebted to discussions of this topic, some over years, with Simon Blackburn, Paul Boghossian, Frank Jackson, Peter Menzies, Karen Neander, Huw Price, Jack Smart, Neil Tennant, and Michael Tooley. I was also helped by comments received when versions of the paper were presented at the University of Sydney and at the Australian National University. The line in the paper may have been particularly influenced by Huw Price. Certainly it fits well with some strands of argument in his book *Facts and the Function of Truth* (Oxford: Blackwell, 1988).

Booo!
Naturalist assumed!

CHAPTER ELEVEN

TRUTH RULES, HOVERFLIES, AND THE KRIPKE–WITTGENSTEIN PARADOX

Ruth Garrett Millikan

[T]he skeptical argument that Kripke attributes to Wittgenstein, and even the 'skeptical solution', are of considerable importance regardless of whether they are clearly Wittgenstein's. The naturalistically inclined philosopher, who rejects Brentano's irreducibility and yet holds intentionality to be an objective feature of our thoughts, owes a solution to the Kripke–Wittgenstein paradox.[1]

The challenge is a welcome one. Although I will argue that the Kripke–Wittgenstein paradox is not a problem for naturalists only, I will propose a naturalist solution to it. (Should the Kripke–Wittgenstein paradox prove to be soluble from a naturalist standpoint but intractable from other standpoints, that would, I suppose, constitute an argument for naturalism.) Then I will show that the paradox and its solution have an important consequence for the theories of meaning and truth. The Kripke–Wittgenstein arguments which pose the paradox also put in question Dummett's and Putnam's view of language understanding. From this view it follows that truth rules must be "verificationist rules" that assign assertability conditions to sentences, rather than "realist rules" that assign correspondence truth conditions. The proposed solution to the paradox suggests another view of language understanding, according to which a speaker can express, through his language practice, a grasp of correspondence truth rules. This will block one route of Putnam's famous retreat from realism:

Too Bad
That Doesn't Happen,
Having read the end of your Point of SCIENTIFIC SCHILL

The point is that Dummett and I *agree* that you can't treat understanding a sentence (in general) as knowing its truth conditions;

1. Brian Loar, "Critical Review of Saul Kripke's *Wittgenstein on Rules and Private Language*", *Noûs* **19** (1985), p. 280.

because it then becomes unintelligible what *that* knowledge *in turn* consists in. We both *agree* that the theory of understanding has to be done in a verificationist way . . . conceding that *some* sort of verificationist semantics must be given as our account of understanding . . . I have given Dummett all he needs to demolish metaphysical realism . . . a picture I was wedded to![2]

(By "metaphysical realism" Putnam means, roughly, the traditional correspondence theory of truth.) Elsewhere I have argued that the distinction Putnam draws between "metaphysical realism" and "internal realism" is illusory, that naturalist arguments for correspondence truth are, inevitably, arguments for truth as correspondence to theory-independent objects, and that there is nothing incoherent in this notion of correspondence.[3] So in giving a naturalist argument to show that grasping correspondence truth rules is no more problematic than grasping verificationist ones, I take myself to be defending the strongest possible kind of correspondence theory of truth and the most flat-footed interpretation possible of the truth-conditions approach to semantics.

I THE KRIPKE-WITTGENSTEIN PARADOX

The Kripke–Wittgenstein paradox, as Kripke explains it, is an apparent dead end we encounter when trying to explain what it is that constitutes a person's meaning something by a word. Kripke takes addition as his central example: what constitutes my meaning addition by "plus" or "+"?

> Although I myself have computed only finitely many sums in the past, the rule for addition determines my answer for indefinitely many new sums that I have never previously considered. This is the whole point, of the notion that in learning to add I grasp a rule: my past intentions regarding addition determine a unique answer for indefinitely many cases in the future.[4]

What is it to "grasp" such a rule? What is it for me to have grasped a rule that determines that 68 + 57 yields the answer 125, in the case that I have

---

2. Hilary Putnam, "Realism and Reason," in *Meaning and the Moral Sciences* (London: Routledge & Kegan Paul, 1978). Michael Dummett's statement is in "What is a Theory of Meaning?" in Samuel Guttenplan, ed., *Mind and Language* (Oxford: Clarendon Press, 1975), pp. 97–139, and in "What is a Theory of Meaning? (II)" in Gareth Evans and John McDowell, eds, *Truth and Meaning: Essays in Semantics* (Oxford: Clarendon Press, 1976), pp. 67–137.
3. In "Metaphysical Antirealism?" *Mind*, 95 (1986), pp. 417–31; reprinted in *The Philosopher's Annual* Vol. IX, 1986 (Atascadero, Calif.: Ridgeview Publishing Co., 1988).
4. S. Kripke, *Wittgenstein on Rules and Private Language* [hereafter *WRPL*] (Cambridge, MA: Harvard University Press, 1982), p. 7.

never happened to add 68 to 57? No such rule is determined merely by extrapolation from previous cases in which I have applied "+" to pairs of numbers; there are always infinitely many functions that accord with a given finite list of such argument–argument–value trios. For example, the "quus" rule might accord:

$$x \text{ quus } y = x + y, \quad \text{if } x, y < 57$$
$$= 5 \qquad \text{otherwise}^5$$

Nor (and this is more obviously a Wittgensteinian theme) can we suppose that my meaning addition by "+" consists in my having given myself general directions for what to do when encountering "+". To give myself general directions would be to lay down a rule of procedure for myself. What then constitutes my meaning by this set of instructions, by this laid-down rule, one procedure rather than another? Certainly this set of instructions does not include a thought of each of the infinitely many sums there are. And my past performances when having this set of instructions in mind do not exemplify a unique general procedure but many such possible procedures. Supplementing the instructions with another set of instructions explaining how to follow the first set leads only to a regress. How then *is* the correct interpretation of the instructions in my mind determined?

Changing the example, Kripke writes

> It has been supposed that all I need to do to determine my use of the word 'green' is to have an image, a sample, of green that I bring to mind whenever I apply the word in the future. When I use this to justify my application of 'green' to a new object, should not the skeptical problem be obvious to any reader of Goodman? Perhaps by 'green', in the past I meant *grue,* and the color image, which indeed was grue, was meant to direct me to apply the word 'green' to *grue* objects always. If the *blue* object before me now is grue, then it falls in the extension of 'green', as I meant it in the past. It is no help to suppose that in the past I stipulated that 'green' was to apply to all and only those things 'of the same color as' the sample. The skeptic can reinterpret 'same color' as same *schmolor,* where things have the same schmolor if . . .[6]

Now it is true that arguments of this sort take hold only if we reject the possibility that intentionality is a *sui generis* feature given to consciousness.[7] We

---

5. *Ibid.*, p. 9.
6. *Ibid.*, p. 20. Kripke's ellipsis points at the end; Kripke's footnotes omitted.
7. Loar claims that Kripke has not demonstrated that intentionality is not this. Kripke's text does however contain several footnotes commenting on the relevant arguments in Wittgenstein's text. I mention these arguments below.

must assume that what comes before the mind, whatever it is that enters or informs consciousness when one means something, does not *itself* determine a use for itself, a purpose for itself, a particular kind of connection that it is to have with one's activities. Rather, whatever comes before the mind is, in this respect, not different from any other item standing alone: "And can't it be clearly seen here that it is absolutely inessential for the picture to exist in his imagination rather than as a drawing or model in front of him? . . ."[8] Wittgenstein argues against the possibility that intentionality is a *sui generis* feature, by showing, for each of a series of cases, that the results of introspection when one means, understands or is guided in accordance with rules, are not the only or the final criteria that we use to determine what we mean or when we understand or are being so guided. What lies before consciousness does not determine its own significance; knowing what one means is not a matter, merely, of apprehending the contents of one's mind. In short, meaning is neither a state of awareness nor an epistemological given. It does not occur encapsulated within consciousness; it is not a state that simply *shows* its content or its significance. If there *is* such a thing as meaning something, say, meaning addition, its nature must lie in part in what is *not* simply given to consciousness.

Nor is it merely because the object thought of or meant is external to mind that meaning has an ingredient not given to consciousness. Meaning to perform a mental activity like adding in the head, that is, having intentions about one's own thoughts, is fully infected with this non-given ingredient. Thus the problem posed is no different for the purest idealist than for the metaphysical realist. Nor is it only "naturalistically inclined philosophers" who need a solution to the Kripke–Wittgenstein paradox. It is anyone who has been convinced by Wittgenstein to doubt Brentano – or, say, convinced after Sellars to reject epistemological "givenness" in *all* of its multifarious forms.

Could it be that the non-given ingredient that pins down what rule I intend to follow for "+" is the *disposition* I have to proceed in a certain way when encountering "+"? Setting aside the problem of what Wittgenstein may have intended as an answer to this question, surely Kripke is right to answer no. Kripke gives two main reasons for his answer. First, people are in fact disposed to make mistakes in arithmetic. Second, the addition function applies to numbers of any magnitude, but "some pairs of numbers are simply too large for my mind – or my brain – to grasp."[9] Nor will it help to take into account dispositions I may have to correct myself or to accept correction from others. Some of my dispositions are dispositions to miscorrect myself. (I often do this when trying to add long columns of figures.) And there are surely conditions under which I would be disposed to accept miscorrection from others.

Kripke concludes, or he claims that Wittgenstein concludes, that there is, indeed, *no fact of the matter what I mean by* "+". This conclusion is what I am

8. Wittgenstein, *Philosophical Investigations* (New York: Macmillan Co., 1953), paragraph 141.
9. *WRPL*, pp. 26–7.

calling the "Kripke–Wittgenstein paradox."[10] Wittgenstein, Kripke claims, offers only a "skeptical solution" to this paradox, a solution that "begins . . ., by conceding that the skeptic's negative assertions are unanswerable."[11] I propose to offer a "straight solution" to this paradox, one that "shows that on closer examination the skepticism proves to be unwarranted."[12]

Kripke distils the essence of the failure of dispositional accounts to capture the nature of rule-following thus:

> A candidate for what constitutes the state of my meaning one function, rather than another, by a given function sign, ought to be such that, whatever in fact I (am disposed to) do, there is a unique thing that I *should* do. Is not the dispositional view simply an equation of performance and correctness? Assuming determinism, even if I mean to denote *no* number theoretic function in particular by the sign '*', then to the same extent as it is true for '+', it is true here that for any two arguments *m* and *n,* there is a uniquely determined answer p that I would give. (I choose one at random, as we would normally say, but causally the answer is determined.) The difference between this case and the case of the '+' function is that in the former case, but not in the latter, my uniquely determined answer can properly be called 'right' or 'wrong'.[13]

---

10. Kripke places a great deal of emphasis on the failure to find anything that "justifies" my proceeding as I do when I follow a rule, and he seems to think of a "justification" as something that must be, by its very nature, open to or within consciousness. Similarly: "Even now as I write, I feel confident that there is something *in my mind* [italics mine] – the meaning I attach to the 'plus' sign – that *instructs* me [italics Kripke's] what I ought to do in all future cases" (*WRPL,* pp. 21–2). And "The idea that we lack 'direct' access to the facts whether we mean plus or quus is bizarre in any case. Do I not know, directly, and with a fair degree of certainty, that I mean plus?" (*WRPL,* p. 40). Indeed, many passages in Kripke's essay suggest that what bothers him the most is not that nothing seems to determine what rule I am following, but that nothing *before my mind* determines it. The feeling is conveyed that Kripke finds the real blow to be that the intentionality involved in rule-following does not reside *within* consciousness. If *that* is what Kripke takes to be the root "Wittgenstein paradox," then all will agree that Wittgenstein made no attempt to give a "straight solution" to it. Nor will I. On the other hand, if that were the main paradox, no one would ever have supposed that a dispositional account would be a "straight solution" to it and Kripke's discussion of dispositional accounts should have been placed not with his account of "Wittgenstein's paradox" but with his discussion of "Wittgenstein's skeptical solution," that is, as an account of what Kripke believed this skeptical solution was not.

  Margaret Gilbert suggests (in conversation) that one paradox may be that meaning strikes one as being something that can be fully constituted at a given time t, whether or not meaning is something that happens within consciousness. And, to be sure, dispositions are usually taken to exist at given times so that a dispositional account might be viewed as an attempt at a straight solution to Gilbert's paradox. Gilbert's paradox, if one finds it paradoxical, is another that I will not attempt to solve. I will merely try to show how there is a fact to the matter of what I mean by "+".

11. *WRPL,* p. 66.
12. *Ibid.*
13. *Ibid.,* p. 24; footnotes omitted.

> The fundamental problem . . . is . . . : whether my actual dispositions are 'right' or not, is there anything that mandates what they *ought* to be?[14]

The problem is to account for the *normative* element that is involved when one means to follow a rule, to account for there being a *standard* from which the facts, or one's dispositions, can diverge.

II GENERAL FORM OF THE SOLUTION

In the case of meaning, the normative element seems to be the same as the purposive element: to mean to follow a certain rule is to have as a purpose to follow it. Whether my actual dispositions are "right" or "wrong" depends on whether they accord with what I have purposed. The possible divergence of fact from a standard is, in this case, simply the failure to achieve a purpose.

Now having as one's purpose to follow a rule might involve having a representation of that purpose in mind, for example, in one's language of thought. But as Wittgenstein observed, any such representation would itself stand in need of interpretation. It would stand in need of a prior rule governing how it was to be taken, that is, how it was to guide one. And that one was to follow this prior rule could not *also* be a represented purpose, not without inviting a regress. To understand what it is to have an explicit purpose that one represents to oneself we must first understand what it is to have a purpose the content of which is *not* represented. Basic or root purposes must be *unexpressed* purposes.

"Intend" strongly suggests an explicitly represented purpose, that is, a purpose that is thought about. So let me use the verb "to purpose" (with a voiced "s"; yes, it *is* in the dictionary) to include this more basic way of having a purpose. We can then put matters this way: root purposing is unexpressed purposing; our job is to discover in what this purposing consists. Let us also distinguish among three ways of conforming to a rule: (1) merely coinciding with a rule (this is the way in which we conform to "quus" rules and to rules to which we have mere dispositions to conform), (2) purposefully following an explicit or expressed rule, and (3) purposefully conforming to an implicit or unexpressed rule. Way (3) involves having an unexpressed purpose to follow a rule and *succeeding* in this purpose. It is the same as displaying a *competence* in conforming to the unexpressed rule or displaying an *ability* to conform to it. Another way to explain our task, then, is to say that we need to learn what a competence in conforming to an unexpressed rule consists in, and how it differs from a mere disposition to coincide with the rule.

---

14. *Ibid.*, p. 57.

My thesis will be that the unexpressed purposes that lie behind acts of explicit purposing are biological purposes; a competence to conform to an unexpressed rule is a biological competence. By a biological purpose I mean the sort of purpose the heart has, or those of the eyeblink reflex, and the human brain. The purposes of these are functions that they have historically performed which have accounted for their continued proliferation. Biological purposes are, roughly, functions fulfilled in accordance with evolutionary design. It does not follow that capacities to perform biological functions are, in general, innate. For example, it is surely in accordance with evolutionary design that the newly hatched chick follows its mother about, but the chick is not born with that disposition. It is not born knowing which *is* its mother, but must imprint on her first. Yet the imprinting, and hence the following, both take place in accordance with evolutionary design. (Later in this paper I will devote considerable space to clarifying how even quite novel biological purposes can emerge as a result of experience and learning.)[15]

Suppose that explicit intending involves something like representing, imaging, or saying something to oneself and then using, or reacting to, or being guided by this representation in a purposeful way, that is, in a way that expresses a competence. My thesis, then, is that the purpose that informs this reacting, that makes it into a competence, is a biological purpose. Similarly, if knowing a language involves having a competence in following certain rules for construction and interpretation of sentences, the purpose that informs this competence, I will argue, is a biological purpose.

III PURPOSIVE RULE-FOLLOWING: COMPETENCE TO FOLLOW A RULE

Let me begin with a very simple example of an organism that displays a competence in conforming to a rule. According to the biologists Collett and Land,

> Males of many species of hoverfly spend much of the day hovering in one spot, thus keeping their flight muscles warm and primed so that they are ready to dart instantly after any passing female that they sight. This chasing behaviour is on such a hair-trigger that all manner of inappropriate targets elicit pursuit (pebbles, distant birds, and midges so small as to be scarcely visible to a human observer) as well as a very occasional female. Although selective pressures have favored a speedy response above careful evaluation of the suitability

---

15. Full details of the notion of biological function that I rely on in this paper are given under the label "proper functions" in my *Language, Thought, and Other Biological Categories* [hereafter *LTOBC*] (Cambridge, MA: Bradford Books/MIT Press, 1984), Ch. 1–2. See also my "In Defense of Proper Functions," *Philosophy of Science* 56 (1989), pp. 288–302.

of the target . . . the response itself is precisely tailored to optimize the capture of objects which are roughly the same size and speed as a con-specific.[16]

Rather than turning toward the target in order to track it, the hoverfly turns away from the target and accelerates in a straight line so as to intercept it. Given that (1) female hoverflies are of uniform size, hence are first detected at a roughly uniform distance (about .7 m), (2) females cruise at a standard velocity (about 8m/sec), and (3) males accelerate at a constant rate (about $30-35\text{m/sec}^2$), the geometry of motion dictates that to intercept the female the male must make a turn that is 180 degrees away from the target minus about 1/10 of the vector angular velocity (measured in degrees per second) of the target's image across his retina. The turn that his *body* must make, given as a function of the angle off center of the target's image on his retina, equals the (signed) angle of the image minus 1/10 its vector angular velocity, plus or minus 180 degrees. According to Collett and Land, whether it is dried peas, male hoverflies, female hoverflies or flying blocks of wood that he spots, that is exactly the rule to which the hoverfly conforms. Taking note that this rule is not about how the hoverfly should behave in relation to distal objects, but rather about how he should react to a proximal stimulus, to a moving spot on his retina, let us call this rule "the proximal hoverfly rule."

I have chosen the proximal hoverfly rule as my first example of rule-following because it seems so unlikely that the hoverfly calculates over any inner representation of this rule in order to follow it. Rather, the hoverfly has an unexpressed biological purpose to conform to this rule. That is, the hoverfly has within him a genetically determined mechanism of a kind that historically proliferated in part *because* it was responsible for producing conformity to the proximal hoverfly rule, hence for getting male and female hoverflies together. This mechanism may account for various other dispositions of the hoverfly, for example, causing him to attract predators by his conspicuous darting movements, or causing characteristic uniform mathematically describable patterns to play on his retina as he turns after the female. But mentioning these latter dispositions does not help to explain why the mechanism has survived, why it has proliferated in the species. Conformity to the proximal hoverfly rule, on the other hand, has helped to explain the reproductive success of (virtually) every ancestor hoverfly, hence to explain the continued presence of the mechanism in the species. Conformity to the proximal hoverfly rule, then – not attracting predators or producing certain patterns on the retina – is a biological purpose of this mechanism, hence of the hoverfly. For similar reasons, a biological function of the heart is to pump blood but not also, say, to make a jazzy sound, and a biological function of the

---

16. "How Hoverflies Compute Interception Courses," *Journal of Comparative Physiology* **125** (1978), pp. 191–204.

eyeblink reflex is to cover the eyes momentarily, but not also to swing the eyelashes in a graceful arc away from entanglement with the eyebrows, nor to point with them at the navel.

The hoverfly displays a *competence* in conforming to the proximal hoverfly rule when his coinciding with it has a "normal explanation," that is, an explanation that accords with the historical norm. That his behaviour coincides with the rule must be explained in the same way, or must fit the same explanation schema, that accounted in the bulk of cases for the historic successes of his ancestors in conforming to the rule. Presumably this normal explanation makes reference to the way the hoverfly's nervous system is put together, how it works, how it is hooked to his retina and muscles, etc. If the hoverfly ends up coinciding with the rule not because his nerves and muscles work in a normal way but only because the wind serendipitously blows him around to face the right direction, he fails to express a competence.[17]

Not just anything a human effects is a human action. Effects that are actions must be intended, or at least foreseen, and must be generated from intentions in a normal way. Effects of human bodily movements that are not actions are called "accidental." Similarly, not just any process that originates in an animal's organs or behavioural systems is a biological activity. Biological activities are only those that express competencies. They correspond to normally fulfilled biological purposes, that is, to what the animal does in accordance with evolutionary design. Conversely, behaviour that fails to express a competence corresponds to what an animal effects, biologically, only by accident. Thus the heart's saying pit-a-pat, the eyelashes' moving away from the eyebrows in a graceful arc and the hoverfly's coinciding, but due only to the wind, with the proximal hoverfly rule are not biological activities, but biological accidents.

To say that a given male hoverfly has a biological purpose to conform to the proximal hoverfly rule is very different from saying either that he himself has a history of having conformed to it (perhaps he has just reached adolescence) or that he has a disposition to conform to it. The normal hoverfly has a disposition to dart off when it sees a flying bird – and also a disposition to squash when stepped on – but these dispositions do not correspond to biological purposes or to competences. Conversely, male hoverflies that are crippled or blind have no disposition to conform to the proximal hoverfly rule, but still it is one of their biological purposes to do so. As male members of the hoverfly species, conforming is the biological norm, the standard for them.[18]

To say that the hoverfly has as a biological purpose to follow the proximal hoverfly rule is also quite different from saying that this rule is the only rule

---

17. For a full discussion of normal ("Normal") explanations for performance of proper functions, see *LTOBC*, Ch. 1 and 2, and my "Biosemantics," *The Journal of Philosophy* 86 (1989), pp. 281–97.
18. On the proper functions of imperfect members of a biological category, see *LTOBC*, Ch. 1–2.

that fits all past instances of hoverfly turns, say, that resulted in hoverfly procreation. Suppose it were so that never in history had a male hoverfly spotted a female that happened to approach him at such an angle as to produce an image on his retina with a clockwise angular velocity between 500 degrees and 510 degrees per second. Then the proximal *quoverfly* rule, "If the vector angular velocity of the target's image is *not* counterclockwise and between 500 degrees and 510 degrees per second, make a turn that equals the (signed) angle of the image minus 1/10 its vector angular velocity, plus or minus 180 degrees; at ease otherwise," fits all past actual cases of successful female encounters. But it is not a rule the hoverfly has as a biological purpose to follow. For it is not because their behaviour coincided with *that* rule that the hoverfly's ancestors managed to catch females, hence to proliferate. In saying that, I don't have any particular theory of the nature of explanation up my sleeve. But surely, on any reasonable account, a complexity that can simply be dropped from the explanans without affecting the tightness of the relation of explanans to explanandum is not a *functioning* part of the explanation. For example, my coat does not keep me warm because it is fur-lined *and red,* nor because it is fur-lined *in the winter,* but just because it is fur-lined. (True, I am making the assumption that the qualifications and additions that convert the proximal hoverfly rule into the proximal quoverfly rule are objectively qualifications and additions rather than simplifications. This assumption rests upon a metaphysical distinction between natural properties and kinds and artificially synthesized grue-like properties and kinds or, what is perhaps the same, depends upon there being a difference between natural law and mere *de facto* regularity. But my project is to solve the Kripke–Wittgenstein paradox, not to defend common-sense ontology. Nor should either of these projects be confused with solving Goodman's paradox.)[19]

To say that the hoverfly has as a biological purpose to follow the proximal hoverfly rule is also quite different from saying that this rule is the only rule that fits the actual dispositions of normal hoverflies or of past hoverflies that managed to procreate. Suppose that, given the principles in accordance with which the hoverfly's turn-angle-determining devices work, engineering constraints necessitated a mechanism normal for hoverflies with a blind spot for clockwise angular velocities between 500 degrees and 510 degrees per second. These particular velocities produce no reaction at all on the part of the male. Then the same proximal quoverfly rule mentioned above fits the actual dispositions of all normal hoverflies, but it still would not be a rule that the hoverfly has as a biological purpose to follow. The hoverfly's biological purposes include the expression only of dispositions that have helped to

---

19. Goodman's paradox is a paradox in epistemology. Kripke, on the other hand, is concerned not about how we could know or discover what someone means by "plus" but about what this determinate meaning *consists* in. Note too that assuming common-sense ontology does nothing, by itself, toward solving Goodman's paradox, which concerns how we can *know* or reasonably guess which entities are the basic ontological ones, *supposing* there to be such.

account for the proliferation of his ancestors. By hypothesis, the disposition to rest at ease when the target's image is counterclockwise and between 500 degrees and 510 degrees per second did not help the hoverfly's ancestors to propagate. It was only the times that the proximal hoverfly rule was obeyed that the ancestors procreated. So the hoverfly resting at ease behind his blind spot is not displaying a competence. It is conformity to the proximal hoverfly rule, not the quoverfly rule, that he biologically purposes, even if normal hoverflies are not especially accurate in fulfilling this natural purpose, in conforming to this ideal.

IV PROXIMAL VS DISTAL RULES

My plan, as I have indicated, is slowly to make plausible the claim that the normative element that is involved when one means to follow a rule is biological purposiveness. Meaning to follow a rule differs from having a disposition to coincide with a rule, in the same way that the hoverfly's biologically purposing to follow the proximal hoverfly rule differs from having a disposition to coincide with it. That is how I aim to solve the Kripke–Wittgenstein paradox concerning what *constitutes* rule-following. At the same time, however, I wish to build a case that language understanding or language competency is competency in the biological sense. And I wish to argue that it is possible to have a biological competence to follow correspondence truth rules, hence that a "realist" theory of language understanding is possible on the biological model. To gain this latter end, we need to discuss distal as well as proximal rules.

Conforming to the proximal hoverfly rule is a means, for the hoverfly, of following a less proximal, or more distal rule: "If you see a female, catch it." Call this "the distal hoverfly rule." To say that conformity to the proximal hoverfly rule is a means to conformity to the distal rule is the same as to say that the mechanism that has historically accounted for the overwhelming majority of ancestor hoverflies' successes at conformity to the distal hoverfly rule begins with conformity to the proximal rule. That is, the normal explanation for conformity with the distal rule contains the specification that the hoverfly first conform to the proximal rule.

Now whether the hoverfly succeeds in following the proximal hoverfly rule depends, for the most part, only upon whether his insides are working right, that is, on whether he is a normal healthy member of his species. But whether, or how often, he manages to conform to the distal hoverfly rule depends upon more. It depends upon conditions that are outside his body and over which he has no control, such as how hard the wind is blowing, whether the females that pass by are in fact of normal size, travelling at the normal speed and, perhaps, whether they are willing. Without doubt, then, hoverflies

219

are worse at conforming to the distal than to the proximal hoverfly rule. That is, their competence or ability to conform to the distal rule is less reliable than their competence or ability to conform to the proximal rule. But that the hoverfly may not be very reliable in his conformity to the distal hoverfly rule bears not at all upon whether it is one of his biological purposes to conform. Compare: it is a biological purpose of the sperm to swim until it reaches an ovum. That is what it has a tail for. But very few sperm actually achieve this biological end because ova are in such short supply. Reaching an ovum is a purpose of the sperm since it is only because ancestor sperm reached ova that they reproduced, thus proliferating the tail. Similarly, it was only when ancestor hoverflies conformed to the distal hoverfly rule that they *became* ancestors.

Turning the coin over, the hoverfly is very reliable in his coincidence with this "overkill rule": "Dart off after everything that flies by you subtending about .5 degrees on your retina, whether it's male, female, animate or inanimate, bird, plane or Superman." But this overkill rule does not correspond to any biological purpose of the hoverfly. True, conforming to the proximal hoverfly rule is one of the hoverfly's biological purposes, and conforming to this rule will *result* in his coinciding with the overkill rule if there are objects other than female hoverflies flying about him (even if there are not). But it is not coinciding with the overkill rule that has helped to account for hoverfly proliferation. Only the times when the distal hoverfly rule was obeyed did hoverfly ancestors procreate.[20]

It is conformity to the distal hoverfly rule that explains the ancestor hoverflies' *successes*. As the hoverfly chases after a distant bird, he expresses no competence except, of course, competence to conform to the proximal hoverfly rule. Conformity to the distal hoverfly rule, not to the overkill rule, is what he biologically purposes, though at the moment he is accidentally, that is, nonbiologically, doing something else.

That is how purposes inform the rule-following behaviour of the hoverfly, how norms, standards, or ideals apply to his behaviours, hence how the hoverfly comes to display competences or abilities to conform to rules rather than mere dispositions to coincide with them.[21] But the unexpressed rules that humans purposively conform to, at least most of those that they purposively conform to when using inner or outer language, are not rules that they are genetically hard-wired to follow, but rules that they have learned. How then can humans biologically purpose to follow such rules? Before

---

20. More precisely, only the distal hoverfly rule would be mentioned in giving a "most proximate normal explanation" of the function of the hoverfly's turning mechanism. See *LTOBC*, and the discussion of "normal explanations" in my "Biosemantics."

21. Notice that it is the reference to evolutionary *history* that has been doing all of the work in explaining how norms come to apply to the activities of an animal, in explaining how there can be a standard from which the facts of individual behaviour diverge. I defend the position that function always derives from history in "In Defense of Proper Functions."

turning directly to the problem of human rule-following, let us examine a more simple case of learned biological purposes, of learned competence – the case of a simpler animal that learns to follow rules.

V LEARNED OR DERIVED RULES AND COMPETENCES

If a rat becomes ill within a few hours after eating a specific food, it will later shun all foods that taste the same. For example, if the rat eats soap and soon becomes ill, thereafter it will refuse to eat soap. Although the rat may have dragged certain nesting materials home or explored new territory just before becoming ill, it will not on that account shun that kind of nesting material or that territory. Nor will it shun foods that merely look the same or that are found in the same place as the food eaten prior to illness.[22] It thus appears that a quite specific mechanism is harbored in the rat, a proper function of which is to produce conformity to the specialized rule "If ingestion of a substance is followed by illness, do not ingest any substance with that taste again." Call this rule the "proximal rat rule." Clearly, following the proximal rat rule is a biological means to following a more distal rat rule, say, "Do not eat poisonous substances"; helping to produce conformity to this rule is a further proper function of the relevant inborn mechanisms in the rat.

Now the proximal rat rule, like the proximal hoverfly rule, tells the animal what to do given certain experiential contingencies. There is a difference, however, in the normal manner of executing these two rules. When the hoverfly conforms to his rule, nothing in his body undergoes a permanent change, but this is not so in the case of the rat. Suppose, for example, that the rat has just become ill after eating soap. In order to conform to the proximal rat rule, in order to avoid henceforth what tastes like soap, the rat's nervous system must first conform to certain preliminary "rules," rules that dictate that a certain sort of permanent change take place in it. The rat, we say, must "learn" in order to conform to his rule. But the fact that the rat's evolutionary history dictates that it is normal for him to undergo learning in order to follow his rule rather than following it directly does not affect the biological status of the rule. That he should follow his rule is one of his biological purposes for exactly the same reason that the hoverfly's rule-following is biologically purposed. Conformity to the rat rule is what his ancestor rats had in common in those cases in which possession of the relevant inborn mechanisms aided them to flourish and proliferate, so it is what the mechanism, hence the rat, biologically purposes.

---

22. The reference is to studies by John Garcia. A bibliography of his papers may be found in *The American Psychologist* 35 (1980), pp. 41–3.

Now the rat that conforms to the proximal rat rule, if he ever becomes ill after eating, ends by conforming to a *derived* proximal rat rule, say, the rule "Do not eat what tastes like soap." Indeed, if a rat becomes ill after eating soap, it immediately becomes one of his biological purposes to follow the rule "Do not eat what tastes like soap." For that he is to follow this derived rule is logically entailed by the proximal rat rule plus the premise that he has in fact become ill after eating soap. Similarly, the hoverfly that currently has an image of appropriate size traversing his retina at a 60 degree angle with an angular velocity of 100 degrees per second currently has as a biological purpose to make a turn of 130 degrees. Notice that the hoverfly has this biological purpose quite independently of whether or not any hoverfly has ever been in exactly this experiential position before. It is theoretically possible, even if unlikely, that no hoverfly has ever had exactly *this* biological purpose before. This is similar to our rat who is sick after eating soap. It is now one of his biological purposes to follow the derived proximal rat rule "Do not eat what tastes like soap" even if it should be true that no other rat in history has ever become sick after eating soap, hence true that no rat in history has ever had this particular biological purpose before.

In this manner, animals that learn can acquire biological purposes that are peculiar to them as individuals, tailored to their own peculiar circumstances or peculiar histories.[23] Although biological purposes are functions fulfilled in accordance with evolutionary design, they need not be innately given purposes. Similarly, biological competences need not be innate. A proper biological activity of an animal can be something that experience has prompted or "taught" the animal to do, experience coupled with an innate mechanism for being guided to learn by experience.

Nor is there need for such mechanisms to be as specialized as the mechanism that conforms the rat to the proximal rat rule. Not long ago many learning theorists believed that all animal learning took place in accordance with principles that were not species specific but universal. Suppose that this were true. Suppose that every species learned in accordance with the principles of one person's favorite general theory of operant conditioning, so that no reference to the particular evolutionary niche of a species was ever needed to explain how its learning mechanisms had historically enhanced its fitness. Then there would have to be some rarefied hypergeneral explanation of how and why these learning principles worked. Such an explanation might make reference, for example, to specific principles of generalization and discrimination used in differentiating stimuli and in projecting what is to count as "the same" behaviour again, that is, reference to universal proximal rules followed during learning. It would have to tell how and why these

---

23. A much more detailed discussion of "derived proper functions" may be found in *LTOBC*, Ch. 2, and in my "Thoughts Without Laws: Cognitive Science With Content," *The Philosophical Review* 95 (1986), pp. 47–80.

particular ways of generalizing and discriminating effected, often enough, isolation or zeroing in on sufficiently reliable causes of reinforcement, and in what universal manner (!) reinforcers are connected with the well-being of animals. Thus it would tell *how* possession of the universal mechanism had normally, that is, historically, enhanced fitness in animals generally. Specific applications of this general explanation schema to individual animals in individual circumstances would then determine which among the various effects of their motions were the proximal and distal biological activities of these individuals, as they learned and applied their learning. Such applications would determine, for example, what specific reliable causes of reinforcement were purposefully being zeroed in on by particular animals at particular times, that is, what these animals were "trying" to learn and, after they learned it, what the specific goals of their learned behaviours were.

Now it is important to note that to fulfil a biological purpose is not always to take a step towards flourishing or propagating; it is not always good for an animal to fulfil its biologically determined goals. For example, a rat might come to have as a biological purpose to follow the derived rule "Do not eat what tastes like soap" even if it were true (I suspect it is true) that soap does not *make* rats sick or does not poison them. Suppose, rather, that the rat eats soap and then becomes ill due to a bout with Rattus enteritis. Still, in order to conform to the proximal rat rule, he must now conform to the derived proximal rule "Do not eat what tastes like soap," for this derived rule is entailed by the proximal rat rule given his situational experience. Yet following this derived rule may, in fact, have no tendency to bring him into conformity with the more distal rat rule "Do not eat poisonous substances." So it can happen that the rat acquires a biological purpose and acquires a competence to conform to a derived rule which does not further the end that is this rule's own *raison d'être*. Indeed, the rat *could* acquire a derived purpose and a competence to behave in a manner that was actually detrimental to him, say, a competence to follow the rule "Do not eat what tastes like corn" when, in fact, unless he eats corn, given his circumstances, he will starve. Compare: the hoverfly, dutifully conforming to the proximal hoverfly rule (the rule that tells how he is to react to a moving image on his retina) may thereby dart off after a bird, who would not otherwise have spotted the hoverfly, hence would not have *eaten* him. Thus it is that an individual may have a biological purpose and a competence to follow a derived rule that has no tendency to further the interests either of the individual or of his species and, more specifically, no tendency to produce conformity to more distal rules toward which following it was, biologically, supposed to be a means.[24]

What an animal is doing in accordance with evolutionary design need not be anything that any member of its species has ever done before. And it need

---

24. For further details on conflicting proper functions, see *LTOBC*, Ch. 2, and my "Thoughts Without Laws."

not be anything that is good for the animal to do. So surely it need not be anything that common sense would call "natural" for it to do. Consider a circus poodle riding a bicycle. It is performing what common sense would call a most "unnatural" act. Yet it is one of the dog's biological purposes to perform that act. Biologically, the (typical circus) dog's distal action is procurement of his dinner. The dog harbors within him an intricate mechanism, operating in accordance with certain largely unknown but surely quite definite and detailed principles, in accordance with which dogs have been designed to develop perceptual, cognitive and motor skills and to integrate them so as to effect procurement of dinner in their individual environments. Living in an unusual environment, the circus dog acquires unusual purposes and competences when he applies his "dog rules" to his environment. But, although he may be making the audience laugh by accident, he is certainly not balancing on that bicycle by accident. He is balancing purposefully or in accordance with evolutionary design – in accordance with another application of the same general principles that procured his ancestors' dinners during evolutionary history.

VI HUMAN RULE-FOLLOWING

Humans are very sophisticated creatures, so we tell ourselves. We not only learn but learn new ways to learn, develop new concepts, and so forth. Further, much of our behaviour results not just from learning but from theoretical and practical inference. But there must still be a finite number of inborn mechanisms, operating in accordance with a finite number of natural principles, having a finite number of biologically proper functions, that account for our dispositions to do these things. Coordinately, there must be a finite number of proximal and distal *"Homo sapiens* rules" that we have as biological purposes to follow, and there must be mechanisms to implement these rules built into the basic body and brain of normal persons.

Consider then any bit of human behaviour produced by biologically well-functioning behaviour-regulating systems, by systems that are not broken or jammed. (Behaviour that results from malfunction is, of course, overwhelmingly unlikely to bear fruit of any interesting kind.) There will be a way of describing this behaviour that captures its aspect as a *biological* activity, a description that tells what proximal and distal biological purposes, and what biological competences if any, the behaviour expresses. This will be so even if the behaviour is totally unique, or systematically self-destructive, or not "natural" by any common-sense standards. But of course there will also be numerous ways of describing the behaviour that fail to express its biological purposiveness, many "quus-like" descriptions – as "pointing toward the navel with the eyelashes" quus-describes the eyeblink reflex. So the question arises, what is the relation of *ordinary* human purposes, of human intentions and meanings, to biological purposes? Are descriptions of human intentional actions quus-descriptions from the standpoint of evolutionary design? Do ordinary human intentions merely, accidentally, *cohabit* with biological purposes?

Surely a naturalist must answer no. Ordinary human purposes, ordinary intentions, can only be a species of biological purpose. To suppose otherwise would be to suppose that the whole mechanism of human belief, desire, inference, concept formation, etc., the function of which culminates in the formation and execution of human intentions, is, as functioning in this capacity, an epiphenomenon of biology, an accidental by-product of systems that nature designed for other purposes. And what would these other purposes be?[25]

This accords with conclusions we reached earlier on the nature of explicit intentions. Explicitly meaning or intending, if this requires representing what one intends, presupposes a prior purposing: purposing to let the representation guide one in a certain way. This is true whether we are talking about representation in an inner medium, say, in a "language of thought," or representation in a public medium – talking, say, about the use of "plus." But this prior purposing cannot be analyzed as the original explicit purposing was analyzed without regress. Rather, a prior unexpressed purposing must be assumed. The reasonable conclusion seems to be that ordinary explicit intending rests on biological purposing – biologically purposing to be guided by, to react this way rather than that to, one's representations. Whether this biological purposing is innate (compare Fodor's version of the "language of thought") or whether it is derived via learning, mechanisms of concept formation, etc., it must *ultimately* derive its content from the details of our evolutionary history.

So unless doing arithmetic results from a total breakdown of the cognitive systems (in which case there may be nothing you purpose when you encounter "plus": how you react to it is accidental under every description) then *whatever* you mean to do when you encounter "plus," that content has been determined by your experience coupled with evolutionary design. But, reasonably, whatever you mean by "plus" is the same as what other people mean who are endowed with the same general sort of cognitive equipment and have been exposed to the same sort of training in arithmetic. This meaning has been determined by the application of *Homo sapiens* rules of some kind to experience. It is likely that these are extremely abstract general purpose *Homo sapiens* rules, in accordance with which human concept formation takes place, and it is likely that the explanation of the efficacy of these rules makes reference to very deep and general principles of ontology. But it is not my task to speculate about the precise form these *Homo sapiens*

---

25. For a more detailed defense of this claim, see my "Biosemantics."

rules take, or about how the experience of standard training in arithmetic elicits from them the capacity to mean plus. Speculation about the specific forms that our most fundamental cognitive capacities take is the psychologist's job.[26]

I believe that these considerations constitute, albeit in very rough and broad outline, the solution to the Kripke–Wittgenstein paradox.

VII TRUTH RULES: VERIFICATIONIST OR CORRESPONDENCE?

I have sketched a theory about meaning in the sense of purposing – both expressed and unexpressed purposing. It remains to connect this theory with the theory of semantic meaning.

Truth rules are rules that project, from the parts and structure of sentences in a language, the conditions under which these sentences would be true. Such rules express, of course, an aspect of the meaning of the sentences. The question is whether the conditions referred to by truth rules are to be understood in a "realist" way as correspondence truth conditions, or in a "verificationist" way as assertability conditions. Dummett's concern about truth rules is this: whatever connection there is between sentences and that which determines their truth has to be a connection that is established via the actual employment of the language. Whatever form truth rules take, realist or verificationist, the *practical* abilities of speakers who understand a language must reflect these rules, indeed, must determine their content. Hence an analysis of the structure of the abilities required for language use and understanding should reveal the kind of rules truth rules are. But, Dummett argues, the only truth rules we could possibly exhibit a practical grasp of are verificationist truth rules.

In Section VIII below, I will claim that Dummett's argument hangs on treating language abilities or competencies, hence the following of language rules, as mere dispositions, or alternatively (perhaps), as taking place wholly within consciousness, and I will add to the arguments already piled up by Wittgenstein and Kripke against the adequacy of this sort of treatment. In the present section, however, I wish to propose a positive thesis. My claim will be that if we interpret rule-following and, in general, purposes and competencies in the biological way, then we can see how, on the contrary, reference to correspondence truth rules might *easily* fall out of an analysis of language competence.

---

26. But, people still persist in asking, How do you know that we really *do* end up meaning *plus* by "plus"? How do you know we don't mean *quus*? Because if we meant quus then "plus" would mean quus, and the way to say that we all mean quus would be "we all mean plus" – which is what I said. Compare Donald Davidson, "Knowing One's Own Mind," *Proceedings and Addresses of the American Philosophical Association* **60** (1987), pp. 441–58, and Tyler Burge, "Individualism and Self-Knowledge," *Journal of Philosophy* **60** (1988), pp. 649–63.

We begin by observing that whatever the content of truth rules may be, realist or verificationist, the intent or purpose of anyone engaged in making sincere assertions in a language must be to conform their sentences to these rules. The sincere speaker purposes to make assertions that are true. It follows that the *way* that the actual practice of a language embodies truth rules is that these are the rules in accordance with which the competent speaker (or thinker), when sincere, purposes to make (or think) assertions. These are rules that he is, as it were, *trying* to follow insofar as he is sincerely speaking (or thinking) *that* language. On the bottom layer at least (perhaps the layer that governs the language of thought) these rules must of course be unexpressed rules. But precisely because truth rules are at bottom unexpressed rules, introspection can give us no handle on what kind of rules they are. Rather, it is necessary to develop a *theory* about truth rules, an explanatory hypothesis about what rules we are purposing to follow when we make sincere assertions.

Assuming a biological standpoint, the question whether truth rules are realist or verificationist can be expressed by asking how "proximal" vs. "distal" truth rules are. The proximal hoverfly rule was a rule about how the hoverfly was to respond to a moving image on his retina, that is, roughly, to sensory stimulations. The distal hoverfly rule was a rule about how the hoverfly was to end up interacting with his more removed environment, namely, with females that entered his life at a distance. "Verificationist" truth rules, as Putnam and Dummett envision these, would be rules that governed responses to prior thoughts and, as Dummett has put it, "bare sense experiences," hence would be proximal rules.[27] "Realist" or correspondence rules, on the other hand, would for the most part be distal rules, rules that governed the manner in which assertions were to correspond to affairs that lie, very often, well beyond the interface of body and world. Convinced by Wittgenstein and Kripke that purposing to follow a rule is not something encapsulated *within* consciousness, we are not compelled to suppose that truth rules have to be rules about what is to happen either in the mind or at the interface between mind, or body, and world. So let us ask what it would be like if truth rules were distal correspondence rules.

The first thing to note is that if truth rules were distal rules they would surely have to be *backed* by proximal rules, rules about how to respond to our thoughts (inference) and to the immediate fruits of our perceptual explorations (perceptual judgement). They would have to be *backed* by rules that determined assertability conditions, the innermost of these conditions being within the mind or brain or at the interface of mind or brain and world. Call these back-up rules "proximal assertability rules." Proximal assertability rules would concern the most proximal conditions under which we should say or think certain things. Conformity to these rules would have, as a biological

---

27. "What is a Theory of Meaning?(II)," p. 111.

purpose, to effect conformity to distal rules, that is, to correspondence truth rules. These truth rules would concern distal conditions under which we should say or think certain things. The truth rules might imply directives with this sort of form: if you have reason to speak (think) about the weather in Atlanta, say (think) "It is snowing in Atlanta" when and only when it is snowing in Atlanta; if you have reason to speak (think) about the colour of snow, say (think) "Snow is white" if and only if snow is white. For a simple biological model here, compare worker honeybees. They (biologically) purpose to follow rules of this kind: when dancing, angle the axis of your dance 10 degrees off the vertical if and only if there is a good supply of nectar 10 degrees off a direct line from hive to sun. (Proposals concerning how humans might *learn* how to (purpose to) conform to distal correspondence truth rules are detailed in *LTORC*.)[28]

Conforming to the proximal hoverfly rule and the proximal rat rule often fails to bring hoverflies and rats into conformity to the distal hoverfly and rat rules. Similarly, conforming to proximal assertability rules might often fail to bring humans into conformity to truth rules. One can unknowingly say what is false even though one has good evidence for what one says. And one frequently fails to say what is true, indeed to say anything at all, because one lacks any evidence at all, either for or against. Also, whether conformity to the proximal hoverfly and rat rules helps to produce conformity to the distal hoverfly and rat rules on this or that occasion often depends upon factors in the hoverfly's or rat's external environment over which it has no control. Similarly, whether conformity to proximal assertability rules would bring us into conformity to truth rules in this case or that might depend upon factors over which we had no control. For example, circumstances responsible for most perceptual illusions are circumstances outside the observer which, normally, he neither controls nor needs to control. Nor is not having enough evidence either to affirm or to deny a proposition typically something that it is within one's control to remedy. The principles in accordance with which biological devices perform functions that are proper to them always refer, in the end, to conditions external to these devices. These are conditions that have *historically* been present often enough to enable a critical proportion of ancestors of those devices to perform these functions, or to perform them a critical proportion of the time, but that cannot be counted on always to be present. All biological devices are fallible devices, even when normal and healthy.[29]

It follows that the proximal assertability rules for a sentence would not *define* its semantics, for they would not determine what its truth conditions were. Rather, following proximal assertability rules would be means that

---

28. Chapters 9, 17 and 18.
29. For amplification of this very crucial theme, see my "Thoughts Without Laws" and "Biosemantics."

were, merely, approximations to the end that was following correspond-ence truth rules – more or less helpful and more or less reliable means to that end. Let us reflect for a moment upon certain consequences of this model.

If proximal assertability rules were rules that we followed only as a more or less reliable means to following distal truth rules, then it would not at least be obvious that those who shared a language in the sense of having competences to abide by the same truth rules would have any need to share proximal assertability rules as well. The male hoverfly follows the distal rule "If you see a female, catch it" by following the proximal hoverfly rule. The male housefly follows the same distal rule by tracking the female rather than by plotting an interception path, employing different proximal means to the same distal end. Now consider how many different ways there are to make a map of a city: for example, by walking about with a yardstick, paper and pencil, by working from aerial photographs, by using surveyors' instruments, etc. Might there not also be various ways to make sentences that map onto the world in accordance with the same truth rules? Is there really any reason to suppose that only one set of proximal assertability rules could effect a reasonably reliable competence to conform to a given set of distal correspondence rules? Consider, for example, how many ways there are to tell whether a solution is acid or whether it has iodine in it. Consider how many alternative visual and tactile clues we use, on one occasion or another, to perceive depth. And consider: were the proximal assertability rules that Helen Keller used when she spoke English the same as those that you use? If not, does it follow that she did not really speak English after all?

Indeed, there is a sense, there is a way of individuating rules, in which it is impossible for people to share proximal assertability rules. Proximal assertability rules that I conform to correlate happenings at the periphery of my nervous system or body with sentences. Proximal assertability rules that you conform to correlate happenings at the periphery of your nervous system or body with sentences. For us to "share a set of proximal assertability rules" could not, of course, be for me to purpose to correlate happenings at the periphery of *your* body with *my* sentences. If I purposed to do that, I would be purposing to conform to a distal rule, not a proximal rule. We could "share proximal assertability rules" only in the sense that our rules ran parallel. But it is not immediately obvious what the point of running parallel to one another with language might be. Why would you take any interest in the sentences I uttered, if these correlated only with what was happening at the ends of my afferent nerves? Only if the proximal assertability rules that you and I used effected relatively reliable conformity to the same *distal* correspondence rules would there be any point in talking to one another. But if agreement is effected on the distal level, what need would there be for agreement on the proximal level? Hence what reason is there to assume, say with Quine, that comparison of only proximal rules *ought* to yield determinate translation between idiolects?[30]

VIII CAUSES OF VERIFICATIONIST MYOPIA

Given a biological approach, then, there are reasons to think that truth rules may be distal correspondence rules, hence that classical truth conditions may do work for semantics. But Putnam and Dummett claim that any such view is unintelligible. Why?

Although there are passages in both Dummett and Putnam that could be given a less sympathetic reading, the reason is not (or at least is not simply) that these philosophers take understanding to be something that must transpire before consciousness. A more explicit theme is that understanding a language is a practical ability, constituted by a set of *dispositions,* in this case, learned responses: "Now when someone learns a language, what he learns is a practice; he learns to respond, verbally and nonverbally, to utterances and to make utterances of his own" (Dummett);[31] "language understanding [is] . . . an activity involving 'language entry rules' (procedures for subjecting some sentences to stimulus control), procedures for deductive and inductive inference and 'language exit rules'. . ." (Putnam).[32] It follows, Putnam and Dummett now agree, that if a language is characterized by certain truth rules, this fact must be one that shows up in the speech dispositions of the language users. And it follows that if there are no *dispositions* to recognize correspondence truth conditions, sentences can not have correspondence truth conditions.

Putnam's phrase "language entry rules" is a reference to Sellars, but, of course, many other central figures have also held that understanding a language must yield to a dispositional analysis, among them Quine, Davidson, many would say Wittgenstein, and, in the philosophy of mind (re: inner language), the functionalists. Despite this distinguished advocacy, surely Kripke's remark about illegitimate "equation of performance with correctness" is applicable here. To be competent in a language involves that one have a practical grasp of its truth rules. About that everyone agrees. But "true" is

---

30. For further discussion of the relation of proximal assertability rules to truth rules see my "The Price of Correspondence Truth", *Noûs* **20** (1986) pp. 453–68, and also *LTOBC*, especially Chapters 8 and 9. Proximal assertability rules are close relatives of what I there called "intensions." (In this essay I am not emphasizing that perception characteristically is an activity involving overt exploration, a fact that was in the foreground when I spoke of intensions in *LTOBC*. Thus the notion "proximal assertability rules" is a somewhat duller tool than I intended "intensions" to be in *LTOBC*.)

31. "What is a Theory of Meaning? (II)," p. 32.

32. "Realism and Reason," p. 110.

clearly a *normative* notion. "True" is how my sincerely uttered sentences are *when they come out right*, when they are, using Kripke's expression, as they "ought to be," when I achieve what I purpose in sincerely uttering them. And no mere set of dispositions, no mere performance, determines a measuring "ought," a standard or norm. No set of dispositions, then, could determine truth rules.

Nor is the normative ingredient in truth provided by the fact that the dispositions that constitute competence in a language must agree with a public norm. Compare games. Consider first a case in which I intend to play the same game as the others do, say, the one they call "chess," but I mistakenly play by different rules than the others. This is a case of playing wrongly in the sense that I have not played the game I intended, or, perhaps, the one others expected me to. Similarly, if I intend to use the same language as the others, but in fact adopt different truth rules, then I speak wrongly, for I have not spoken the language I intended, or that others expected me to. This is called "not knowing the language" or "making mistakes in the language." Second, consider a case in which I have no intention to play with the chess pieces as the others do nor do the others expect me to. Then playing by different rules is just playing a different game. It is neither playing chess wrongly nor doing anything else wrongly. The linguistic parallel to this is called "speaking a *different* language." But speaking wrongly in the sense of speaking *falsely* is still a *third* possibility. Speaking falsely is not just a way of being out of step, nor is it just marching to the beat of a different drummer. Suppose we call it a "rule" of chess that you are supposed to checkmate your opponent. Then speaking falsely is like failing to checkmate the opponent. Better, it is like failing to pick up one straw without moving the others when playing jackstraws. Just as learning the rules better is not the cure for losing at chess or jackstraws, learning the community's language better is not the cure for bad judgement. And just as whether one succeeds at jackstraws, that is, at not moving the other sticks, does not depend on any agreement with the community, neither does whether one succeeds in speaking truly in one's language. To purpose to follow certain truth rules is to set a standard for *oneself* – a standard that one may fail to meet.

It is because purposes set standards that "true" is a normative notion and that no set of dispositions could determine truth rules. Similarly, although Dummett and Putnam are right that semantic meaning must be resident somehow in language competence, no set of dispositions equals a competence. First, a disposition does not express a competence unless it is a disposition informed by a purpose. My disposition to fall if left unsupported is no competence, nor is the hoverfly's disposition to chase birds. Conversely, having a competence does not, in general, imply that one has any particular dispositions. If I know how to A – say, to sharpen a drill bit – it doesn't follow that I have a disposition to succeed in A-ing if I try. Perhaps my hands are too cold, or the only grindstone available is not the kind I am practiced at using, or you insist on joggling my elbow. Though I know how to walk, sometimes I trip when I try. Recall the hoverfly, who exhibits a competence whenever he conforms to the distal hoverfly rule in a normal way, yet, due to the inconstancy of conditions outside him, often does not manage to conform to it at all. Nor are there specified conditions under which a person must succeed in order to know how. If I can only sharpen the bit using one sharpening tool whereas you know how to use another, then normal conditions for exercise of my ability to sharpen a drill bit will be different from normal conditions for exercise of yours; each may fail where the other succeeds. Knowing how to do A entails, at best, only that there are *some* normal conditions under which one succeeds in doing A.

Now there is an evident reason why knowing how to A does not, in general, entail having any simple disposition to succeed in A-ing. The reason is that most know-how involves *distal* action, and there is no such thing as a simple *disposition* to involvement with anything distal. How one interacts with things at a distance always depends upon what lies in between, on surrounding conditions. Simple dispositions can concern only reactions to and actions upon that which *touches* one or, perhaps, what is inside one. It follows that to assimilate language competence to a set of dispositions directly begs the question against distal truth rules. There is no need for tortuous arguments to demonstrate that truth rules must then be verificationist. On a dispositional account, to "grasp" correspondence truth rules for each sentence in one's language would be to have a "capacity . . . to evince recognition of the truth of the sentence when and only when the relevant condition is fulfilled" (Dummett).[33] But if a "recognitional capacity" is a disposition, it must be a disposition to respond to a proximal stimulus, there being no such thing as a disposition to respond to something distal. And dispositions to respond to proximal stimuli with sentences could correspond, at best, to assertability conditions, certainly not to distal correspondence truth conditions. QED.

Compare the hoverfly. Assuming that his insides are working right, what he has a *disposition* to do is, at best, to conform to the proximal hoverfly rule. Does it follow that he has no ability to catch females?

It is significant, I think, how close the dispositional view of language understanding is to the more classical view that understanding takes place wholly within consciousness. On the classical view, understanding must ultimately involve relations only to things that touch the mind. On the dispositional view, understanding still involves only what touches the mind or, say, the nervous system. It is easy, then, to slip back and forth between two ways of interpreting the Dummett–Putnam attack upon realist truth.[34] Yet

---

33. "What is a Theory of Meaning? (II)," pp. 80–1.
34. I will not attempt to prove that Dummett and Putnam themselves do some sliding, but on Putnam, see *LTOBC*, Epilogue.

232

what Kripke has shown is that *neither* view of language understanding is a tenable view. Hence, whatever may be said for or against the positive theory of rule-following that I have offered, the verificationist vision is surely unnecessarily nearsighted. If Kripke (and Kripke's Wittgenstein) are right, then *whatever* the status of rule-following, we have no reason to think that the following of correspondence truth rules is any more *problematic* than is the following of verificationist truth rules.

On the other hand, perhaps what is most puzzling about the following of any kind of language rules is how one could "know" these rules without having a prior language, a prior way of "meaning" or thinking of these rules. Yet surely even the medium of thought, even whatever is currently before the mind or in the head, stands in need of interpretation. Knowing the rules is not a disposition, nor can it be explained in the end by reference to prior representations of the rules. The biological account agrees with both of these considerations.[35]

35. Earlier versions of this paper were read at the University of Wisconsin (Madison), Western Michigan University, the University of Maryland, Trinity University, the University of New England (Australia), Australian National University, Monash University and Vanderbilt University. I am grateful to the members of these departments, to Margaret Gilbert and John Troyer, and to unknown referees for *The Philosophical Review*, for helpful comments and suggestions.

CHAPTER TWELVE

KRIPKE ON WITTGENSTEIN ON NORMATIVITY[*]
George M. Wilson

In Saul Kripke's *Wittgenstein on Rules and Private Language*,[1] there are two main characters: a semantical skeptic and Ludwig Wittgenstein. Kripke himself, we can suppose, is the narrator. In the course of his narrative, the narrator often speaks for one or the other of the characters, and, when the characters are in agreement, he sometimes speaks for both. However, unlike Dr. Watson and Holmes, Kripke's Wittgenstein does not assent to all the skeptic's chief conclusions. Rather, Kripke's characters are related more in the manner of the governess and Mrs. Gross in *The Turn of the Screw*. The skeptic sees 'the super-natural' where Kripke's Wittgenstein sees only the skeptic's own delusion. Many commentators on Kripke's text have not done a good job of negotiating the question, "Whose voice is speaking in this passage? And now, who speaks in that one?" The upshot has been serious misunderstandings of the structure and content of the implicit dialogue that Kripke depicts in his book. Of course, the misunderstandings do not arise solely out of a deficient sense of 'point of view'; other factors encourage and support the confusions. These factors also need to be diagnosed. In any case, I will argue that the commentators have often been wrong about what the skeptic assumes, wrong about what Kripke's Wittgenstein concludes, and wrong, correlatively, to read some of the central arguments in a topsy-turvy fashion. My aim is to set these matters straight, commenting, where it seems especially illuminating to do so, upon the mistakes of several of Kripke's major critics.

I have noted that Kripke represents his characters as agreeing upon certain major issues. Upon what do they agree? Most notably, we are informed that they agree upon 'the skeptical conclusion.' And, what is that? Kripke varies

---

* This essay is dedicated to the memory of David Sachs.

1. Saul Kripke, *Wittgenstein on Rules and Private Language* (Cambridge, MA: Harvard University Press, 1982). Page citations in the main text are all to this book.

his formulation of the thesis throughout the book, but here are two reasonably characteristic statements of the point. "Now Wittgenstein's skeptic argues that he knows of no fact about an individual that could constitute his state of meaning plus rather than quus" (p. 39). Or again, "But then it appears to follow [from the skeptic's argument] that there was no *fact* about me that constituted my having meant plus rather than quus" (p. 21). And yet, even these explicit formulations can leave one troubled, for, in their larger context, they seem dangerously ambiguous. One might be tempted to suppose, for example, that, suitably generalized, they say:

> It is never a fact that a speaker means something by a term,

or

> There are no facts that ascriptions of meaning could correctly describe,

or, considering other aspects of the discussion,

> There are no (possible) facts that could constitute truth conditions for meaning ascriptions.

It is not merely that these statements might bear the sense of these crude paraphrases. In addition, each paraphrase roughly formulates a significant doctrine that figures in the developing argumentation. Hence, we will want to sort out at least three issues. How are the various 'skeptical' claims to be construed? Where do they stand within the different arguments that the protagonists deploy? And, returning to our first concern, which character voices any particular argument, and who is it that speaks for any given conclusion?

Since it will be important, as we proceed, to be as clear as possible about what Kripke's skeptic does and does not affirm, I will begin by attempting to state, in some detail, the perspective from which, as I see it, his skeptical arguments are developed. Here, for example, is an early statement by Kripke of one of the skeptic's basic presuppositions. "I, like almost all English speakers, use the word 'plus' and the symbol '+' to denote a well-known mathematical function, addition. . . . By means of my external symbolic representation and my internal mental representation, I 'grasp' the rule for addition. One point is crucial to my 'grasp' of this rule. Although I myself have computed only finitely many sums in the past, the rule determines my answer for indefinitely many new sums that I have never previously considered. This is the whole point of the notion that in learning to add I grasp a rule: my past intentions regarding addition determine a unique answer for indefinitely many new cases in the future" (pp. 7–8). Shortly afterwards, Kripke continues, "The basic point is this. Ordinarily, I suppose that, in computing '68 + 57' as I do, I do not simply make an unjustified leap in the dark. I follow directions I previously gave myself that uniquely determine that in this new instance I should say '125'. What are these directions?" (p. 10). These and related remarks lead into the summary statement of the skeptic's challenge that is offered on page 11. I quote that summary almost in full.

> [T]he challenge posed by the skeptic takes two forms. First, he questions whether there is any *fact* that I meant plus, not quus, that will answer his skeptical challenge. Second, he questions whether I have any reason to be so confident that now I should answer '125' rather than '5'. The two forms of the challenge are related. I am confident that this answer also accords with what I *meant*. Neither the accuracy of my computation nor of my memory is under dispute. So it ought to be agreed that *if* I meant plus, then unless I wish to change my usage, I am justified in answering (indeed compelled to answer) '125', not '5'. An answer to the skeptic must satisfy two conditions. First, it must give an account of what fact it is (about my mental state) that constitutes my meaning plus, not quus. But further, there is a condition that any putative candidate for such a fact must satisfy. It must, in some sense, show how I am justified in giving the answer '125' to '68 + 57'. The 'directions' mentioned in the previous paragraph, that determine what I should do in each instance, must somehow be 'contained' in any candidate for the fact as to what I meant. Otherwise, the skeptic has not been answered when he holds that my present response is arbitrary.

It is these thoughts that we need to review with some care.

The skeptic, it seems, begins with a skeletal but plausible conception of what it is to mean something by a term. Restricting ourselves, first of all, to the exemplary case of addition, the conception runs as follows. If, during a certain period, I meant addition by "+", then, during that time, I must have adopted some *standard of correctness* for my actual and potential applications of the term. Meaning something by "+" essentially involves having a *policy* about what is to count as a correct and incorrect application of the expression. Moreover, the skeptic supposes, the wanted standard of correctness is, in this example, specified for me in terms of the arithmetic operation of addition itself. As a matter of mathematical fact, independently of my or anyone else's linguistic practices, the addition function yields a unique numerical value for any pair of natural numbers. This general arithmetic fact constitutes the basis for a suitable standard of correctness. What I must do to establish the standard for myself, the skeptic maintains, is to adopt a *rule* or a *commitment* to the effect that *correct answers* to queries of the form $\lceil j + k = ? \rceil$ are given

236

by the values of the addition operation for the pairs of numbers that, query by query, are in question. Having adopted this linguistic rule for "+", correct applications of the term are *governed by* the infinite table of values that addition generates. Alternatively, we can say that, in meaning addition by "+", I must successfully 'single out' the addition function and, correlatively, form the *intention or purpose, concerning just that function,* that it is to determine correct applications of my use of the term. Hence, my acceptance of the linguistic commitment 'justifies' my answers to queries framed from "+" (when those answers are correct) in the sense that it supplies me with the standard of correctness that my applications of "+" are supposed to track.[2]

It is precisely at this juncture that the skeptic interposes his disturbing challenge. It is my contention that the skeptic does not doubt that the skeletal conception of what is involved in meaning addition by "+" is right. What he does doubt is that this conception can be intelligibly filled in with an account of *how* I (or any other speaker) achieve the adoption of the specified linguistic policy or commitment. What, he asks, does my adopting such a conception concretely consist in? In particular, what are the facts about me in virtue of which *it is addition* that governs correct applications of "+" for me and not some other initially similar but divergent arithmetic operation? What is it about me that makes it the case that I employ addition, and not (say) Kripke's quaddition, as my standard of correctness? In the discussion above, it was claimed that I must, in some manner, 'single out' addition and form an intention, about that function, that it is to settle correct applications of my use

---

2. In this paragraph, I have deliberately used somewhat different formulations. That is, I speak of adopting a commitment, a policy, a rule, and also of forming a certain intention. I have done so in order to avoid whatever significant issues might be raised if one were to try to choose between them. On the other hand, I believe that none of the main questions discussed in this essay would be affected by such a choice. Also, in the second quotation from Kripke given above, he speaks of 'giving oneself directions' where I would use one of the locutions just mentioned. To my ear, this phrase of Kripke's too much conveys the idea of performing (outwardly or inwardly) a certain kind of speech act, and this distorts the general conception that the skeptic has in mind. In particular, the choice of words is particularly unfortunate when it is conjoined with Kripke's description of the first response to the skeptic's problem. The would-be response is stated in this way: "Rather I learned – and internalized instructions for – a *rule* which determines how addition is to be continued" (p. 15). This proposal is clearly rejected, but the similarity in formulation can suggest that the skeptic's basic conception of what must be involved in meaning addition by "+" is here being rejected. Rather, it seems to me, what is proposed and rejected is the idea that I *establish* which arithmetical operation is to constitute the standard of correctness for my use of "+" by giving myself a linguistic definition or set of instructions that specify the operation in question. But then, the obvious reply – given in Kripke's text – is that, because the puzzle about what it is I mean by a term is a completely general one, the puzzle will arise again and with equal force with respect to the relevant terms in the verbal definition or instructions I formulated for myself. Although this proposal is rejected, the skeptic's idea that, if I mean addition by '+', then something about me 'singles out' addition as that which governs my use of the term remains in place. In the first quotation, he speaks of 'grasping a rule', and I have similarly talked about 'adopting a rule.' But, standing by itself, these locutions can be understood as meaning something like 'accepting a linguistic or symbolic *formulation* of a rule.' So understood, the confusion just described can arise again. So I have been at some pains to counter this impression.

of "+". Well then, the skeptic asks, in what specific manner do I accomplish the task of 'singling out' addition so as to form the required intention concerning it?[3]

The ensuing skeptical argument purports to show that there are no acceptable answers to these questions. Some of the proposals that the skeptic considers cite facts about me that do not single out any particular arithmetic operation whatsoever. Other proposals cite facts which, if they do identify a specific function at all, wrongly identify an operation other than addition. All of them fail to explain how I have acquired a linguistic policy that is directed, as it should be, upon the addition function. The skeletal conception with which we started cannot be determinately grounded in facts about me that render it intelligible that it is addition that I have meant by "+".

As Kripke repeatedly emphasizes, the skeptic's problem is a general one: it concerns the meaningfulness of any speaker's use of a term. To lay hold of the broader point of view, it will be helpful to rehearse these last reflections in a more general fashion. Thus, let $\lceil\phi\rceil$ be any term which a speaker X proposes to use as a general term or predicate. That is, $\lceil\phi\rceil$, as X is to employ it, is to apply correctly or incorrectly, as the case may be, to the members of some open-ended domain of objects D. In particular, and without significant loss of generality, we can assume that $\lceil\phi\rceil$ is to be a 'descriptive' term for X – a term that is applied correctly or incorrectly, in a given case, depending upon facts about the specific character of the candidate item. As before, the skeptic insists that X will not mean something by the term $\lceil\phi\rceil$ unless she supplies for herself a standard of correctness for the envisaged use. But, from where is the appropriate standard to be derived? Well, let us take it for granted that each member of D (considered at a time when the pertinent item exists) exempli-

---

3. I realize that these formulations suggest that the facts about X that the skeptic will accept as relevant to his challenge are restricted, as it were, to 'individualistic' facts about X. Much of Kripke's discussion tends to carry the same suggestion – in some cases rather strongly. This suggestion leaves the skeptic open to the charge that he has illegitimately excluded, from the beginning, a kind of social version of a 'straight' solution to his puzzle. Thus, very roughly, one might hold the following. First, it would be granted that there are facts about members of a linguistic community – in virtue of *their* complex, cooperative use of a term $\lceil\phi\rceil$ – that establish properties $P_1 - P_n$ as the standards that govern correct applications of [ϕ] among *them* or in *their* language. Second, it would be held that an individual member X of the community will mean $P_1 - P_n$ by $\lceil\phi\rceil$ only if his or her linguistic dispositions concerning $\lceil\phi\rceil$ situate him/her as a competent $\lceil\phi\rceil$-user in that community. Whatever the merits or demerits of this vaguely specified approach, I take it that Kripke holds that his skeptic rejects it and rejects it for reasons similar to the ones given in his main exposition of the skeptical problem. See, in particular, the brief remarks on p. 111. I assume that Kripke is here denying that Wittgenstein would accept the first plank in the approach adumbrated above, i.e., that there are facts about the linguistic community, even taken collectively, that constitute some set of properties as standards of correctness for their use of $\lceil\phi\rceil$. Again, I will make no attempt to assess the force of the considerations available to the skeptic against a position of this kind. However, I do mean to suppose in the text that the skeptic's arguments for his skeptical conclusion are to be understood as including non-individualistic solutions of this ilk. For many, I suspect, the skeptic's arguments will seem truly disturbing only if this supposition is made.

fies a range of determinant properties and does not exemplify a host of others. We can presume that the fact that a D-member has a certain property or the fact that it does not obtains independently of our beliefs about the matter and independently of whatever forms of language use we may have put in place. So, it seems, the standards of correctness for the descriptive predicates are to be established in terms of these properties of the D-members – in terms of these objective predicable conditions, realized or not as they may be, by the various objects in D. The skeptic repeats that what X must do if she is to mean something by $\ulcorner\phi\urcorner$ is to adopt the linguistic commitment that $\ulcorner\phi\urcorner$ is to be applied to a D-item v just in case v has just *these* properties, e.g. the properties $P_1 - P_n$. Varying the formulation, X is to have the intention, concerning $P_1 - P_n$, that $\ulcorner\phi\urcorner$ applies to v iff v exemplifies those conditions.

We should notice, since this will become important as we proceed, that X's meaning something by $\ulcorner\phi\urcorner$, thus conceived, ensures that the meaning of $\ulcorner\phi\urcorner$ for X enjoys a certain intuitive *normativity*. For an unbounded number of objects in D, X's semantic policy for $\ulcorner\phi\urcorner$ determines, when relevant facts about the D-items are fixed, whether or not *it is correct* to apply $\ulcorner\phi\urcorner$, on X's use, to the objects in question. Actually, as this formulation suggests, this determination of correctness is a two-stage affair. By adopting her semantic rule, X thereby determines *what has to be the case* if $\ulcorner\phi\urcorner$, as she means it, is to apply. It is determined, as we have said, *which properties* a candidate for $\ulcorner\phi\urcorner$ ascription is to have. But now, whether $\ulcorner\phi\urcorner$ *does* apply to an object v (as it is at a time t) depends also upon the facts about v's character at t. It depends upon whether that character 'accords with' the defining properties, $P_1 - P_n$. With this qualification understood, we can say that, on the present conception, meaning determines correctness and so is normative in relation to the speaker's prospective practice.

These considerations place us in a position to describe succinctly how the skeptic's negative argument proceeds. First, we have just observed that the skeptic endorses a natural and powerful conception of the normativity of meaning. He holds that

N_s) If X means something by a term $\ulcorner\phi\urcorner$, then there is a set of properties, $P_1 - P_n$ that govern the correct application of $\ulcorner\phi\urcorner$ for X.

However, as we also observed in our discussion of "+", the skeptic insists that, if certain properties are to function as conditions of correct applicability for X's use of $\ulcorner\phi\urcorner$, then there must be concrete facts about X which establish that it *is* just those properties which she has successfully singled out and about which she has formed a proper semantic commitment. The existence of conditions of applicability for a term must be intelligibly *grounded* in facts about the speaker's psychological and/or social history.[4] Therefore, the 'grounding constraint' says that

---

4. If one goes back to Kripke's summary statement of the skeptic's challenge, one finds the grounding condition indicated in the following statement: "The 'directions' . . . that determine

G) If there is a set of properties, $P_1 - P_n$, that govern the correct application of $\lceil \phi \rceil$ for X, then there are facts about X that *constitute* $P_1 - P_n$ as the conditions that govern X's use of $\lceil \phi \rceil$.

Acceptance of this constraint moves us into the territory that the skeptic attacks. Naturally, the skeptic defends a number of skeptical-sounding conclusions, but what I take to be the basic skeptical argument attempts to show that the grounding constraint cannot be satisfied. That is, what I will call "the basic skeptical conclusion" states that

BSC) There are *no* facts about X that constitute any set of properties as conditions that govern X's use of $\lceil \phi \rceil$.

This is the conclusion for which the skeptic argues on a case-by-case basis. He investigates a range of suggestions, purporting to exhaust the possibilities, concerning the sorts of facts about X which might be thought to establish a set of properties as conditions of correct ascribability, and he tries to demonstrate that each of these suggestions is unacceptable. BSC), then, sums up the purported results of these investigations. In this essay, I will not attempt to assess the cogency of the case-by-case argument for BSC).

Nevertheless, simply setting up the structure of the skeptic's overall position in this form raises a number of significant questions. For example, I mentioned, at the beginning of this essay, that when Kripke frames what he calls "the skeptical conclusion," he tends to favor formulations such as

S) There are no facts that constitute X's meaning something by a term [ϕ].

It was this sort of formulation that seemed so provocatively elusive. But how, one may wonder, is my BSC) a plausible version of the troublesome form of words? Here, I believe, there are two related but distinguishable connections to be made. First, from the skeptic's viewpoint, BSC) simply says that there are no facts about X that constitute anything (i.e., any set of properties) as that which X means by $\lceil \phi \rceil$. After all, the skeptic thinks that what X means, if anything, by $\lceil \phi \rceil$ is a particular set of properties and that X's meaning some such set of properties by $\lceil \phi \rceil$ just is a matter of X's use of $\lceil \phi \rceil$ being governed by the properties in question.

However, there is another conclusion, potentially expressible by S), to which the skeptic is also directly committed. On the present reconstruction,

---

what I should do in each instance, must somehow be 'contained' in any candidate for the fact as to what I meant." Given the way in which I have formulated the issues, I would be inclined to put the point in this way. *The properties,* which constitute the standards for my use of $\lceil \phi \rceil$, and which thereby determine how I should apply $\lceil \phi \rceil$ in each instance, must somehow be 'contained' in any candidate for the fact as to what I meant. That is to say, the fact as to what I meant must itself partially consist in facts about me that establish which properties are to be my standards of correctness in using $\lceil \phi \rceil$.

the skeptic has held a view from the outset about the type of fact that X's meaning something by $\lceil \phi \rceil$ would have to consist in. In other words, the view says that statements of the form $\lceil X$ means ψ by $\lceil \phi \rceil \rceil$ uniformly purport to describe a fact of a certain kind, i.e., the fact that the relevant properties do govern X's use of $\lceil \phi \rceil$. But, the skeptic also contends that there can be no facts of that type unless they contain more specific facts about the speaker that fix for her the linguistic standards of correctness she is to pursue. And now, since BSC) is the thesis that no such standard-fixing facts exist, the skeptic concludes that there are and can be no facts that would be truly describable as $\lceil X$'s meaning something by $\lceil \phi \rceil \rceil$. There are no facts in the world to be correctly recorded by these ascriptions of meaning.

It will emerge, as we proceed, that it is important to keep these two connections to S)-style formulations sharply in mind. Although, as I have just indicated, the skeptic endorses both conclusions, the conceptual situation shifts dramatically when we turn to the framework of what Kripke calls "the skeptical solution." I will argue that this framework also incorporates BSC) (the skeptic and the skeptical solution agree on this), and, from a point of view different from the skeptic's, the skeptical solution agrees to the first of the reformulations offered above.[5] However, the thought expressed by my second formulation is quite a different matter. For reasons I will present later, the skeptical solution need not adopt the position that meaning ascriptions do not correctly describe or state facts about the speaker in question. But it will be easier to explain the import and the rationale for this remark only after the framework of the skeptical solution has been erected.

As I indicated above, since the skeptic draws several surprising conclusions, it is dangerous to speak of 'the' skeptical conclusion. It has probably not escaped notice that the three premises, N_s), G), and BSC), jointly entail the *radical* skeptical conclusion that

RSC) No one ever means anything by a term.

Kripke's skeptic plainly is committed to this. But what are we to say about Kripke's Wittgenstein in this connection? Kripke asserts that Wittgenstein accepts 'the' skeptical argument and agrees to its skeptical conclusion. Does

---

5. When the skeptic affirms that there are no facts about X which establish some particular set of properties as that which X means by $\lceil \phi \rceil$, he presupposes that meaning ascriptions of the form $\lceil X$ means ψ by $\lceil \phi \rceil \rceil$ say that X's use of $\lceil \phi \rceil$ stands in the 'meaning-relation' (as he conceives of this) to a set of properties indicated by $\lceil \phi \rceil$. Hence, his affirmation threatens to entail that X does not mean anything by $\lceil \phi \rceil$. However, the proponent of the skeptical solution rejects this crucial presupposition. As we will see later, it is central to the skeptical solution the skeptic has, in this manner, misconstrued the character of the meaning ascriptions from the very beginning. Thus, if we say, as I do, that the proponent of the skeptical solution endorses *this* affirmation of the skeptic, perhaps we should also say that he, unlike the skeptic, employs "means by" within scare quotes in this context and that the scare quotes are to signal the fact that he agrees to the claim only when "means by" is used as the skeptic (wrongly) understands it. See Kripke's remarks on what is essentially this same complication on pp. 76–7.

this mean that Kripke thinks that Wittgenstein also holds or is committed to RSC)? The answer, I will urge, is "No," but to see *how*, on my reading of Kripke, this can be so will force us to explore some difficult terrain. In my judgement, the skeptical conclusion that Kripke's Wittgenstein accepts is just BSC), and it is the skeptical argument for *that* result that he endorses.

Consider, to begin with, an important remark that Kripke makes on pages 70 and 71; "Nevertheless I choose to be so bold as to say: Wittgenstein holds, with the skeptic, that there is no fact as to whether I mean plus or quus. But if this is to be conceded to the skeptic, is this not the end of the matter? What *can* be said on behalf of our ordinary attributions of meaningful language to ourselves and to others? Has not *the incredible and self defeating conclusion* [emphasis added], that all language is meaningless, already been drawn?" The question that closes this passage refers to RSC), and the discussion that ensues unequivocally affirms that Wittgenstein does not draw this conclusion. In fact, it is natural to read Kripke as saying that it is a chief objective of the skeptical solution to explain why RSC) does not follow from BSC). Note that, in this quotation, RSC) is described as "incredible and self-defeating," and it seems obvious, in context, that this characterization is meant to reflect Wittgenstein's attitude also. So, Kripke does not suppose that Wittgenstein embraces RSC).

However, if Kripke's Wittgenstein accepts BSC) and rejects RSC), then the resulting conjunction has an immediate, important consequence. That is, according to Kripke's interpretation, Wittgenstein is committed to rejecting N_s) also, and that is the thesis that incorporates the skeptic's affirmation of the normativity of meaning. How plausible is this as part of a reading of Kripke's account of Wittgenstein? Many will wish to object that Kripke's Wittgenstein surely shares with the skeptic his emphasis upon the claim that meaning is normative. Any construal of Kripke's book that holds that its author represents Wittgenstein as repudiating 'normativity' must be mistaken.

In many ways, this objection goes to the heart of the reading of Kripke I propose, and it will take the remainder of the essay to develop fully my response. Here I can only adumbrate the strategy I will pursue. It will be my position that we need to be careful to distinguish a broad and somewhat schematic condition on meaning that articulates its normative character from the skeptic's more specific account of how normativity arises for a speaker's application of a term. I fully agree that Kripke's Wittgenstein, in rough harmony with the skeptic, accepts this normativity condition, and, guided by passages in Kripke's book, I will try to formulate the schematic condition as we proceed. Further, as I will try to show, not only does Kripke's Wittgenstein accept the condition, but from within the skeptical solution, he constructs a distinctive account of the *basis* of the normativity condition. On the other hand, N_s) encapsulates the skeptic's alternative conception of the basis of normativity, and this conception, I believe, *is* one that Kripke's Wittgenstein denies.

In any case, the following is my present hypothesis. The skeptic is committed to this argument:

N$_s$)
G)
BSC) therefore
RSC;

Kripke's Wittgenstein is not; rather he is committed to the 'contrapositive' argument:

G)
BSC)
~ RSC) therefore
~ N$_s$)

Having just allowed that this hypothesis will require an elaborate defense, I hasten to add that, if it can be defended, there is a major interpretative benefit to be gained. Moreover, the benefit is accrued in relation to interpretative issues to which other commentators on Kripke have inadequately attended.

At the very beginning of his presentation of the skeptical solution, Kripke stresses that Wittgenstein rejects what he (Kripke) calls the "classical realist" theory or picture of meaning. Kripke provides a brief description of the sort of view he has in mind in this passage:

> The simplest, most basic idea of the *Tractatus* can hardly be dismissed: a declarative sentence gets its meaning by virtue of its *truth conditions,* by virtue of its correspondence to facts that must obtain if it is true. For example, "the cat is on the mat" is understood by those speakers who realize that it is true if and only if a certain cat is on a certain mat; it is false otherwise. The presence of the cat on the mat is a fact or condition-in-the-world that would make the sentence true (express a truth) if it obtained. (p. 72)

That Kripke believes that Wittgenstein rejects this classical realism has been widely noted, but he later makes a stronger claim whose import deserves deeper consideration. On page 85, Kripke writes,

> In this way the relationship between the first and the second portions of the *Investigations* is reciprocal. In order for Wittgenstein's skeptical solution of his paradox to be intelligible, the 'realistic' or 'representational' picture of language must be undermined by another picture (in the first part). On the other hand, the paradox developed in the second part, antecedently to its solution, drives an

important final nail (perhaps the crucial one) into the coffin of the representational picture.

Now, what does Kripke mean when he tells us that the skeptical paradox "drives a final nail into the coffin of classical realism"? It is my assumption that he means that Wittgenstein rejects classical realism because, perhaps along with other reasons, Wittgenstein supposes that the skeptical argument offers him the grounds for a definitive argument against the classical realist position. But, then, how is this argument supposed to run? If we see, as I think we should, that the skeptic develops his paradox from a conception of meaning that is itself classical realist, then, given my suggestion above, the argument is readily discerned. In effect, N_s) is a condensed statement of a central aspect of what the classical realist believes about meaning, and I have just outlined the way in which Kripke's Wittgenstein has a *reductio* of precisely that thesis.

When I first introduced and motivated N_s), I devoted some space to trying to convey what I take to be the skeptic's picture of what is involved when a speaker means something by a term. It was a part of my intention, in devoting as much space as I did to this conception, to bring out, at least implicitly, the way in which the skeptic himself is a (skeptical) classical realist. It is true that, when Kripke introduced classical realism (named as such) into his discussion, he focused on the idea that the meaning of a *sentence* arises from its supposed correlation with 'realist' truth conditions, i.e., with *a possible fact* whose realization in the world will render the sentence true. By contrast, I focused on *general terms* and on the thought that their meaningfulness depends upon their correct application being governed by *properties* or objective and exemplifiable conditions. However, these variant styles of formulation are easily intertranslatable. If, for example, in a sentence $\ulcorner \alpha$ is $\ulcorner \phi \urcorner \urcorner$, $\ulcorner \alpha \urcorner$ names an object o and $\ulcorner \phi \urcorner$ ascribes a property P to o, then $\ulcorner \alpha$ is $\ulcorner \phi \urcorner \urcorner$ is true just in case the possible fact of o's being P obtains. So, to repeat: the skeptic has a classical realist background, and N_s) is his credo. Kripke's Wittgenstein endorses the skeptical argument to BSC), agrees also to the grounding constraint G), but, reasonably enough, denies the "insane and intolerable" RSC).[6] These components generate his *reductio* of N_s). Unlike the skeptic, Kripke's Wittgenstein sides with common opinion that people often mean something by the terms and sentences they use. But he claims to have shown that those sentences cannot have classical realist truth conditions (for sentences) nor classical realist satisfaction or truth-of-conditions (for terms). Hence, the meaningfulness of language for its users cannot consist in that.

---

6. The characterization of a skeptical conclusion as being "insane and intolerable" occurs on page 60. I am taking this to refer to the radical skeptical conclusion, but, even in context, this is not so clear. Kripke simply says that *the* skeptical conclusion is insane and intolerable. But he cannot mean here 'the skeptical conclusion' with which Wittgenstein is supposed to agree. It has to be some conclusion drawn from the skeptic's argument which the skeptical solution is supposed to block. Admittedly, such remarks are confusing.

I am reassured that my reading of Kripke's book is controversial by David Pears's discussion of the same material in his *The False Prison*, vol. 2. My last proposals simply contradict the interpretative impression he has formed. Pears states that the targets of Wittgenstein's attack are "Platonizing" accounts of meaning – theories that, as he puts it, hold that "the guidance given by a rule is complete, covering every possible case in advance and leaving nothing to be contributed to what counts as compliance by the mind of the person who is following it."[7] Now, although a lengthy process of sorting out and weighing would be required to support the claim, it strikes me that Pears's 'meaning Platonism' does not differ essentially from Kripke's 'classical realism' about meaning. Suppose that I am right about this, and consider a central objection that Pears makes to Kripke's views. "[I]t can be shown that the passages in the *Philosophical Investigations* which Kripke interprets as expressions of skepticism about rule-following are really nothing of the kind: they are part of a reductive argument directed against Platonizing theories of meaning."[8] I do not find Pears's exegesis of Kripke's argumentation easy to follow, but, details aside, I do not believe that this passage could have been written unless its author had failed to distinguish adequately the issues about which the skeptic and the skeptical solution agree from those about which they distinctly disagree. What I have been urging is that, if one does so distinguish, a major *reductio* of classical realism – what Pears calls "Platonism" – about meaning is present in the text and serves as a prolegomena to the skeptical solution. I conjecture that Pears does not believe that there can be a *reductio* in Kripke similar to the one that he outlines in his book because he supposes that Kripke holds that Wittgenstein shares the skeptic's conception of normativity. But then, N$_s$) represents a 'Platonizing' account of meaning, and so, Kripke's Wittgenstein cannot be arguing against that. As I acknowledged earlier, the appearances in support of Pears need to be explained.

Crispin Wright and Paul Boghossian also structure Kripke's reading of Wittgenstein quite differently than I do.[9] A few pages earlier, I signaled the fact that there is an issue about which of the skeptical conclusions Kripke's Wittgenstein is supposed to accept – an issue about the extent to which the skeptical solution is in agreement with the skeptic's position. It is precisely at this juncture, I believe, that Wright and Boghossian, in company with other commentators, commit a crucial error. But the issues are delicate and need to be developed with some care.

A symptom of my larger differences with Wright and Boghossian is to be found in their judgement that there exists a puzzling lacuna in Kripke's argumentative strategy. Both philosophers are well aware that Kripke's

---

7. David Pears, *The False Prison*, vol. 2 (Oxford: Oxford University Press, 1988), p. 465.
8. *Ibid*. p. 457.
9. Crispin Wright, "Kripke's Account of the Argument Against Private language," *Journal of Philosophy* 81 (1984): pp. 759–78. Paul A. Boghossian, "The Rule-Following Considerations," *Mind* 98 (1989), pp. 507–49 (this volume Ch. 9).

Wittgenstein rejects (classical realist) truth conditions in a global fashion, i.e., that he holds

S2) *No* sentence has classical realist truth conditions.

But, Boghossian in particular charges that Kripke has neglected to specify how the skeptical solution arrives at S2). (He does think that the gap can be filled in and is prepared to suppose that Kripke sees the connection that he, Boghossian, supplies.)[10] Both authors also correctly record that the favored formulation of the skeptical conclusion is

S) There are no facts that constitute X's meaning something by a term $\lceil \phi \rceil$,

but they construe this to mean something like

S*) There are no facts about X that assertions of the form $\lceil X$ means ψ by $\lceil \phi \rceil \rceil$, even when they are correct by ordinary criteria, *describe truly.*

In response to this supposed result, they suggest that the skeptical solution incorporates a certain 'projectivism' about meaning at its core. Wright summarizes both the provocation and response in this way: ". . . Kripke's Wittgenstein may be seen as first, by the skeptical argument, confounding the ordinary idea that our talk of meaning and understanding and cognate concepts has a genuinely factual subject matter, and then, via the skeptical solution, recommending an alternative projective view of its content."[11] Thus, the skeptical solution is thought to feature the 'projectivist' thesis that sentences of the form $\lceil X$ means ψ by $\lceil \phi \rceil \rceil$ do not, as part of their semantic content, ever purport to describe facts. This, of course, is meant to take the sting out of S*). For if $\lceil X$ means ψ by $\lceil \phi \rceil \rceil$ does purport to describe facts about X, then the truth of S*) ensures that all such meaning ascriptions are either false or somehow incoherent. The projectivist thesis guarantees that S*) does not have this consequence and encourages us to search for an alternative account of the semantic function or functions of meaning ascriptions. Neither Wright nor Boghossian tries to elaborate such an alternative, but, in the light of relevant parts of Kripke's presentation, one might be led to suggest, for example, that the semantic function of such ascriptions is to confer license upon or to acknowledge the license of a speaker to be a competent user of $\lceil \phi \rceil$ within the prevailing linguistic practices.[12] This at least hints at what

10. See Boghossian, "Rule-Following Considerations", p. 524 (this volume Ch. 9). See also Wright, "Kripke's Account", p. 769.
11. Wright, "Kripke's Account", p. 761.
12. For remarks that could suggest such a view, see Kripke, p. 92. However, it should be clear that I do not take Kripke, in such passages, to be proposing a projectivist account of the semantic function of meaning ascriptions. He is merely attempting to bring out certain features of their assertability conditions and their 'role and utility' in relevant language games.

'projectivism' might amount to here, but, for present purposes, the details do not matter.

Therefore, on this construal of Kripke, the skeptical solution presents us with S*), and it seems plausible that a simple consequence of this is

S3) Sentences of the form ⌜X means ψ by ⌜ϕ⌝⌝ do not have classical realist truth conditions.

But now, Boghossian tells us that he cannot find in Kripke an explanation of what justifies the inference from S3) to the globally generalized S2), and, as I mentioned, he offers an explanation of his own. And yet, by my lights, there is no gap to be filled: Wright and Boghossian have got Kripke's argumentative structure back to front. It is my contention that the global S2) is derived directly as part of the *reductio* of N$_s$) – it is an immediate result of that general argument. Naturally, S3) is also accepted, but it merely follows as an instance of S2). There is no reason to hunt for a route from S3) back to S2).

My deeper disagreement with Wright and Boghossian, however, concerns a prior question. In my opinion it is highly doubtful that such a projectivist thesis figures in the skeptical solution. I find this thesis not only implausible on its own, but irrelevant to the true concerns of Kripke's Wittgenstein. Projectivism about meaning ascriptions is supposed to blunt the consequences of 'the skeptical conclusion', S*), but Kripke's Wittgenstein is not committed to S*). Kripke's skeptic *is* probably so committed, but, as we noted before and as we will see again shortly, that is another matter. It is easy to become tangled up in trying to formulate the issues properly. Contributing to the potential tangle is the fact that the version of skeptical conclusion Kripke spotlights (i.e., S): "There are no facts that constitute X's meaning ⌜ψ⌝ by ⌜ϕ⌝" can be read, with roughly equal naturalness, as expressing either S*) or S3). My claim is that only the S3) reading is correct. Moreover, Kripke's employment, in his book, of the phrase "states facts," where that applies to sentences, sometimes helps to encourage the confusion.[13]

The first point to be stressed is that S*) and S3) are not equivalent, at least, they are not when S*) bears a sense to which projectivism might be an appropriate response. I have already granted that it is plausible that S3) follows from S*), but the converse cannot be assumed to hold in the present dialectical context. More broadly, from

---

13. On the whole, when Kripke says that a sentence does not 'state facts,' he seems to mean that the sentence does not have classical realist truth conditions. Or, so I interpret him. After all, talk of facts in relation to the question of sentence meaning is introduced when Kripke introduces the classical realist account of meaning. But, in some passages, his usage is not so clear. For example, on page 73, he says, "Since the indicative mood is not taken as in any sense primary or basic, it becomes more plausible that the linguistic role even of utterances in the indicative mood that superficially look like assertions need not be one of 'stating facts'." Especially when this is read along with n. 62 at the bottom of the page, 'stating facts' here seems to mean "used to describe [or: report] facts" as I have been employing this phrase.

i) $\lceil P \rceil$ does not have classical realist truth conditions

it does not follow that

ii) $\lceil P \rceil$, even if 'correct', does not describe facts,

or, more guardedly and more to the present point, it would seem to be Wittgenstein's view that the inference is unsound. Consider what Wittgenstein says about 'family resemblance' terms such as his famous example "game."[14] Leaving aside everything else in his remarks on the topic, I take it that he contends that there is no single property and no single set of properties that govern the correct application of these terms. "Game" does not have classical realist truth (satisfaction) conditions. As an item of Wittgenstein interpretation this is not very controversial. However, I cannot see that the 'family resemblance' doctrine commits him, in any way, to the position that sentences like

a) This activity is a game,
b) John is playing a game,

and so on, do not, even when asserted correctly, describe facts. Such a commitment would surely be quite surprising. We have the conviction, I believe, that statements such as these *are, in some reasonable sense,* used to describe facts. There seems to be nothing projective about the content of such sentences. It is not, for instance, a part of their semantic function to express some attitude of the speaker's or to effect some sort of performative pronouncement. True utterances of a) and b), we want to grant, do function somehow to describe facts, and there is no reason why Wittgenstein could not agree with our conviction here.

One may well feel some hesitation over the questions just raised, because limited reflection makes it patent that the notion of a 'fact-describing' sentence is vague and problematic. One would like some minimal account of what the notion involves, and I feel certain that there are a number of non-equivalent but palatable accounts that could be developed. Nevertheless, through all the variations that might be played, a) and b) should come out on the 'descriptive' side. Further, nothing in the skeptical solution, as Kripke articulates it, precludes us from drawing a distinction (or, several alternative distinctions) between sentences that are used to describe facts and sentences that are not. That is, this distinction (or these distinctions) would be elaborated in terms of the framework that constitutes the skeptical solution.

As Kripke presents the skeptical solution, a meaningful sentence will have both assertability (justification) conditions and a "role and utility" within the

---

14. Wittgenstein, *Philosophical Investigations* (Oxford: Basil Blackwell, 1958), §§31–36.

language games in which it figures.[15] Kripke does not say much about the concept of the 'language game role and utility' of a sentence, but the road seems open to delineating the view that some sentences, given their overall use in the relevant language games, do have the role of describing (or stating or registering) facts. By contrast, other varieties of sentences, given their characteristic uses, will have other non-descriptive roles. Perhaps one will wish to grant, in a Wittgensteinian spirit, that the specific language game roles of sentences that count as 'describing facts' may bear only a family resemblance to one another. But, however the details might go, the envisioned distinction will be built as an added story upon the skeptical solution so that, presumably, the former will not contradict any component of the latter.

How will meaning ascriptions be classified by such a distinction? It is obvious that this will depend crucially on the particular character of the distinction that is drawn. My point here is that, at least in the absence of such a further distinction, the skeptical solution is or should be *agnostic* about the truth of S*). Hence, the skeptical solution need not and, in my opinion, does not incorporate projectivism about meaning ascriptions. Notice that if the inference from i) to ii) above were sound, then the global rejection of classical realist truth conditions in S2) would enjoin a projectivist view of the content of all sentences. Whether for this reason or another, Wright thinks that Kripke's Wittgenstein is unwittingly stuck with this extreme position. Criticizing this supposed consequence. Wright says, "it is doubtful that it is coherent to suppose that projectivist views could be appropriate quite globally. For, however exactly the distinction be drawn between fact-stating and non-fact-stating discourse, the projectivist will presumably want it to come by way of a *discovery* that certain statements fail to qualify for the former class: a statement of the conclusion of the skeptical argument, for instance, is not *itself* to be projectivist."[16] I am urging that Kripke's Wittgenstein, properly construed, can endorse the second sentence of this passage wholeheartedly. Of course, if we mistakenly think that an argument for S3) – or, indeed, an argument for S2) – is itself an argument for S*), then we will feel forced to inflate the skeptical solution with a projectivist remedy. But, I have also argued, on any reading of S*) that is plausible in the dialectical context, such a conflation just *is* a mistake.

I am not sure that Wright and Boghossian are actually guilty of conflating S*) with S3). It may well be that they understand S*) as a proposition, stronger than S3), which represents the central skeptical conclusion, the conclusion with which Wittgenstein is said by Kripke to agree. If this is the case, then, for reasons already sketched, they are mistaken about this different point. I explained earlier why Kripke's skeptic may well be committed to

---

15. The concept in question is first introduced on pages 75–6. More on this notion, in relation to the "+" example, is found on pages 91–3.
16. Wright, "Kripke's Account," p. 770.

something like S*). The skeptic believes that, if a correct form of normativity is to be engendered, then X's meaning something by $\lceil \phi \rceil$ must be constituted by there being a set of properties to which X is committed as the conditions of correctness for her use of $\lceil \phi \rceil$. But, the skeptic also holds that, if there are or even could be facts of that type, there must be, constitutively, further facts about X that determine what that set of properties is. And now, the skeptic argues at length, there are and can be no such further facts. In other words, there cannot be any facts of the type that, on the skeptic's view, instances of $\lceil X$ means ψ by $\lceil \phi \rceil \rceil$ purport to describe. However, I also pointed out earlier that all of this rests on the skeptic's conception of normativity, encapsulated in N_s), or equivalently, on the classical realist picture of meaning that backs it up. In addition, it was a main thesis of that part of my discussion that Kripke's Wittgenstein decisively rejects N_s) and the 'classical realism' that goes with it. So, it *is* a mistake to imagine that Kripke's Wittgenstein buys into S*). He follows the skeptic only as far as BSC) and its consequences.

It is instructive to glance at Wright's general conception of how the skeptical argument proceeds. In broad terms at least, I suspect that many commentators share this conception.[17] In any case, Wright says,

> The initial target class of putative facts comprises those which you might try to express by claims of the form 'By E, I formerly meant so-and-so.' The relevant idealization will involve your total recall of all facts about your previous behavior and previous mental history, it being assumed that facts about your former meanings must be located in one of those two areas if they are located anywhere. The argument will then be that, even in terms of the idealization, no such claim is justifiable. It follows that your previous life in its entirety is empty of such facts, and hence that there are none.[18]

Now, as Wright and others have indicated, if this *is* the argument in outline, its basic strategy is deeply problematic. Kripke's Wittgenstein is deemed to start out from an assumption about the kinds of potentially relevant facts that exist and then to seek to 'locate' among these a suitable subject matter for ascriptions of meaning. But, given the types of facts that the skeptic appears willing to countenance (e.g., "facts about your previous behavior and previous mental history") locating a subject matter for such statements can involve nothing less than some form of reduction of meaning to the already

---

17. For example, Warren Goldfarb seems to have a similar notion of the strategy of the skeptical argument in "Kripke on Wittgenstein on Rules," *Journal of Philosophy* 82 (1985): pp. 471–88 (this volume Ch. 6). See his discussion on pages 473–80. For example, consider, "It [the skeptical argument] questions whether, if everything there is were laid out before us, we could read off the correct ascriptions of meaning to people. . . Thus, it is the notion of fact, of 'everything there is', that is to provide the ground of the challenge" (p. 474).

18. Wright, "Kripke's Account," p. 762. Boghossian sees the argument in very similar terms.

accepted factual base. This has the consequence that it is open to the skeptic's opponent to reject the presupposition that a reduction is either possible or required. Why not say from the outset that, among the facts that exist for X to recall, is, e.g., the fact that X meant addition by "+", and that fact is just what it is and not another thing.

This conception of the argument misconstrues the kind of facts the skeptic wants specified and misunderstands the skeptic's reasons for his challenge. No wonder it winds up with a false idea of what the skeptical conclusion is. To reiterate once more, the classical realist and, hence, the skeptic believe that, if X means something by a term, then there is a specific set of properties about which X has formed an intention (commitment, policy) that these properties are to be the standards for correct uses of her term. It is probably fair enough for the classical realist to resist an unmotivated demand for a reductive account of what it is to have the semantic intention or purpose in question, but it is much harder, without falling back on dogmatism or superstition, to turn aside the question, *"How* does X succeed in picking out the set of properties with which her intention is supposedly concerned?" There must be some way she does this and something to say about that way. *This* is where the 'facts about X' are needed – they are to be facts about how X's intention comes to be about just *this* set of properties and not any of *these* others. The skeptic argues that his question has no answer, and Kripke's Wittgenstein agrees.

We have reached the point at which it is imperative to say something positive about the question of the normativity of meaning. I have maintained that Kripke's Wittgenstein rejects N_j), and, so far, this is the only brand of 'normativity' we have. How, then, do I propose to explain the definite indications in Kripke's text that he thinks that Wittgenstein accepts, even insists upon, the normative character of meaning.

To make a beginning, consider what Kripke says in the passage that most directly formulates the idea that meaning is normative. He explains,

> Suppose I do mean addition by "+". What is the relation of this supposition to the question how I will respond to the problem '68 + 57'? The dispositionalist gives a *descriptive* account of this relation: if '+' meant addition, then I will answer '125'. But this is not the proper account of the relation, which is *normative,* not descriptive. The point is not that, if I meant addition by '+', I *will* answer '125', but that, *if I intend to accord with my past meaning of '+', I should answer '125'.*   (p. 37, these last italics are my own)

Now, although there may be various questions to be raised about this passage and about the context in which they are set, one point seems fairly clear. The normativity of meaning is to be explained in terms of the correctness of a certain kind of 'normative' conditional concerning meaning: e.g., the kind of conditional of which the italicized sentence that concludes the quotation is an instance.

In some ways, Kripke's overview of the issue is presented more perspicuously in a segment of his summary account of the strategy of the skeptical solution.

> ... [W]e must give up the attempt to find any fact about me in virtue of which I mean 'plus' rather than 'quus', and must then go on in a certain way. Instead we must consider how we actually use: (i) the categorical assertion that an individual is following a given rule (that he means addition by 'plus'); (ii) the conditional assertion that "if an individual follows such-and-such a rule, he must do so-and-so on a given occasion (e.g., if he means addition by '+', his answer to '68 + 57' should be '125'"). (p. 108)

These remarks tell us explicitly that it is an essential task of the skeptical solution to provide, in the terms that it allows itself, an account of the acceptability of these normative conditionals about meaning. Thus, although the word "normativity" is never used in the later stages of Kripke's exposition, it is my belief that these and similar conditionals are to serve to define the concept that the word expresses.[19]

Let me, therefore, attempt to state more explicitly and more generally what it is for meaning to be normative. Kripke never offers such a general formulation, and, in the light of various qualifications he suggests, my formulation may be no more than a first approximation to a fully adequate explication of the concept. Nevertheless, I take it that the normativity of meaning rests upon the correctness of a generalized conditional of the form

N) For each of an unbounded range of (actual and possible) cases, if there is something that X means by $\ulcorner \phi \urcorner$ during t, then, were the question to arise, X *must* [or: *should*] apply $\ulcorner \phi \urcorner$, as she meant it at t, to the case in question.[20]

---

19. For example, in Kripke's summary statement of the skeptic's challenge (which I quoted earlier), he says, "So it ought to be agreed that *if I meant plus, then unless I wish to change my usage, I am justified in answering (indeed compelled to answer) '125', not '5'.*" The conditional I have italicized is another variant formulation of the sort of condition that is meant to define the normativity of meaning. Indeed, that is its role in this passage, although, of course, the term 'normativity' has not yet been introduced.

20. The too brief qualification, "as she meant it [[$\ulcorner \phi \urcorner$]] at t" is intended to do the following work. Suppose that a question about whether or not $\ulcorner \phi \urcorner$ applies to some object o arises at some time t^* that falls outside the period t mentioned in the relevant meaning ascription. Suppose also that X then incorrectly denies that $\ulcorner \phi \urcorner$ applies to o. At best, X's denial is grounds for denying that, *at t^*,* X means such-and-such (for whatever interpretation of X's use of $\ulcorner \phi \urcorner$ is in question). X's denial, by itself, does not provide grounds for deciding anything about what X did or did not mean *during t.* To connect the denial at t^* with the question of what X meant by $\ulcorner \phi \urcorner$ during t, we need the assumption that what X means by $\ulcorner \phi \urcorner$ at t^* is the same as what X meant [or: will mean] at t.

As I have already indicated, both the skeptic (or, more broadly, the classical realist) *and* the proponent of the skeptical solution are to be understood as assenting to N). Where they differ and differ radically is over the grounds there are for so assenting.

Why the classical realist accepts N) has been made all too familiar by our previous discussion. Since meaning something by $\lceil \phi \rceil$ is thought to involve there being properties that govern X's application of the term, X must or should ascribe $\lceil \phi \rceil$ to any item that has just those properties. That is, X must ascribe $\lceil \phi \rceil$ to an object from this class if, respecting the standards of correctness she herself has set, her ascription is to be, in fact, correct. Further, there will be an indefinitely large range of actual and possible cases that satisfy these standards.

The skeptical solution depicts this conception of how normativity arises as the product of a bizarre and ultimately incoherent mythologization of banal linguistic facts – of an interrelated complex of facts about familiar linguistic practice. The general character of the mistake with which the classical realist is charged can be illustrated with a simpler example whose moral is more transparent. Imagine that someone says this: "If Jones already knows *now* that Judy will divorce Jim in two weeks, then Judy *must* divorce Jim in two weeks."[21] It would be an outlandish misconception of what has been said if some Martian, learning English, were to interpret this 'normative' conditional to mean: knowledge that Judy will divorce Jim in two weeks is a psychological state, realized in Jones at the present moment, which, through its power to act upon the future, will somehow necessitate Judy's divorce from Jim in two weeks' time. In the face of such a misunderstanding, we would want to explain that the speaker was simply asserting that, in this case as in others, its being the case that P is semantically required (along with other conditions) to sustain the judgement that Y knows that P. The conditional assertion is being used to remind us that Judy's divorcing Jim in two weeks is required to sustain the judgement that Jones knows now that such a divorce will take place.

Kripke's Wittgenstein contends, in a similar vein, that the classical realist supposes that, if X *now* means something by $\lceil \phi \rceil$, then this entails that there is something available *now* to X's language faculty that determines, *modulo* facts about the various candidate items, whether $\lceil \phi \rceil$ applies correctly or not. But, according to the skeptical solution, this picture reverses the true order of

---

In fact, a formulation that explicitly conveys this condition would make N) clearer, but it also would make N) rather complicated and hard to read. As a compromise, I have settled for the briefer but possibly misleading phrase mentioned above. Since the condition that I have just explained will play no real role in the discussion below, I thought that the danger of misunderstanding could be accepted. On the other hand, I wanted N) to acknowledge the condition both because it is obviously needed and because Kripke several times mentions the condition briefly in formulations he gives.

21. For comparison, consider Wittgenstein's remarks in section 187. I am not at all clear, however, that the use I have given in my example indicates the idea that Wittgenstein had in mind in this passage.

'determination' and, in the process, grotesquely distorts the nature of the 'necessity' in play. The real basis of N) can be illustrated by suitable reflections on the following case.

We are wondering what Ralph means by the word "table" these days, and we notice that Ralph, his senses and intellect in normal working order, is situated so as to have a plain view of what we deem to be an exemplary table. But Ralph judges that this exemplary item is not a table. "That is not what I would call 'a table'," he insists. In virtue of his surprising claim, Ralph thereby supplies us with defeasible warrant for denying that he means table by "table," or, at least, for withholding judgement that this is what he means. Insofar as we regard ourselves as being thus warranted, we could naturally express the content of our warrant with the words, "If Ralph means table by 'table,' then he *must* apply 'table' to this object." The "must" in the statement simply registers a *requirement* that we are prepared to impose for judging that Ralph means table by "table." We require Ralph to agree with us that this paradigm is a table. Moreover, the requirement is a *primitive* requirement. It is established by our first and fundamental procedures in ascribing meaning, and it is not based upon a 'theory', e.g., about what speech behaviour happens to be correlated with meaning 'table' by some term. In other words, what the normative conditional requires of Ralph constitutes an *assertability condition* for judgements about whether his use of the word means 'table'. Compare these reflections on Ralph with what Kripke says about similar conditionals. "By such a conditional we do not mean, on the Wittgensteinian view, that any state of Jones guarantees his correct behavior. Rather by asserting such a conditional we commit ourselves, if in the future Jones behaves bizarrely enough (and on enough occasions), no longer to persist in our assertion that he is following the conventional rule of addition" (p. 95). It is these and similar remarks in Kripke's book that I am trying to stress and elucidate.[22]

It will be useful to sketch, however crudely, the general pattern that the skeptical solution is invoking. By doing so, we can comprehend more precisely how Kripke's Wittgenstein agrees to N). Hence, where $\ulcorner \phi \urcorner$ is an arbitrary term employed by X, let $\ulcorner \psi \urcorner$ be a term or phrase that might specify a possible interpretation of X's use of $\ulcorner \phi \urcorner$. I will say that an object o (as it is at a given time) is a *paradigmatic sample* for $\ulcorner \psi \urcorner$ within a designated linguistic

---

22. In his famous discussion of linguistic stereotypes, Hilary Putnam says, "The theoretical account of what it is to be a stereotype proceeds in terms of the notion of a *linguistic obligation*; a notion we believe to be fundamental to linguistics and which we shall not attempt to explicate here. What it means to say that being striped is part of the (linguistic) stereotype of 'tiger' is that it is *obligatory* to acquire the information that stereotypical tigers are striped if one acquires the word 'tiger'. . . ." "The Meaning of 'Meaning'" in *Minnesota Studies in the Philosophy of Science*, vol. VII, edited by Keith Gunderson (Minneapolis, 1975), p. 171. But see all of pp. 169–73. It is interesting to compare Putnam's notion of 'linguistic obligation' to the treatment of the modals in the normative conditionals proposed by the skeptical solution. I do not mean to suggest that Putnam expects his concept of 'linguistic obligation' to do the same overall theoretical work that Kripke's Wittgenstein expects from his treatment of the relevant modal terms.

community just in case 'competent' members of the community generally agree in being prepared to ascribe ⌜ψ⌝ to o when o has been presented to them under familiar, favorable 'test circumstances.' By "competent members of the community," I have in mind members who are competent in ascribing ⌜ψ⌝, and they are to be the members who, having been subjected to a standard regimen of training in the use of ⌜ψ⌝, regularly and systematically apply ⌜ψ⌝ in overall agreement with one another. Given the role of the paradigmatic samples in relation to ascriptions of meaning to individual speakers, it follows that both positive and negative warrant for these ascriptions *presuppose* the existence of general agreement in the pertinent judgements of community members. This is a point much emphasized by Kripke in his development of the skeptical solution.[23] In addition, it should be noted that various remarks in Kripke's presentation suggest several refinements and modifications that may be in order here. For example, some passing phrases hint at the idea that we might stipulate that competent ⌜ψ⌝-users should normally be disposed to ascribe ⌜ψ⌝ to paradigmatic samples, optimally presented, "confidently and without hesitation."[24] In any case, I trust that the intuitive concept is clear enough. The paradigmatic samples for ⌜ψ⌝ should more or less coincide with the objects that competent ⌜ψ⌝-users would, as a matter of course, be inclined to treat as samples in the ostensive teaching of ψ.[25]

We can now arrive at N) by generalizing the earlier reflections on Ralph's prospective use of the word "table." Suppose that we are entertaining the possibility that X means something by ⌜φ⌝ during t, and let ⌜X means ψ by ⌜φ⌝ during t⌝ represent any hypothesis that we have occasion to consider. Finally, let o be one of the paradigmatic samples for ⌜ψ⌝. As Ralph's case has illustrated, the skeptical solution maintains that we are entitled to affirm the normative conditional

n) If X means ψ by ⌜φ⌝ during t, then, were the question to arise, X must apply ⌜φ⌝ to o.[26]

---

23. For a discussion of agreement under that label see page 96. But much material on pages 88–100 is relevant.

24. For invocation of the concept of ascriptions made "confidently" and "unhesitatingly," see pages 86, 87, and 96.

25. Pears, in *The False Prison*, holds that he differs from Kripke, not only over the existence of a certain kind of *reductio* in the *Investigations*, but over Kripke's supposed failure to see the importance in Wittgenstein's thought, of "calibration on standard objects" (as he puts it). See, e.g., page 464 for the charge and chapter 14 for an account of what it amounts to. Re-reading Kripke in the light of the discussion of the role of what I am calling "paradigmatic samples," one might investigate the amount of difference between Pears and Kripke over even this topic. Notice that, since Kripke tends to develop his discussion quite extensively in terms of his "addition" example, the importance of "standard objects" or "paradigmatic samples" does not have great salience in his text.

26. Here and in the discussion that follows I drop the condition "as she meant [⌜φ⌝] at t" and the modest complications that would ensue in the discussion below if it were to be included. Nothing of significance, except simplicity, turns on this. See my n. 20.

As was also explained before, we are entitled to affirm instances of n), according to the skeptical solution, because n) is used to state a requirement that we impose upon the meaning ascriptions exhibited in the antecedents of these conditionals. The requirement is that X must ascribe $\lceil \phi \rceil$ to o if the judgement that X means ψ by $\lceil \phi \rceil$ is to sustain its warrant. Actually, two questions of warranted assertability are tied together here. A member of the community is warranted in asserting a given instance of n) just in case failure to ascribe $\lceil \phi \rceil$ to o in favorable test circumstances warrants denying that X means ψ by $\lceil \phi \rceil$. The skeptical solution tells us that this is a requirement that we impose in our actual practice of assigning meanings to speakers' words and that we recognize, at least implicitly, that this is the case. So, on this basis, we are entitled to accept n).

However, we assumed nothing special about the object o. We are equally entitled to accept a generalization of n) which is prefixed by "For each paradigmatic sample, o, for $\lceil \psi \rceil$." This generalization of n) merely formulates the wider principle upon which each of the n)-style specialized requirements is based. The proponent of the skeptical solution believes that the same examination of what we do in ascribing meanings that convinces us of the propriety of instances of n) convinces us of the principle as well. Our realization that each instance is warranted provides us with warrant for the generalization. Finally, since we are concerned with both actual and possible paradigmatic samples for $\lceil \psi \rceil$, it is safe to assume that the range of these samples is unbounded – that it is indefinitely large in number. This point and the fact that $\lceil \psi \rceil$, the putative interpretation for X's use of $\lceil \phi \rceil$, has been an arbitrary term or phrase throughout guarantee that our generalization of n) entails N). And this is where we wanted to be. From the perspective of the skeptical solution, there are clearcut reasons to endorse the 'thin' normativity of meaning that N) is meant to capture.

To conclude this outline of the view I take Kripke to impute to Wittgenstein, let me briefly return a final time to the vexed issue of 'projectivism' in this domain. It has been a central tenet of my account of the skeptical solution that it does not include a projectivist explication of meaning ascriptions. However, in the light of the considerations just expounded, we possibly should allow that the skeptical solution does offer a projectivist conception of the 'hardness' of the semantical "must." That is, it may be that the reading of the modal terms embedded in instances of schema n) is projectivist in character. I hesitate over this point because of uncertainties I feel about what the doctrine of projectivism does and does not involve. In any case, the following is true. The skeptical solution denies that these normative conditionals are made true by some range of semantical facts generated by a set of standards that members of the linguistic community, individually or collectively, have pre-established as the basis of correct and incorrect application. This is the upshot of BSC). By contrast, the skeptical solution asks us to see the acceptability of the relevant n)-instances as the manifest expression of linguistic commitments or requirements imposed by the community in its actual practices of ascribing meanings. Perhaps this deserves to be called a 'projectivist theory' of the normative conditionals, and it may be of substantial philosophical interest if this is so. But, however this may be, projectivism of this sort does not seem to entail that meaning ascriptions (or, for that matter, the normative conditionals themselves) do not purport to state facts about a speaker's use of a term. For the reasons sketched earlier, that is a conclusion that Kripke's Wittgenstein has no obligation nor incentive to embrace.

The route to this result has been slow and laborious. But it has seemed to me important to be cautious here. In the first part of the essay, I argued that commentators have been seriously confused about the issue of the normativity of meaning. Noticing that Kripke says that both the skeptic and his Wittgenstein concur that meaning is normative, they fail to see that Kripke's Wittgenstein repudiates the skeptic's conception of normativity. Even this way of putting the matter verges on the paradoxical unless we distinguish sharply between two questions, "What condition or conditions define the normativity of meaning?" My answer to this has been, "The conditions laid down in N) or some improved version thereof." Here the two protagonists agree. The second question is, "What are the facts about meaning or about ascriptions of meaning in virtue of which the N-type conditions are satisfied?" Over the answer to this question, the skeptic and the skeptical solution diverge fundamentally. It is at the juncture of their divergence, I believe, that the heart of the whole topic is exposed.

A number of his critics have objected to Kripke's framing of Wittgenstein's investigation of 'following a rule' in terms of a debate about semantic *skepticism*. Some have denied that Wittgenstein's chief objective was to overcome a global skepticism about meaning; more have felt uncomfortable with the notion that Wittgenstein's views can be characterized as being even partially skeptical. To a considerable extent, it seems to me, these complaints tend to reflect the commentator's own attitudes toward classical realism about meaning. If one finds the classical realist account, whatever its local difficulties, to be natural, powerful, and intuitively persuasive, then Wittgenstein is likely to appear more plausibly in the role of a skeptic. On the other hand, if classical realism seems little more than a seductive and widely influential theory of truth and meaning, then Wittgenstein will probably arrive on stage as the subtle, commonsense therapist of a philosophical illusion. I doubt that there will turn out to be much substance to quarrels of this sort about the felicity of Kripke's drama of skepticism. Beyond this, these worries and complaints tend to miss one of the key factors that motivates Kripke's talk of skeptical problems and skeptical solutions. What is missed is the essence of Kripke's analogy to Hume.

Late in his book, Kripke gives a concise, instructive summary of the intended analogy. He says, "Wittgenstein's skepticism about the determination of future usage by the past contents of my mind is analogous to Hume's skepticism about the determination of the future by the past. . . . The paradox can be resolved only by a 'skeptical solution of these doubts', in Hume's classic sense" (pp. 107–8). We are presently well situated to grasp the comparison that this and similar remarks propose. Hume thinks that he can refute the idea that causation is an ontologically primitive relation between pairs of concrete events, a relation that implies that a cause necessitates its effect. Correlatively, his skeptical solution attempts to explain what we legitimately mean when we assert, e.g., "Event C caused E'" and "If the cause occurs, its effect must ensue." Of course, these analyses or explications purport to eschew the theses already repudiated in the previous skeptical stage. Similarly, Kripke's Wittgenstein denies that meaning something by a term or sentence involves the grasping of a something that semantically 'necessitates' the way the term or sentence is to be correctly used. The new skeptical solution tries to explain the content of meaning ascriptions in terms of their role and utility in the relevant language games, and the normative conditionals about meaning, which the classical realist misconstrues as describing a super-rigid semantical determination, are explained in terms of the requirements that our use of standard criteria for meaning ascriptions engender and enforce. I have wanted to emphasize the exact character of the analogy, because it is a significant virtue of my reading of Kripke that it enables us to make accurate sense of this. Many other readings do not.

Whether Kripke's interpretation is true to the thought of the actual Wittgenstein is another topic, one that I have not pursued. Nevertheless, I will close by making just one broad comment on this subject. In §185 the famous case of the wayward adder is introduced, and in §186 we find the following exchange.

> To carry it out correctly! How is it decided what is the right step to take at any particular stage?—"The right step is the one that accords with the order—as it was *meant.*"—So when you gave the order +2 you mean that he was to write 1002 after 1000—and did you also mean that he should write 1868 after 1866, and 100036 after 100034, and so on—an infinite number of such propositions?—"No: what I meant was, that he should write the next but one number after *every* number that he wrote; and from this all those propositions follow in turn."—But that is just what is in question: what, at any stage, does follow from that sentence. Or, again, what, at any stage, we are to call "being in accord" with that sentence (and with the *mean*-ing you then put into the sentence—whatever that may have consisted in).[27]

---

27. Wittgenstein, *Investigations.*

It is notable that, in this passage, Wittgenstein, who so often seems elusive, flatly asserts, "This is just what is in question." And we are told what that question is, i.e., "What, at any stage, follows from the cited sentence?" In §189 and §190, what I take to be a variant formulation of the question is employed: "What, at any stage, does a formula or the meaning of a formula determine as the next step?" From §190 through §243 many of the remarks are, indeed, focused on various facets of this question. Or, rather, the question under philosophical investigation in this section is, "*What is it* for a formula or the meaning of a formula to determine the next step?" (However, we need to be careful not to build in too much about the form an answer to this question has to take.) Now, I have argued that this is what Kripke claims Wittgenstein's central question to be, and it is the question that his dialectic is meant to address. But, this point will not be apparent if we misunderstand the issues he frames in terms of 'the normativity of meaning' or if we miss the fundamental position that they occupy in his exposition.

Further, it is clear that Wittgenstein believes that we are deeply and recurrently tempted to give an unsatisfactory answer to the problem about 'determination by meaning' – to form a wildly misleading picture of what meaning determination involves. In a more positive vein, many of the remarks in the 'following a rule' section are intended to help us set matters straight. Again, if my exegesis of Kripke is right, it is the skeptic (*qua* classical realist) who gives expression to the misleading picture and to the unsatisfactory account it prompts. Correspondingly, the skeptical solution, by assembling a configuration of reminders about the nature and force of our practices in teaching and ascribing meanings, has the goal of shattering the bad picture by showing us the relevant plain facts that otherwise would be hidden. I realize, naturally, that these last observations of mine still leave it quite open whether the finer-grained execution of Kripke's interpretation mirrors the details of Wittgenstein's remarks accurately, but they do indicate that Kripke correctly portrays the basic structure of Wittgenstein's philosophical concerns. Even this modest assessment has been frequently denied. In any case, we will certainly be in no position to test Kripke's text against Wittgenstein's if we read the former through a pair of spectacles that invert the arguments he presents.[28]

28. Earlier versions of this essay were read to colloquia at the University of Michigan, the University of Maryland, the University of Western Ontario, and the University of Connecticut at Storrs. I am grateful in each instance for helpful discussion that substantially improved the evolving work. I also want to thank the following individuals for help and encouragement: Margaret Gilbert, Jerry Levinson, Ed Minar, Bill Taschek, and especially Mark Wilson.

CHAPTER THIRTEEN

MEANING, USE AND TRUTH

On whether a use-theory of meaning is precluded by the requirement
that whatever constitutes the meaning of a predicate be capable
of determining the set of things of which the predicates is true
and to which it ought to be applied.

Paul Horwich

For a large class of cases—though not for all—in which we employ the
word "meaning" it can be defined thus: the meaning of a word is its
use in the language.   Wittgenstein (1953, §43)

The purpose of this paper is to defend Wittgenstein's idea – his so-called "use-theory" of meaning – against what is perhaps the most influential of the many arguments that have been levelled against it. I'm thinking of Kripke's critique of "dispositionalism", which is a central component of his celebrated essay, *Wittgenstein on Rules and Private Language.*[1] Kripke argues that meaning a certain thing by a word is *not* a matter of being disposed to use it in a certain way. And his argument has been well-received. Most commentators, whatever they say about Kripke's *overall* line of thought (leading up to his "sceptical conclusion" about meaning), tend to agree at least that the use-theory has been elegantly demolished.[2] My main objective is to combat this impression.

Just what Wittgenstein himself had in mind is not entirely clear; but that's not my topic. Rather, what I want to do here is to explore and support a certain version of the use-conception of meaning – one which seems to me to

---

1. Cambridge, MA: Harvard University Press, 1982. Kripke takes himself to be sympathetically presenting Wittgenstein's view of meaning, not attacking it. Thus, despite §43 (on which he does not comment) he does not read Wittgenstein as identifying the meaning of a word with dispositions for its use. However, the criticism of Kripke in what follows does not concern his interpretation of Wittgenstein, but solely the effectiveness of his argument against that reductive thesis.

2. See, for example, Paul Boghossian, "The Rule-Following Considerations", *Mind*, 98 (1989), pp. 507–49 (this volume Ch. 9); Simon Blackburn, "The Individual Strikes Back", *Synthese*, 10 (1984), pp. 281–301 (this volume Ch. 3); Warren Goldfarb, "Kripke on Wittgenstein on Rules", *Journal of Philosophy*, 82, (1985) pp. 471–88 (this volume Ch. 6); Crispin Wright, "Kripke's Account of the Argument Against Private Language", *Journal of Philosophy*, 81, (1984), pp. 759–78.

have some attractive features (and which I believe can be pinned on Wittgenstein). This version involves the following interlocking elements:

(i) There are *meaning-properties*. So, for example, a certain sound has, in English, the property of meaning *dog* (or, to be more explicit, meaning *what "dog" means in English*); a different sound has that same property in French; other English words have other meaning-properties; and so on.

(ii) Each such property has an underlying nature. The property of "being water" is constituted by a more basic property, "being H_2O", whose possession by something (e.g. the contents of a certain glass) explains why it has the characteristics in virtue of which we identify it as water; similarly, the property of "meaning *dog*", for example, is constituted by an underlying property whose possession by a word explains why that word has the characteristics symptomatic of its meaning *dog*.[3]

(iii) The underlying natures of meaning-properties are non-intensional. After all, the systems that display those properties are, in the end, nothing but physical objects.

(iv) The non-intensional underlying natures of meaning-properties are basic regularities of use, explanatorily fundamental generalizations about the circumstances in which words occur. For it is on the basis of assumptions about what is meant by words that we explain when they are uttered; and conversely, it is on the basis of how words are used that we infer what is meant by them. Therefore, a *basic* use-regularity could explain the characteristics symptomatic of a meaning-property and could thereby satisfy the condition for constituting that property.

As I said, perhaps this isn't really Wittgenstein's view. I tend to think that it is. But my aim here is to defend the account of meaning itself and not its attribution to Wittgenstein.[4]

---

3. I am assuming that for a property U to constitute a property S it is necessary, not merely that U and S be co-extensive, but that there be a certain explanatory relationship between them: namely, that the holding of U by something explain why it has the properties that correlate with S and on the basis of which S's presence is identified. Some philosophers would be inclined to say that in such cases U and S are identical, that constitution is identity. I myself find that step dubious; but nothing here hinges on whether or not one takes it.

4. Part of the difficulty of interpreting Wittgenstein's remark is to find a reading of it that accommodates two somewhat conflicting constraints: first, that his identification of meaning with use be genuinely illuminating; and second, that it not be a controversial theory – that it conform with his therapeutic, anti-theoretical metaphilosophical outlook. One strategy of interpretation would be to note that in ordinary language the words "meaning" and "use" are often interchangeable: "How is that word used?", "The word 'bank' has two uses". But if this were what Wittgenstein had in mind, then although his thesis would indeed be uncontroversial, it would not be interesting. For ordinary characterizations of "use" can perfectly well involve *intensional* notions – notions closely affiliated with the notion of meaning (e.g. "It is used to refer to dogs", "It is used to express the belief that snow is white", etc.). So we would not have

The following discussion will be divided into three parts. To begin with I want to review briefly the distinction between two conceptions of truth: the traditional view (which I'll call *inflationary*) according to which truth is a substantive property whose underlying nature it is the job of philosophy to articulate, and a more recent *deflationary* view according to which an adequate account of truth is given (roughly speaking) by the schema

"*p*" is true iff *p*.

In the first part of my discussion I will quickly describe these competing conceptions and indicate why I think the deflationary view is correct.

In the second part I will rehearse Kripke's well known argument against the reduction of meaning-facts to facts about dispositions of use. The main thrust of this argument is that such a reduction could not accommodate the representational and normative character of meaning: the fact that we *are* disposed to apply a predicate in certain cases could not determine the set of things to which it *truly* applies and to which we *ought* to apply it.

In the third part I will show that Kripke's argument can be saved from a fallacy of equivocation (with the term "determines") only by presupposing an inflationary conception of truth. So if, as I believe, the inflationary conception of truth is incorrect, Kripke's argument against the use-theory is unsound.

1. TWO VIEWS OF TRUTH

It is commonly supposed that the word "true" stands for a property that is profound and mysterious. (Here I want to emphasize "property", "profound" and "mysterious".) That truth is a *property* almost goes without saying. We do, after all, distinguish two classes of statement: those that are true and those that aren't – so truth is what members of the first class have in common. That truth is *profound* is indicated by the striking depth, generality and variety of the principles in which it figures: truth is the aim of science, true beliefs

---

achieved what Wittgenstein appears to want to achieve: namely, a demystification of meaning and related concepts. On the other hand, if one construes "use" non-intensionally – if one insists that the use of a term be characterized in purely non-intensional (e.g. behavioural and physical) terms – then although the thesis promises to demystify meaning, it seems far from obviously correct; and to propound it would appear to violate Wittgenstein's metaphilosophy. Perhaps the solution to this dilemma is to suppose that Wittgenstein takes it to be obvious that conclusive criteria for what someone means lie in their behaviour, and draws the conclusion that the meaning of a word consists in non-intensional aspects of its use. He would perhaps regard the controversial character of this idea not as symptomatic of philosophical theorizing, but rather as the consequence of confusions that lead us away from what is in fact implicit in our discourse, and toward various mistaken conceptions of meaning. What follows, however, is intended merely as a defence of the use theory of meaning, and not as an exegesis of Wittgenstein.

facilitate successful action, meanings are truth conditions, good arguments preserve truth, and so on. And, finally, that truth is *mysterious* is shown by the inability of philosophers, after hundreds of years of attempts, to say what it is. We have tried "correspondence with reality", "mutual coherence", "pragmatic utility", "verifiability in suitable conditions", and various other analyses; but every such proposal has encountered devastating objections. Either there are straightforward counterexamples, or the analysis contains notions just as problematic as truth itself. Thus truth threatens to remain a great enigma. We need to know what it is, in order to assess and explain the many important principles in which it appears; but we just can't seem to make much progress.

A way out of this impasse is offered by the deflationary conception, according to which truth is not susceptible to conceptual analysis and has no underlying nature. No one doubts that the English sentence, "snow is white", is true if and only if snow is white.[5] And, for a large range of cases, this equivalence can be generalized. Thus, instances of the so-called "disquotational schema",

$$\text{``}p\text{'' is true iff } p,$$

are typically uncontroversial (though exceptions must be made because of the liar-paradoxes). Traditional appproaches acknowledge this but don't think of the schema as providing the sort of definition or theory that is needed and, as we have seen, attempt to achieve this end with some further principle of the form

$$\text{``}p\text{'' is true iff ``}p\text{'' has property } F$$

(such as correspondence to reality, provability, etc.), which is supposed to specify *what truth is*. But the deflationary view is that the search for an analysis is misguided, that our concept is exhausted by the uncontroversial schema, and that there is no reason at all to expect that truth has any sort of underlying nature.[6]

This view is best presented together with a plausible account of the *raison d'être* of our notion of truth: namely that it enables us to compose

---

5. More accurately, one ought to speak of a sentence as *expressing a truth* rather than as *being true*; and it is in this first sense that I intend my use of the truth-predicate to be understood.

6. For a more detailed and exact characterization and defense of the deflationary position, as I see it, see my *Truth* (Oxford: Basil Blackwell, 1990). For other versions of the view, see W. V. Quine, *Pursuit of Truth* (Cambridge, MA: Harvard University Press, 1990), Ch. 5; Stephen Leeds, "Theories of Reference and Truth", *Erkenntnis*, 13 (1978), pp. 111–29; Hartry Field, "The Deflationary Conception of Truth" in Macdonald, Graham & Wright (eds), *Fact Science and Morality* (Oxford: Basil Blackwell, 1986); and Michael Williams, "Do We (Epistemologists) Need a Theory of Truth?", *Philosophical Topics*, 14 (1986), pp. 223–42.

generalizations of a special sort which resist formulation by means of the usual devices – the words "all" and "every" and, in logical notation, the universal quantifier. Suppose, for example, we wish to state a certain form of the law of non-contradiction:

Nothing is both green and not green, or both tall and not tall, or both good and not good, and so on.

We need a single statement that will capture this "infinite conjunction". We can obtain it as follows. The truth schema tells us that

Nothing is both green and not green

is equivalent to

"Nothing is both green and not green" is true.

Similarly for the other conjuncts. Therefore our initial infinite list may be converted into another such list in which the same property, *truth,* is attributed to every member of an infinite class of structurally similar objects (namely sentences). Consequently this second list can be captured as an ordinary generalization over objects:

Every sentence of the form "Nothing is both F and not F" is true.

It is in just this role that the concept of truth figures so pervasively in logic and philosophy. Or so one might argue by showing that principles such as "truth is the aim of science", "true beliefs facilitate successful action", and "good arguments preserve truth" involve the notion of truth, as in the above example, merely as a device of generalization. Insofar as this can be shown, and since truth's ability to play that role requires nothing more or less than the disquotational schema, there can be no reason to suppose that truth has an underlying nature. Just because most of the properties we encounter have one, we should not assume that all do. Such an assumption about truth – the inflationary view – would seem to be a paradigmatic Wittgensteinian example of a philosophical misconception and pseudo-problem generated by an overdrawn linguistic analogy.

The distinction between inflationary and deflationary conceptions of truth is exactly paralleled by competing conceptions of *being true of* and *reference.* Thus, virtually no matter what is substituted for *"F"* or *"N",* it is uncontroversial that

"F" is true of something iff it is F

and

> "N" refers to something iff it is identical to N

According to the deflationary point of view there is nothing more to our concepts of *being true of* and *reference* than is conveyed by our acceptance of these schemata. This is in sharp contrast to the traditional and still prevailing inflationary view according to which, given these schemata, it still remains to be said what the relations of *being true of* and *reference* really are. Some inflationary philosophers attempt to analyse these notions in terms of causal or counterfactual relations (e.g. Evans, Devitt, Stampe, Fodor); others try to do it in terms of idealized applicability (e.g. Dummett, Putnam, Wright); others attempt "teleological" reductions (e.g. Dretske, Papineau, Millikan). But no such approach has ever seemed satisfactory. From a deflationary point of view this is only to be expected since there are no underlying natures to be analysed here.

The deflationary conceptions of *truth, being true of* and *reference* go hand in hand with one another. These notions are interdefinable, so any substantive analysis of one would imply substantive analyses of the others. And any argument for deflationism with respect to one of the notions (based, say, on the utility of semantic ascent) will be convertible into an argument for deflationism about the other notions too.

2. KRIPKE'S ARGUMENT AGAINST THE USE-THEORY

The core of Kripke's sceptical treatment of meaning (1982) is his argument against what he calls the dispositional theory: the view that the meaning of a word consists in dispositions regarding its use. As I reconstruct it, Kripke's reasoning is as follows:

(1) Whatever constitutes the meaning of a predicate must determine its extension (the set of things, sometimes infinite, of which the predicate is true and to which one should apply it).
(2) The use of a predicate does not determine its extension.

Therefore:

(3) The meaning of a predicate is not constituted by its use.

There's no initial reason to question this argument's validity. The first premise seems clearly correct, as long as we restrict our attention to terms whose extensions are context-insensitive. For, in that domain, any two synonymous predicates are co-extensional. Moreover, if predicates v and w have the same meaning-constituting property, they must have the same meaning. Consequently, if v and w have the same meaning-constituting property, then they have the same extension. In other words, just as premise (1) says, the extension of a predicate is a function of the property that constitutes its meaning.

But on what grounds does Kripke maintain the second premise: that the *use* of a predicate does *not* determine its extension? The reasoning goes roughly as follows. How *could* the use of a predicate possibly determine its extension? For if we consider the things to which we are actually disposed to apply a given word w, that set of objects is bound to diverge from the true extension of w. Our capacities are limited; mistakes occur; so w will inevitably be applied to certain things outside its extension and will fail to be applied to certain things inside its extension. In order to be able to accommodate these discrepancies it would be necessary to identify certain extremely favourable epistemological circumstances, M, such that in those ideal conditions the application of w would coincide with its extension. We would then be in a position to say that, in a sense, the use of w determines its extension; for we could identify *the use of w* with *how we are disposed to apply w in circumstances M;* and that would give us the right set. But the insurmountable difficulty with this strategy, says Kripke, is that we cannot specify the circumstances M in a satisfactory way. In order to be sure of arriving at the correct set the only characterizations of M we could offer would be along the lines of "circumstances in which mistakes are not made"; but that amounts to "circumstances in which, if we mean F we apply w to Fs", which is blatantly circular.

Paul Boghossian, who provides a clear and sympathetic exposition of Kripke's argument, puts the central point as follows:

> If a dispositional theory is to have any prospect of succeeding, it must select from among the dispositions I have for "horse", those dispositions which are *meaning-determining*. In other words, it must characterize, in non-intensional and non-semantic terms, a property M such that: possession of M is necessary and sufficient for being a disposition to apply an expression in accord with its correctness condition.
> (Boghossian, 1989, p. 532)

He proceeds to argue on holistic grounds (and quite persuasively) that, no such property M is specifiable.

3. HOW THE USE OF A PREDICATE DETERMINES ITS EXTENSION

A vital feature of Kripke's argument – an aspect on which, I believe, insufficient critical scrutiny has been brought to bear in the responses to his book – consists in the conceptions of *determination* that are deployed. According to Kripke, in order that our use of a predicate "determine" its extension, it must be possible to, as he puts it, "read off" the extension from the use. Thus he says:

> [The dispositional analysis] gives me a criterion that will tell me what number theoretic function j I mean by a binary function symbol "f" ... The criterion is meant to enable us to "read off" which function I mean by a given function symbol from my disposition.
>
> (Kripke, 1982, p. 26)

> According to [the dispositionalist], the function someone means is to be *read off* from his dispositions . . ..   (p. 29)

And this way of picturing the situation is repeated in Boghossian's exposition:

> ... it ought to be possible to read off from any alleged meaning-constituting property of a word, what is the correct use of that word. And this is a requirement, Kripke maintains, that a dispositional theory cannot pass: one cannot read off a speaker's disposition to use an expression in a certain way what is the *correct* use of that expression . . ..   (Boghossian, 1989, p. 509)

But what exactly is this "reading off" requirement? Let us look back to the way in which we saw it being applied in the justification of premise (2) – the premise that use does not determine extension. First the use-property of w was imagined to be something from which it follows that

> w would be applied (in conditions M) to something iff that thing is a member of S.

Second this relation between w and S was supposed to be what constitutes the semantic relation

> S is the extension of w.

Then, given these assumptions, it was appreciated that we would be able to *read off* the extension of any predicate from its use.

Generalizing from this example, it would seem that in order to be able to read off the extension of any word w from its meaning-constituting property $U(w)$, there would have to be a fixed, uniform relation R satisfying the following two conditions: first, that we can deduce from $U(w)$ that w bears R to some set S; and second, that each predicate stands in R to a single set, namely, to the extension of the predicate. That is to say, in order to read off the extension of w from its meaning-constituting property, you simply

(a) scrutinize the meaning-constituting property of w,

(b) infer that w bears R to set S,

(c) deploy the assumption that, for any w and S, w bears R to S, if and only if w has extension S,[7]

(d) conclude that S is the extension of w.

It is only in this "reading off" sense of the word "determination" (call it "DETERMINATION") that Kripke makes it plausible (and Boghossian even more plausible) that the use of a predicate does not DETERMINE its extension. But in that case, his argument against the constitution of meaning by use threatens to be invalidated by equivocation. For the claim of the first premise – that what constitutes meaning *does* determine extension – is uncontroversial only if we construe it (as we did above) as saying merely that any two predicates with the same meaning-constituting property are co-extensional. Thus the premises we can establish are

(1) What constitutes meaning determines extension

and

(2) Use does not DETERMINE extension

from which, evidently, the distinctness of use from what constitutes meaning cannot be inferred.

In order to respond effectively to the present objection it would be necessary to remove the equivocation. There are two obvious strategies for attempting to do this: either argue that whatever constitutes the meaning of a predicate must DETERMINE its extension, even in the strong, "reading off" sense; or argue that the use of a predicate does not determine its extension, even in the weak, functional sense. But neither of these strategies looks promising.

The first one appears to be what Kripke mainly has in mind (although he also seems to sympathize with the second). However the first strategy is affiliated with an inflationary conception of truth. For the assumption that what constitutes the meaning of each predicate DETERMINES its extension

---

7. One might object that in order to *read off* the extension of a predicate w from the fact that w bears relation R to set S one needs merely the assumption that "w bears R to S" is *sufficient* for "w has extension S", and not that it is necessary; for it might be that various different relations $R2$, $R3$, . . ., are what determine extensions within different semantic categories of predicate. However, to the extent that we allow this flexibility and suppose the number of such extension-determining relations to be large (the limit being the supposition that each predicate bears a different relation to its extension) it becomes (a) increasingly unclear that the extension of each predicate could not be read off its meaning-constituting property (i.e. increasingly unclear that Kripke's second premise is correct); and (b) increasingly unnatural to speak of the various extensions as being "read off".

implies that there be a way of reading off a predicate's extension from whatever property constitutes its meaning. This implies, as we have just seen, that there be non-semantic necessary and sufficient conditions for *being true of* – some account of the form

w is true of the members of S iff $R(w, S)$

where $R(w, S)$ is deducible from whatever non-semantic property constitutes the meaning of w. For it is only via such an account that we can infer the predicate's extension from the property underlying its meaning. But the existence of any such theory is plausible only if *being true of* has some non-semantic underlying nature. And that is precisely what deflationism denies.

Thus the first way of trying to remove the equivocation from Kripke's argument is motivated by an inflationary point of view. To repeat: having shown us that the *use* of a predicate does *not* DETERMINE (in the "reading off" sense) its extension, then, in order to conclude that use does not constitute meaning, he must suppose that what constitutes the *meaning* of a predicate *does* DETERMINE its extension. He must suppose, in other words, that each meaning-constituting property relates the predicate possessing it, in a uniform way, to the extension of the predicate. But that assumption can seem plausible only if it is taken for granted that *being true of* is a substantive relation – that it has some unified naturalistic analysis and is not wholly captured by the schema

"F" is true of exactly the Fs.

So if deflationism is correct, Kripke's argument is unsound.

The only remaining hope of salvaging something from the argument would be to adopt the second strategy mentioned above. Here we drop the "reading off" requirement, we forget strong DETERMINATION, and we reject the inflationary conception of *being true of* with which these notions are associated. Instead we operate throughout with the weak form of determination according to which the thesis that meaning determines extension is simply the thesis that synonymous predicates must be coextensional. The second strategy is to suggest that these uncontroversial ideas about meaning are in tension with the use-theory – to show that two predicates may have the same use but different extensions.

Kripke appears to think that this can be done by means of the following thought experiment. Imagine that there is a foreign community whose use of the predicate "quus" has been, always will be, and would, in all hypothetical circumstances, be just the same as our use of "plus", but whose predicate is true of a slightly different set of triples of numbers – the difference concerning only numbers that are so ungraspably huge that neither we nor they have the capacity to talk about them. If this really is possible, then usage doesn't determine extension (even in the weak, non-"reading off" sense) and so cannot constitute meaning.

The trouble with this argument is that it assumes the very thing that it is supposed to establish: namely, that a word whose use is *exactly* the same as the use of our word "plus" might nonetheless have a different extension. To insist, without justification, on there being such a possibility is simply to beg the question against the use-theory of meaning. What does seem intuitively right is that there are possible *complex* expressions – definable in terms of "plus" – whose extensions diverge from that of "plus" in the slight way imagined. But no complex expression – since it will inevitably bear certain use-relations to its constituents – can have exactly the same use as a primitive expression. Therefore, in order to construct his counterexample to the use-theory, Kripke must assume that the term "quus" satisfies the following three conditions: (1) that it be a *primitive* term (on a par with "plus"); (2) that it be co-extensive with one of those possible, complex expressions whose extension diverges very slightly and remotely from that of "plus"; and (3) that its use (including the absence of dispositions regarding the divergent cases) be identical to our use of "plus". But it is plausible to suppose that "quus" would acquire such an extension only if, either it were defined in terms of some word meaning the same as "plus", or it were applied in some *definite* way to certain triples that, given our limitations, are beyond our definite range of application of "plus"; and in neither of these cases would it be correct to say that the use of "quus" is *exactly* like our use of "plus". Thus what Kripke needs to assume in order to construct a counterexample is intuitively implausible and simply begs the question against the use-theory of meaning.[8]

But why, one may be tempted to insist, should our dispositions for the use of "plus" be associated with *plus* rather than one of the other functions with which these dispositions are consistent? It appears to be impossible to explain, on the basis of our practice with a word, why it should mean what it does, and why it should happen to apply to one set of entities rather than another.[9]

---

8. It might be thought that my claim that Kripke is begging the question is itself begging the question: i.e. that it reflects an unjustified assumption on my part about who has the burden of proof. But such a complaint would neglect the facts (a) that there are independent reasons (sketched at the beginning of this paper) for taking the use-theory very seriously; and (b) that Kripke does not so much as hint at what factors, other than use, might underpin the difference between meaning *plus* and *quus* – let alone justify any such assumption.

9. Here we must of course separate the epistemological issue – given the use of a predicate, what puts us in a position to say that its extension is such-and-such rather than so-and-so? – and the explanatory issue – why, given the use of a predicate, is its extension such-and-such rather than so-and-so? The question that is raised and addressed in the text concerns explanation, but let me say a quick word here about the epistemological situation.

In the case of a predicate of our own language (e.g. "horse"), we master its use (without necessarily being able to characterize that use explicitly) and we arrive at our knowledge of its extension by means of the stipulation

"horse" is true of exactly the horses

Well, yes and no. For suppose that the property

w means *plus*

is constituted by the property

w's use is so-and-so.

In that case we surely do explain why a certain word means *plus* if we point out that its use is so-and-so. This is not to say, however, that we can explain *why* this particular use-property constitutes that particular meaning-property. And in fact I think that nothing of the sort can reasonably be expected. For such an explanation could be given only if there were some general principle by which a term's meaning could be extracted from a characterization of its use. Thus the prospect of such an explanation goes hand in hand with the reading off requirement, with strong DETERMINATION of extensions by meanings, and with the inflationary conception of truth.

Notice moreover that the existence of an inexplicable constitutive relation between properties is perfectly normal. One can't explain why it is that water is made of H_2O, or why it is that the underlying nature of redness is to reflect certain wavelengths of light. The best we can do, in such cases, is to *justify* the thesis of constitution by showing how the underlying property gives rise to the characteristic symptoms of the more superficial one. In the same way, although we cannot – and should not be expected to – explain how it comes about that w's meaning *plus* is constituted by w's use being so-and-so, we might well be able to explain, by reference to a use-property it possesses, why w has the features on the basis of which it is recognized as meaning *plus,* and we could thereby justify the reduction of its meaning to that use-property.[10]

So I am left believing that the use of a predicate *does* determine (weakly)

---

which partially defines "is true of". We do not infer the extension of "horse" from its use. The situation is rather that we apply the extension-determining stipulation only to those predicates that we use. Thus it is by definition that we know that "horse" is true of horses, and not of "quorses".

In the case of foreign words the situation is slightly different. Their extensions are determined by principles such as

w means the same as "horse" $\rightarrow$ (w is true of exactly the horses).

Therefore the knowledge that a foreign word has the same use and therefore the same meaning as "horse" will be the basis for inferring its extension.

10. Christopher Peacocke in *A Study of Concepts* (Cambridge, MA: MIT Press, 1992) has developed an ingenious and sophisticated form of the use theory of meaning, whose general character is very much in tune with the view of meaning defended here. I must part company with him, however, when he maintains that the accounts of how concepts are constituted by their inferential roles must be supplemented by what he calls a "determination theory" – a theory that would enable us to derive (i.e. read off) the referent of each term from the facts underlying its meaning. For it is precisely the main point of this paper to argue that there is no such theory, nor any need for one.

(continued overleaf)

its extension, and does, therefore, determine (weakly) the infinitely many contexts to which it ought to be attributed.[11] There appears to be no sense of "determination" in which both of Kripke's premises are correct; and so his argument against the use-theory of meaning does not succeed.[12]

Needless to say, this does not prove that the theory is correct. There are many other serious and well-known objections to it: Exactly how are we to identify *which* of the regularities in a word's use constitutes its meaning? Can behaviourism and implausible forms of holism be avoided? Can compositionality be explained? What about meaningful sentences that are not used? What about words (like "and" and "but") with the same semantic content yet different uses? I am hopeful that these further challenges to the use-theory of

---

Consider a concept F whose identity is specified by a certain inferential role. The "determination theory" in this case, Peacocke suggests, might be that *the referent of F is whatever would make the defining rules of inference come out valid.* But what I have been arguing here is, first, that such a theory is unnecessary since, once the concept F has been identified, its referent is specified disquotationally and trivially as the set of Fs; and second that the view that we need such a theory is motivated by an incorrect (inflationary) conception of truth and inference. A further objection, applicable to this particular determination theory, is that we simply have no reason to assume that concept-constituting rules of inference *must* be valid; what constitutes the concept is our *following* the rules, not their correctness.

11. Granting that the use of a predicate does determine its extension – i.e. does determine to what we may truly apply it – I can imagine someone complaining that I had missed the real point of Kripke's argument. For isn't his real point that meaning has *normative* consequences – implying what one *ought* to say? Whereas a pattern of use, even if it does determine what it would be *true* to say, does not have intrinsic normative consequences.

The simple answer to this objection is that we must indeed deploy a further principle, something along the lines of

> one ought to speak the truth,

if we are going to be able to derive, from the *use* of the word "plus" (say), that one *ought* to assert a certain infinity of sums. But the same goes for the *meaning* of "plus". What one ought to say follows from the *meaning* of "plus" no more than it follows from the *use* of "plus" – unless the norm of truth-speaking is assumed.

12. Kripke presents his skeptical considerations as raising the same problems for both *meaning* and *rule-following*, barely distinguishing between these two cases. Presumably he takes meaning to be a special case of rule-following, and infers that insofar as there are difficulties in identifying the facts in virtue of which a certain rule is being followed, the same difficulties must arise in identifying the facts in virtue of which a certain thing is meant by a word. More specifically, it would seem that what Kripke has in mind is that (in the case of predicates) to mean *F-ness* by a word *w* is to follow the rule:

> Apply *w* to a thing iff it is *F*.

Thus, saying something false will be a matter of failing to properly follow such a rule.

Couched in these more general terms, my central point is that a dispositionalist analysis of what it is to follow rule D need not (and often will not) itself make reference to the generalization D. It need not have the form:

> For any person A and generalization D, A follows D iff #(A, D)

which would enable one to *read off*, from the facts constituting it, that the rule D is being followed. And it would nonetheless be perfectly possible that the constituting facts *determine* (in the weak, functional sense) which rules are being followed.

meaning can be met; but if and how this may be done must remain to be seen. What has been shown, I believe, is that the reduction of meaning to use is not put under any pressure whatsoever by the fact that words, in virtue of their meanings, are applied correctly to some things and incorrectly to others. For the problem in identifying which property underlies a given meaning is to find one that explains the behaviour – no matter whether correct or incorrect – on the basis of which that meaning is attributed. There is no need for this property to be one from which the correct applications can be "read off".[13]

---

13. For their valuable comments on earlier versions of this paper I would like to thank Ned Block, Paul Boghossian, Brian Loar, Scott Soames, Scott Sturgeon and Timothy Williamson.
   For further development of the line of argument presented here, see Chapters 4 and 10 of my *Meaning* (Oxford: Oxford University Press, 1998) and my "Why Words Mean What They Do" (forthcoming).

CHAPTER FOURTEEN

KRIPKE'S NORMATIVITY ARGUMENT[1]

José L. Zalabardo

I INTRODUCTION

In *Wittgenstein on Rules and Private Language*,[2] Kripke presented an argument to the effect that there can be no facts as to what someone means by a linguistic expression. In this argument, a central role is played by the contention that meaning is a normative notion. Some of the most popular accounts of what meaning facts consist in are rejected on the grounds that they fail to accommodate the normative character of meaning. This aspect of Kripke's dialectic plays a crucial role in his rejection of dispositional accounts of meaning, and it is rightly perceived as undermining, if successful, currently fashionable information theoretic accounts of semantic notions. Assessments of its success vary widely. Whereas for some writers the normative character of meaning constitutes an insurmountable obstacle for dispositional accounts, advocates of the information theoretic program have generally failed to acknowledge that their proposals are invalidated by this aspect of the notion. This debate rests largely on a tacit consensus on how Kripke's normativity argument should be interpreted. My main goal in this paper is to question this consensus. I shall argue that a certain widespread interpretation of the argument is incorrect, as it misrepresents the nature of the constraint that Kripke takes the normativity of meaning to impose on a successful account of meaning facts.

1. This paper was presented at a symposium on the philosophy of Saul Kripke organised by the Instituto de Investigaciones Filosóficas, UNAM, in Mexico City. Thanks are due to that audience, especially to Saul Kripke and Scott Soames. I have also benefited from comments by Harold Noonan, Greg McCulloch and an anonymous referee.
2. Cambridge, MA: Harvard University Press, 1982. Hereafter *WRPL*.

It will simplify matters to focus on a specific kind of meaning facts, namely the facts that are supposed to determine which objects satisfy a predicate, as meant by a speaker at a time. I shall further restrict my attention to the bearing of the normativity of meaning on a specific approach to predicate satisfaction, to which I shall refer as *the realist approach*. According to the realist approach, the satisfaction conditions of a predicate are determined by a property to which the predicate bears a certain relation. Whether a predicate is satisfied by an object is determined, on the realist approach, by whether the object exemplifies the property to which the predicate bears this relation. Information theoretic accounts of satisfaction facts, as they are standardly construed, are instances of the realist approach, in which predicates are connected to the properties that determine their satisfaction conditions by a causal-nomological relation.

I shall start by outlining, in Section II, the line of reasoning that is generally taken to underlie Kripke's contention that dispositional accounts cannot accommodate the normative character of meaning facts. Then, in Section III, I shall argue that a crucial ingredient of this line of reasoning is missing from Kripke's discussion. In Section IV, I shall contend that Kripke's normativity argument should be construed along different lines. I shall end by suggesting, in Section V, that the target of Kripke's argument, as I propose to construe it, is not restricted to information theoretic accounts of satisfaction, or any other specific account of the nature of the relation that is supposed to pair each predicate with the property that determines its satisfaction conditions. Kripke's argument, I shall contend, can be seen as putting pressure on the realist approach – on the very idea that satisfaction is to be explained by reference to properties to which predicates bear a certain relation.

II THE STANDARD NORMATIVITY ARGUMENT

Let me start then by presenting the line of reasoning that is generally taken to be behind Kripke's contention that dispositional accounts cannot accommodate the normative character of meaning. I shall refer to this line of reasoning as the *Standard Normativity Argument*. The Standard Normativity Argument arises from a certain interpretation of the claim that meaning is normative. On this interpretation, the claim amounts to the thought that the meaning of a linguistic expression licenses the application to its uses of a family of notions that we may naturally characterize as 'evaluative.' Jerry Fodor offers an extensive catalogue of the members of this family. He spells out the claim that meaning is normative as the thought that 'some ways of using symbols are *wrong*,' that 'there are *mis*representations; and that they are things to be avoided,' that we 'should prefer' some ways of using symbols to others, that 'misrepresentations are . . . to be deplored,' or that 'misrepresentation is a bad thing.'[3] On this reading, then, what the normative character of meaning amounts to is the propriety of applying concepts such as these to our uses of meaningful expressions. In the case of predicate satisfaction, the normative character of satisfaction facts would amount to the thought that we can speak of applications of predicates to objects as right or wrong, good or bad, praiseworthy or deplorable, etc., according to whether the object of predication satisfies the predicate in question. As Paul Boghossian puts it,

> Suppose the expression "green" means *green*. It follows immediately that the expression "green" applies *correctly* to *these* things (the green ones) and not to *those* (the non-greens). The fact that the expression means something implies, that is, a whole set of *normative* truths about my behavior with that expression: namely, that my use of it is correct in application to certain objects and not in application to others. . . . The normativity of meaning turns out to be, in other words, simply a new name for the familiar fact that . . . meaningful expressions possess conditions of *correct use*.[4]

This interpretation of the normative character of meaning provides the first premise of the Standard Normativity Argument:

(A) The fact that determines the satisfaction conditions of a predicate licenses evaluative claims about ascriptions of the predicate.

The Standard Normativity Argument is supposed to invalidate dispositional accounts of predicate satisfaction on the grounds that they cannot accommodate this feature of satisfaction facts. Satisfaction facts, the thought goes, cannot be dispositional, because dispositional facts cannot license the relevant evaluative claims. From the fact that a speaker is disposed to apply a predicate to an object, it doesn't follow that he *should* do so, that doing so is a *good* thing, or that he *ought to be praised* for doing so.[5]

The Standard Normativity Argument supports this conclusion with two further premises:

(B) Dispositional facts are descriptive.
(C) Descriptive facts cannot license evaluative claims.

From (A), (B) and (C), the Standard Normativity Argument concludes that dispositional accounts of predicate satisfaction are unacceptable:

---

3. All these quotations are taken from Jerry Fodor, 'A Theory of Content, II: The Theory,' in *A Theory of Content and Other Essays* (Cambridge, MA: MIT Press, 1990), pp. 128–9.
4. Paul Boghossian, 'The Rule-Following Considerations' *Mind* 98 (1989), p. 513 (this volume Ch. 9).
5. See *Ibid.*

[handwritten annotation: Goals & I thinking about how Boston Celtics games support terrorism — /RA]

therefore (D) Dispositional facts cannot determine the satisfaction conditions of predicates.

Is the Standard Normativity Argument sound? Its validity is hardly controversial. (D) is a straightforward consequence of (A)–(C). If there is a problem with the argument, it has to concern the acceptability of its premises. Premises (A) and (B) seem unassailable. The satisfaction conditions of a predicate determine the class of objects to which it is correct to apply it. And any reasonable account of which facts are descriptive can be expected to include dispositional facts in this category.

Premise (C) may be more problematic. It is a straightforward statement of the familiar Humean injunction against the derivation of ought-claims from is-claims. Indeed, the basic thought behind the Standard Normativity Argument is perfectly expressed by the famous passage in the *Treatise*:

> In every system of morality, which I have hitherto met with, I have always remark'd, that the author proceeds for some time in the ordinary way of reasoning, and establishes the being of a God, or makes observations concerning human affairs; when of a sudden I am surpriz'd to find, that instead of the usual copulations of propositions, *is*, and *is not*, I meet with no proposition that is not connected with an *ought*, or an *ought not*. This change is imperceptible; but is, however, of the last consequence. For as this *ought*, or *ought not*, expresses some new relation or affirmation, 'tis necessary that it shou'd be observ'd and explain'd; and at the same time that a reason should be given, for what seems altogether inconceivable, how this new relation can be a deduction from others, which are entirely different from it.[6]

As a demand for a justification for the passage from descriptive to evaluative claims, Hume's point is perfectly appropriate, and no less valid about 'systems of semantics' than about systems of morality. But premise (C) of the Standard Normativity Argument makes a stronger claim. It asserts that, at least in the case of semantics, the justification that would be required for drawing evaluative conclusions from descriptive premises cannot be supplied. This places the burden of proof squarely on the proponent of the Standard Normativity Argument. Premise (C) would have to be supported by an argument to the effect that the descriptive character of claims about speakers' dispositions and the normative character of claims about how they should use linguistic expressions invalidates inferences from the former to the latter.

---

6. David Hume, *A Treatise of Human Nature*, 2nd ed., L. A. Selby-Bigge and P. H. Nidditch, eds (Oxford: Oxford University Press, 1978), p. 469.

III KRIPKE AND THE STANDARD NORMATIVITY ARGUMENT

The Standard Normativity Argument encapsulates a widespread interpretation of Kripke's claim that the normative character of meaning invalidates dispositional accounts of meaning facts.[7] It is, at any rate, the line of reasoning that Fodor seems to have in mind in his brief discussion of 'Kripkensteinian' worries about the normative force of meaning. It is possible to find some textual evidence for the attribution to Kripke of the Standard Normativity Argument. 'A candidate for what constitutes the state of my meaning one function, rather than another, by a given function sign,' he writes, 'ought to be such that, whatever in fact I (am disposed to) do, there is a unique thing that I *should* do. Is not the dispositional view simply an equation of performance and correctness?' (*WRPL*, p. 24). And later on:

> The dispositionalist gives a *descriptive* account of this relation [between the meaning that I ascribe to "+" and my response to the problem "68 + 57"]: if "+" meant addition, then I will answer "125." But this is not the proper account of the relation, which is *normative,* not descriptive. The point is *not* that, if I meant addition by "+", I *will* answer "125," but that, if I intend to accord with my past meaning of "+", I *should* answer "125." (*WRPL*, p. 37)

These passages seem to indicate that, according to Kripke, dispositional accounts fall prey to the illegitimacy of inferences from descriptive premises to normative conclusions. But, as we have just seen, if Kripke presents a successful argument along these lines, we should be able to extract from his discussion a justification for the Humean injunction, at least in the case of dispositional accounts of meaning. In this section I want to consider whether such a justification can be found in Kripke's text.

Kripke's detailed discussion of dispositional accounts starts with the claim that a speaker's dispositions cannot determine how he should use an expression because they are finite, whereas the question of how an expression should be used should in principle receive an answer in infinitely many cases (cf. *WRPL*, pp. 26–8). How I am disposed to apply a predicate cannot determine how I should apply it because facts about which objects I should apply the predicate to are bound to outstrip facts about which objects I am disposed to apply it to. There will always be objects for which the normative question should receive an answer but with respect to which I have no disposition either way.

---

7. Paul Boghossian has given the clearest presentation of this reading of Kripke's normativity considerations (cf. 'The Rule-Following Considerations'). Boghossian attributes this reading to Simon Blackburn, Crispin Wright and John McDowell (cf. *ibid*., pp. 532–3), and at least in the case of the first two, this attribution seems incontestable. See Simon Blackburn, 'The Individual Strikes Back,' *Synthese* 58 (1984) pp. 281–302 (this volume Ch. 3) and Crispin Wright, 'Kripke's Account of the Argument against Private Language,' *Journal of Philosophy* 81 (1984), pp. 759–77.

The claim that dispositions are finite has not gone uncontested.[8] However, my goal here is not to assess this line of argument against dispositional accounts, but to consider whether it can be used to fill the gap that we have detected in the Standard Normativity Argument. And it is hard to see how the claim that dispositions are finite could perform this task. What we are looking for is an explanation of why inferences from dispositional premises to normative conclusions are rendered invalid by the descriptive character of the former. To obtain this explanation from the finite character of dispositions would require showing, on the one hand, that the finiteness of dispositions follows from the descriptive character of dispositional facts, and, on the other, that it is in virtue of its normative character that the question of how I should apply a predicate has to receive an answer in infinitely many cases. But it is far from clear how we could try to establish either of these claims, and if they cannot be established, the finite character of dispositions cannot be adduced in support of premise (C) of the Standard Normativity Argument, independently of whether it can be invoked to undermine dispositional accounts through a different route. At any rate, even if the finiteness of dispositions could be used to support premise (C), it is hard to believe that Kripke intends it to play this role, as he seems to make no attempt to connect the descriptive/normative contrast with the finite/infinite one.

The second line of reasoning that Kripke deploys against dispositional accounts arises from the reflection that an admissible account of meaning facts has to make room for the possibility that speakers fail to use linguistic expressions the way they should (cf. *WRPL*, pp. 28–30). In the case of predicate satisfaction, an admissible account of satisfaction facts would have to make room for the possibility that speakers apply predicates incorrectly. This consideration is devastating against what Kripke characterizes as the 'crude' dispositional account (cf. *WRPL*, p. 27). This account operates with a notion of disposition according to which speakers are disposed to do whatever they in fact do. An account of predicate satisfaction based on this notion of disposition would obviously fail to make room for the possibility of incorrect predicate ascriptions, and it can be dismissed on these grounds.

But the proponent of this crude dispositional account is a straw man. The dispositional accounts of predicate satisfaction currently on offer follow the more sophisticated model that Kripke goes on to consider (cf. *WRPL*, pp. 30–2). According to the more sophisticated version of the dispositional account, the property that determines the satisfaction conditions of a predicate is singled out in terms of how the speaker would apply the predicate under certain 'ideal' conditions. An immediate consequence of the appeal to ideal conditions is to defuse the objection that invalidates the crude dispositional account. For the conditions under which a speaker ascribes a predicate may fail to be ideal, thus opening the possibility of incorrect predicate ascriptions.

8. Cf. e.g., J. Fodor, 'A Theory of Content', pp. 94–5.

[handwritten: Sophisticated Dispositionalism]

This approach to predicate satisfaction enjoys a good deal of popularity nowadays, as it is the model followed by most information theoretic accounts of the notion.[9] According to these accounts, the property that determines the satisfaction conditions of each predicate is to be singled out as the property that would cause the predicate to be 'tokened in the belief mode' under certain conditions.[10] Thus it seems reasonable to assume that if the sophisticated dispositional account could be shown to be incapable of accommodating the normativity of satisfaction facts, the same conclusion would have to be drawn for information theoretic accounts of satisfaction.

Kripke goes on to consider other arguments that do bear on sophisticated dispositionalism. First, he argues, correctly, that it would be circular to construe ideal conditions in terms of semantic or normative notions (cf. 30). Proponents of information theoretic accounts accept this constraint, and see it as their main task to provide a non-circular specification of ideal conditions such that the property to whose instances a speaker would apply a predicate under those conditions is the property that determines the satisfaction conditions of the predicate, as meant by the speaker.

Kripke then points out a family of important difficulties faced by the attempt to specify ideal conditions non-circularly in such a way as to effect the right pairings of predicates and properties. They are generated by the fact that speakers' mistakes are often systematic, and hence, presumably, likely to arise even under conditions that we would expect to result only in correct uses of expressions (cf. 31–2). This is no doubt a serious hurdle for the information theoretic program. But few of its proponents are under the illusion that they face an easy task. In any case, our main concern is whether these considerations could be used to support the injunction against inferences from descriptive premises to normative conclusions on which the Standard Normativity Argument relies. And it seems to me that they are not even intended to play this role. These considerations, if successful, would yield the result that it is impossible to provide a systematic specification, in non-intentional, non-normative terms, of which property determines the satisfaction conditions of each predicate which yields the right property-

---

9. However, not all dispositional accounts are information theoretic. Cf. Carl Ginet, 'The Dispositionalist Solution to Wittgenstein's Problem about Understanding a Rule: Answering Kripke's Objections,' in P. A. French, T. E. Uehling, Jr., and H. K. Wettstein, eds, *Midwest Studies in Philosophy, Volume XII: The Wittgenstein Legacy* (Notre Dame, IN: University of Notre Dame Press, 1992) pp. 53–73.

10. Cf. J. Fodor, 'A Theory of Content, I: The Problem,' in *A Theory of Content and Other Essays,* p. 60, where a number of influential information theoretic accounts are presented as following this model. Fodor claims that his most recent version of the information theoretic account doesn't follow this pattern (cf. 'A Theory of Content, II', 90). See Paul Boghossian, 'Naturalizing Content' in G. Rey and B. Loewer, eds, *Meaning in Mind: Fodor and His Critics* (Cambridge, MA: Blackwell, 1991), pp. 71–3, where this claim is contested.

predicate pairings.[11] But this is not the way in which the Standard Normativity Argument is supposed to undermine information theoretic accounts of satisfaction facts. The thrust of the Standard Normativity Argument is that, even if such a specification were available, the dispositional facts in terms of which it would single out the property that corresponds to each predicate could not be identified with satisfaction facts. For satisfaction facts have normative consequences, and dispositional facts, being descriptive, could not have consequences of this kind. This feature of the argument is explicitly highlighted by some of its advocates. Thus Crispin Wright writes:

> Even at the most fundamental level, then, and when nothing interferes with the exercise of a disposition, there should be a distinction between what somebody's understanding of E requires and the use of that expression which he actually makes; it is just that, if nothing interferes with the exercise of the disposition, the use he makes *will* be the use required of him.[12]

And, according to Boghossian, this is Kripke's own view:

> Kripke seems to think that even if there were a suitably selected disposition that captured the extension of an expression accurately, the disposition could still not be identified with that fact of meaning, because it still remains true that the concept of a disposition is descriptive whereas the concept of meaning is not. In other words, according to Kripke, even if there were a dispositional predicate that logically covaried with a meaning predicate, the one fact could still not be identified with the other, for they are facts of distinct sorts.[13]

I have been arguing that, cogent as they may be, the considerations adduced by Kripke against dispositional accounts fail to support this particular line of objection against them. This is the conclusion drawn by Jerry Fodor, who fails to see how the Standard Normativity Argument is supposed to undermine information theoretic accounts of predicate satisfaction. He writes:

> requiring normativity to be grounded suggests that there is more to demand of a naturalized semantics than that it provide a reduction of such notions as, say, extension. But what could that "more" amount

---

11. For other arguments against the feasibility of this task, see Paul Boghossian, 'Naturalizing Content,' and J. Zalabardo, 'A Problem for Information Theoretic Semantics,' *Synthese* 105 (1995) pp. 1–29.
12. Crispin Wright, 'Kripke's Account of the Argument against Private Language,' pp. 771–2.
13. Boghossian, 'The Rule-Following Considerations,' p. 332 (see volume Ch. 9). Cf. also Simon Blackburn, 'The Individual Strikes Back,' p. 291 (this volume Ch. 3), where this claim is attributed to Kripke and endorsed.

to? To apply a term to a thing in its extension *is* to apply the term correctly; once you've said what it is that makes the tables the extension of "table"s, there is surely no *further* question about why it's *correct* to apply a "table" to a table. It thus seems that if you have a reductive theory of semantic relations, there is no job of grounding normativity left to do.[14]

Fodor's point is that if we could specify systematically in non-intentional, non-normative terms the property that determines the satisfaction conditions of each predicate, we would be entitled to treat the facts invoked by this specification as the satisfaction facts – at any rate, that we would not be prevented from treating them in this way by the reflection that satisfaction facts have normative consequences. I have been suggesting that this assessment of the situation is not refuted by any of the Kripkean arguments against dispositionalism that I have sketched.

why not?

In fact, Fodor suggests in passing a different line of reasoning that might be seen as supporting the injunction against is/ought inferences in semantics. He continues:

> In short, I'm not clear how – or whether – "open question" argu-
> ments can get a grip in the present case. I am darkly suspicious that
> the Kripkensteinian worry about the normative force of meaning is
> either a non-issue or just the reduction issue over again; anyhow, that
> it's not a *new issue*. (*Ibid.*, p. 136)

Thus, for Fodor, Kripke's normativity argument rests in the end on an open-question argument. In his view, Kripke's point is that we cannot draw evaluative conclusions from descriptive premises concerning speakers' dispositions because an open question argument would invalidate these inferences. The reasoning would, presumably, go as follows. How a speaker would apply a predicate under ideal conditions cannot be the fact that determines how he should apply it because we can meaningfully ask whether the applications that he would endorse under ideal conditions are the ones that he should endorse.

Would this line of reasoning succeed in barring the passage from descriptive premises to evaluative conclusions in this case? I want to suggest that this argument is unlikely to carry much conviction. The problem is that the proponents of naturalistic reductions of semantic notions see their task as on a par with other theoretic reductions, such as the identification of water with H_2O or of heat with kinetic energy.[15] The proponents of information theoretic semantics aim at revealing the nature of predicate satisfaction, and

---

14. 'A Theory of Content, II,' p. 135.
15. Cf. Hartry Field, 'Tarski's Theory of Truth,' *Journal of Philosophy* **69** (1972) pp. 347–75, for an explicit statement of this way of conceiving the task.

of the attending normative facts, precisely in the sense in which the nature of water is revealed by its identification with a certain molecular structure.

Hence semantic naturalists can be expected to react to open-question arguments along lines that would be perfectly proper in the case of other theoretical identifications. No doubt we can meaningfully ask whether water is H_2O, but the meaningfulness of this question doesn't undermine the identification of water with H_2O – the claim that whether something is water is determined by whether it has that molecular structure. Similarly, semantic naturalists would concede that we can meaningfully ask whether a speaker should ascribe a predicate to the objects to which he would ascribe it under certain conditions. But the meaningfulness of this question, they would contend, doesn't undermine the claim that how the speaker should apply the predicate is determined by how he would apply it under those conditions.

I am not suggesting that semantic naturalists are right in thinking that the task of elucidating predicate satisfaction should be looked upon as having the same nature as the task of discovering the hidden essence of water. There may be telling considerations against this assimilation.[16] I have only argued that this way of conceiving the task of explaining satisfaction would receive no immediate challenge from the Standard Normativity Argument, unless the ban on inferences from descriptive premises to normative conclusions could be justified in the case of semantics, and that neither the arguments explicitly offered by Kripke, nor an open-question argument, can justify this ban. If semantic naturalists could overcome the difficulties raised by Kripke and others, and provide a systematic, non-circular account of which property determines the satisfaction conditions of each predicate, the Standard Normativity Argument would fail to undermine the identification of satisfaction facts with the facts invoked by the naturalistic account.

To sum up, in this section I have contended that, in his discussion of dispositional accounts, Kripke offers no support for the crucial premise of the Standard Normativity Argument – the injunction against inferences from descriptive premises to normative conclusions. One may be tempted to conclude from this that Kripke fails to offer adequate support for his contention that dispositional accounts cannot accommodate the normative character of meaning. Notice, however, that this diagnosis rests on the assumption that the Standard Normativity Argument is the line of reasoning that Kripke offers in support of this contention. And the absence from Kripke's text of support for the crucial premise of the argument should surely be treated as evidence against this assumption. It should make us question the

---

16. I have argued against this way of understanding the task of explaining predicate reference in J. Zalabardo, 'Predicates, Properties, and the Goal of a Theory of Reference,' *Grazer Philosophische Studien* 51 (1996), pp. 121–61. Cf. also Hilary Putnam, *Reason, Truth and History* (Cambridge: Cambridge University Press, 1981), p. 47, for an argument against the assimilation of the task of explaining reference to the scientific explication of pre-theoretic notions.

attribution to Kripke of the Standard Normativity Argument. This attribution would be hard to resist if no other line of reasoning could be found in Kripke's discussion to underpin his claim that dispositional accounts cannot grasp the normative dimension of meaning. The Standard Normativity Argument would then have to be attributed to Kripke, so to speak, by default. But if we could find in his discussion of dispositional accounts a different line of reasoning in support of this claim, then the attribution to him of the Standard Normativity Argument would lose much of its point. I want to suggest that this is in fact the situation. A strand in Kripke's discussion of dispositional accounts that we have so far overlooked provides an alternative line of reasoning in support of the contention that speakers' dispositions cannot ground normative claims concerning their predicate ascriptions.

IV KRIPKE'S NORMATIVITY ARGUMENT

At the end of his discussion of dispositional accounts, Kripke offers a gloss on their inability to ground normative claims about predicate ascriptions. The problem is that 'the fact that an answer to the question of which function I meant is *justificatory* of my present response is ignored by the dispositional account' (*WRPL*, p. 37). The reason why dispositional facts cannot ground normative claims about my responses is, it seems, that dispositional facts are not justificatory of my responses. The difficulty that dispositional accounts face with respect to normative claims is presented as arising from the connection between normativity and justification.

How are we to understand Kripke's claim that meaning facts have to be justificatory of my responses? Earlier on he rephrases the claim by imposing on a candidate for a fact that determines what I mean the following basic condition: 'that it should *tell* me what I ought to do in each new instance' (*WRPL*, p. 24; cf. also p. 11). Satisfaction facts have to ground claims about how I should apply predicates by telling me which applications to endorse. Dispositional facts cannot ground such claims because they don't meet this condition – they don't tell me which objects to apply each predicate to.

Kripke elaborates on this condition when he considers a version of dispositionalism according to which how I should respond now is determined by my past dispositions. On this account, if I want to be faithful to my past understanding of '+', I should now answer '125' when queried about '68 + 57' because in the past I was disposed to give this response. Kripke offers the following reply to this proposal:

> how does any of this indicate that – now *or* in the past – "125" was
> an answer *justified* in terms of instructions I gave myself, rather than
> a mere jack-in-the-box unjustified and arbitrary response? Am I

> supposed to justify my present belief that I should answer "125" . . .
> in terms of a *hypothesis* about my *past* dispositions? (Do I record and
> investigate the past physiology of my brain?)   (*WRPL*, p. 23)

The point is that if the answer I should now give were determined by my past dispositions, justifying my present response would require acquiring information about how I was disposed to answer in the past. But this information is not directly available to me now. Hence justifying my present response would require forming a hypothesis about my past dispositions. But this is not how I proceed. I do not 'record and investigate the past physiology of my brain.' As Kripke puts it when he is considering a different proposal,

> I immediately and unhesitatingly calculate "68 + 57" as I do, and the meaning I assign to " + " is supposed to *justify* this procedure. I do not form tentative hypotheses, wondering what I should do if one hypothesis or another were true.   (*WRPL*, p. 40)

Hence, Kripke is rejecting this version of dispositionalism on the grounds that, if my past dispositions determined how I should now answer '+'-questions, the procedure that I employ for answering these questions would not be justified.

We can gain a better understanding of Kripke's reasoning if we consider more generally the kind of situation exemplified by '+'-questions. Some procedures for answering questions of a certain kind K are justified, while others are totally arbitrary. Whether a given procedure for answering K-questions is justified can be expected to depend on which facts determine how K-questions should be answered, and on how the procedure is related to these facts. Thus a hypothesis concerning which facts determine how K-questions should be answered generates a criterion of adequacy for the procedures that we may want to use for answering them: if a procedure for answering K-questions is to be justified, it has to be suitably related to those facts. Conversely, a hypothesis concerning which procedures for answering K-questions are justified generates a criterion of adequacy for accounts of which facts determine how K-questions should be answered: the facts that play this role will have to be related to those procedures in such a way as to render them justified.

In his rejection of the view that how I should now answer '+'-questions is determined by my past dispositions, Kripke is invoking the latter kind of criterion. He is arguing that a successful candidate for a fact that determines how I should answer '+'-questions has to be related to the procedure that I actually employ for answering these questions in such a way as to render the procedure justified. My past dispositions cannot determine how I should answer '+'-questions because they fail this test.

But how does a procedure for answering K-questions have to be related to the facts that determine how they should be answered in order for the procedure to be justified? Kripke seems to think that if the correct answers to '+'-questions were determined by the past physiology of my brain, the only justified procedure for answering these questions would be to 'record and investigate' the relevant physiological facts. This suggests that, for Kripke, a procedure for answering K-questions would not be justified unless it involved *conscious engagement* with the facts that determine how these questions should be answered. Kripke doesn't provide a precise characterization of this requirement, nor does he offer any support for it, but it seems clear that a principle along these lines underlies his argument against treating my past dispositions as determining how '+'-questions should be answered.[17]

This line of reasoning can be equally deployed against the sophisticated dispositional account of predicate satisfaction. When I'm trying to decide whether to apply a predicate to an object, I do not consider what decision I would reach under ideal conditions. Facts about what I would decide under ideal conditions are not directly available to me. For one thing, I don't know which conditions count as ideal – under what conditions I would decide to apply a predicate precisely to the objects that satisfy it. Hence taking these facts into account would require forming 'tentative hypotheses' – about which conditions are ideal and about how I would respond under those conditions. But I form no such hypotheses. I reach my decisions 'immediately and unhesitatingly.' At any rate, the procedures that I employ do not take into account facts concerning how I would apply predicates under ideal conditions.[18]

It follows from this, the argument continues, that if facts about how I would apply predicates under ideal conditions determined how I should apply them, my procedures for applying predicates would not be justified. Therefore these facts cannot determine how I should apply predicates. And since satisfaction facts have to effect this determination, the argument concludes, facts about how I would apply predicates under ideal conditions cannot be identified with satisfaction facts. They cannot be the facts that determine the satisfaction conditions of predicates.

What I am suggesting, then, is that we can find in Kripke's text an argument which, when applied to the case of predicate satisfaction, would have roughly the following structure. It would have the following three premises:

---

17. Warren Goldfarb has also seen that a principle along these lines is at play in Kripke's discussion of dispositionalism. He writes: 'Now Kripke, in saying the "fact must show how I am justified," does seem to mean that the justifications must in some sense be transparent' (Warren Goldfarb, 'Kripke on Wittgenstein on Rules,' *Journal of Philosophy* 82 (1985), p. 478) (this volume Ch. 6).

18. Some predicates are associated with fairly elaborate application procedures, while others are applied on the basis of brute classificatory propensities. As I am using the notion, procedures for applying predicates are meant to include both kinds of case. They could be as minimal as, say, checking whether an object is red by looking at it. Notice also that I am not assuming that each predicate will be associated with a single procedure. We often have several methods for deciding whether to apply a predicate to an object.

(1) The procedures that I use for deciding whether to apply a predicate to an object must be justified.

(2) The procedures that I use for deciding whether to apply a predicate to an object would only be justified if they involved conscious engagement with the facts that determine which objects I should apply each predicate to.

(3) I decide whether to ascribe predicates to objects without considering whether I would do so under ideal conditions.

From premises (2) and (3), the argument infers

(4) If facts about how I would apply predicates under ideal conditions determined which objects I should apply each predicate to, the procedures that I use for deciding on the application of predicates would not be justified.

And from (4) and (1), the argument draws the anti-dispositionalist conclusion:

(5) Facts about which objects I would apply each predicate to under ideal conditions do not determine which objects I should apply each predicate to.

This is, I submit, the main line of reasoning offered by Kripke in support of his claim that dispositional accounts cannot accommodate the normative character of satisfaction facts. I shall refer to it as the *Justification Argument*.

The presence of this argument in Kripke's dialectic doesn't strictly rule out the possibility that he sees the Standard Normativity Argument as providing additional support for his contention that dispositional accounts of satisfaction cannot accommodate normativity. But, as I suggested above, the fact that we have found a different line of reasoning to this effect makes the attribution to Kripke of the Standard Normativity Argument lose much of its point.

One could try to ground this attribution on the passages that I quoted at the beginning of Section III, in which Kripke seems to object, in general, to inferences from descriptive premises to normative conclusions. But the context in which these passages occur makes this interpretative line extremely dubious. Of his conclusion that 'the relation of meaning and intention to future action is *normative,* not *descriptive*' (WRPL, p. 37) he says in the following paragraph that it shows 'that in some sense we have returned full circle to our original intuition', i.e., the reflection that meaning facts have to be justificatory of my present response. What may have sounded like an endorsement of the Standard Normativity Argument is presented as, in effect, making the central point of the Justification Argument.

The same can be said of the other text quoted at the beginning of Section III, in which Kripke contends that meaning facts 'ought to be such that, whatever in fact I (am disposed to) do, there is a unique thing that I *should* do' (*WRPL*, p. 24). For the following paragraph starts with what appears to be a summary of the preceding discussion: 'So it does seem that a dispositional account misconceives the skeptic's problem – to find a past fact that *justifies* my present response.' Once again, a passage that seemed to lend support to the attribution to Kripke of the Standard Normativity Argument is presented as a statement of the Justification Argument.

Be this as it may, whether Kripke's attack on dispositional accounts of meaning *also* involves the Standard Normativity Argument is perhaps only of academic interest. The important point is that Kripke offers a different line of reasoning in support of his claim that dispositional accounts cannot accommodate the normativity of meaning. Discussions of Kripke's normativity considerations have often failed to take notice of this line of reasoning.[19] Jerry Fodor, for one, dismisses 'Kripkensteinian' worries concerning normativity with no discussion of the point that meaning facts have to be justificatory of speakers' responses. The main lesson is, then, that those, like Fodor, who think that Kripke's normativity considerations pose no threat to their preferred account of meaning facts would not be entitled to this conclusion unless they could supply a strategy for dealing with the Justification Argument. In the remainder of this paper I shall make some remarks on how one might try to resist this argument.

V RESISTING THE JUSTIFICATION ARGUMENT

That the conclusion of the Justification Argument follows from its premises seems beyond any doubt. Hence resisting the conclusion would require challenging one of the premises. I shall consider each of them in turn. One could try to challenge premise (1) by contending that my procedures for deciding on predicate ascriptions need not be justified. Someone who attempts to defend an information theoretic account of predicate satisfaction along these lines could concede that, since my procedures do not take into account how I would apply predicates under ideal conditions, the claim that the satisfaction conditions of my predicates are determined by these dispositional facts would render the procedures unjustified. But he would contend that, surprising as it may be, this corollary should not be taken as a refutation of the dispositional account. He would accept Kripke's remark that

---

19. There are some exceptions. In his review of Kripke's book (*Noûs* **19**, 1985), Brian Loar emphasized the importance of this line of reasoning for Kripke's dialectic (cf. p. 275). Warren Goldfarb has also identified this strand of Kripke's argument. Cf. his 'Kripke on Wittgenstein on Rules,' pp. 477–9 (this volume Ch. 6). Ruth Millikan also registers, in a footnote, this aspect of Kripke's dialectic. Cf. Ruth Garrett Millikan, 'Truth Rules, Hoverflies, and the Kripke–Wittgenstein Paradox,' *Philosophical Review* **99** (1990), pp. 327–8, n. 10 (this volume Ch. 11).

identifying meaning facts with facts to which my access is indirect 'is already to take a big step in the direction of skepticism' (*WRPL*, p. 40), but he would insist that this is a step that we have to take.

I won't say much about this position, because it is probably the least appealing strategy for resisting the conclusion of the Justification Argument. I only want to emphasize that the skepticism that it urges us to accept is very radical indeed. It would involve treating all our predicate ascriptions so far as blind, arbitrary, unjustified stabs in the dark, since they arise from procedures that are not suitably related to satisfaction facts. We could only escape this predicament by abandoning our arbitrary application procedures, and adopting instead procedures that took into account how we would apply predicates under ideal conditions. This would involve forming hypotheses concerning which conditions are to be treated as ideal and which predicate applications we would endorse under those conditions.

We are entitled to wonder whether this massive disregard of the procedures that we actually employ for ascribing predicates leaves something recognizable as an account of the satisfaction conditions of predicates *as meant by us*. But even without invoking any sort of conceptual link between meaning and use, it is hard to find any appeal in an account of satisfaction facts which forces upon us this disparaging assessment of our actual practices for ascribing predicates.

Another strategy for resisting the conclusion of the Justification Argument would be to reject premise (2). The proponent of this strategy would concede that an account of satisfaction facts which renders our procedures for applying predicates unjustified would be totally inadmissible, and that we ascribe predicates without considering what we would do under ideal conditions. But he would contend that our procedures may have this feature and still yield justified predicate ascriptions, as he would reject the idea that a justified procedure for ascribing predicates needs to involve conscious engagement with the facts that determine how predicates should be applied. In other words, the proponent of this strategy would try to save an information theoretic account of satisfaction by rejecting Kripke's account of how a procedure for answering a question should be related to the fact that determines how the question should be answered in order for the procedure to be justified. The procedure, he would contend, could fail to involve conscious engagement with the fact and still be justified. We can expect the proponent of this strategy to substitute an account according to which a procedure for answering a question is justified so long as it reliably tracks the facts that determine how the question should be answered.

These are, of course, the familiar moves of externalist accounts of justification.[20] This is not the place to undertake an assessment of these

---

20. For externalist accounts of epistemic notions, see, e.g., A. Goldman, 'Discrimination and Perceptual Knowledge,' *Journal of Philosophy* 73 (1976), pp. 771–91 and D. Armstrong, *Belief, Truth and Knowledge* (Cambridge: Cambridge University Press, 1973), chs. 12 and 13.

accounts.[21] In this connection I would only like to register the fact that the Justification Argument relies on an anti-externalist premise. If justification could be construed along externalist lines, the argument could not be used to undermine information theoretic accounts of justification, as their proponents might be able to contend that facts about how I would apply predicates under ideal conditions are justificatory of my procedures – so long as these procedures reliably track those facts.

Let me turn now to the third way in which the conclusion of the Justification Argument could be resisted. One could try to defuse the argument by rejecting premise (3) – the claim that my procedures for ascribing predicates do not take into account which ascriptions I would endorse under ideal conditions. Recall that, as I have presented the project, the information theoretic account of satisfaction is an instance of the realist approach. It construes satisfaction facts by pairing each predicate with a property, whose instantiation conditions determine the satisfaction conditions of the predicate. According to information theoretic semantics, these pairings can be specified in terms of how a speaker would apply predicates under ideal conditions. Suppose, for the sake of the argument, that information theoretic semantics could provide a systematic, non-circular specification of which property determines the satisfaction conditions of each predicate that gets these property-predicate pairings right. Call this the *IT-specification* and the facts that it invokes the *IT-facts*.

In order to use the Justification Argument against the identification of satisfaction facts with the IT-facts, we would need to establish (premise 3) that our procedures for ascribing predicates do not involve conscious engagement with the IT-facts. This claim may seem to follow from the unquestionable fact that my procedures for deciding on the ascription of a predicate do not involve forming a hypothesis as to which property is such that, under ideal conditions, I would apply the predicate precisely to its instances. But the proponent of this line of reasoning could protest that conscious engagement with the IT-facts does not require forming such hypotheses. It is enough, he might contend, that I consciously engage with the property that the IT-specification pairs with each predicate – even if I don't know that the property can be specified in this way. But we are assuming that the property that the IT-specification pairs with each predicate is, as a matter of fact, the property that determines its satisfaction conditions. Hence, he would conclude, so long as the procedures that I use for ascribing a predicate involve conscious engagement with the property that determines its satisfaction conditions, the procedures can be said to involve conscious engagement with the IT-facts.

---

21. For a promising line of attack on epistemological externalism, cf. B. Stroud, 'Understanding Human Knowledge in General,' in M. Clay and K. Lehrer, eds, *Knowledge and Skepticism* (Boulder, CO: Westview Press, 1989).

This conclusion is open to question. One may wonder whether conscious engagement with the property that the IT-specification pairs with each predicate amounts to conscious engagement with the IT-facts themselves. But I propose to leave these worries aside and accept, for the sake of the argument, that if the procedures that I use for ascribing a predicate involved conscious engagement with the property that determines its satisfaction conditions, the Justification Argument would not undermine an information theoretic account of satisfaction.

Notice that this concession doesn't render the information theoretic account immune to the Justification Argument. All it does is to make it as safe as the realist approach of which it is an instance. On the realist approach, the satisfaction conditions of each predicate are determined by a property with which the predicate is connected. If the procedures that I use for ascribing a predicate could be described as involving conscious engagement with the property with which the predicate is so connected, the facts in terms of which the realist approach construes satisfaction would justify these procedures. Hence, in these circumstances, we wouldn't be able to object to the realist approach on the grounds that satisfaction facts have to be justificatory of my procedure for applying predicates. What I am conceding is that under these circumstances this line of reasoning would not undermine the information theoretic account either. However, if the realist approach fell prey to this line of reasoning, its information theoretic version would naturally fall with it. I would like to end with a few remarks about this possibility.

Bringing the realist approach under pressure from a version of the Justification Argument would involve arguing that my predicate-ascribing procedures cannot be described as involving conscious engagement with the property that determines, on the realist approach, the satisfaction conditions of each predicate. That the procedures can be so described may seem totally uncontroversial. At least in the cases that the empiricist tradition treats as basic, such as predicates of colour, shape, etc., it seems hard to deny that I decide on the application of a predicate to an object by 'bringing to consciousness' the property with which it is connected, in order to determine whether it is present in the object under consideration. Let me refer to this description of the procedure as the *Classical Empiricist Picture*.[22]

The Classical Empiricist Picture cannot be directly applied to all our predicates, as some will be connected with properties of which we cannot be

---

22. Wilfrid Sellars identified this picture as central to the traditional empiricist account of sense perception. Cf. Wilfrid Sellars, 'Empiricism and the Philosophy of Mind,' in H. Feigl and M. Scriven, eds, *Minnesota Studies in the Philosophy of Science, Vol. I: The Foundations of Science and the Concepts of Psychology and Psychoanalysis* (Minneapolis: University of Minnesota Press, 1956), pp. 286–8. The picture is also present in the Fregean conception of senses as objective, extra-mental, reference-determining entities which the mind is nevertheless capable of grasping. Kripke discusses briefly the bearing of the rule-following considerations on this view (cf. WRPL, pp. 53–4).

said to be aware. But it would seem possible in principle to deal with these cases by treating our access to these properties as derived from our grasp of those that we can bring to consciousness, presumably by means of the theoretical links between the predicates associated with the two kinds of property. Be this as it may, in the cases in which it is directly applicable, the Classical Empiricist Picture provides a very natural account of our access to the facts that determine the satisfaction conditions of predicates, according to the realist approach. And so long as the Classical Empiricist Picture goes unchallenged, the facts in terms of which the realist approach construes satisfaction can be said to justify my predicate-ascribing procedures.

If, on the contrary, the Classical Empiricist Picture had to be rejected, the way would be open to using a version of the Justification Argument to undermine the realist approach. For rejecting the Classical Empiricist Picture would amount to giving up the claim that our predicate-ascribing procedures can be described as involving conscious engagement with the property that determines, on the realist approach, the satisfaction conditions of each predicate. But can the Classical Empiricist Picture be seriously challenged? I want to suggest that the rule-following considerations can be naturally construed as aiming at this goal. The Classical Empiricist Picture attributes to the human mind a capacity for conscious engagement with properties. This capacity enables us to bring a property to consciousness in order to determine its presence in, or absence from, an object. That we have conscious episodes that we are inclined to describe in these terms is not open to question. What is not so clear is that we are entitled to this description. No doubt we have inclinations to classify objects as satisfying or failing to satisfy, say, the predicate 'red.' According to the Classical Empiricist Picture, these responses are guided by a property to which we have conscious access. But it seems reasonable to ask on what grounds the proponent of the Classical Empiricist Picture claims to be entitled to describe our classificatory responses in these terms, rather than as brute inclinations to answer one way rather than another, accompanied by the *illusion* that they are guided by our awareness of a property. What I am suggesting is that the rule-following considerations can be construed as mounting an attack on the description put forward by the Classical Empiricist Picture. This seems to be the point of Wittgenstein's discussion of episodes of 'grasping the meaning of a word in a flash,' or of the private linguist's acts of inner ostension. For in both cases his goal seems to be to undermine the claim that in these episodes the subject can be construed as bringing to consciousness an item by which his responses are guided.

I shall not try to develop this argument here. I only wish to emphasize that if we were forced to abandon the Classical Empiricist Picture, the only way, short of embracing skepticism, to save the realist approach to satisfaction from the Justification Argument would be to adopt an externalist account of the justification of our procedures for deciding on predicate ascriptions. On the resulting position, the satisfaction conditions of predicates would still be determined by the instantiation conditions of properties, but our predicate ascriptions would not be informed by any kind of conscious access to the properties that play this role. They would result from 'blind' classificatory propensities, but so long as these propensities reliably tracked the instantiation conditions of the properties with which predicates are associated, our verdicts would be considered justified. If the Classical Empiricist Picture had to be abandoned, the fate of the realist approach would turn on the viability of this position, but an assessment of its prospects will have to be left for another occasion.

GUIDE TO FURTHER READING

Wittgenstein's main texts on rule-following are:

Wittgenstein, L., *Philosophical Investigations* (Oxford: Basil Blackwell, 1958), especially §§138–242.
Wittgenstein, L., *Remarks on the Foundations of Mathematics* (Oxford: Basil Blackwell, 1978), especially section VI.

Kripke's reading is contained in:

Kripke, S., *Wittgenstein on Rules and Private Language* (Oxford: Basil Blackwell, 1982).

The sections below are not mutually exclusive: works are listed in the "general" category when they do not fit easily into only one of the others. The list is not intended to be exhaustive. Not all of the items are directly focused on Kripke or Wittgenstein: many have been included in virtue of their contribution to the philosophical issues which arise in the light of the rule-following considerations.

1. REDUCTIONIST, DISPOSITIONALIST, NATURALISTIC RESPONSES TO THE SKEPTICAL ARGUMENT

Boghossian, P., "Naturalizing Content", in G. Rey and B. Loewer (eds) *Meaning in Mind: Fodor and his Critics* (Cambridge, MA: Blackwell, 1991).
Chomsky, N., *Knowledge of Language* (New York: Praeger, 1986).
Crane, T., *The Mechanical Mind* (Harmondsworth: Penguin, 1995).
Fodor, J., *Psychosemantics* (Cambridge, MA: MIT Press, 1987), chapter 4.
Fodor, J., *A Theory of Content and Other Essays* (Cambridge, MA: MIT Press, 1990), chapters 3 and 4.

Ginet, C., "The Dispositionalist Solution to Wittgenstein's Problem about Understanding a Rule: Answering Kripke's Objections", in P. A. French, T. E. Uehling, Jr., and H. K. Wettstein (eds) *Midwest Studies in Philosophy, Volume XII: The Wittgensteinian Legacy* (Notre Dame: University of Notre Dame Press, 1992).

Heil, J. and Martin, C., "Rules and Powers", in J. Tomberlin (ed) *Philosophical Perspectives* 12: *Language, Mind, and Ontology* (1998).

Horwich, P., "Critical Notice of Kripke's *Wittgenstein on Rules and Private Language*", *Philosophy of Science* 51 (1984).

Horwich, P., "Wittgenstein and Kripke on the Nature of Meaning", *Mind and Language* 5 (1990).

Horwich, P., *Meaning* (Oxford: Oxford University Press, 1998), chapters 4 and 10.

Loar, B., "Critical Notice of *Kripke's Wittgenstein on Rules and Private Language*", *Noûs* 19 (1985).

Loewer, B., "A Guide to Naturalizing Semantics", in B. Hale and C. Wright (eds) *A Companion to the Philosophy of Language* (Oxford: Blackwell, 1997).

McManus, D., "Boghossian, Miller and Lewis on Dispositional Theories of Meaning", *Mind and Language* 15 (2000).

Margalit, A: "How to Outsmart the Rules: A Comment", in E. Ullman-Margalit (ed) *The Scientific Enterprise* (Kluwer, 1992).

Miller, A., "Boghossian on Reductive Dispositionalism: The Case Strengthened", *Mind and Language* 12 (1997).

Miller, A., *Philosophy of Language* (London: UCL Press, 1998), chapter 6.

Miller, A., "Horwich, Meaning and Kripke's Wittgenstein", *Philosophical Quarterly* 50 (2000).

Millikan, R., *Language, Thought, and Other Biological Categories* (Cambridge, MA: MIT Press, 1984).

Millikan, R., "Speaking Up for Darwin", in G. Rey and B. Loewer (eds) *Meaning in Mind: Fodor and his Critics* (Cambridge, MA: Blackwell, 1991).

Smart, J. J. C., "Wittgenstein, Following a Rule, and Scientific Psychology", in E. Margalit (ed.) *The Scientific Enterprise* (Kluwer, 1992).

Soames, S., "Skepticism About Meaning: Indeterminacy, Normativity, and the Rule-Following Paradox", *Canadian Journal of Philosophy*, supp. vol. 23 (1998).

Tennant, N., *The Taming of the True* (Oxford: Clarendon Press, 1997), chapter 4.

Thornton, T., *Wittgenstein on Language and Thought* (Edinburgh: Edinburgh University Press, 1998), chapters 1 and 2.

Zalabardo, J., "A Problem For Information Theoretic Semantics", *Synthese* 105 (1995).

2. THE SKEPTICAL SOLUTION, SEMANTIC NONFACTUALISM AND SOLITARY LANGUAGE

Bar-On, D., "On the Possibility of a Solitary Language", *Noûs* 26 (1992).

Blackburn, S., "Wittgenstein's Irrealism", in J. Brandl and R. Haller (eds) *Wittgenstein: Eine Neubewehrung* (Vienna: Holder-Pichler-Temsky, 1990).

Blackburn, S., "Wittgenstein, Wright, Rorty and Minimalism", *Mind* 107 (1998).

Boghossian, P., "The Status of Content", *Philosophical Review* 99 (1990).

Boghossian, P., "The Status of Content Revisited", *Pacific Philosophical Quarterly* 71 (1990).

Byrne, A., "On Misinterpreting Kripke's Wittgenstein", *Philosophy and Phenomenological Research* 56 (1996).

Davies, D., "How sceptical is Kripke's 'Sceptical Solution'", *Philosophia* 26 (1998).

Davies, S., "Kripke, Crusoe and Wittgenstein", *Australasian Journal of Philosophy* 66 (1988).

Devitt, M., "Transcendentalism About Content", *Pacific Philosophical Quarterly* 71 (1990).

Edwards, J., "Response-Dependence, Kripke, and Minimal Truth", *European Review of Philosophy* 3 (1998).

Hoffman, P., "Kripke on Private Language", *Philosophical Studies* **47** (1985).

Humphrey, J., "Kripke's Wittgenstein and the Impossibility of Private Language: Same Old Story?", *Journal of Philosophical Research* **21** (1996).

Humphrey, J., "Quine, Kripke's Wittgenstein, Simplicity, and Sceptical Solutions", *Southern Journal of Philosophy* **37** (1999).

Kraut, R., "Robust Deflationism", *Philosophical Review* **102** (1993).

Kremer, M., "Wilson on Kripke's Wittgenstein", *Philosophy and Phenomenological Research* **60** (2000).

Miller, A., *Philosophy of Language* (London: UCL Press, 1998), chapter 5.

Soames, S., "Facts, Truth-Conditions, and the Skeptical Solution to the Rule-Following Paradox", in J. Tomberlin (ed.) *Philosophical Perspectives* 12: *Language, Mind, and Ontology* (1998).

Tennant, N., *The Taming of the True* (Oxford: Clarendon Press, 1997), chapter 3.

Thornton, T., *Wittgenstein on Language and Thought* (Edinburgh: Edinburgh University Press, 1998), chapter 3.

Williams, M., "Blind Obedience: Rules, Community, and the Individual", in K. Puhl (ed.) *Meaning-Scepticism* (Berlin: De Gruyter, 1991).

Wilson, G., "Semantic Realism and Kripke's Wittgenstein", *Philosophy and Phenomenological Research* **83** (1998).

Wright, C., "Kripke's Account of the Argument Against Private Language", *Journal of Philosophy* **81** (1984).

Wright, C., "Does PI §§258–60 Suggest A Cogent Argument Against Private Language?", in J. McDowell and P. Pettit (eds) *Subject, Thought and Context* (Oxford: Oxford University Press, 1986).

Wright, C., *Truth and Objectivity* (Cambridge, MA: Harvard University Press, 1992), chapter 6.

Wright, C., "Comrades Against Quietism: Reply to Simon Blackburn", *Mind* **107** (1998).

3. McDOWELL ON KRIPKE'S WITTGENSTEIN

Blackburn, S., "Rule-Following and Moral Realism", in S. Holtzmann and C. Leich (eds) *Wittgenstein: To Follow a Rule* (London: Routledge & Kegan Paul, 1981).

Ebbs, G., *Rule-Following and Realism* (Cambridge, MA: Harvard University Press, 1997), chapter 5.

McDowell, J., "Non-Cognitivism and Rule-Following", in S. Holtzmann and C. Leich (eds) *Wittgenstein: To Follow a Rule* (London: Routledge & Kegan Paul, 1981).

McDowell, J., "One Strand in the Private Language Argument", *Grazer Philosphiche Studien* **33/34** (1989).

McDowell, J., "Intentionality and Interiority in Wittgenstein", in K. Puhl (ed.) *Meaning-Scepticism* (Berlin: De Gruyter, 1991).

McDowell, J., "Meaning and Intention in Wittgenstein's Later Philosophy", in P. A. French, T. E. Uehling, Jr., and H. K. Wettstein (eds), *Midwest Studies in Philosophy, Volume XII: The Wittgensteinian Legacy* (Notre Dame: University of Notre Dame Press, 1992).

McDowell, J., *Mind and World* (Oxford: Oxford University Press. 1994), Lecture V.

Miller, A., "Rule-Following, Response-Dependence and McDowell's Debate With Anti-Realism", *European Review of Philosophy* **3** (1998).

Miller, A., "Rule-Following and Externalism", *Philosophy and Phenomenological Research* (forthcoming).

4. PETTIT ON RULE-FOLLOWING AND RELATED MATTERS

Haukioja, J., Rule-Following, Response-Dependence and Realism, unpublished PhD thesis, University of Turku, 2000.

Pettit, P., "Affirming the Reality of Rule-Following", *Mind* 99 (1990).

Pettit, P., "Realism and Response-Dependence", *Mind* 100 (1991).

Pettit, P., *The Common Mind: An Essay on Psychology, Society, and Politics* (Oxford: Oxford University Press, 2nd edn 1996).

Powell, M., "Realism or Response-Dependence", *European Review of Philosophy* 3 (1998).

Summerfield, D., "On Taking the rabbit of Rule-Following Out of the Hat of Representation: A Response to Pettit's 'The Reality of Rule-Following'", *Mind* 99 (1990).

Wright, C., "Euthyphronism and the Physicality of Colour: A Comment on Mark Powell's 'Realism or Response-Dependence'", *European Review of Philosophy* 3 (1998).

5. WRIGHT ON RULE-FOLLOWING, JUDGEMENT-DEPENDENCE AND RELATED MATTERS

Blackburn, S., "Circles, Finks, Smells and Biconditionals", *Philosophical Perspectives* 7 (1993).

Diamond, C., *The Realistic Spirit: Wittgenstein, Philosophy, and the Mind* (Cambridge, MA: MIT Press, 1991), Chapter 7.

Divers, J. and Miller, A., "Best Opinion, Intention Detecting, and Analytic Functionalism", *Philosophical Quarterly* 44 (1994).

Edwards, J., "Best Opinions and Intentional States", *Philosophical Quarterly* 42 (1992).

Hale, B., "Rule-Following, Objectivity, and Meaning", in B. Hale and C. Wright (eds) *A Companion to the Philosophy of Language* (Oxford: Blackwell, 1997).

Holton, R., "Intention Detecting", *Philosophical Quarterly* 43 (1993).

Johnston, M., "Objectivity Disfigured" (Appendix 3), in J. Haldane and C. Wright (eds) *Reality, Representation, and Projection* (Oxford: Oxford University Press, 1993).

McDowell, J., "Reply to Wright", C. McDonald, B. Smith, and C. Wright (eds) *On Knowing One's Own Mind* (Oxford: Oxford University Press, 1998).

Miller, A., "An Objection to Wright's Treatment of Intention", *Analysis* 49 (1989).

Rosen, G., "Objectivity and Modern Idealism: What is the Question?", in M. Michaelis and J. O'Leary-Hawthorne (eds) *Philosophy in Mind: The Place of Philosophy in the Study of Mind* (Kluwer, 1994).

Sullivan, P., "Problems For a Construction of Meaning and Intention", *Mind* 103 (1994).

Thornton, T., "Intention, Rule-Following, and the Strategic Role of Wright's Order-of-Determination Test", *Philosophical Investigations* 20 (1997).

Wright, C., *Wittgenstein on the Foundations of Mathematics* (London: Duckworth, 1980), Chapters 2 and 12.

Wright, C., "Rule-Following, Objectivity and the Theory of Meaning", in S. Holtzmann and C. Leich (eds) *Wittgenstein: To Follow a Rule* (London: Routledge & Kegan Paul, 1981).

Wright, C., "Rule-Following, Meaning, and Constructivism", in C. Travis (ed.) *Meaning and Interpretation* (Oxford: Blackwell, 1986).

Wright, C., "On Making Up One's Mind: Wittgenstein on Intention", in Weingartner and Schurz (eds) *Logic, Science, and Epistemology* (Vienna: Holder-Pichler-Temsky, 1987).

Wright, C., "Moral Values, Projection, and Secondary Qualities", *Proceedings of the Aristotelian Society Supp.* volume 62 (1988).

Wright, C., "Realism, Antirealism, Irrealism, Quasi-Realism", *Midwest Studies in Philosophy* 12 (1988).

Wright, C., "Wittgenstein's Later Philosophy of Mind: Sensation, Privacy, and Intention", in K. Puhl (ed.) *Meaning-Scepticism* (Berlin: De Gruyter, 1991).

Wright, C., *Truth and Objectivity* (Cambridge, MA: Harvard University Press, 1992), Appendix to chapter 3.

Wright, C., "Self-Knowledge: The Wittgensteinian Legacy", in C. McDonald, B. Smith, and C. Wright (eds) *On Knowing One's Own Mind* (Oxford: Oxford University Press, 1998).

Wright, C., *Rails to Infinity* (Cambridge, MA: Harvard University Press, 2001) (contains many of the papers by Wright listed above).

6. GENERAL

Baker, G. and Hacker, P., *Wittgenstein: Understanding and Meaning* (Oxford: Blackwell, 1980).

Baker, G. and Hacker, P., *Wittgenstein's Philosophical Investigations* (Oxford: Blackwell, 1983).

Baker, G. and Hacker, P., *Scepticism, Rules, and Language* (Oxford: Blackwell, 1984).

Baker, G. and Hacker, P., *Wittgenstein: Rules, Grammar, and Necessity* (Oxford: Blackwell, 1985).

Blackburn, S., *Spreading The Word* (Oxford: Oxford University Press, 1984), chapter 2.

Boghossian, P., "Review of McGinn's *Wittgenstein on Meaning*", *Philosophical Review* 98 (1989).

Budd, M., *Wittgenstein's Philosophy of Psychology* (London: Routledge, 1989).

Carruthers, P., "Ruling Out Realism", *Philosophia* (1985).

Ebbs, G., *Rule-Following and Realism* (Cambridge, MA: Harvard University Press, 1997).

French, P., Uehling, T., and Wettstein (eds), *Midwest Studies in Philosophy, Volume XII: The Wittgensteinian Legacy* (Notre Dame: University of Notre Dame Press, 1992).

Gampel, E., "The Normativity of Meaning", *Philosophical Studies* 86 (1997).

Goldfarb, G., "Wittgenstein, Mind, and Scientism", *Journal of Philosophy* 86 (1989).

Goldfarb, G., "Wittgenstein on Understanding", in French, P., Uehling, T., and Wettstein (eds): *Midwest Studies in Philosophy, Volume XII: The Wittgensteinian Legacy* (Notre Dame: University of Notre Dame Press, 1992).

Hacker, P., *Wittgenstein: Meaning and Mind* (Oxford: Blackwell, 1990).

Hanfling, O., *Wittgenstein's Later Philosophy* (London: Macmillan, 1989).

Heal, J., *Fact and Meaning* (Oxford: Blackwell, 1989).

Holtzmann, S. and Leich, C. (eds), *Wittgenstein: To Follow a Rule* (London: Routledge & Kegan Paul, 1981).

Kusch, M., *The Rule-Following Considerations: A Defense of Kripke's Wittgenstein* (forthcoming).

McGinn, M., "Kripke on Wittgenstein's Sceptical Problem", *Ratio* (1984).

McGinn, M., *Wittgenstein and the Philosophical Investigations* (London: Routledge, 1997), Chapter 3.

McManus, D., "The Epistemology of Self-Knowledge and the Presuppositions of Rule-Following", *The Monist* 78 (1995).

Malcolm, N., *Nothing is Hidden* (Oxford: Blackwell, 1986).

Malcolm, N., "Wittgenstein on Language and Rules", *Philosophy* 64 (1989).

Peacocke, C., "Rule-Following: The Nature of Wittgenstein's Arguments", in S. Holtzmann and C. Leich (eds) *Wittgenstein: To Follow a Rule* (London: Routledge & Kegan Paul, 1981).

Pears, D., *The False Prison* volume 2 (Oxford: Oxford University Press, 1988).

Puhl, K. (ed.), *Meaning-Scepticism* (Berlin: De Gruyter, 1991).

Putnam, H., "On Wittgenstein's Philosophy of Mathematics", *Proceedings of the Aristotelian Society supp. vol.* 70 (1996).

Read, R., "The Unstatability of Kripkean Scepticisms", *Philosophical Papers* 24 (1995).

Sartorelli, J., "McGinn on Content Scepticism and Kripke's Sceptical Argument", *Analysis* 51 (1991).

Scruton, R., "Critical Notice of Kripke's *Wittgenstein on Rules and Private Language*", *Mind* 93 (1982).

Summerfield, D., "*Philosophical Investigations* 201: A Wittgensteinian Reply to Kripke", *Journal of the History of Philosophy* 28 (1990).

INDEX

340 9464

Philosophy of music / music constraint

So I say may be intentions can be reduced, but they must not be denied entirely & if they aren't I should be able to use them to answer the skeptic

How is it

4854 9464